BRIDGES

BRIDGES

by

Aart Jurriaanse

ANCIENT WISDOM REVEALED

Paperback Edition

BRIDGES
PUBLISHING

First paperback edition 2007
Revised Edition 2001
First published 1978

Cover Painting: "The Seven Spheres" © by Soham Holger Gerull,
Petersberg-Steinhaus, Germany

Published by: in Cooperation with:
Bridges Publishing   "Sun Centre"
Hans-Juergen Maurer   School of Esoteric Philosophy
P.O. Box 207   5, Almond Drive
79002 Freiburg   Somerset West 7130
Germany   South Africa

www.verlaghjmaurer.de or www.bridges-publishing.de
info@verlaghjmaurer.de

ISBN 978-3-929345-32-2

BUILDING BRIDGES

May these thoughts contribute towards bridging the gap between man and man, nation and nation, race and race; between the past, the present and the future; between science and religion, religion and religion; between the tangible and the intangible, unconsciousness and consciousness, darkness and light; between the material and the spiritual, the not-self and the Self, the personality, the Soul and the Monad; between man and the Spiritual Hierarchy of Perfected Men and of Angels; and may all these bridges eventually lead to synthesis within the human race and the realisation of the One Humanity, the One Soul, the One Universe and the One Supreme Being.

Contents

PART TWO: Man on the Path of Life

INTRODUCTION

Universal Principles

These thoughts are not expressed for the East or the West; for people with white, black or yellow skins; for English, Germans, Chinese or Jews; for Roman Catholics or Protestants; for Moslems, Christians or Buddhists; for the religious minded, the agnostic or the scientist; they deal with the basic principles of life and the Laws of Nature, which are applicable to every single human being and therefore also to all of humanity. But neither are these so-called 'Wisdom Teachings' limited to the human kingdom – they are also relevant to every other kingdom of nature, such as the mineral, vegetable, animal and spiritual kingdoms. In fact the 'Ageless –' or 'Ancient Wisdom' teachings are all-inclusive, never ending and perpetually apply to all of Creation ... the whole Universe.

The approach that will be followed is objective but leads to subjective and philosophic considerations which are altogether non-denominational viewed from the religious standpoint. These principles are fundamental and can therefore be studied by the occidental or oriental, the devotionally inclined, the mystic, agnostic or scientist. The stage to which the individual can advance will solely depend on personal limitations of intellect, mind and spiritual consciousness but progressive development could eventually lead him far beyond the relatively narrow precincts dealt with in this treatise. Should the envisioned unfoldment not occur during the present life, then it is bound to manifest in the course of some future incarnation. Although these concepts are treated at a relatively simple level, it is realised that with a large percentage of the world population being in an early stage of mental development, this comparatively unsophisticated approach will still be beyond the reach of many. The basic principles can, however, always be satisfactorily interpreted to any individual by appropriate adaptation of these concepts.

The beauty of these tenets is that each person can find his own level of adjustment according to his specific stage of development of intellect, mind and spirit and according to the position he occupies in his particular physical and social environment. Furthermore his subsequent progress, whether fast or slow, will depend purely on himself. There may be the occasional individual who, although accepting these premises, does not have the inclination for further study or development. Should this be the case, there probably will be some sound esoteric reason, even though the man may not be aware of it. Occasionally there will also be those who apparently have reached their ceiling or 'high-water mark' of development for a particular life; such an apparently static phase may only prove to be of a temporary nature but in exceptional instances such a condition might remain relatively stable for the duration of that particular life.

On the other hand there is an unlimited scope for study and expansion of consciousness for those who feel the inner urge. As the result of persistent study and meditation, new vistas and spiritual fields of exploration will systematically be revealed before the awakening inner eye of the dedicated aspirant. He will experience growing light and understanding and an ever deepening feeling of love and goodwill towards his fellow men and this will find expression as a growing urge to be of service to his daily associates, his community, humanity as a whole and finally to his Spiritual Leader and thus to contribute towards the realisation of the Divine Plan.

May the thoughts reflected in the following pages serve as an introduction for these aspirants, to be used as a stepping stone in their spiritual development or as a refresher to bring back to the mind that which was already learnt or experienced in some previous existence, thus serving as a bridge leading to the study of more advanced teachings.

Although the principles of the Ageless Wisdom doctrines remain basically unalterable throughout the ages, practically each separate individual, depending on his physical, mental and spiritual constitution, will become aware of different facets of the One Truth. He will attach his own nuances of interpretation to these, depending on the influence of his environment and that intricate combination of forces and energies to which each individual is constantly subjected. The picture he eventually paints will then be coloured by the shades of those aspects which have made the deepest impression on his specific complex of characteristics. It is because of this that it will be found that no two versions of the Truth will ever be identical. This will, however, make no difference to and should actually serve to broaden the outlook of the intuitive and understanding student, who will realise the underlying reasons for this diversity and who will be able to discover the linking and continuous thread of gold running through and connecting all genuine renderings.

The Ever Changing Pattern of the Universe

ENERGY ... what a comprehensive term! The whole Universe, all that is manifested, all that has been, is or ever will be, all consists of energy and nothing but energy – 'free' energy; energy bound or limited to greater or lesser extent in the myriads of forms and shapes in manifestation; energy temporarily apparently locked up in the densely compacted atoms of minerals; energy in the more diffusely arranged atoms of gaseous substances; inexhaustible streams of energy contained in that invisible, intangible, unrecorded reservoir which man in his ignorance has termed 'empty space'.

The above is a most clumsy and inadequate description of the all-inclusive energy of which the Universe is comprised and only reflects that infinitesimal fraction of the Whole which the restricted mind and intellect of even highly developed human beings can visualise or conceive. Furthermore the concept of 'energy' may be glibly discussed but not even the most highly qualified scientists know what this fundamental power or faculty really is. This mysterious but basic principle underlying all life and manifested existence may be variously described according to its many known qualities and properties and even practically applied in many ways to the benefit (or destruction) of man but for the rest these energies and forces either just have to be accepted for what they are, without undue concern about their hidden and inexplicable origin and quality, or else they can be broadly designated as divine gifts, totally beyond the comprehension of man.

Energy is manifested in a never ending range of qualities, strengths and combinations which man often tries to differentiate by commonly used terms, such as – Spirit, Matter, Life, Light, Electricity, Vitality, Will, Power, Love, Wisdom, Intelligence, Beauty, Knowledge and Idealism. This treatise will in the first instance make a study of various known aspects of these energies, of the extent to which they may be invoked by man and the commensurate response that may be expected. The point that will be stressed, however, is the fact that all energies, whether moving freely through space or whether temporarily confined within the walls of an atom, remain in constant motion. The power determining this movement may be only enough to support the electrons in an atom or otherwise of sufficient potency to guide and support celestial bodies or even whole constellations on their predetermined orbits through the heavens.

One of the consequences of this perpetual but systematic motion of all energy is that no form of creation, nothing on Earth or in the rest of the Universe, ever remains stable. Everything that IS remains in a perpetual state of modification and adaptation and may be classified as being in the stage of:

(a) *Involution* – during which energies are in the process of being bound or converted into various structures or forms.

(b) *Evolution* – during which the different created forms are in the process of being altered, adapted and improved, thus to become better suited to ever changing demands, circumstances and environment.

(c) *Devolution* – the process of breaking down, effected either through sudden changes or otherwise by the progressive dissolution of forms, thereby releasing or liberating energy.

The present stage in human development, together with that of the physical environment in which he has been placed, has only been reached after vast aeons of time stretching utterly beyond man's conception. But strictly speaking it is incorrect to refer to a 'present stage', because a point of *status quo* is never attained, as the various processes of change continue endlessly. Some of these developments take place so gradually, however, that they are hardly noticeable to the relatively restricted perceptive faculties of the human being. Furthermore it should be remembered that in man these progressive changes occur not only in his physical body but probably even more important are those demonstrated in his more elusive aspects, that is in his emotional, mental and spiritual unfoldment.

The flow of energy does not follow an even tenor but is characterised by pulsations or cycles, exhibiting periods of higher and lower concentration of energy and evoked activity. This can be compared with the process of in- and out-breathing, so typically exemplified in nature by the ebb and flow of the ocean tides, the perpetual sequences of day and night, the annual succession of the seasons and the recurrent birth, death and rebirth of man.

To keep pace with these ever varying and developing conditions exacts severe demands on man's resourcefulness, versatility, vitality and perseverance, which may lead either to suffering, agony and even destruction or alternatively to the highlights of the expanding consciousness and eventually to spiritual liberation and exaltation.

Humanity is at present experiencing the throes of one of its most radical periods of transition. To enable it to make suitable adjustments and to reap the maximum benefits from evolving conditions, it is essential that man should have a reasonable concept of the energies and forces responsible for these changes. He has been endowed with a reasoning mind which distinguishes him from the animal kingdom and by means of this questing and probing instrument, he has been enabled to effect some influence in the direction of these energies and thus also on the course of his own life and development. Man was never intended to be just an inanimate puppet to be buffeted hither and thither by every chance circumstance or 'wind of change'.

A brief survey therefore will be made of some of the many energies and forces influencing man's existence on Earth, to determine what action can be taken to co-operate with the beneficial forces or how to avoid or to counteract the detrimental effects or otherwise how to control and guide such energies in the desired direction.

The Path of Experience

Who and what is Man? What is the sense and purpose of existence? What is Life and where must it all lead? What have I done that I should experience all this suffering? These are only a few of the questions which are daily being asked by thousands throughout the world who are weighed down by heavy burdens, who feel desperate, insecure and uncertain and are consequently searching for deeper values on which their hopes for the future may be founded.

In the following pages an attempt will be made to draw the veils obscuring the mind's eye slightly apart and thus to throw perhaps a little more light on to a terrain that to many has so far been shrouded in absolute darkness. Although a beam of light may be thrown on the Path that lies ahead and on to the signboard indicating the direction and destination of the road, this is a path which each man must walk on his own – alone and yet not alone, because the man who honestly, sincerely and selflessly strives to serve his fellow man may rest assured that he will always be guided and inspired from subjective levels to ever brighter *Light*, to a more understanding and inclusive *Love* and to more profound *Wisdom*. In the early stages of his development he may, however, remain totally unaware of the helping hands which will constantly serve to protect him and to guide him along his determined Path.

Mankind stands at the portals of a New Age. Bridges with the past are being broken down rapidly and systematically, one after another, usually resulting in stupendous disruption and the upsetting of all that characterised previous generations. Because man as a rule is not ready and prepared for such demolishment, these changes are often accompanied by excessive pain and suffering which may appear unnecessarily severe and merciless. However, have every confidence that humanity's fate rests in safe and benevolent hands and is being guided by the Lord of the World according to His carefully considered Purpose and Plan.

It should also be realised that nothing in all the Universe ever happens haphazardly. Although the average human being, bound as he is by physical, emotional and mental limitations, may not be able to fathom the reasons for all these changes which for him are so often fraught with distress and misery, there nevertheless *must* be and actually *is* adequate justification for each and every happening. Furthermore these apparent adversities must not be seen as a form of chastisement meted out by a discontented Father to His defecting children but merely as the implicit effects of the natural Law of Cause and Effect, combined and co-ordinated with the immutable and to man oft incomprehensible Divine Plan; they may also be regarded as the experiences and lessons of life which actively contribute towards the development and shaping of the character of each individual.

Although man, with the free will with which he has been endowed, is to some extent able to affect the course of events within the elements of time and space and in some instances can therefore either retard or expedite the trend of occurrences as far as these may concern his personal life and conditions, the final issue and destination has been determined by Higher Authority and cannot be modified or deviated by the 'little wills of men'.

The Tibetan's Teachings

It should be clearly understood that the thoughts to be expressed are definitely not the product of the writer's 'fertile brain'. Neither does he presume to be qualified to proclaim his own teachings. This treatise is merely an attempt at producing an abbreviated and simplified interpretation of the tenets of that profound sage, *Djwhal Khul* (D.K.) – commonly known as 'The Tibetan' – and at sharing his thoughts with those who perhaps may not have access to his complete writings.

The original manuscripts were *telepathically dictated* to Alice A. Bailey (A.A.B.) who agreed to act as the Tibetan's amanuensis and who over a period of thirty years, stretching from 1919 to 1949, recorded his directed thoughts. This original rendering was subsequently published progressively in a series of eighteen volumes, comprising a total of nearly 10,000 pages of text. (For a complete list of these books see the Appendix).

It is hoped that the present work may serve as an introduction to esoteric study in general, perhaps leading interested students to a clearer understanding of the more comprehensive and in places rather abstruse original writings.

Actually it is of no importance through which channels these principles are relayed or from what source they originate, as long as the correct message is conveyed to its intended destination – humanity. Come to think of it, from where did the Tibetan obtain all his knowledge? Although he must be regarded as an exalted and refined instrument, he is again merely a channel through which thoughts, knowledge and wisdom, inspired primarily from some higher divine source, have been directed to humanity.

It should also be realised that as these divine inspirational thoughts are being passed down, step by step, from spiritual to material levels, the instruments used for this transference are of ever decreasing quality and become coarser and coarser. It stands to reason that as these channels become cruder and are no longer qualified by true intuition and divine wisdom, that the standard of the teachings will suffer proportionately and that they will thus become relatively distorted. These distortions are, however, not always due to faulty instruments but in many cases adaptations have to be made because the original message or concepts, in their pristine and elevated form, are beyond the understanding of the average, materially oriented human being.

Fundamental Nature of the Philosophies

The principles to be reflected are basically of a philosophic nature and are intended for the average man of intelligence, with the purpose of possibly opening some new vistas of thought and thereby perhaps even a new approach to life. The concepts involved have already proved acceptable to men from all walks of life and an attempt will be made to avoid emotional aspects and as far as possible to retain a rational, logical, impersonal and detached approach.

These views may perhaps lead the unbiased scientist to totally unexpected visions on certain long-standing problems and even to a fresh outlook on certain old and accepted tenets and premises. In some instances this might result in the opening up of vast new vistas and the possibilities for further research. As far as this is concerned there seem to be special opportunities waiting in the fields of electrical energy, light, sound and colour. There also seem to be vast possibilities for exploration of the realms of the invisible and intangible or the so-called *etheric* world – a field which today has already been tentatively approached and designated as 'extra sensory perception' (E.S.P.). When more is known of and closer contact has been established with the etheric realm, a totally new approach will be uncovered to both medical practice and the closely related and rapidly developing science of psychology. But more about this in its proper context.

The man with a religious outlook will also find, once he allows himself to read and think with an open and unprejudiced mind and therefore without being constantly limited and fettered by prescribed dogmatism, that new light will suddenly dawn for him on various problems that have consciously or unconsciously been puzzling him for many years. Dogma with its doctrines may have its uses but when it leads to suppression of free thought and an avoidance of careful and objective consideration and analysis of unsolved problems of the practised religion, then it is certainly indicative of mistakenly applied accents. God has endowed man with an intelligent and reasoning mind and it can surely not be argued that his questing thoughts are meant to be applied to every field of knowledge and all terrains of life *except religion* – that most important aspect of subjective existence, which should really constitute the background and quality of every conscious being – the spiritual well-being!

There are of course those who actually have so little confidence in their so-called 'faith' that they are afraid to discuss their religion, to submit it to the light of reason or to listen to or read about diverging views, as this might lead to doubt and uncertainty. However, a faith that rests on such insecure foundations can surely never be of much use to anyone; religion with its accompanying faith should form the mainstay of life and should in fact represent a raft of safety to which man can cling when he is being swept away by the turbulent currents which daily course through the uncertainties of life and when every other support seems to be failing him.

Remember that life, with its constant processes of development and evolution, can never remain static – there has either to be progress or otherwise retrogression, or devolution is bound to set in. The same assertion is valid in the case of religion. As man's mind unfolds a growing urge inevitably develops to penetrate deeper into the arcana of the subjective realms – to pierce or at least to lift slightly that dense veil that has up to now obscured his view. And actually the power to obtain more 'Light on the Path' is at the disposal of each and every individual. It is only a question of becoming aware of the opportunities and for the urge to arise and to move forward towards the beckoning Light. The degree of success that will eventually crown the aspirant's efforts will depend on the motives and purposefulness underlying his striving and the perseverance that is maintained.

The basic truths can of course never be altered but at the same time the Absolute Truth will never be fully comprehended by the mind of man while he is still inhibited by physical limitations. What can however be altered, adjusted and expanded, is man's interpretation of that which is being revealed to him and the subsequent sound application of his findings in his daily living and being. This in turn will lead to a closer approximation to and understanding of the final Truth. These studies should thus help to lead the aspirant to ever expanding horizons and to bridge some of the chasms between illusion and Reality.

Today the average man is more or less fully occupied with his daily range of activities, which vary between wide limits according to his individual qualities, his environment and circumstances and the position he occupies in the human community and the particular aims and objectives to which he aspires. Man's material concerns, as a rule, engage his attention to such an extent that only a small percentage of human beings are consciously aware of the existence of the subjective worlds which are so intimately associated with the dense physical conditions. To the majority of men the latter still remain the only conscious form of life and existence. The surrounding spiritual world, which is actually closely interwoven and interrelated with the physical is, however, very real and it is only because of man's limited range of perception that the presence of this more ethereal realm cannot be registered at this stage of his existence.

An attempt will be made to create a picture of the constitution of man; of how the human kingdom links up and is related to the other kingdoms of nature; to indicate how the physical and subjective worlds are closely integrated and associated and how our planet, the Earth, forms part of the solar system, which in turn only represents an atom in the greater whole of the Universe. It will also be indicated that these physical forms which man observes are merely the material or lowest reflection of spiritual Existences or Entities, which are finally synthesized in that inconceivable and indescribable concept – the Supreme Power.

So many human beings plod through life in a daze, unable to fathom something of the meaning and purpose behind it all, instinctively clinging to physical existence because of their fear of 'death' and the 'unknown beyond' which must inevitably terminate each individual term of life on Earth. Meanwhile in their daily struggle they seem to be experiencing an apparent constant series of reverses, leading to a never ending sequence of either or both physical and mental pain and suffering, which in most cases seems to be relieved by little real pleasure or happiness. In an effort to drown their sorrows or to create some sense of security, confidence or exhilaration, many turn to the use of alcohol; others again avail themselves of narcotics, in this way trying to escape from the daily problems and afflictions but thereby only transferring temporarily to an astral world of glamour and illusion and deferring the day of reckoning when life will have to be faced again with an increased load of tribulations. Still others, especially those just entering the path of life, try to cram in as much pleasure as possible in order to escape from the responsibilities of life. After a phase of such hectic living, many of these youngsters come to accept that this mad hunt after pleasure is but a chimera which in the end leads them nowhere.

It is hoped that a description of some aspects of the subjective realms may serve to make more men aware of this nebulous and undefined terrain which, nevertheless, forms such an intimate, although usually unrealised, part of all human existence and which inevitably has to play such an important and even conscious role in the future development of each and every child of man.

Life's Problems

When man's unfolding intellect is afforded the time to ponder on life's problems, then the following are a few of the challenging questions that are apt to obtrude themselves into the explorative mind:

What is the nature of the Universe; is it circumscribed in any way and if so, where lie its boundaries and to what extent is it consciously, intelligently and methodically planned and controlled? How does our planet, the Earth, fit into this bigger scheme? What role is man supposed to play in this set-up? What is Life and what is its purpose? What happens at death and after death? Is there any form of life hereafter? Should man be immortal, then how does this comply with the fact that the physical body decomposes and disintegrates after death? Is there some form of subjective life and what about 'heaven' and 'hell'? Do our lives consist of just a series of incoherent and fortuitous incidents and circumstances or are we being guided by some subjective Entity towards a specific and planned purpose or objective? Should there be a basic purpose, then there must definitely also exist some Supreme Guiding Power or Deity – where and of what nature is this Deity and how or through what channels does IT function? What are the relationships between this Deity, humanity and the other kingdoms of nature? To what extent can man depend on the guidance of this Deity and to what extent can these sustaining Forces be invoked?

These and many similar questions keep arising in the inquiring mind of the thinker. A thoughtful survey of the human family immediately discloses the never ending diversity between its individual components. Actually no two single members will be found who are identical in all respects. These differences occur within wide limits, not only with regard to the physical appearance and characteristics of individuals, groups and races but also when their emotional, mental and spiritual make-up is taken into consideration, as well as the conditions and environment of their existence.

An unbiased consideration of the widely varying conditions and circumstances under which each of the millions of individuals in the world are living; of the wide disparity that exists in the allocation of material and worldly goods with which they have been favoured; of the varying degree of intelligence with which individuals have been endowed; and finally the extent of spiritual unfoldment that is evinced – all such contemplation must lead the observer to the final choice between either of two premises:

Firstly, if each individual should only be afforded a single life and therefore only a single opportunity of redemption on Earth, as professed by the protagonists and dogmatists of certain religions, then according to human criteria this could only be regarded as a grave form of injustice. Why should some individuals under these circumstances be granted every opportunity in life and others hardly anything at all? No! Impossible! No righteous Father would ever tolerate such a position!

The *second* inference is that which has been propounded for thousands of years as part of the Ancient Wisdom teachings and seems to be the only logical conclusion that can be arrived at when all available evidence is carefully weighed. This is that all human beings are in a constant state of spiritual evolution towards an eventual common destination but that for various reasons the individuals (souls) composing mankind are at different stages and levels of development. Some are still near the bottom of the ladder, whilst others have already climbed to much higher rungs. This development of the human being is stimulated by the experiences gained during the activities of a physical life on Earth but as a single life would be hopelessly inadequate for all the experiences and lessons that life has to offer and because each individual has to undergo the full range of all possible experiences, each being has to return over and over again to this physical 'vale of tears'. All this will, however, be dealt with in greater detail and in proper context in the course of the following pages.

The Expanding Consciousness

With regard to the comprehension of many of the subjective principles, an attempt will be made to explain matters as clearly as possible. Those who have the necessary affinity and sensitivity for these studies will, however, soon realise that many of the deeper and esoteric concepts cannot be expressed in human words. Human thought is exploring a field for which, as yet, there exists no adequate language and for the expression of which the exact terms are still lacking. As the student persists, however, his consciousness will gradually expand, until he unexpectedly becomes aware of a new form of discernment – his intuition is awakening and he is conceiving certain subjective and abstruse principles which could never be explained in words.

Most of the tenets under consideration can be approached from several aspects and are consequently being dealt with under different headings. Such apparent repetition in varying context should, however, be seen in true perspective, as it serves to present or clothe the thought in a different garb, thus leading to a clearer understanding of the various facets contained in the principle or truth under examination.

Classification of the Contents

The contents of this book are classified under numerous subject headings, some of which only comprise a brief paragraph. Although it is realised that this system has certain disadvantages and has led to some sacrifice of fluency and facile readability, this practice has notwithstanding been deliberately introduced to contribute towards greater clarity of expression and definition of concepts, which to many readers may prove new, strange and perhaps not readily understandable. This way of classification will also be of assistance to the student who wishes to avail himself of the numerical references given in the

"Reference Index". These references should facilitate the gaining of more complete information on specific subjects from the Tibetan's teachings.

The intention is certainly not to supply light reading for relaxation but, on the contrary, to provide something for mental stimulation. To many the thoughts expressed and the approach that is being followed with regard to spiritual matters will be something new and a careful study of the relative principles will be required to arrive at a clear understanding of what is involved. It has therefore been felt that lucidity in the presentation of the subject matter is of more importance than the use of a perhaps more flowing arrangement to afford easier reading.

A. J.
Pretoria, April 1978

PART ONE

Man in the Universe

SUMMARY

Contrary to usual procedure, this book is being introduced with a brief survey of what is to follow, since the subject to be dealt with is complicated and comprehensive and the many aspects are so intimately intertwined that it is impossible to start the story with a few simple facts and then gradually to deploy the theme into its broader principles. This means that from the start certain terms and concepts will have to be introduced, which can only be elaborated or explained at a later stage. This might not matter to those already somewhat acquainted with these philosophies but might prove rather confusing to those who have had no previous contact with this line of thought. As the present treatise is intended primarily for the newcomer a brief review of what the subject comprises will enable the student to become somewhat better oriented to a philosophy of life and to points of view which may prove to be a totally new approach to him.

First of all it will be stressed that the whole Universe, with all it embraces, consists of *Energy* – energy in its myriad forms of manifestation; energy freely moving in space, supporting the celestial bodies and at the same time the carriers of those powers and forces which interrelate everything in the universal system, synthesising it all into the *One Whole*.

An attempt will be made to give some faint idea of who and what *man* is, the position he occupies in the overall picture and something of the role he has to fulfil in the Divine Plan. It will be briefly explained how man is constituted of three separate bodies – the physical, the emotional and the mental vehicles, with their functions co-ordinated by the soul. The three 'material' bodies are mortal, 'return to dust' at death and merely serve for the temporary accommodation of man's immortal aspect, the soul, during a single span of life. The soul (or Monad) in turn is but a spark of the divine Over-Soul.

The soul is in a process of constant evolution and, for some divine reason incomprehensible to man, it needs physical experience on Earth for its development and it is in order to gain this experience that the soul is *reincarnated* over and over again, each time into a new body and a fresh set of circumstances and environment, with the purpose of undergoing every possible phase of trial and experience that can be provided by physical life. The real inner conscious man is therefore the soul, a spiritual entity. Death of the physical body is thus not something to be feared and should often even be welcomed, as it only means a change in the state of consciousness and field of activity and a temporary release from physical limitations, till the soul is again ready for the next incarnation.

As the soul gains the required experience, it gradually begins to dominate the physical instrument or personality and step by step guides it to the life of *perfection* which is the ultimate objective of physical life on Earth. During this process of spiritual evolution the human unit undergoes certain marked expansions of consciousness, which enable him to obtain a deeper awareness and more intimate contact with spiritual levels which previously remained hidden to the uninitiated mind. For the sake of convenience these expansions of awareness are called '*initiations*'.

After the soul has attained perfection on physical levels, there is no further motivation for return to a material body, except perhaps in the case of some specific mission on behalf of humanity. There is, however, no end to spiritual development and after the soul becomes absorbed in its even more exalted reflection, the *Monad*, its further evolution is continued in spiritual realms. Contrary to commonly entertained views, spiritual life is characterised by intense activity, either on behalf of humanity or otherwise on behalf of one of the sub-human kingdoms.

A brief description will also be given of the constitution of the *Spiritual Hierarchy*, that is to the extent that the limited human mind can conceive and understand existence on these higher planes and dimensions. It will be explained how the developing spiritual entity, after having gained even deeper consciousness and wisdom in the course of its more exalted activities, eventually reaches the stage known as a *Master of Wisdom*. These Entities, each in charge of their own group of disciples, are working under direct control of the Master of Masters, the *living Christ*, who still remains directly and actively concerned with the onerous task of uplifting, guiding and redeeming humanity. A study will be made of the little realised but close relationship between Humanity and the Hierarchy of Masters on the one hand and how this combination is again linked with the Planetary Logos, the Lord of the World.

The brief recapitulation set out above cannot even be regarded as a skeleton or framework of what is to follow. It is merely intended to give the beginner some faint indication of the lines of thought which are to be developed. It should, however, always be remembered that even with the elaboration of somewhat greater detail, these thoughts should only be regarded as a mere introduction to a never ending and ever expanding course of study which will eventually lead the ardent and persistent student, step by step, onto the Path of ever increasing Supernal Light.

THE ANCIENT WISDOM

The origin of this philosophy, these thoughts, teachings or whatever they may be called, cannot be fathomed by the ordinary human mind and fades away into the mists of time. These principles date back to far beyond recognised historical times; back firstly to forgotten Lemuria and subsequently to ancient Atlantis. The actual past existence of these continents and civilisations is today still queried by many historians and scientists.

Yes, in the very first paragraph a highly contentious statement is already being made and those interested in these thoughts will find throughout these studies that concepts are being dealt with which in many respects transcend the usual mental approach and as such may evoke attitudes of distrust, resistance or misgiving. The man in the street is averse to thoughts of an esoteric nature, these being new and strange to him, challenging him to use his mind. A large percentage of human beings are as a rule mentally lazy, finding it much easier to reject such 'far-fetched and ridiculous' ideas, rather than to consider them carefully and without prejudice.

These thoughts are therefore intended for those who are prepared to think for themselves and who are willing and even keen to explore and ponder deeply on those aspects of life which are not immediately obvious or which do not necessarily conform with the accepted physical and emotional patterns of daily living. As far as the thought life is concerned, there is of course no normal person today who does not at times involuntarily reflect on the inner or hidden meaning of life, even if only to meditate fleetingly on such matters as the real significance of death and whether there perhaps may not be some truth in the belief of certain people that death is not the absolute and final end of life, with the prospect that there may remain some form of continued spiritual existence after parting from the physical body.

But even those who normally function on the mental plane will entertain widely different views as to the existence, influence and nature of the spiritual realms. On the one extreme there are those who, in public, will vigorously repudiate the possibility of any spiritual existence but on the other hand there are also many who are earnest believers in the continuity of life and that human destiny is guided by unknown subjective Entities or a Supreme Power of some nature. There are also those who are consciously aware of inner guidance, who endeavour to identify themselves with their soul, sometimes also referred to as the 'Christ Within'. Others speak of the 'Immanent God' as the more personal reflection of 'God Transcendent', responsible for the Universe as a whole. At any rate these concepts vary within extremely wide limits and should these views prove possible of careful analysis, it is doubtful whether any two individuals will ever be found entertaining exactly similar ideas as to the details of their religious beliefs or their interpretations of the unrevealed worlds of spirit.

To many so-called religious people, their religion is something purely emotional or devotional, which they do not allow to be subjected to mental dissection. In the majority of these instances they have been indoctrinated since the cradle with religious dogma of some nature. The result is that these individuals have grown into the habit of blindly accepting certain beliefs and it never even seems to occur to them to question these credos and to give them some deeper consideration. The impression is sometimes gained that these devotees do not want to subject their beliefs to penetrating thought, because deep within themselves there is a feeling of doubt and uncertainty and that they are not prepared to subject their beliefs to the pure light of reason because they are afraid that this moral support, on which they have been relying since early youth, might be swept away from under their feet.

The Ancient or Ageless Wisdom as such must definitely not be considered as a religion, although many of the basic principles have in the past and will again in the future be incorporated into various religious precepts. It is merely a study or philosophy by means of which it is endeavoured to understand and set out logically the existing relationship between man and the rest of the Universe of which he forms such an infinitesimal but nonetheless intimate part; it is the urge to arrive at a better understanding of man's own nature and basic constitution; of how physical man is related to the spiritual aspects of life; of the role he has played in the past and is destined to play in the future, with the realisation of the Divine Plan. An attempt will be made to describe or define energy, what its functions are and the extent to which it can be controlled or affected by the human being. It is therefore a study of the inter-relationship of man with all that constitutes his environment and the reciprocal effect of the respective energies and forces resulting from such contact; this scrutiny may be approached from many aspects, points of view and different levels of knowledge, depending on the stage of development of the observer.

Therefore, although these esoteric studies cannot be considered as representing a religion, these tenets may readily lead to religious practice, that is to the formulation of man's invocative appeal for help from spiritual realms and the response evoked to these needs. In fact, all the hundreds of religions or religious sects which today occur throughout the world are founded on the basic principles of the Ageless Wisdom – principles and truths that have been interpreted, adapted and propounded by various Prophets, Messengers,

Teachers or Leaders over the ages, to meet the requirements of specific groups or peoples under particular circumstances. Although originating from the same fundamental verities, some of these teachings have in the course of time been distorted beyond all recognition. These misrepresentations have in some instances been due to faulty interpretation, to mistakes that have crept in through handing down traditions from generation to generation and in other instances regrettably to deliberate falsification to suit the selfish objectives of ambitious individuals.

A fascinating aspect of these teachings is that each individual will attach his own interpretation to what he is taught and that these separate conceptions will then vary according to each person's specific physical, emotional and mental constitution and stage of development; these have in turn been affected by the numerous and varying streams and forms of energy to which the individual has been subjected in his particular circumstances and environment. The extent to which the student will benefit from these studies will of course largely depend on his spiritual development or as it is called – the spiritual age of the soul.

To make the statement that the origin of the Ageless Wisdom dates back for thousands and even millions of years is again only a relative truth. Teachings certainly were passed on to the human beings of that time but those would be of a much simpler and more practical nature than the precepts imparted today and could probably be compared with the rudimentary facts of life forming part of the elementary education of present day children.

The Wisdom teachings in their pristine form are derived from some divine Source quite beyond human conception. Although these teachings fundamentally remain unaltered, they are nevertheless adapted from age to age and civilisation to civilisation, not only to suit the requirements of the peoples of a particular age and environment but also to match the mental development of humanity in each particular era. During Lemurian times for instance, man was mainly physically oriented, with all his faculties concentrated on the feeding, protection and reproduction of the physical body but as yet exhibiting relatively little signs of emotional reaction and with the mind still totally dormant. Gradually the emotions began to awaken but it was only many aeons later, during the Atlantean age, that the emotional life started to play a more important role and progressively came to dominate physical stimulus, with the mental life making its first appearance. It is only during the present or Aryan age that the mind is obtaining a stronger grip on mankind and even now merely a minority of individuals can really be regarded as fully mentally focussed. Today the majority of humanity must still be classified as belonging to the Atlantean type, as they are as yet largely emotionally inclined, with the mental body only playing a secondary function. The under-developed and purely Lemurian type is, however, rapidly disappearing from the human community.

The previous paragraph could perhaps be summarised as follows:

Man	Polarisation	Awakening to
1. Lemurian	Physical	Emotional life
2. Atlantean	Emotional	Mental life
3. Aryan (modern)	Mental	Intuitional/Spiritual life

It therefore stands to reason that the teachings presented to Lemurian man or even those provided in the days of Atlantis, though based on the same virginal principles or spiritual truths, could not possibly have been cast in the same mould as is required today. Teachings offered to the present day man of average intelligence would have been totally incomprehensible to the primitive Lemurians as well as to the large majority of the somewhat further advanced Atlanteans. And thus the picture will steadily keep on modifying, the teachings being progressively adapted and elevated to higher planes to keep tread with the evolving mental and intuitive capacity of man.

Although it is quite right that man should avail himself of the scriptures, traditions and teachings contributed by prophets and teachers of past ages, who were delegated to guide man along the Path, it need never be feared that the source of fresh versions of these Divine Truths will ever become exhausted; as man intellectually matures and becomes receptive for more penetrating aspects of the Truth, these are bound to be provided from some source or another. Consciously or unconsciously man ever evokes that teaching for which he is ready and in need and this teaching inevitably must and will reach him and at the same time will clarify and amplify much of the deeper and hidden meanings in older scriptures – meanings which previously either escaped his notice or remained obscure to the casual or unprepared student.

Although Buddha, the Christ, Mohammed or some other Master may be quoted as the direct authority for certain teachings, it should always be remembered that these loved and revered Teachers are again but channels for the transmission of the Divine Truths which originate from some Supernal Source. These Truths would of course be totally incomprehensible to the ordinary human being if received in their pristine purity and they are consequently stepped down from one spiritual level to the next in ever simplified form. As these teachings are brought down to lower planes through channels of constantly descending mental order, they finally become manifested on the physical plane as human speech or the written word. In this process some of its spiritual qualities necessarily had to be sacrificed, thus becoming more circumscribed and limited in expression and in the meaning conveyed. Distortion and misrepresentation of the communications may be so severe that the original ideas become hardly recognisable.

One of the important responsibilities of the aspirant on the Path of Truth is to strive toward an ever expanding consciousness, thereby contacting ever higher and purer sources of Truth. In doing so he himself will become an increasingly efficient channel for the distribution of the benefits he has received and which should be passed on to his fellow man. It should always be remembered that nobody is ever favoured with deeper spiritual knowledge for purely personal or selfish advantage; whatever man is granted in this respect is credited to his personal account merely for redistribution to humanity as a whole, through any avenues that may be at his disposal. It stands to reason that before an instrument can be used effectively on behalf of his fellow man, such an individual will first need adequate training to qualify him for the expected task and thus to ensure reasonable competence. With the experience and knowledge gained during this process of instruction, the aspirant – or tool – must of course benefit considerably in his personal capacity; this, however, should never become his primary motivation.

III

ALL IS ENERGY

Scientists and esotericists have at last reached one point of agreement and that is the truth of the age-old postulate that "All that IS, is Energy". But that still does not throw much more light on this subject. Man is inclined to talk glibly about 'Energy' but meanwhile as with other concepts such as 'Life' and 'Spirit' even scientists, although they may be thoroughly acquainted with many of their relative properties and qualities, do not know what these principles really are, what their esoteric significance is, nor whence and how they originate. These principles form an intrinsic part of daily existence and of 'nature' and are blandly accepted and taken for granted by both scientists and the world at large but without anyone being able to explain or clearly define what they really are.

Actually scientists at times are most inconsistent with regard to their attitude towards different aspects of subjective life, some aspects of which they blindly and blithely accept without further argument (because of their ignorance) but in other instances very similar tenets or facts of life are rejected because they cannot be substantiated by certain stringent demands of 'scientific proof'. There are however indications that there is a definite change in the tide of opinions and during recent years several scientists have for instance been persuaded to acknowledge the reality of telepathy, the existence of an etheric body, as well as to several other aspects of "extra sensory perception" (ESP) and it is hoped that this will prove to be the thin end of the wedge which will eventually lead to the shattering of the wall of self-satisfaction and self-assuredness with which science has for so long surrounded itself and which has been the cause of serious limitation with regard to the extension of their field of activity and service. Once this restricting wall has been breached, allowing a broader outlook and a realisation and acknowledgement of the existence of subjective realms, it will lead science to a better understanding of these hidden spheres and a consequent far more rapid progress in development. Such collaboration with the esoteric field will eventually prove of inestimable benefit to mankind.

The final step which largely contributed to the recognition that all matter is in fact nothing but energy, bound and restricted into physical form, was the success of experiments culminating with the 'splitting' of the atom during the last phases of the world war which ended in 1945. The rather sudden termination of this war may be ascribed mainly to the fear engendered by the destructive power of this newly discovered nuclear weapon. Apart from the strategic and scientific potentialities of this new discovery, intellectual man was dumbfounded by the unbelievable quantity of energy which proved to lie locked up in a single minute atom. New vistas of potential future energy sources were suddenly revealed to the human eye – but what a pity that these forces should first of all be harnessed in warfare for the destruction of fellow men.

'Spirit' is but a synonymous designation of energy and another ancient adage states that 'matter is spirit at the lowest level of its cyclic activity and spirit is matter at its highest'. Matter is therefore merely the densest manifestation of energy.

All energy, of whatever nature, is in a constant state of movement, vibration or cyclic activity. Limited perception brings the human being under the illusion that a great deal of energy is permanently locked up in certain physical forms and that energy in that state lies perfectly dormant. Take for instance a piece of rock which according to geologists may already have been formed many millions of years ago; to the uninitiated mind such a piece of rock is absolutely lifeless, inert and inanimate. But microscopic examination with present day equipment and evidence by modern science will testify to the deceptive nature of this appearance and that this rock is really constituted of myriads of live atoms, differing considerably from the inanimate consistency so often ascribed to them in earlier days. Each of the individual component atoms is in actual fact a miniature 'living' unit, characterised by a central nucleus around which one or more electrons revolve in a field of energy, which could be compared with planets orbiting around a central sun in a solar system – "as above, so below". Subsequent investigations have determined that even the nucleus and its surrounding electrons can again be subdivided into still smaller units, which may finally be resolved into the constituent basic forces and energies.

But apart from the constant and cyclic movement of energy within each atom, the atom is also characterised by a process of 'breathing'. If any form of matter is pictured as consisting of millions of these minute and more or less closely united atomic particles, then the inclination would be to consider that, depending on the density of the material concerned, these atoms would lie so closely packed that there could hardly be room for anything between them. But this is not the case, because every atom, whatever its nature, is actually surrounded by a minute layer of energy, the so-called '*etheric body*' which will subsequently be discussed in greater detail. The atom not only absorbs energy systematically from this etheric surround when 'breathing in' but also 'breathes out' by constantly radiating energy through the atomic wall into this surrounding layer. Some kinds of atoms are relatively stable, the intake of energy more or less balancing the output but there are others which definitely radiate more energy than is absorbed and such atoms are then gradually 'decomposing'. This is a process that may proceed slowly over millennia or otherwise it may take place fairly rapidly. The other extreme is where the atom is broken up suddenly and an explosive action is caused by the released energy – the atom is 'split'!

With these considerations in mind one not only has to come to the conclusion that 'all that IS, is *Energy*' but furthermore that all is *Life*, all is *Spirit* and all is *Divine*. (And to these vital and comprehensive expressions each student will attach his own interpretation!) It is all a question of degree or relativity – life is contained in all matter, whether a mineral, a flower, an animal, a human being or finally a spiritual or divine Entity. The difference only lies in the extent to which manifested energy has been bound and restricted, its relative density, rarity or freedom and, most of all, the relative degree of development of its consciousness. *Consciousness* is one of the distinguishing features of the soul, which according to the sages is the product of the interaction between spirit and matter – a definition which really goes beyond the understanding of the ordinary man. Consciousness could perhaps be better described as the awakening awareness of the reasoning mind. There are again innumerable degrees or stages of consciousness, which in broad terms may be classified as sub-consciousness, instinctive consciousness, self-consciousness and eventually spiritual consciousness.

In whatever way the question of energy is approached, there is one tenet which should always be clearly kept in mind, namely that *nothing whatsoever in nature ever remains stable and unchanged* – energy perpetually remains alive and consequently keeps on vibrating, moving and flowing and thus must also constantly affect matter in the phantasmagoria of the multiple forms of its manifestation, which persistently and ceaselessly keep on changing, transmuting, reforming or reincarnating all there is. These changes may be sudden or even of an explosive and destructive nature or else so gradual that it cannot be registered by the most sensitive instruments devised by science but change there always *must* and *will* be. In other words, there is a sustained process during which energy becomes either bound or *involuted* into form or after further interaction and in the course of time, the form grows, changes or adapts itself to an inconstant environment and thus evolves and the process is known as *evolution*. As time proceeds and energy action continues, the stage is reached when the form has served its transitory purpose and destruction, decomposition, withdrawal of energy or *devolution* sets in, during which process the stored or restricted energy is again released to continue on its cyclic passage. The nature and rate of the latter process will depend on the dictates of Life or the Will and Purpose of the supreme Guiding Power working through Its many channels of manifestation which of course also include man.

Although fundamentally all creation consists of energy, this energy is expressed or revealed in many more ways than is immediately apparent to normal observation and what the average man registers through his senses are merely the physical, emotional and mental effects, which represent but a relatively small fraction of the greater Whole. But even within the discernible range, energy is manifested in countless ways as evidenced in the diverse forms of matter, such as dense minerals, fluids, vapour, gases and plant and animal life in their fantastic diversity. These in turn are influenced, activated or controlled by less tangible forms of 'free' energy, such as *Life*, *Love* and *Electricity*, which are again responsible for such secondary displays as temperatures and the many human emotions and reactions so typical of human existence and which are accountable for the many different expressions of involution, evolution and devolution.

Life is that divine expression of energy with which man is constantly surrounded in his daily activities, which is usually just casually accepted or taken for granted because normally he remains relatively unaware of these impulses until circumstances focus his attention on this all-embracing power in which all manifestation is immersed. Once aware of this energy, this One Life, he can merely accept it, appreciate it and apply it to best advantage but as with all other forms of energy the essence of its nature can never be fully grasped by the circumscribed mind.

Yes, *Love* is also an energy and actually one of the most potent forces by means of which man is being guided along his evolutionary path. This active energy comprises far more than the limited sentimental or sensual connotation so readily attached to the word in its more restricted daily application. It should furthermore be remembered that Love is not only demonstrated in its positive reflections, such as goodwill, sacrifice, understanding, loving discrimination, tolerance, courage and wisdom but also in its many contrasting or negative features, as for instance hate, antagonism, intolerance, criticism, suspicion, selfishness and fear. But much more about these expressions in their proper context.

This brings us to *Electricity*, which although not visible can be very distinctly sensed when contacted in certain minimum concentrations. Electricity is an energy which man knows how to 'generate', accumulate and then to utilise in numerous ways, having become acquainted during the past century with many of its properties and characteristics but which nevertheless still remains an enigma as to what it intrinsically really is. (Another of these inexplicable 'energies'). Man talks about 'generating' electricity, which means 'bringing it into existence' or in other words 'creating' it. But in fact man can never newly 'create' any form of energy – he can merely transform it. Energy is indestructible but man has been granted the privilege, the intelligence and ability deliberately to convert or transpose certain forms of energy and then to recast it into new moulds with altered qualities and appearance and thus to adapt it to his requirements.

There are energies which have temporarily been confined in forms in which they have *apparently* been lying dormant for millions of years but at some stage or other such energy will again be released to continue its perpetual and cyclic activities through the Universe, this time perhaps assuming a totally fresh garb from which new patterns of application may arise.

The so-called 'generative process' for producing electricity often consists of some means of rapid and controlled friction and the subsequent gathering and accumulation of the energy that is set free. Actually this 'generation' is merely a technique that has been devised to concentrate and conduct some of the diffuse energy contained within the etheric surround of the materials used. Science is today becoming aware of the electromagnetic fields which in stronger or weaker concentrations are present in or enclose all that lives – each and every form, whether a single atom, a mineral, plant or human being, has its own electric field, which under specific conditions serves either to radiate or to attract energy.

Notwithstanding the important role that electricity already plays in modern human activities, the Tibetan gives the assurance that in this respect a vast terrain for exploration and discovery still remains unrevealed and that further research will lead to fascinating new disclosures and technical applications as yet undreamed of, which will drastically affect human existence.

As a further example of 'free' energy, special mention should of course be made of *sunlight*, as this constitutes one of the principal sources of energy, not only for our planet Earth but for the whole of our solar system which is constantly bathed in the energies of which this light is the symbol or recognisable reflection. The average man is hardly consciously aware of the potent effect which sunlight has either directly or indirectly on his daily living. The majority just take it for granted, not realising the fantastic amount of energy and power that is systematically being poured into the atmosphere by these rays, affecting all that lives and exists. Science is, however, gradually awakening to the enormous potentialities for extended practical application lying locked up in this source of energy which has ever been at man's disposal but which so far has remained relatively neglected and not nearly developed to its full capacity. More and more research is being undertaken to find practical methods of utilising this energy to better advantage for man's industrial, domestic and agricultural requirements.

These energies, all originating from the One Source, have been differentiated into several subsidiary streams, reaching our Earth from many secondary sources, each containing their varying attributes and evoking the diversity of effects and qualities which characterise not only all visible and tangible manifestation in our material world and the Universe as a whole but also those even vaster but undefinable realms which remain hidden and undiscernible to ordinary human senses.

In the chapters that are to follow, some of these ideas and principles will be amplified in proper context. One of the main objectives of esoteric study is to make man more consciously aware of some of these energies, of himself as an intelligent tool in the hands of subjective Guides, that he is in possession of certain spiritual and even divine powers enabling him to manipulate these energies at will and that he can thereby evoke results which may be utilised not in the first instance for personal benefit but to the advantage of humanity as a whole, as well as towards uplifting the other kingdoms of nature with which he is consciously or unconsciously associated.

III. 1. The Etheric World

To obtain a better understanding of what is to follow, it is first of all essential that the student should clearly picture in his mind how the etheric world pervades and interpenetrates all that exists.

In the previous chapter it was described how every atom and every form is composed solely of energy – energy that has been confined and is retained in atoms of varying densities. The energy within the atom wall remains in constant movement or circulation and is for ever bombarding its restricting walls with the result that a limited amount of this energy does succeed to pierce its barrier and to escape. The energy which has percolated in this way however retains an affinity with and is attracted by the bulk of energy still under restriction and consequently becomes spread as a thin layer tightly surrounding each and every atom. This mantle is what is known as the ***etheric body*** or the ***aura*** of the atom.

The etheric body performs several important functions. It is for instance electrically charged, resulting in either a positive or negative field, which in turn will affect the attractive or repulsive action of one kind of atom towards another. The etheric layer is also the channel along which energies and forces are conducted and because it encloses the atom can either serve to protect it to a limited extent against undesirable outside influences or otherwise it may allow desirable rays to be absorbed by the essence of the atom.

As a rule atoms do not occur as separate units as they are usually grouped with various other atoms into molecules of matter, which are again massed together to create the myriads of combinations composing the endless variety of forms fulfilling the requirements of nature. Atoms may therefore be considered as the bricks needed for the construction of the various forms and the thin layer of etheric matter surrounding each atom may be regarded as the mortar with which the atoms are being held together. It also acts as a plane of partition enabling each atom to retain its individuality, when for some reason the life or other motivating force which has served as the binding agent is withdrawn. Should this happen, then the state of cohesion which held the form together will also lapse and disintegration will set in, releasing the atoms or molecules for ultimate regrouping under new conditions.

Because each individual atom has and retains its etheric body, it goes without saying that any composite form must be similarly equipped. And so it is. Every form has its etheric surround, the width or depth of which will vary within wide limits, depending on the virility of the life force contained within the body and the amount of energy which is consequently being radiated. In the case of human beings the etheric aura may vary from only a thin layer, to a surround of many inches deep, corresponding to the intensity of the inner radiating forces. It will also take on different colours in accordance with the emotional life of the individual and his degree of spiritual development. Discerning clairvoyants or higher entities with clairvoyant vision can, as a rule, by just a quick look at a person's aura, determine from its colour and brightness what his main characteristics are and under what emotional stresses he is functioning.

As described, the etheric body not only encloses every form but actually interpenetrates the form with an intricate and continuous etheric network, reaching down to every cell, molecule and atom. It is this pervasive mesh which is responsible for the interchange of energies – that is both the energy emitted or radiated and the energies being absorbed from external sources and which will exert their influence on the form. In a later chapter it will be described in greater detail how this **etheric web** is concentrated at several points of distribution, called the **etheric centres** and also how this etheric framework underlies the nervous system in the animal or human physical body.

The etheric web not only constitutes an intrinsic part of every form on our planet but this system is carried forward throughout our solar system and eventually beyond this complex, to include every other star, constellation and galaxy within the infinite macrocosm. It is this etheric network which serves as the channel for the flow of all energy and life-essence and it is through this system that each and every form is eventually linked up with every other form, not only within our Earth life but throughout the solar system and the Cosmos in its totality. Although these concepts really go beyond all human comprehension, it is because of this interlinked system that every action of whatever nature, from a flash of thought up to a nuclear explosion must have *some* influence on all the rest of the great Surround. There are of course many impulses that are so slight that the vibrations which they set in motion can hardly be registered. Others again may be sufficiently violent to have their effects throughout the ethers. And in this way our planet, with all that it encompasses, is persistently being subjected to forces that have been generated from sources from within its sphere of normal interaction or its ring-pass-not and in addition to constant streams of impulses or rays of energy issuing forth either from sources within the surrounding solar system or otherwise from wider stretching celestial spheres.

The etheric network is therefore that element which synthesises all of creation into one inseparable and interdependent whole and it is consequently of the greatest importance to realise that, whatever happens to any one part of the system, must inevitably be reflected by a reaction of a corresponding nature somewhere in the remaining part of the whole. Notwithstanding greatly improved astronomical equipment, it remains practically impossible for man, living on his relatively atom-sized little planet, to register or realise the influence of major disturbances in the starry heavens. Nevertheless, whether he is consciously aware of these influences or not they will take their course and must inevitably leave an imprint of some nature. These universal laws which apply to the macrocosm are naturally just as valid for man's more circumscribed conditions – as above, so below! In his daily existence this means that every single thought fostered in the mind, every action that is taken, whether deliberate, accidental or involuntary, has been triggered by some prior activity, vibration or influence. Furthermore every such action *must* inevitably be followed by a corresponding repercussion in the surrounding etheric sphere and these vibrations must again be demonstrated by some effect on physical, astral, mental or spiritual levels either separately or combined: the **Law of Cause and Effect** or **Karma**. Because such effects are not always immediately noticeable or are evidenced on levels not perceptible to the actor, there is often the tendency to disregard or disparage such consequences. Be assured, however, that every thought or action, whether for good or bad, must and will have a comparable reaction in the ethers, even though the sequel may be somewhat obscure and retarded or results may be produced on some unexpected terrain or level, where these effects are not always recognised as such or are not directly associated with the original impulse.

III. 2. **The Seven Rays of Energy**

It has already been stated that all that IS consists of energy, has been built from energy and by energy and will eventually be resolved again into the elements of energy that were temporarily bound and limited to form. Furthermore, all the forms that have arisen from such 'condensed' energy are constantly and consistently being impacted, activated, supported and maintained by streams of energy in its many grades, qualities and potencies as supplied through etheric channels. This principle is applicable to all forms within the Universe, whether a sun, a planet, a man or an atom.

These streams of energy are not present as a haphazard conglomeration of forces of undetermined quality but all originate from supernal sources and are sent forth, guided and controlled for specific purposes and functions under a divine blueprint or Plan and must eventually evoke specific results as visualised and ordained by some Higher Entity. These Plans are far beyond human conception.

The nature and origin of Primordial Energy, the Will of the Almighty, will forever remain an obscure and incomprehensible secret to the human mind but apparently the potency of this fundamental energy is such that with direct contact it would annihilate any material form known to man. According to the Ageless Wisdom, this Primordial Energy successively passes through a series of Celestial Entities or Bodies, during which process the energy becomes subdivided and dispersed to such an extent that it is considerably moderated before it ever reaches our solar system.

These universal streams of energy, the so-called *Rays of Energy*, are reticulated on a septenary basis; each of the seven Primary Rays, when passing through a specific Higher Life, is split up into seven subsidiary rays, each with its own particular properties and qualities with which every form along its line of progress will be permeated and animated.

Our own planet receives its energy supplies from a variety of sources, of which the following are of main importance:
1. The sun as the focal point of our solar system.
2. Rays that reach the Earth via each of the seven planets.
3. Radiations from solar systems beyond our own.
4. Energies emanating from the Logic Life of our planet with its hierarchical system.
5. Energies and forces contained within our immediate etheric environment.

This whole complex of interrelated and interacting energies and evoked forces is, however, so intricate that the human computer (brain) cannot cope with it. Let the student therefore not concern himself unduly with attempts to unravel the exact source of the many energies – let it suffice that they exist and that the evolution of every individual is determined by their influence. What is of importance is that every form, whether plant or man, during a manifested life is moulded by Seven Rays of Energy and that during that specific life one of these major rays will exert a predominating influence.

Each ray is distinguished by its own special attributes and the qualities and characteristics of individual forms will largely be determined by the predominating ray under whose influence this life came into being and supplemented by the effect of subsidiary rays playing a complementary role.

As far as human being are concerned it should be remembered that we are firstly considering a most complex combination of energies and forces – a group of related and interrelated energies functioning in a field of energy. The being for ever keeps on striving towards a point of balance but a *status quo* can never be attained, because the incoming energies never abate and continually keep on varying and changing, thus constantly evoking new conditions and problems. This, however, is what produces growth and evolution – or degeneration. Secondly, the study of man becomes even more involved because of the several subjective bodies which constitute his being, each of which is in turn subject to its own specific set of ray influences. This often results in internal conflicts when a quality in one vehicle is brought to face a diametrically contrasting tendency in another body.

Man thus has to contend with and find his way through life by attempting to reach near-balance between contending forces which may be acting simultaneously upon his several component vehicles. The Rays to be considered are:

1. The Soul ray.
2. The Personality ray.
   (a) The ray of the Mental body.
   (b) The ray of the Astral body.
   (c) The ray of the Physical body.

In esoteric studies the Seven Rays are often referred to by numbers, allocated according to the following classification:

The Three Rays of Aspect:

Ray I   :   The Ray of Will or Power.
Ray II   :   The Ray of Love-Wisdom.
Ray III :   The Ray of Activity, Adaptability or Intelligence.

The Four Rays of Attribute:

Ray IV   :   The Ray of Harmony, Beauty, Art or Unity.
Ray V   :   The Ray of Concrete Knowledge or Science.

Ray VI   :   The Ray of Abstract Idealism or Devotion.
Ray VII :   The Ray of Ceremonial Law or Magic.

Each Ray is distinguished by both positive and negative qualities and it will largely depend on the application of man's own free will as to which of these characteristics will be allowed to assume predominance.

By a study of the attributes of these Rays and an objective and unprejudiced analysis of the inner driving forces and inclinations, a fair idea can be arrived at of the Ray pattern controlling one's own soul and personality. A progressive recognition of the energies concerned will open the way to collaboration and encouragement of the relative virtues of these forces and a corresponding resistance to the negative influences. It will be noticed that a considerable degree of overlapping occurs between the characteristics of the different Rays and this makes it even more complicated for the beginner to determine in which of the constituting vehicles of manifestation these influences are experienced. However, as the student advances with his studies and self-analysis and the consciousness progressively expands, ever increasing light will become available, enabling dividing lines to become more clearly discernible.

The main distinguishing features of these Rays can be briefly enumerated:

Characteristics of the Seven Rays

Their Virtues

Their Failures

RAY I: Will or Power.
Vision; power to good; leadership; strength; courage; steadfastness; truthfulness arising from absolute fearlessness; force of will; singleness of purpose.

Solitariness; power for evil; pride; ambition; wilfulness; hardness; arrogance; desire to control others; obstinacy; anger.

Objectives: Tenderness; humility; sympathy; tolerance; patience.

RAY II: Love-Wisdom.
Divine love; wisdom; tact; calm; strength; patience and endurance; love of truth; faithfulness; intuition; clear intelligence; serene temper.

Selfishness; suspicion; over-absorption in study; coldness; indifference to others; contempt of mental limitations in others.

Objectives: Love; compassion; unselfishness; energy.

43

Their Virtues	Their Failures

RAY III: Activity, Adaptability or Intelligence.

Mental illumination; philosopher; broad views on abstract questions; sincerity; clear intellect; capacity for concentration; patience; caution.

Impractical; unpunctual; idle; intellectual pride; coldness; isolation; inaccuracy in detail; absent-mindedness; obstinacy; selfishness; critical.

Objectives: Sympathy; tolerance; devotion; accuracy; energy; common-sense.

RAY IV: Harmony, Beauty, Art or Unity.

Strong affections; sympathy; physical courage; generosity; devotion; quickness of intellect and perception.

Veiling of intuition; self-centredness; worrying; inaccuracy; lack of moral courage; strong passions; indolence; extravagance.

Objectives: Serenity; confidence; self-control; purity; unselfishness; accuracy; mental and moral balance.

RAY V: Concrete Knowledge or Science.

Accuracy; truthfulness; justice (without mercy); perseverance; common-sense; uprightness; independence; keen intellect.

Power to isolate; mental separation; harsh criticism; narrowness; arrogance; unforgiving; lack of sympathy; prejudice.

Objectives: Reverence; devotion; sympathy; love; wide-mindedness.

RAY VI: Abstract Idealism or Devotion

Inclusiveness; idealism; sympathy; devotion; single-mindedness; love; tenderness; intuition; loyalty; reverence.

Violence; fanaticism; suspicious; jealous love; overbearing; partiality; self-deception; sectarianism; prejudice; superstitious; bad temper.

Objectives: Strength; self-sacrifice; purity; truth; tolerance; serenity; balance; common-sense.

Their Virtues   **Their Failures**

RAY VII: Ceremonial Law or Magic.
Creativity; thinker; organiser; strength;   Over-stressed routine; super-
perseverance; courage; courtesy; metic-   stitious; formalism; bigotry; pride;
ulous; self-reliance.   narrowness; poor judgement; arro-
                                             gance.

Objectives: Synthesis; tolerance; humility; gentleness; love.

In all these considerations it should be kept in mind, however, that the dominating Ray
of our solar system is the great cosmic Second Ray of Love-Wisdom and that these two
basic principles of Love and Wisdom are the main guiding and controlling powers underlying the functioning of our whole system, determining both the Quality and Purpose of
our Deity. Basically every unit of life and every form in manifestation is therefore governed by love and wisdom and although the influence of all the Seven Rays will always
be present, they must be seen as only the secondary aspects of the over-ruling cosmic Ray
of Love-Wisdom.

IV

THE UNIVERSE

To obtain a somewhat more comprehensive concept of Deity and a more balanced perspective of the relative position which man, on his little planet Earth, occupies in the overall picture, an attempt will be made to sketch an approximate outline of how the Universe is constituted, as seen from the very limited and material outlook of man. With regard to the last remark it must be pointed out that physical manifestation, in both the microcosm and macrocosm, is only the reflection on the very lowest plane of that which exists in far greater splendour on several higher spiritual levels, where so many of the shortcomings and limitations of physical existence are not in evidence. But if a clear conception of the grandeur of the infinite physical Universe already far supersedes man's mental capacity, then it becomes absolutely futile even to attempt considering the nature of the corresponding spiritual Universe. Let it therefore suffice to mention that these spiritual spheres do exist and that they are of far greater importance than the tangible replica which man is registering through his senses.

Descriptions will therefore only refer to our objective Universe or to that insignificant part of it which man has observed by means of his senses, which have been fantastically amplified by the use of modern instruments today available to photography, radio and optical astronomy. The interpretation of these observations have furthermore been greatly facilitated by modern computers.

During the past few decades astronomy has made extremely rapid progress as a result of improved equipment and the break-through with space investigations. It is expected that this progress will be sustained for some time and that some older concepts will be rendered obsolete. New astronomic or scientific discoveries will however never seriously disturb basic Ancient Wisdom teachings, because these as a rule are not concerned with the minutiae of material life but deal with the broader and underlying spiritual principles. Furthermore both the Wisdom teachings and scientific knowledge originate from the same Spiritual Source so any discrepancies would only be due to faulty human interpretation. Therefore any deeper knowledge, whether of science or esotericism, both of which may be regarded as criteria of human development, must inevitably serve to bring these two approaches closer to each other, till they finally merge into a united effort on behalf of humanity.

In this connection it should also be realised that the rapid scientific strides which have been accomplished during this century are not so much due to man's increased mental powers but progress should rather be ascribed to enhanced sensitivity or in other words to the fact that his mental equipment has unconsciously developed into a more receptive instrument with which to register those impulses and ideas with which he is systematically being inspired from higher planes.

But to return to Earth. Until the middle ages man still had the presumption, or rather the ignorance, to consider that his great planet formed the centre of the starry heavens and that the Sun and all the celestial bodies orbited around this focal point of existence. Copernicus, born about five hundred years ago, was the first scientist to conclude that in fact it was the Earth that revolved around the Sun. It took many years to convince the world and especially the orthodox Church, of this reality, which already for ages had been one of the familiar doctrines of the Ageless Wisdom. However, only to substitute the Sun as the centre of the Universe instead of the Earth made no notable difference to astronomy and it was only with the coming of the twentieth century and the introduction of powerful new telescopes that astronomy began to move out of the doldrums with totally revised conceptions as to the constitution of the Universe.

Today there is no acknowledged centre of the celestial expanse, because of the gradual acceptance of the infinity of the heavens and the infinite can of course have no centre. What is, however, being more pertinently realised, is the comparative insignificance not only of our planet but even of our solar system, when seen in relation to the Whole.

Although it is impossible for the finite mind to envisage this immeasurable immensity, available evidence indicates that this whole fantastic complex is in a constant state of cyclic and *ordered* movement and that behind all this there *must* be some incomprehensible Master Mind or Power, Whose Will and Purpose guides and controls the whole system. Apparently it is all a question of wheels turning within wheels. To begin with there is our own solar system with its central Sun and ten *known* planets orbiting around it. If our solar system were to be looked at from some outer heavenly body – through human eyes – merely the Sun would be noticeable as a single star, as the planets would be invisible because of their limited size and also because they generate no light of their own as does the Sun. Thus there are innumerable solar systems comparable to ours, although varying considerably in size and composition and apparently many of the billions of stars in the firmament are but the suns of similar systems, with their planets as yet remaining invisible. The next step in this sequence is that a number of solar systems are again associated and each of them, as separate units or entities, is orbiting around some central unit, thus forming a super-system. Several of these super-systems in turn revolve around another and greater synthesised focal point, thus forming a constellation. And so the cumulative process continues and expands interminably, creating ever larger and larger and ever more complicated entities, until all are eventually and paradoxically synthesised into that inconceivable, infinite Whole – the ONE.

That these super-human concepts can be so readily and superficially sketched, is an indication of the relative shallowness of the human mind which can form no real conception of that which has been described. It is still largely a question of words and nothing but words. But these ephemeral word pictures do have some value: as man advances from stage to stage, gradually gaining ever deeper insight, knowledge and understanding of the Truth, he is adding new touches of paint to his picture, scraping off or obliterating that which has served its purpose in the past. And thus, with the brighter light of increasing knowledge and expanding consciousness, the subject is steadily projected into clearer perspective, allowing the distorted images of the past to be discarded and to be superseded by greater verities.

Although few people can conceive the real immensity of astronomic data, a few comparative spatial facts and dimensions might nonetheless serve to leave some faint impression of the vastness of the heavens:

The distance between the Earth and the Moon is 238,000 miles (384,000 km), with the Sun 93 million miles (150 million km) away.

Light travels at the inconceivable speed of 186,282 miles *per second*.

The range between celestial bodies is expressed in terms of *light-years*, that is the distance covered by light in one year – in round figures this represents about 6,000,000,000,000 miles.

Our nearest star is 4 $^1/_3$ light-years distant.

The galaxy or milky-way associated with our solar system, is some 100,000 light-years in cross section.

Millions of galaxies have been identified in recent years and it is estimated that several billions actually exist. Each galaxy in turn consists of many billions of stars or solar systems.

Revolutionary discoveries within the last few decades have shattered a number of older views on astronomy and meanwhile fresh information keeps pouring in from all sides, reflecting new approaches and trends:

According to astronomers 'empty space' contains a considerable amount of 'star dust' from stars that have exploded or disintegrated. It is maintained that from this material future celestial bodies will again be reconstructed. There is also the belief that all space is filled with streams of active energy in a perpetual state of movement, only varying in potency, concentration and density. When such energy becomes focalised in a specific region by Powers beyond human ken and when the concentration of energy is raised to certain levels, then atoms and eventually molecules of matter will begin to manifest. This process of concentration and compression, when sustained, will generate such tremendous heat that this primary matter will be in the form of glowing vapour, which with the course of aeons will be compressed to a seething molten mass. To what extent star-dust will be included in the process is still unknown. This, in broad terms, seems to be the way in which new heavenly bodies come into existence.

The tenet that all energy and therefore also all matter for ever remains in a state of motion or change, logically also holds good for the macrocosm. This means that though celestial bodies orbit along planned courses, which to human perception may appear fixed and permanent, these orbits do alter with the course of time. In rare instances these changes may even be sudden. As with all else, cosmic bodies are also unstable and the processes of involution, evolution and devolution or birth, growth, death and dissolution also proceed in the heavens but in terms of human calculation these changes may operate over periods of billions of years. New bodies are created and progressively move through the various stages of densely concentrated energy, followed by the nebulous, the fiery vapour and the molten lava phases, which are then succeeded by cooling and coagulation, only eventually to be terminated again by dissolution. All these different phases of growth, development and disintegration may apparently be witnessed in the heavens.

A great deal of information is today being gathered about the chemical composition, density, temperature, velocity and other characteristics of the stars by analysing their light and radiations. This radio astronomy is developing into a new and fascinating science. In addition optical astronomy is also being considerably promoted by improved photographic techniques used in combination with spectroscopes and telescopes and with electronic equipment playing an ever increasing role.

When stars are observed, the average man as a rule does not realise that the light they radiate may have taken thousands of years to reach us and that what is seen today only reflects the position as it existed ages ago. Therefore celestial phenomena now being observed may in fact be millions of light-years away and could actually have disintegrated and disappeared many ages ago. Yes, all is relative!

Certain dying stars, after burning out, are known as 'collapsed stars' or 'white dwarfs'. These celestial corpses are of such incredible density, that a teaspoon of their material could exceed a ton in weight. In other instances stars apparently end their physical cycle by exploding and leaving only a nebula of star-dust and debris.

A number of puzzling discoveries have been made in recent years, some of which are so unexpected and seem so far-fetched, that further corroborative evidence is required before the information will be generally released.

Scientists are coming to the conclusion that it is highly improbable that ours is the only form of intelligent life in the Universe. No *organic life*, as understood by man, could possibly exist on a fiery star but no valid reasons can be raised why such life could not be maintained on certain cooled planets associated with these stars. It has, however, not yet been determined whether it is a general rule that stars are attended by planets. Planets, when no longer in a glowing state, do not emit sufficient light and are also too small to be recognised with present optical equipment. Astronomers have, however, determined by indirect techniques that at least some of the stars must also be accompanied by planets. If the fact is then considered that there are billions and billions of stars and that a fair percentage of these can probably be regarded as solar systems, each with planets orbiting around their central sun, then it seems only reasonable to conclude that widespread life must also occur throughout the firmament. It would certainly be against all laws of reason and probability that our puny, insignificant little planet, this minute atom in the

Macrocosm, should be the only place in the manifested Whole where some form of intelligent life occurs. No, this just cannot be! It is far more likely that the heavens are teeming with life – life in all its wonderful diversity and stages of development and possibly of a far more advanced nature than man can imagine.

It is only natural that man should be inclined to invest the rest of creation with a similar pattern of existence to that with which he is familiar. Because he has no other standard for comparison it is difficult for him to visualise any other form of life – to him the human being is the acme of creation. Because man needs certain specific and minimum conditions of environment with which to sustain life, such as a moderate climate, water, basic food supplies and the atmosphere he breathes, he considers all these as essentials for existence. There are probably not many who consciously realise that it is not only the human being who has adapted himself over the ages to environmental conditions but that the great variety of other forms, belonging to the lower kingdoms of nature, have followed a similar pattern. Over the aeons there have been constant changes in climate, atmosphere and other aspects of the physical environment to which the existing forms of life necessarily adjusted or else had to disappear from the scene. It is therefore life that conforms to the environment and not vice versa – and that is how potential life on other spheres should also be considered. Although no other planet in the greater system may have conditions closely corresponding to ours, this would therefore certainly not preclude the presence of life forms on such bodies. On the contrary, it is possible that a great variety of other forms of life, adapted to their specific circumstances and perhaps totally differing from ours, may have made their appearance; beings may even abide there with cultures and civilisations far in advance of our earthly development. At this stage, however, there seems to be little prospect of convincingly solving these speculations as to life on other planets.

This contemplation of the Universe, coupled with the few odd facts derived from astronomy and science, have been given to convey some faint conception of the majesty and immensity of the incredible Universe in which our planet moves and has its being. Seen in comparison with the infinite Whole (which is really beyond man's mental capacity), the insignificant planet which has fostered humanity is less than the smallest speck of dust – only an infinitesimal atom. Could this picture only be conceived by man then it should provide ample food for thought and might contribute to greater mental balance and humility. Does the thought not occur that life on Earth must merely be a preliminary step in man's development, leading to something far greater and more comprehensive than the milieu of his planet can possibly provide? If man on Earth is an atom of the greater Whole, then why should he, if actually an immortal and perpetually evolving entity, remain limited and cloistered within his present small sphere? Must this evolutionary process not carry him, in the course of millennia, far beyond the opportunities provided by the Earth's 'ring-pass-not'?

Surely the time must come when the divine urge for development must lift him even above the spiritual confines of this planet, to play a still more exalted role in the divine Plan for the Greater Cosmos. Ponder on this!

V

THE PLANES OF EXISTENCE

A n abstruse subject will now be briefly dealt with. It concerns one of the basic principles on which the Ageless Wisdom is founded and should therefore be introduced at this stage even if only perfunctorily. With sustained study a clearer insight into these complicated concepts will progressively be acquired.

Everything that average man can sensitively observe, all that he can see, feel, hear, smell or taste, belongs to the *physical plane*. This plane therefore encompasses the four lower kingdoms of nature, that is the human, animal, vegetable and mineral realms or all dense matter including all fluids, vapours and gases.

Beyond the gaseous stage an even more rarefied or subtle phase exists, which is not normally perceivable to man and is known as the *etheric world*. Please note that the etheric, though insubstantial, nonetheless still belongs to the physical plane and not to the spiritual.

Closely associated with the physical plane is the *emotional or astral plane*. This is the region on which the majority of human beings are as yet largely focussed through their lower minds. As indicated by the name, it is the plane of emotional living – of hope and fear, of sentimental or sensuous love and hate, of happiness and suffering and above all it is the plane of glamour and illusion.

Next comes the *mental plane*, the plane of the mind. An ever increasing number of the more developed human beings, the thinkers of the world, are becoming oriented on this level, although often still standing hesitantly with one foot on the emotional step.

The mental plane in turn gives access to the four spiritual levels, the lowest of which is the *intuitional or buddhic plane*, providing the normal abode for the soul. This is consequently the objective to which the awakening personality aspires in its urge for fusion with its higher counterpart. Still higher follow successively the *spiritual or atmic plane*, then the *monadic plane* and finally the *divine plane* or plane of the Logos.

In descending order, the seven planes of our solar system therefore consist of:

Spiritual and Formless Planes:
1. Divine Plane (The plane of the Deity)

2. Monadic Plane (Plane of the Monad)

3. Spiritual or Atmic Plane

4. Intuitional or Buddhic Plane (Plane of the Soul)

Personality and Physical Planes:

5. Mental Plane

6. Emotional or Astral Plane

7. Physical Plane (including the Etheric Plane)

These seven planes collectively constitute the '*Cosmic Physical Plane*', which in turn represents the lowest of the *Seven Cosmic Planes*, namely:

I. Cosmic Divine; II. Cosmic Monadic; III. Cosmic Spiritual; IV. Cosmic Intuitional;
V. Cosmic Mental; VI. Cosmic Astral and VII. Cosmic Physical Planes.

   The above may theoretically be acceptable to the student but while the mind of the average man remains inhibited by his physical environment, he cannot yet differentiate between the various spiritual levels of our solar system and the cosmic planes are of course something totally beyond the range of his conception.

VI

The Essence of Life

'GOD is LIFE'

Our planet could be regarded as a living Entity, representing the manifested physical body of our planetary Logos or Deity. It is the Life of the Logos which animates, vivifies and correlates all that is to be found on the seven planes of existence; it is in this One Life 'in Whom we live and move and have our being'; it represents the informing, ensouling Life of the Earth, with all that it contains.

Try to conceive that no form of whatever description, whether a galaxy, a planet, a man or an atom, can ever lead a separated or detached existence. Each and every form is part of the One Life and each form is but a fraction or component of a greater form and every form in turn is again an aggregate of subsidiary forms or lives. All these forms are the expression of the indwelling or ensouling Life – that quality which interrelates and binds each and every form through the etheric body into the ONE WHOLE.

The fusion of life essence with substance produces consciousness – the reflection of the soul. The degree of consciousness exhibited will vary according to the natural receptivity of the form, with its point in evolution and with the relative position it occupies in the overall chain of development.

'God' is a concept beyond the limited understanding of the human mind and because 'God is Life' it is consequently just as futile to attempt explaining what Life is. There are those who are under the delusion that man may some day succeed in creating new life but these bemused individuals still have to learn that Life can never be 'created', because all that exists already contains life. Every form is therefore but a manifestation of Life – of Divinity. Life is that power which sustains the form and which consistently demonstrates its presence by some kind of activity or 'livingness'. Therefore Life is but another manifestation of energy and as a divine principle it can never be destroyed. Strictly speaking and viewed from the spiritual aspect, it is therefore impossible to 'take life' – one can only 'pass on' the life essence from one form or channel to another and from one life experience to the next, until eventually the Will of God is realised.

The problem of '*taking life*', regarded superficially, contains several paradoxes but if carefully pondered upon and considered from the right perspective, will gradually become clearer. Life should never be taken indiscriminately and in this respect follow the dictates of the conscience or intuition or in other words the Soul. On the other hand it should be realised that no physical movement or action of any nature can be taken without destroying life of some sort. Thus all physical existence is therefore dependent on the destruction or rather the transmuting of life. Therefore '*lives dwell upon lives and are nourished by the comprehensive life – by Life itself*', till the time arrives when the evolutionary process of such life is expressed through the life of man, leading him consecutively through many lives, till he finally attains to spiritual levels. Then can man permanently relinquish the process of cyclic return to the world of matter; then the portals are opened to him for entry into the reality of LIFE where there will no longer be the needs of a physical body insistently clamouring for nourishment to be derived from lesser lives.

In this connection it should be remembered that *sacrifice* is one of the basic laws of our solar system and that through sacrifice the fundamental Plan and Purpose which sustains all existence is brought to fruition. And part of this Plan is that the higher should subsist on the lower, yielding the lesser life to the greater, thereby simultaneously incurring increased responsibility for the greater. This accruing burden from bounties received or taken from lesser lives must however again be redeemed and this is what entails cyclic return of the greater, partly with the unconscious urge of contributing towards the upliftment of the lower kingdoms. This rotating pattern proceeds from the vegetable life feeding on the mineral, the animal on the plant and eventually man receiving sustenance from both plant and animal life. And still the wheel of life inexorably rolls on, until such time when the personality sacrifices itself to the greater – the Soul – and the Soul is in turn absorbed in the Monad and the Monad is finally assimilated in LIFE or GOD the Great Unknown, the ONE, Who is reflected in all existence and manifestation.

One of the most distinctive features of the conscious life of man is that consciousness is simultaneously coupled with a '*free will*'. This free will constitutes one of the essential requirements for human evolution and it is therefore a factor that may not be overlooked or interfered with. By destroying *conscious life* – in contradistinction to that of lesser or unconscious life – the pursuance of the normal progress or activity is impeded, the expression of the spontaneous free will is tampered with and the course of natural law is being obstructed. Therefore normally man should not take the life of man.

All lives are however subject to adjustment according to circumstances of time and space and notwithstanding the clear injunction about not destroying conscious life, there are circumstances under which such drastic action not only becomes expedient but essential and should be regarded as an exigency or duty which should be responded to by the individual, the group or organisation on whose shoulders destiny has placed the karmic responsibility for the solution of that specific problem. In such instances it is not so much the nature of the deed or activity that should prove decisive but rather the underlying motivation. For example, war under ordinary circumstances represents mass murder but on the other hand conditions may occur when the motives impelling such action are lofty and pure and where such action not only becomes right and justified but should even be regarded as a sacrifice and an altruistic duty.

Similarly when a man is forced to kill in defence of the weak and innocent and without hate or rancour in his heart, such slaying cannot be considered as murder and will therefore not be added to his karmic liability.

And so the Wheel of Life for ever keeps on revolving, evolving from form to form and life to Life; from mineral, to plant, to animal, to man; evolving in man from the brute physical, through the emotional, to the mental and on to the Soul; and still for ever on and on … from lesser light to greater Light … till all merges into the ONE LIGHT, the ONE LIFE.

VII

THE KINGDOMS OF NATURE

No human mind, constituting only an infinitesimal part of the Whole, can possibly encompass and conceive the Ultimate but the contemplator can at least make an attempt towards a better understanding of himself, of the human race of which he forms a part and of the environment by which he is influenced and on which he involuntarily must also have some effect, depending on the role he is fulfilling. Once the position which man occupies in the overall pattern can be clearly visualised, he will be far better qualified to avail himself of life's circumstances and opportunities and to acquit himself more efficiently of his allotted task or self-imposed objective. To obtain a reasonable perspective of his position in this framework, it is advisable to work from the general to the particular and that is why in a previous chapter an endeavour has been made to give some idea of the nature of the Universe and of the relative insignificance of our planet in this greater Whole.

But even if the attention is diverted from the illimitable Universe, to be focussed merely on our little planet, then the task of understanding that which is observed remains prodigious. To human perspective the dimensions of this sphere of his activities remain immense and in many respects incomprehensible in its totality. The question arises how the many facets composing this formidable structure are related and co-ordinated, how all these expressions of the One manage to function without undue interference and without resulting in utter chaos and exactly where and how man fits into the scheme and what role he is supposed to fulfil.

To create some order out of this apparent confusion of creation, the Sages of old have classified the manifested world into what have become known as the seven kingdoms of nature:

Plane	Kingdom
Physical	1. The Mineral Kingdom
	2. The Vegetable Kingdom
	3. The Animal Kingdom
Dual	4. The Human Kingdom
Spiritual	5. The Kingdom of Souls
	6. The Kingdom of Planetary Lives
	7. The Kingdom of Solar Lives

It will be noticed that the human kingdom occupies the central position, constituting the link between the three sub-human kingdoms and the three spiritual kingdoms. This intermediate position is reflected in man's dual nature, namely his purely physical attributes which, through the medium of his soul are in turn related to his spiritual qualities, enabling him to function simultaneously in the world of matter and the world of spirit. Actually one of the major functions of humanity is to serve as a channel for the distribution of energies from the higher to the lower realms and to play an active role in the development and uplifting of the latter. This is where man's provocative challenge lies – to improve himself constantly as a sensitive and receptive instrument to supernal influences and then to serve as an effective channel for transmitting these energies to lower elements in the evolutionary system.

The average man, perhaps partly because of early religious training, is as a rule aware of 'something' beyond his immediate physical, emotional and mental existence. Actually what he is contacting is the spiritual world and most probably this contact is being effected through the soul, of whose presence he is as yet not consciously aware. Figuratively speaking, however, the soul is knocking at the door of his consciousness and is demanding admittance and recognition. But while this perception is still vague, undefined and perplexing, man usually either ignores it or pushes it into the background of his mind. Gradually and by reflection and study, a deeper identification with the soul will, however, be established and this will be coupled with clearer understanding of what the buddhic plane or kingdom of souls implies. To the ordinary human being the two higher spiritual kingdoms will, however, remain an enigma and therefore, apart from recognising that these higher spheres of evolutionary development exist, they will be given no further consideration at this stage.

Before dealing with the seven kingdoms of nature, another fundamental truism should perhaps be introduced to afford some further food for thought. It is taught in the Ageless Wisdom that during the course of aeons, every single atom has to pass progressively through forms in every stage and every phase of evolution, from the mineral, through the vegetable, animal and human bodies, to the spiritual. Ponder on these implications!

The material kingdoms all form an integral part of the physical body of the Planetary Logos. This classification of nature into separate kingdoms remains rather arbitrary with regard to the lines of division and there will always be a certain degree of overlapping, as sharp distinctions between the main groupings cannot be drawn and marginal forms will always occur. This must be regarded as typical of evolution on all levels as far as biological populations are concerned and where individuals in every possible stage of development will always be found. Where such populations are divided into groups and classes, it becomes inevitable that transitional stages and specimens will be found which could justifiably be classed into either of adjoining or related groups.

A few of the salient characteristics of the lower kingdoms can be briefly outlined.

As far as quantitative representation is concerned, the ***Mineral Kingdom*** is by far the most important. It not only constitutes the crust of the Earth on the surface of which the other material kingdoms have been deployed and are fulfilling their varied functions but the core also consists of minerals, probably largely in a molten state. Furthermore minerals compose the skeleton, both figuratively and literally, on which the vegetable, animal and human kingdoms are founded. The minerals also largely provide the basic source of nutrients for the three higher kingdoms. Thus plants are for the greater part rooted in mineral soil, from which dissolved minerals are derived as nourishment and incorporated in their systems. Plants in their turn serve to feed the animal world, during which process the minerals are transferred into the structures in which the lives on this higher plane are centred. And finally, both plants and animals again provide the fourth or human kingdom with sustenance, thereby introducing the minerals to this level.

With regard to the four lower kingdoms, it can be said that through the ages they have successively evolved, one from the other and with certain limitations this process is still continuing. In the evolutionary process each kingdom therefore acts as the mother from which the succeeding ones are born and the offspring thus depends upon and draws life and sustenance from the preceding kingdom from which it has sprung.

The mineral kingdom represents the densest expression of the life of God in substance and its outstanding characteristic, which has become so apparent with the development of nuclear physics, is the imprisoned or unexpressed power contained within its constituent atoms. In this connection it should be clearly realised that 'matter is spirit at the lowest point of its cyclic activity and spirit is matter at its highest'. Earth substance is therefore nothing but tangible etheric substance or energy that has been reduced or compressed into manifestation as dense and tangible objective matter. But this process of condensation represents only the involutionary part of the picture and reflects only one cycle in an unending spiral of the evolutionary plan, because eventually this Earth substance must again be progressively transmuted back into the originating energy. This restoration or resolution, when taking its normal course over the aeons, is called *radiation* and may proceed at a very slow and gradual tempo or under other circumstances more rapidly. Man has, however, succeeded in partially controlling this process by artificial means and can now scientifically release the incredible amount of energy locked up in certain atoms. These discoveries have placed powers in the hands of modern man, which if abused or injudiciously applied could prove self-destructive and fatal to all civilisation. On the other hand, with discriminative use, it could prove of great blessing to humanity and a valuable source of energy.

The next in order of succession is the *Vegetable Kingdom*, in which life forces for the first time become distinguishable as 'growth' when the manifested form begins to react to external factors, such as light, temperature and moisture. This means that there are indications of sentiency but not yet of consciousness.

From these remarks it should not be concluded that the mineral kingdom is completely insensitive. On the contrary, it is all a question of degree and once it is known what to look for and if the necessary instruments are available for recording reactions to which our senses may perhaps be insufficiently attuned, it will be found that all minerals will for instance react to heat and cold by evincing a certain amount of expansion or contraction. This property is most evident in metals and science has for instance availed itself of the exceptional sensitivity of mercury in the construction of thermometers to register relative changes in temperatures.

As the Tibetan has already repeatedly prophesied, scientists are at long last becoming aware of the fact that all forms are surrounded by an etheric body or as science refers to it, an electromagnetic field, in which energy impulses of many kinds are registered. Recognition of this surround has formed part of esoteric teachings for centuries but was consistently rejected by science and treated with so much disdain that research in this direction was for long totally discouraged. Discovery of this new terrain must mainly be ascribed to improved radionic, electronic and photographic instrumentation, which have enabled scientists to penetrate several new spheres of investigation which before remained obscure. It does not matter whether the etheric body is known as an 'electromagnetic field' or by any other designation – what signifies is that this 'discovery' has led to a sudden widespread interest throughout the scientific world and that deeper delving into these hidden aspects of nature are now assured and must inevitably lead to a better understanding of that which so far has largely remained unacceptable because of its impalpability and invisibility.

Now that scientists have acknowledged the actual existence of various aspects of what has commonly become known as 'extra sensory perception' (E.S.P.) their appetites have in many instances been whetted and they are realising that an unlimited field of research is lying fallow, simply crying out for exploration by men of initiative and imagination. Just the first glimpses have been granted into what is proving to be a most exciting new world, the existence of which was hardly ever imagined. With the awakening of science to this new domain, it is expected that further discoveries and developments will be rapidly forthcoming and that new vistas will be opened up, throwing light on to concepts stretching far beyond the wildest fancies of ordinary man.

One of the major results of this vertical extension of human knowledge will be a corresponding expansion in consciousness of humanity and this must in turn lead to horizontal unfoldment and a much better understanding and closer linking between science, religion and practical daily living. And finally such developments must unavoidably result in improved human relationships and also to a better acquittal of man's unrealised function and responsibility, namely serving as a link, channel and mediator between the higher and the lower kingdoms.

These general reflections are not as digressive and inappropriate in the present context as might be considered on first impression. Certain investigators have come to the conclusion that plants are not only extremely sensitive to vital factors of their environment, such as the relative position of the sun and moon, light intensity and colour, temperature, moisture, soil nutrients and atmospheric conditions but that they will even react to music or at least certain ranges of sound. There are also indications that plants may show response to the human voice and to emotional and mental emanations directed even unconsciously towards them; this may be reflected as an attractive or positive reaction towards certain individuals, in contrast to a comparable negative response towards others. Does this not tend to confirm the old-fashioned belief that some people have 'green fingers' and a knack of handling plants with success and others not? Yes, it should be realised that plants are living entities with a delicate sentiency, comparable with an early form of instinctive consciousness. What a wonderful field for research is awaiting the worker with the needed vision and sensitivity! Apparently the time has arrived for these revelations!

One of the main functions of plant life is to transform minerals into a form which animals or man can assimilate as sustenance. In this process of conversion or transmutation, dissolved minerals are combined with atmospheric and solar energy or 'life' to produce organic plant material. This represents a further terrain where knowledge is still most inadequate and which will lend itself well to deeper investigation; this must then inevitably lead to an awareness of the existence of the **Deva Realm**. A detailed consideration of the Devas, those invisible natural builders of the etheric world, would entail a vast separate study. Therefore, let it suffice for present purposes to say that the Deva-evolution develops parallel to that of humanity and that these two evolutions cannot be separated altogether, as in several respects they are too closely associated and integrated. The Devas are for instance the actual etheric builders of all that constitutes physical form in nature and eventually each and every form, whether a crystal, a plant or the physical body of animal or man, may be regarded as representing one of the myriads of forms taken on by Devas. It is realised that for the novice in esoteric thought this concept will not be readily acceptable but let this not cause undue perplexity at this stage, as with the pursuance of these studies it will be found that the many separate pieces of this jigsaw puzzle will gradually begin to sort themselves out to form a clearer pattern. Actually it is this Deva-realm to which ancient legends about fairies, gnomes, goblins, imps and vixens symbolically refer. Yes, there is a background of truth to many of these fairy tales!

(See also: XVII – "Devas and Elementals")

The vegetable kingdom, with its profusion of beauty of form and colour, fulfils par excellence the function of decorating our globe. These ornamental properties, together with the attractive perfumes exuded, are the characteristics providing the magnetism which plants exert on insects, animals and man.

The evolution of plants, exemplified by its magnificent trees, its fascinating flowers, charming and attracting man and beast alike with their lovely form, odour and colour, could in its own sphere be considered as one of the most advanced of the natural kingdoms. In addition vegetation is an absolute essential for providing a wide range of nutrients, of fibre for clothing and many other materials, of timber and its variety of derived products and for numerous other requirements of the two higher kingdoms.

It should also be mentioned that the human kingdom is playing an important and active role in the development and evolution of plant life, by selective breeding, developing many new varieties and by artificial propagation, cultivation, fertilising, etc. and thus stimulating plant life and food production on a large scale. On the other hand man has also been responsible for several negative aspects, for instance being guilty of large scale destructive exploitation of natural forests, for over-grazing, denudation and deterioration of natural pastures, which have often led to serious soil erosion and even encroachment of desert conditions.

In considering the *Animal Kingdom* it should be pointed out that in common with the vegetable kingdom, an extremely wide range of types and species occurs, varying from unicellular to relatively highly developed forms. Furthermore there are the marginal cases where it is difficult to decide in which of the two kingdoms the form should be classified. Although these are points of interest, they do not really affect the issues with which these studies are concerned. Neither is it necessary to go into detail about the various subdivisions occurring in the animal kingdom, such as the insects, reptiles, bird-life, mammals, etc. What is of importance for present purposes is that it should be realised that all of this realm also remains in a perpetual state of change and evolution and that within each group or type representative specimens will be found at practically every stage of development.

Because of this wide and individual variation within species, it may often prove deceptive to refer to the evolution of a species as a whole. In each species individuals will, however, be found which have reached relatively superior positions in their respective evolutionary patterns. Noticeable differences may for instance occur not only in bodily qualities but also in intelligence or instinctive reaction within such species as dogs, cats, horses and even elephants.

The main difference between man and animal lies in the respective degree of *consciousness* displayed. The human being is qualified with what is called *self*-consciousness, while the higher animals are generally guided by *instinctive*-consciousness or a consciousness controlled by natural instinct rather than by a *reasoning mind* as with mankind.

The degree of consciousness exhibited will be determined by the presence or absence of the soul, that vague spiritual quality, which because of its ephemeral nature cannot be pinned down and truly defined in human words. It is that divine spark with which *animal-man* was endowed and by means of which he was raised into the human kingdom. As the whole spiritual evolution of man is centred around the concept of the soul and as this theme will recur over and over again in subsequent pages, it will not be enlarged upon at this stage. For present purposes let it suffice that the lives of the domestic animals referred to above, such as dogs and horses, are guided by what is esoterically known as a *group-soul*. Some of the more outstanding members of these higher animals have, however, as a result of many ages of close association with man, developed such a relatively high form of intellect and awareness that they are already closely approximating the early stages of self-consciousness and are therefore being prepared for eventual transfer to the lower levels of the human kingdom – towards which over the aeons the animal kingdom as a whole is slowly evolving.

These esoteric studies are so broadly based, that it is difficult to gather the many strings together and to weave them simultaneously and smoothly into a systematic design, with a clearly defined pattern. This seems a suitable stage, however, for a few more words about *animal-man*, the prehistoric and brute prototype of the human being.

There was a time, millions of years ago, when man's progenitors, and by this is understood self-conscious human beings, had not yet made their appearance on Earth. The Sages estimate that it was some twenty-one million years ago when animal-man as such first became distinguished in the animal world. These precursors of intelligent man cannot be described with any degree of certainty but according to deductions based on archaeological research, these humanoids probably had an upright posture but otherwise they still very much resembled present day man-apes. It should be noted that these animal-men, being without self-consciousness, are not yet classified as human beings.

According to Ancient Wisdom teachings the birth of humanity dates back some fifteen million years, to what has become known as the Lemurian race. The land of Lemuria was situated in a region today mainly covered by the Pacific ocean, stretching from somewhere between Australia and Indonesia in the West to the Americas. The early Lemurians were the first animal-men to become '*individualised*', that is they were the first to be individually endowed with a soul of their own, instead of having to share and to be guided en masse by a common group-soul. Individualisation is regarded as the portal of entry into the *Human Kingdom*.

The rest of this treatise will mainly be devoted to a description of the many aspects of the human kingdom but with the accent falling on the spiritual evolution of man and a consideration of the many ways and means at his disposal, firstly to attain personal development and subsequently towards realising his higher objectives of service to his fellow man and contributing towards the realisation of the Divine Plan.

VIII

A Retrospective Glance Over The Ages

This is no attempt at a complete review of the past but presents only a quick backward look to obtain a general idea of the pre-history of man. To many this will mean a totally new approach, because the average man today is hardly aware that intelligent beings existed more than a couple of thousand years ago.

It is only some decades ago that many theological students still believed that the Earth and paradise were created not more than about 5,000 years before the time of the Christ's appearance in Palestine. There are some die-hards who even now persist in this belief – people who do not think for themselves, blindly adhering to their own literal and biased interpretation of the Bible and closing their eyes to fresh disclosures by science and the dictates of reason. A somewhat different version but one which basically reflects the same bigoted attitude, characterised by a total lack of imagination, insight and vision, is also encountered among certain conservative scientists who are reluctant to accept new findings by colleagues who are exploring new and more subjective fields of thought. According to the conservatives these new findings are too far-fetched, deviating too far from old and accepted principles – these intangible terrains had in the past been condemned as being beneath scientific consideration.

On the other hand it is largely owing to the progressive scientists of today that certain concepts contained in the Ageless Wisdom teachings, which previously were systematically rejected by the average man, are now beginning to be generally accepted. Take for instance the question of the age of the Earth, which scientists not so many years ago used to estimate in terms of a few million years. Today, with improved equipment and new scientific systems of dating, it is realised that our planet is far older than ever considered possible. Epochs are now calculated in terms of many millions and even billions of years and man is becoming aware of the relatively narrow span of time covered by our present civilisation and the very limited period to which so-called reliable historic records are applicable. Year by year archaeologists and palaeontologists are making further discoveries by means of which a few more dabs of colour are added to the picture of prehistoric times and happenings but so far this painting remains incomplete, with only vague outlines indicated and much further detail required, before the theme will become recognisable.

Looking back it will be realised that fairly complete and authenticated historical data are available at most for a few centuries, beyond which both the quantity and quality of even reasonably reliable facts and details rapidly decrease. Turning back the clock of time a mere 2,000 years, to that most important historical period when Christ walked on Earth in a physical body, it is found that many of those notable events are only indefinitely or inaccurately recorded, thus giving rise to serious dissension between individuals and groups. Furthermore, except for the very early years of his life and again the last few years devoted to his teaching, terminating with his crucifixion and resurrection, very little is known of the intermediate years of the life of this historic figure. Going beyond the time of the Christ, the cloud of obscurity rapidly settles over the past, gradually enshrouding the whole picture with impenetrable darkness and only an occasional salient fact hesitantly emerging perhaps as far back as 2-3,000 B.C. And beyond that ... nothing!

This last statement is somewhat exaggerated, because scientists have been able to draw some remarkable conclusions even about the remote past, by means of archaeological explorations and excavations of ancient cities, dwelling places or cave shelters. By investigating various fossil remains, a few more secrets of the hidden past have been disclosed, thus lighting an occasional beacon in the surrounding firmament of darkness.

The position could be summarised by comparing it to the view obtained from a strong lamp set up in the open and throwing a beam of light into the surrounding darkness. The immediate foreground will be brightly lit, with every object clearly distinguishable but within a short distance the brightness rapidly fades, shadows are thrown and outlines become blurred. At increasing distances from the source of light, the clarity progressively diminishes, till even the most prominent objects become indistinct, eventually fading altogether into the all-embracing darkness. But wait – in the distance a few points of light unexpectedly flicker on in the obscurity; a few lamps have been lit and are shining forth from behind the windows of an occasional cottage occupied by some pioneers. These lights now serve as beacons to the intrepid stranger trying to find his way through the black of night.

If man were to remain solely dependent on his own knowledge and scientific ingenuity, a great deal of ancient and prehistoric facts would forever remain hidden to him. In many respects this would not be of major importance, as man should rather keep his eyes focussed on the future, instead of allowing himself to be retarded by projecting himself too ardently into the past. Many past happenings may prove of interest from the romantic point of view but otherwise most of these events no longer directly concern modern man and might as well remain buried and forgotten. However, for a fuller appreciation of man's position in the overall framework of daily living and of understanding how he fits into the greater Plan, he must acquire a general picture of his origin and gradual evolution over the ages. Fortunately, however, recourse can be had to certain esoteric sources – the Ancient Wisdom. Actually some of this arcane history is also vaguely referred to in the Bible but in most cases the meanings are so shrouded in parable and symbolism that they remain hidden to the ordinary man.

No doubt many will reject this version of ancient history because at this stage it cannot be substantiated by factual data that can readily be confirmed. Under the circumstances it must be left to the intuitive decision of each student as to whether the authenticity of these assertions can at least provisionally be accepted as a workable basis on which to build, till such time as more convincing evidence comes to hand, serving either to confirm these assumptions or to prove them untenable. In any event it seems preferable to work from some logical supposition, rather than to have no point of reference at all on which to build.

And now for some of these historical events. As a matter of interest, first try to visualise panoramically the events covered by a single century; then slowly let your imagination roam back over the known historical ages covered by the two millennia since the birth of Christ. But even this comparison cannot faintly convey a concept of what is encompassed by a period of a million years! No – it is very doubtful whether any human mind can bring such a period of time into true perspective. Nonetheless, the following periods are given as an indication of the relative sequence of events.

1. About twenty-one million (21 M) years ago *animal-man* made his appearance on the world scene, as a separate species in the animal kingdom. Please note that these specimens were as yet mindless and thus should still be regarded as animals but with the physical build and appearance of primitive human beings.

2. Some 2 M years later or 18 M years ago, a group of Beings from other planetary schemes were brought to Earth to assist in arousing the *mind* of animal-man. This band formed the nucleus of those superior Beings who subsequently became known as the **White Brotherhood** or the *Hierarchy of Masters of Wisdom*. Their headquarters was established on etheric levels and is referred to by esotericists as 'Shamballa'. Although located in the etheric realm, Shamballa is recognised as occupying a definite position in space.

3. After a further lapse of 1 M years or about 17 M years ago, it was decided that more effective results would be obtained if representatives of the Brotherhood were to function in dense material bodies on the physical plane, thereby being in direct contact with animal man and thus enabling them to serve as practical Guides and Leaders to the evolving race. The first outpost of this Fraternity was established at a place then known as Ibez, located somewhere in the central regions of South America. Aeons later remnants of this original culture were still traceable in the ancient Maya institutions. A second branch became rooted in Asia, giving rise amongst others to the appearance and work of the Himalayan and Southern Indian adepts. In this connection the Tibetan prophesies that at some future date much of the mystery still enshrouding pre-history in general and the early history of the Near East, the Gobi desert and Central Asia in particular, will be revealed with the discovery of certain ancient monuments and records. Some of these will be found above ground and others in subterranean strongholds where many of these archaic chronicles are still intact and have been safely conserved as convincing testimony to the truth of these ancient historical facts.

4. At the end of the previous chapter it was briefly described how some 15 M years ago these efforts of the Brotherhood led to the '*individualisation*' of animal-man, resulting in the appearance of the first true but still most primitive human beings. This might be regarded as the birth of the human kingdom. Historically this original race of men has become known as *Lemurians,* named after their country Lemuria, situated somewhere in the region now occupied by the Pacific ocean and probably also including parts of both North and South America.

5. After a protracted period of some three million years of slow development, the greater part of Lemuria was destroyed by volcanic action and disappeared below the seas, leaving only a number of smaller islands where once there had been a vast continent. Some remnants of the race escaped, however, to become the founders of the future *Atlantean* race, which originated about 12 M years ago. Where Lemuria lay to the West of the Americas, the continent of Atlantis was situated mainly East of these continents, comprising a region now mostly covered by the Atlantic ocean and stretching far out from the Americas towards Europe and North Africa.

Little detailed knowledge of these two early human races is available but a general description can be given of the various stages through which they evolved.

The spark of mind, the first distinctive attribute of the soul, which served to lift the Lemurians from the animal into the human kingdom, remained for a long time somewhat dormant and barely noticeable by awakening the physical consciousness. In the course of time, this gradual awakening of the self produced men still largely retaining their animal tendencies but who were distinguished by their selfish nature and an overruling desire for satisfying the various physical appetites. On the emotional level, only the primitive forms of emotion, such as fear of physical pain and sexual desire, were as yet apparent. However, at times the first vague indications of an awakening of the love nature, combined with an indefinite urge towards something better and higher could be detected – the embryonic appearance of what in ages to come would develop into a primitive form of aspiration.

It is of course impossible for modern man clearly to visualise or understand the mind, or rather the lack of mind, of those primitive stone-age men whose level of existence differed so radically from that of the present. Even today those on differing levels of development find it extremely difficult to understand each other's mentality and approach to life, each group entertaining and accentuating those values which to them, at their particular stage, appear to be of paramount importance.

The awakening of the principles of desire and emotion indicated the approach of the Atlantean phase, when man no longer remained satisfied with simple physical or animal existence. He was developing an acquisitive nature and began surrounding himself with that which he wanted. In addition the leaders of the race began to display the first signs of mental unfoldment, just as today in the Aryan race there are ever increasing signs of intuitional development. This primitive mental perception was applied towards acquiring more material possessions for satisfying the ever increasing desires. Gathering of possessions inevitably led to the renouncing of certain freedoms so representative of the purely nomadic life of the hunter and this in turn led to the establishment of larger and more permanent groups than just the family units, eventually giving rise to the development of the first urban communities.

In those early days of Lemuria and Atlantis the primitive masses were led by their priest-kings, assisted by adepts, initiates and disciples, the direct descendants of the erstwhile White Brotherhood, who as yet still formed the only real source of intelligent and spiritual guidance.

With the development of the Atlantean race mainly focussed on the stimulation of the desire nature, this era became characterised by an overruling tendency to excessive sexual relationships, resulting in a rapidly increasing population with low moral standards. In the course of time this dominating accent on satisfying emotional desires led to utter perversion and decadence. The efforts of the White Brothers at mitigating these conditions proved futile and with their rapidly declining influence and authority, a major crisis was precipitated. The Hierarchy finally came to the decision to withdraw its representatives to etheric levels and to liquidate the degenerated elements of the race. As happened previously with Lemuria, the destruction of Atlantis, including most of its population, was achieved by cataclysmic convulsions of the Earth's crust and the subsequent submergence of the greater part of the continent.

According to H.P. Blavatsky in **The Secret Doctrine** this inundation of the mainland of Atlantis took place several million years ago. A few large islands were, however, allowed to survive the disaster and these provided a sanctuary for some favoured and more advanced groups who were spared to serve as points of nucleus for the partial restoration and regeneration of the race and to permit man's evolutionary process to proceed without undue interruption.

About 850,000 years before our present time, the larger part of these islands were in their turn swallowed by the seas, leaving only one relatively small remnant "West of the Pillars of Gibraltar", which Plato referred to as Poseidonis (or Atlantis). This remaining fragment finally also disappeared below the waters about 9,000 B.C. but not before a number of survivors had been allowed to escape and to introduce civilisation where they settled, in parts of what today are known as Europe, the Mediterranean regions and the near and middle East.

It is this submergence of Atlantis which gave rise to the symbolic biblical chronicle about the Deluge and Noah's Ark. Furthermore the story of the Old Testament is largely founded on the post-diluvian experiences and development of these Atlantean survivors and their descendants.

During the aeons of human existence the White Brotherhood has ever been present to support man in his perpetual struggle towards greater light. During the Lemurian and early Atlantean cycles, they moved amongst men in physical presence, fulfilling the role of rulers, priests and political leaders. Subsequently, with elements of the Dark Forces fulfilling their part in providing man with the necessary experience, the Hierarchy retired to subjective levels but nevertheless maintained their support. The Dark Forces originated with the development of desire and emotion, which in turn led to man's realisation of his dual nature – the perpetual conflict between the good and the bad and man's free will to choose between these alternatives.

It can be said that human history is largely the history of *Spiritual Messengers*, who periodically and in times of urgent need have made their appearance on Earth from divine Realms, to aid, inspire, reveal and redirect man's efforts. It is the history of the presentation of new ideas and of the re-accentuation of ancient verities and principles. The teachings provided should really suffice mankind in its interminable struggle towards perfection, if it were not for the indolence, selfishness, perversity and misapplication of the free will of the individual. Nonetheless, from these joint efforts of both the Teachers and mankind as a whole, new cultures and civilisations have progressively evolved, which are step by step contributing towards the final realisation of the divine Plan and Purpose.

The history of mankind could also be seen as the history of man's approach to God, of his invocative demand for Light and for contact with the Most High and of the pouring in of the Light evoked. It remains for ever an irreversible Law that every earnest invocative appeal issuing from the *heart* of man *must* inevitably evoke a commensurate response and when mankind in desperation sounds forth a united appeal, a Saviour or World Teacher has ever issued forth from the Secret Place to bring fresh revelation, hope and incentive towards fuller spiritual living.

Then again human history could also be regarded as the recording of the cumulative effect of streams of living energy from outer space, impinging without intermission on Earth and on mankind in its many and varying stages of evolutionary development. All that has happened in the past, and is occurring at present, is the cumulative effect of these energies, pouring systematically and cyclically through nature and through that part of nature that is called humanity. It is therefore all a question of reception and distribution, of sensitivity and reactivity to these energies and therefore of its absorption and dispersion. The key to so many of humanity's troubles has been its tendency selfishly to take and retain; not to release and again eagerly and graciously to surrender that which was so freely granted; to accept greedily but not to share willingly, to grasp and not to give and spread.

IX

MAN KNOW THYSELF

Man represents a mere atom of the Divine and only by a better understanding of this small fragment can he hope to attain a clearer concept of the greater Whole, of God.

The well known Delphic injunction reads: 'Man know Thyself' – what a tall order and what an impossible direction! But although man will never be able to know himself completely, he certainly can make an effort to understand this complex entity as far as his mental and intuitive unfoldment will allow. At any rate it will be found that the endeavour to penetrate the mysteries of life is not only a most demanding but also a very rewarding task. As the student step by step advances along the Way, intriguing new facets continually emerge, unexpected secrets demand solution and challenge and urge him on to ever greater effort and dedication in his striving towards brighter Light and finally towards more effective service of the Plan.

The honest and informed physician and scientist will probably be the first to admit his limitations and relative lack of knowledge of many of the more delicate physiological aspects of man's intricate physical system. But the physical body only represents the material reflection of that which exists on subjective planes – a fact of which the ordinary man remains blissfully unconscious. Man is the sum total of an intricate range of complexes, psychoses, neuroses, instincts, intuitions and intellectual fixations – the product of the action of numerous energies and forces from either extraneous sources or from his environment. On the other hand the individual remains limited and conditioned by his instrument of expression, the physical body and can express no more than the condition of his nervous system, brain and glands will permit. The degree to which these qualities of the instrument have been developed varies between wide limits – from the primitive Lemurian consciousness, which luckily is only rarely encountered, to divine perfection. Mankind represents a complete range of specimens encompassing all phases of development between these two extremes.

Man is the product of the two poles, Spirit and matter and the result of this union is an individualised 'son of God' or a unit of the divine Self. In *essence* man is therefore divine but this is as yet only rarely demonstrated in daily life. These same principles are referred to in the following two biblical phrases: "I have said, Ye are Gods." (John 10:34) and "Know ye not that ye are the temple of the Holy Spirit?" (Cor. 3:10). Man is thus Spirit or the Self or Soul, working through the matter of the physical body or 'not-Self', by means of the mind. The outer tangible appearance, the form, is only an automaton, obedient to whatever forces or energies are controlling the subjective surround which conditions each specific individual; his life conduct will depend on whether the emotional, the mental or the egoic (soul) forces predominate.

Man is therefore an aggregate of forces which dominate him serially and (or) simultaneously; these colour his nature, furnish his quality and determine his 'appearance'. For ages he has been wielded and dominated by these forces, his evolution being shaped accordingly. As he progressively arrives at a clearer understanding of these forces and how they affect him as an individual, he gradually begins to discriminate between them and to decide which of these are to preponderate. Eventually the stage is reached when first the soul and subsequently the Spirit or Monad take over final control.

The basic assumption that all men are 'sons of God', and therefore brothers, has led to the adage which is commonly and sometimes conveniently used these days, that '*all men are equal*'. This is quite correct up to a point: God has made all men *potentially* equal; they are all spiritual brothers and form part of the one humanity; they all function in physical bodies that have been endowed with a spark of Deity; they are all of the same origin and work towards the same final spiritual destination. Therefore as far as these divine attributes are concerned, all men are definitely equal and jointly compose one brotherhood. As with all else in life this basic assumption is, however, of a relative nature and can very readily be misconstrued. Certain politically oriented movements have for instance seized upon this phrase as a motivation for demanding 'one man, one vote', apparently conveniently forgetting that allowance should be made in practical life for differences in respect of the stage of evolutionary unfoldment of the spiritual, mental and emotional qualities, for varying racial attributes and corresponding national and religious characteristics. A careful survey of any normal human community will soon determine that only a relatively small percentage of the population is capable of independent and discriminative thought and that the large majority have not as yet outgrown the Atlantean stage. They are therefore liable to be swayed or led by effective *emotional* propaganda rather than by their own mental convictions. Hence political systems based on such a slogan may accomplish desired objectives but will represent the abuse of a basic truth improperly applied, causing maladjustments and with possible harmful consequences.

Every human being is but the personification of a spark of Deity, being impelled into incarnation by some inexplicable urge for physical experience. All sons of men are unconsciously striving towards the same final objective but each individual has to follow his own particular path to reach that destination. For life after life the soul returns into physical incarnation to gain further experience in the world of matter on its prolonged and wearisome path. Every incarnation is undertaken with the purpose of supplementing past experience and to enrich and expand the soul by further specific tests and trials, to encourage the development of attributes which so far have been lacking. And that is why exactly identical individuals will never be encountered: each is qualified for his (the soul's) particular purpose in life by his own character, attributes and capacities which, to those who have the required insight, will indicate the point in spiritual evolution attained by the individual. These personal variations in quality and character will also be accentuated by the surroundings and circumstances in which destiny has decreed that a particular life should find its expression. This will be demonstrated by differences in race, colour of skin, language, culture and mental and physical characteristics – those qualities provided by divinity to compose that intricate tapestry of human living which in its totality constitutes the divine Plan, not only for human development but for the whole of Creation.

The preceding generalities serve to emphasise the desirability of better knowing and understanding oneself – as far as the intellect and intuition will allow. To obtain a more comprehensive insight into the threefold instrument in which the soul finds expression during a human lifespan, it is essential that a more detailed analysis be made of how man is constituted and is differentiated into three aspects or 'bodies' and how these bodies are co-ordinated and synthesised to form a single and effectively operating unit. This instrument, the personality, composed of the physical, emotional and mental bodies, will determine man's temperament, the profession he chooses and the quality of his daily activities; they will decide his reaction to impacting energies; they will provide him with the colouring of his character, his abilities and aptitudes, his deficiencies and limitations, which will jointly impel him and determine his path through life.

These features will be considered and analysed in more detail in the following chapter. Some of these concepts will prove to be new, strange and perhaps difficult to accept but, with sustained study, the beauty and logic of these thoughts will be better appreciated and it will become apparent how perfectly these patterns begin to fit snugly together into the larger jig-saw, to produce a picture of which, as yet, only a vague outline is being revealed to the gradually unfolding but still largely obscured vision of man.

X

THE CONSTITUTION OF MAN

Man is the manifestation in physical matter of the spiritual Monad, a single spark of the One Spirit. The final objective as far as man, the individual, is concerned, is that his physical life and activities should be brought under complete and conscious control of the Soul, the reflection of the Monad or the Christ within. Through that control he must dominate circumstances and make environment the instrument with which to manipulate matter. In this process he has to work in, with and through energy or, as it is also known, electric force, which has to be applied and directed through three types of form, manifested as:

The *mental body* – the first aspect,
The *astral or emotional body* – the second aspect,
The *physical body* – the third aspect.

The mental vibration holds the key to the situation and by means of the *Will* seeks to co-ordinate the functions of the physical body. In some respects it endeavours to link up the consciousness with the three forms but it may also repulse and cause separation.

The astral vibration deals with the quality of the individual, determines his attractive or repulsive aspects and also contains the psychic element.

The dense physical level is where consciousness or Spirit is reflected in the material form.

The force holding the three forms together and allowing them to function as a coherent whole, is contained within the *vital or etheric body* which is controlled by the *seven centres of energy;* these centres are responsible for the vitalisation and co-ordination of the bodies and they correlate these forms with the soul, the main centre of consciousness.

The correct way of representing the constitution of man would be in the descending order of Monad – Triad – Soul – Personality. But as this exposition is primarily intended for the average man, who is still mainly self-centred, it will perhaps be better understood if the personality is used as the point of reference and if his path of unfoldment is indicated in rising order – the Path of Return to the Father's home.

The principal items, as set out below, will subsequently be considered in greater detail:

I. The Personality:

The physical plane man or lower self.

The 'personality' is a triple concept, composed of:

1. The physical body, containing the dual aspects of
   (a) the etheric or vital body.
   (b) the dense physical body.
2. The emotional or astral body.
3. The mental body, including the lower or concrete mind.

II. The Soul:

Also known as the Ego, Higher Self, Inner Ruler, the Christ Within or the Son of Mind.

The Soul is not a body. It is the linking or middle principle, representing the *relation* between spirit and matter; the link between God and His form; the Christ principle.

The Soul is that which provides consciousness, character and quality to all manifestations in form and it is therefore also the inner guide of the personality. The degree of progressive spiritual unfoldment in man is an indication of the extent to which the Soul is asserting its influence, till eventually the lower self is fully controlled by the Soul and the doors are opened to the higher spiritual influences – to the energies from the Monad, the Father.

The highest aspect of the Soul is represented by the *Higher or Abstract Mind*, which simultaneously is the lowest aspect and therefore the connecting link, between the Soul and …

III. The Spiritual Triad:

This is the triple reflection of the Monad, through which the Father functions at lower levels. It is expressed as:

1. Spiritual Will,
2. Intuition, Love-Wisdom, the Christ-Principle,
3. Higher or Abstract Mind.

The Triad stands, on a higher level, in the same relationship to the Monad as the Personality respectively stands to the Soul – the lower being the instrument through which the higher is functioning.

IV. The Monad:

Or Pure Spirit, the Father in Heaven, reflecting the triplicity of Deity:

1. Divine Will or Power   The Father
2. Love-Wisdom   The Son
3. Active Intelligence   The Holy Spirit.

Direct contact between the Monad (the Triad) and personality is only effected when man is nearing the end of his journey of experience in the three lower worlds and when the gap in consciousness between Spirit and matter has been bridged by the 'Lighted Way'. The personality then becomes a direct instrument of service under the direction of the Monad, by-passing the Soul which then becomes redundant and is absorbed within the Monad.

It is realised that the above classification will at first appear artificial and unrealistic to the student. The trouble is that of all the aspects indicated, only the dense physical is tangible and can be registered by direct contact and this is the only form of existence of which the average man is consciously aware. The other expressions are all to a greater or lesser extent subjective and to what measure the individual is or becomes aware of them will depend on the stage of development of his inner consciousness. All of man's spiritual evolution is centred around his consciousness and its gradual unfoldment. With some entities this process may be fairly rapid and with others again much slower, requiring sometimes numerous lives before any noticeable spiritual progress is evinced.

In the previous paragraph reference has been made to the multiplicity of lives. The subject of *reincarnation* will again be dealt with but it is desirable to introduce this theme now in order to acquaint the student gradually with the concept of the continuity of existence, which really underlies the whole principle of spiritual evolution. An unbiased consideration of the many unfamiliar and esoteric facts of life related to this issue, must inevitably lead the observer to the conclusion that it would be impossible to crowd all the experiences needed for the evolution of a primeval mind, from its elementary condition to the consummate perfection of the higher consciousness and intuition of the adept, during only one single span of existence in the material world.

It will be realised that as a rule the experience gained in any one life is relatively limited and inclined to be rather one-sided, depending largely on where and under what circumstances the individual was born and the degree of innate intelligence at his disposal. It will be found that some have to plod through life with a minimum of intellect, no educational facilities, no money or worldly goods and often under-fed – or generally speaking, with hardly any advantages or opportunities. In contrast there are those who seem to be favoured by destiny, who are born in favourable environmental conditions and who appear to have every advantage that life has to offer. But apart from the circumstances which may determine the tone and quality of a man's life and irrespective of the nature and diversity of his activities, the full range of experiences to be gained in one short span on Earth will remain negligible when considering what is needed for his spiritual unfoldment. What man requires for a complete and balanced development comprises the full gamut of experiences that life can offer. That would include in the first instance 'individualisation', then progressively moving through the primitive physical stages as symbolised by the Lemurian phase, followed by lives typical of the Atlantean phase which furnish the opportunity for developing the emotional aspects and then gradually moving up the scale to lives for unfolding the mental attributes, till eventually the intuitional and spiritual planes are reached.

Therefore if the individual is to gain every possible kind of experience, he will also have to travel through lives in the divers races, qualified by the many differing characteristics, with skin colours varying between black, red, brown, yellow and white; he will have to experience lives in the bodies of men and of women; live in the orient and the occident, in the polar regions and under tropical conditions; experience want, famine and abundance; the life of the slave, of the servant and of the master – in short every phase of life that can be conceived. It is to garner the riches and essence drawn and distilled from these experiences in physical form that the soul has, during the course of ages, returned over and over again for additional experiences, each time to a better equipped body and to different surroundings and circumstances.

(See also: X. 6 (g) – "Reincarnation")

This diversion from describing the constitution of man may seem out of place but has been given deliberately to provide a background for visualising and understanding the relative purpose and function of the dense physical body, supported by the several subjective complements of which the Monad avails itself during physical manifestation.

In the course of the following pages repeated use will be made of the terms *etheric body*, *astral* or *emotional body* and *mental body*. It must be explained that such wording should be interpreted in a figurative sense and not too literally. The etheric or vital body directly encloses and interpenetrates the physical body and to a considerable extent conforms to the latter and may therefore with justification still be regarded as a tangible 'body'. The astral and mental 'bodies', however, although esoterically regarded as material, are merely vague spheres of focus or reservoirs of energy closely associated with the physical body, wherein either the emotional or mental forces have been concentrated; they are only called 'bodies' for the sake of convenience.

X. 1. **The Etheric Body**
(The Vital Body)

It has already been described how every atom is surrounded by an electric energy field, which science knows as the electromagnetic field; how every form, whether minute, a man or a planet, is composed of atoms in their myriads; that these combined atoms individually retain their etheric shroud, which serves as the attractive or binding medium between atoms. Throughout every physical form there thus exists, down to atomic levels, a reticulated network of etheric matter which internally forms a dense grid and on the outer surface is intimately linked to form a joint etheric body surrounding each and every form. The etheric bodies of all individual forms on a planet are again linked to compose the etheric body of the planet, star or any other heavenly body. Similarly all celestial bodies are synthesised by the cosmic ether into the One Universe, THE ONE.

This cosmic etheric system, intimately connected with and reticulated down to the tiniest atom, could be regarded as the nervous system of the Universe, through which all energies and forces are canalised and distributed and it is the medium through which all the forms are interrelated, leading to reciprocal association. This network serves a double purpose: as a medium for conducting the incoming and, simultaneously, as an avenue for the outgoing forces. In the case of human beings it is along these etheric channels that invocative appeals may be directed to Higher Spheres and along these same paths responses are evoked and manifested.

The Tibetan has repeatedly prophesied that science would in the near future become aware of the etheric world. This is now rapidly being realised. In the past it appeared as if there existed some organised resistance on the part of scientists against acknowledging these phenomena of nature which actually fulfil such a logical and essential role in the daily processes of life. Thus any reference to the etheric sphere was generally disclaimed as unproved, as illusion or otherwise that science was not interested in the supernatural. Meanwhile evidence about the existence of an etheric world has been steadily accumulating as a result of what at first appeared to be the fortuitous findings of occasional research workers in different parts of the world. This in turn led to more purposefully designed investigations by a few inspired researchers, somewhat less hide-bound than most of their colleagues and who were prepared to outface ridicule for the sake of their convictions. These workers are now rapidly exposing a fantastic new field for exploration. Thus the authenticity of *telepathy* or thought communication, irrespective of distance or the use of physical equipment, has already withstood some severe tests. Furthermore, many excellent photographs have been published of etheric emanations from plants, animals and human beings – usually referred to as electromagnetic radiation. Similar electro-encephalographic recordings have also been made, yielding most unexpected results and there are workers who have since come to the conclusion that plants not only show a form of consciousness but that they even demonstrate etheric reaction or a kind of emotion to events occurring at some considerable distance.

A beautiful terrain for further investigation has thus been opened up and it is expected that this fascinating new direction will be attracting considerable attention from workers in many countries and that rapid advance in several respects will be attained in the near future. It is also hoped that this work will bring both the medical profession and psychologists to a realisation of the vital role the etheric body is playing in both physical and mental health.

The vital body is a material body, though composed of subtler material than that of the dense physical body. It is essentially a transmitter of energies and not a generator; it is a clearing house for all the forces reaching the physical body and the condition of the 'etheric centres' (See: X. 1 (a)) will largely determine the extent to which the relatively free flow of forces is affected. It is the receiver of Life Forces, transmitting them to the physical body through the nervous system, the blood stream and the endocrine system.

Although of a tenuous nature, the vital body nonetheless remains the foundation and framework on which the material body is constructed, underlying and sustaining every part of the tangible body. It provides the network of 'nadis' (See: X. 1 (b)) which forms the etheric counterpart of the nervous system. Therefore any debility or congestion occurring in the etheric system itself or any deficiency in the relation or co-ordination between this inner structure and the outer form, will immediately be reflected in the physical, emotional or mental condition of the individual concerned. Free and unimpeded flow of energy between the various vehicles must therefore be regarded as an essential for retaining good health conditions. Now that science is 'discovering' the etheric world, this must in due course also affect the views and approach of the medical fraternity.

The etheric body has no distinctive life of its own. With the 'death' of the physical body, the vital body withdraws its occupation and these etheric forces are then dissolved into the surrounding general etheric reservoir.

To conclude it can therefore be stated that the vital body is the field where two worlds meet – the subjective or spiritual and the world of matter. It represents the most important feature of man's response apparatus, not only qualifying the five senses and affording the needed contact with the world of matter but simultaneously providing the channel for the expanding consciousness to register the subtler worlds. Once control is taken over by the soul, this will also be the portal through which entry into spiritual realms will be furnished.

X. 1 (a) Centres of Energy (Etheric Centres)

The vital body is composed entirely of numerous lines of force. At certain spots these lines cross each other and thus form focal points or centres of energy. Where many such lines of force cross each other large centres of energy are formed and esotericists thus recognise seven major centres which play a most important role in life functions. These centres are situated in that part of the vital body which parallels the spine and surrounds the head of the individual. In addition to the seven major centres, twenty-one lesser centres are also distinguished and numerous pinpoints of these energy nodes are distributed throughout the vital body. Although the seven major centres are often referred to as being situated respectively in the solar plexus, the heart, throat or head, this may prove confusing as they definitely do not occur within the physical body itself but are distinctive focal points in the surrounding etheric vehicle, situated in positions more or less corresponding to the organs with which they are associated.

The following is a diagrammatic arrangement of the seven major force centres as they appear in man's etheric body [see next page]. The endocrine gland related to each centre is also indicated, as well as certain physical organs with which they are directly correlated.

These seven centres are present in the etheric vehicle of each individual. In the life of the average man some of these centres may remain more or less dormant and a gradual

77

awakening and vivification will only take place in accordance with spiritual unfoldment. In this connection aspirants need a special word of warning, because grave danger threatens the man who, in his eagerness to obtain results, resorts to improper practices and experiments to arouse the fires of the system. If by unlawful means he should actually succeed in intensifying these fires, his ignorance or wilfulness may eventuate in serious consequences by actually burning and destroying either vital body or brain tissue, which then might induce various forms of affliction or even mental aberration.

The balanced man should strive to lead a life of disciplined altruism, characterised by sustained training, refining and purifying of his lower vehicles, thus gradually bringing

The Seven Centres of Energy

1.
Head Centre
Pineal Gland
Brain

2.
   Alta Major Centre   **Eye or Ajna Centre**
   Carotid Gland   Pituitary Body
   Spinal Column   Eyes, Ears, Nose

3.
Throat Centre
Thyroid Gland
Vocal, Bronchial, Lungs

4.
Heart Centre
Thymus Gland
Heart

Diaphragm ——————————————————————————————

5.
Solar Plexus Centre
Pancreas
Liver, Stomach, Gall Bladder

6.
Sacral Centre
Gonads
Reproductive System (Male and Female)

7.
Centre at Base of Spine
Adrenal Glands
Spinal Column
(polar opposite to Head Centre)

them under soul control. The mental vehicle should be equipped by persistent and suitable study and disciplined thought-life. If in addition these efforts are then co-ordinated by dedicated, suitably directed and selfless service to humanity, this will ensure that the aspirant's vibrations are stabilised and are raised to the required intensity. He will then find that, although the centres have received no direct attention, they have followed a natural and parallel course of development and that their functioning and radiation will be adequate to all the demands of his particular circumstances. Therefore by conforming to esoteric laws he has awakened the etheric fires without running any risks.

During this process of development it will be found that the centres are at various stages of unfoldment, some still being dormant, while others may already be functioning and whirling vigorously. For the average man the centres below the diaphragm will prove to be more active than those above. Those beginning to aspire towards spiritual unfoldment will have the lower centres in an active state, with the heart and throat centres slowly awakening, whilst with fairly advanced disciples the ajna centre will also be vivifying. When the head centre is coming into vibrant activity, the disciple is nearing the initiate stage and it now only remains to bring all the centres into co-ordinated and rhythmic vibration.

Each individual will follow his own specific pattern of development, depending on the combination of Rays to which his vehicles are subject, the time factor and the complex of influences determining his existence.

The vital centres are in the nature of distributing agencies and electric batteries, providing dynamic force and qualitative energy to man; they are whirlpools of force swirling etheric, astral and mental matter into activity of some kind, thus producing definite effects upon outer physical manifestation. Through their constant activity man's quality appears, his ray tendencies begin to emerge and his point in evolution is clearly indicated.

The physical body is held together by the forces from the centres which synthesise them into a coherent, energised and vital whole. In this respect it should be noted that the ***thread of consciousness*** is anchored in the head centre and the ***life thread*** in the heart centre. When subsequently dealing with the endocrine system, it will also be pointed out that this system is a product of the seven centres and that the vitality and activity of the glands will vary according to the condition of the centres.

Each of these centres is related to certain types of incoming energy. When the energy reaching the etheric body is not related to a particular centre, then that centre remains quiescent and unawakened; when it is correctly related and the centre is sensitive to its impact, then that centre becomes vibrant and receptive and develops as a controlling factor in the life of the man.

All men differ from each other as to life emphasis, the condition of their centres, the glandular responses in the physical body and therefore in the various inhibitions of the flesh as reflected in their relative state of health. It is in this respect that the work of the physician and the psychologist must eventually go hand in hand. It is therefore expected that the medical science of the future will largely rest upon the science of the centres and that diagnosis and possible cure will usually become based upon this knowledge.

At some future stage when more is known about the etheric vehicle and its force centres, the advanced student will control the centres by power of thought. Through meditation and right practices the centres will then be brought under direct control of the soul, which is something quite different from the control of the centres by the lower mind – but for this the majority of men are not yet ready.

With the exception of adverse health conditions caused by accidents, wounds, infections or epidemics, it may be said that most diseases arise from disturbed conditions of the centres, resulting in ineffective control of energy or energy that has become overactive, misdirected, is lacking or is retained instead of being transmuted or directed into the proper channels.

X. 1 (b) Carriers of Energy ('Nadis')

The etheric network within the physical body is characterised by millions of tiny streams or lines of energy, to which the Eastern esotericist has given the name of 'nadis'. As the English language contains no suitable word to express this concept, it will also be incorporated in this text for the sake of convenience. These nadis are the carriers of energy and they underlie the nervous system, which they nourish, control and galvanise; they thus determine the nature and quality of the nervous system.

All energies influencing or controlling the physical body, whether originating from the astral plane or from higher spiritual levels, must utilise the etheric system and therefore also these carriers of energy, to effect the necessary contact. The type and quality of energy carried by the nadis for reciprocal interchange with the nervous system will consequently depend in the first instance on the man's focus of consciousness, his psychic sensitivity, the potency of his aspiration and desire, the set of Rays impinging on his vehicles and finally the stage of his spiritual evolution. On the other hand, the network of nadis within the physical body will also closely relate this internal etheric system to the seven main etheric centres located in the aura surrounding the physical vehicle, thus simultaneously linking the individual body with the comprehensive etheric system.

The nadis therefore represent the mechanism through which energies are externalised or manifested through the super-imposed nervous system and form the point or rather the area where contact is made between the subtle subjective energies and forces and the dense physical body. The nerves in their turn relay the impulses received to the physical brain. This same procedure also functions in the reverse order and when the brain reacts to impulses from the mind, these will be channelled via the nervous system to the nadis and thence through the etheric centres on into the etheric world, as directed by the brain. This is what happens with 'thought direction' which is the underlying principle of telepathy.

X. 1 (c) **The Third Eye**

A great deal has already been written in esoteric literature about the 'Third Eye' and it seems that more clarity is required about this little understood mystic organ. However, although descriptions and explanations may provide some mental concept of this 'eye', real inner understanding can never be reached until by gradual spiritual unfoldment a measure of practical experience of vision through this 'eye of the soul' is first of all gained – another of these esoteric paradoxes!

A few synonymous expressions will be found to be partly descriptive and will perhaps give some idea of the functions of the third eye. For instance: the spiritual eye; the mirror of the soul; the eye of the soul; the all-seeing eye; the eye of the magician; the eye of vision; the inner eye; the director of energy.

The third eye exists in etheric matter and is an etheric centre of force situated just in front of the forehead, at the midpoint between the two physical eyes. Although associated with the *pineal gland*, it must not be confused with the latter, which is distinctly a small physical gland at the back of the brain. The third eye should be regarded as the etheric correspondence of the pineal gland and it is only as the latter attains full activity that the 'eye' will be functioning effectively, indicating the 'fully awakened' stage in man.

The third eye is also the instrument of the Will or Spirit and thus becomes the 'Director of Energy'.

This 'eye' provides the aspirant with inner vision of the subjective realms and therefore with clairvoyance and will also afford the proficient worker with effective control over many of the energies governing the behaviour of matter.

Until the eye is functioning, even if only partially and periodically, man cannot comprehend and fully appreciate the nature of the energy which he is actually capable of wielding and therefore of the potential powers at his disposal. Eventually this eye will give him the powers of the white magician and that is why it is also called the 'eye of the magician'. It is by directing energies with the third eye that thought-forms are energised and vivified, sweeping the lesser builders ('devas') into any particular line of activity. (For 'Devas' see Ch. XVII)

The third eye is thus the directing agency in all mental creative work, thus also forming the basis of all practical creation. By fixing the inner eye upon the object of contemplation, a steady stream of energy is produced, which when focussed upon the objective engenders vitalisation and activity. As a rule this process operates unconsciously but by means of meditation and contemplation the qualified student learns to apply these principles deliberately and at will, although with discrimination.

It is through the medium of this 'all-seeing eye' that the 'Master of Wisdom', or the perfected man, can at any moment put himself in touch with his disciples, wherever they are or can communicate with other members of the Spiritual Hierarchy throughout the etheric realm. This eye serves him as an instrument for directing and controlling energies and holding thought-forms which he may have created within his sphere of influence and upon his path of service and it is through this medium that he directs currents of energy to help and stimulate his disciples and groups in any place and at any time.

Visualisation also stimulates the development of the third eye and forms, ideas and thought abstractions can thus be mentally clothed and brought into etheric being.

There are mainly two procedures which are responsible for the development of the *pineal gland*. Firstly this may be stimulated by energies emanating from the soul itself and acting via the etheric centres. This downflow of egoic or soul energy stems in the first place from awakening the centres through meditation and spiritual activities; the energy impinges on the gland, which in the course of years will gradually develop and begin to unfold itself to start a new cycle of activity. The pineal gland may, however, also be stimulated by a rational physical life and by disciplining the body to the laws of spiritual unfoldment. This will mean leading a regulated life, avoiding meat and stimulants such as nicotine and alcohol and practising moderation in all things. In this way the gland will progressively lose its atrophy and become vitalised.

To sum up it can therefore be said that the third eye constitutes the window of the soul, whereby it looks inwards into the three worlds of human existence, revealing the nature of the interior worlds, the Kingdom of God and the Divine Plan; it directs the energy of the soul on the physical plane and lastly it links the awakened man of the physical plane with the astral or subjective world, enabling him to function there in full consciousness. It therefore enables man to become aware of that which previously remained hidden to his senses; a world of fantastic new realities is opened up to his etheric vision and the nature and quality of the realm of souls and that of the Hierarchy is revealed to him in all its beauty. Actually these new perceptions are animated more distinctly and become more authentic to the observer than the world of physical experience ever could have been.

X. 1 (d) The Spiral or Kundalini Fire

There is no known word in any Western language for this hidden, subjective power, therefore the name under which it was described by the ancient mystics is retained in this commentary. The adjective 'kundalin' means 'coiled' and refers to the dormant power or energy present in every human being and lying like a coiled serpent *in the etheric body* at the base of the spine. This coiled serpent has been biding its time for ages, waiting for the day when the soul would begin to take charge of its rightful domain – the personality or the combination of the physical, astral and mental bodies.

This 'spiral' force, while still asleep, is the static form of creative energy which serves to vitalise the whole body. When awakened and beginning to 'uncoil', this electric, fiery force proves to be of a spiral nature and hence the symbolic description of 'serpent power'.

As the kundalini force is aroused, it will steadily increase the vibratory action of the etheric centres and consequently also that of the physical, astral and mental bodies through which the vital body finds expression. This animating activity will have a dual effect, firstly by eliminating all that is coarse and unsuitable from the lower vehicles and secondly by absorbing into its sphere of influence those lofty qualities which will serve to raise the energy content of the vital body of the evolving individual.

One of the objects of activating the spiral fire and its progress up the spine to the head, is to awaken the pineal gland, which again results in the opening of the third eye and the consequent revelation of the subtler planes of spiritual life. By sustained meditation, by study, disciplined living and selfless service to humanity, the entire system will step by step be aroused, bringing the lower man under the influence of the soul; this will ensure a simultaneous and parallel awakening of the etheric force centres and the dormant forces at the base of the spine. When this process is carried forward with care and under suitable direction, the awakening will take its course gradually and normally and without incurring any danger.

Should attempts be made, however, to accelerate the natural unfoldment unduly by various exercises or other artificial means, then the aspirant is letting himself in for trouble. Breathing exercises should, for instance, never be undertaken without expert guidance and then only after years of spiritual application, devotion and service. Concentration upon the etheric centres with the object of activating them should also be avoided, as this will only lead to over-stimulation and the opening of doors on to the astral plane – once opened these doors are difficult to close again. Students are also specifically and strongly warned against following intensive meditation programs lasting for hours or against practices which aim at arousing any particular centre or the kundalini fire. The average student is already stimulated to such an extent by present day life activities, that excessive meditation, breathing exercises, a fanatical diet, curtailment of sleep and undue interest and emphasis upon psychic experiences, will be inclined to upset his mental balance and may cause irreparable damage. The raising of the kundalini force, if brought about ignorantly and prematurely, may lead to serious nervous trouble, inflammation of the tissues, spinal disease and brain trouble but if allowed to proceed progressively and naturally through disciplined living, it will finally serve to open the gates to higher realms.

X. 1 (e) **The Etheric Web**

The term 'etheric web' refers to partitions of etheric matter, separating various etheric force centres or forming dividing walls between different stages or spheres in the development of consciousness. As the consciousness evolves, one etheric obstruction after another is successively dissolved, leading to constantly improved vision, greater light and therefore also increased responsibility.

There is for instance the web separating the lower physical consciousness of the brain from the astral plane. With man's spiritual development this etheric web is subjected to a lengthy process of demolition and gradually the first 'rents' in the web will appear. It is through these rents that the student first becomes conscious of inner happenings and can make his first contacts with the Soul. As the head centre increases in activity, it becomes receptive to occasional flashes of illumination from higher planes through this torn web. With passing time this will happen more frequently and, with more rents appearing, that particular web begins to disintegrate.

Each of the force centres within the etheric body, situated along the spine and up towards the head centre, are also separated by such etheric webs or discs and during the course of the aspirant's unfoldment, all these must be progressively destroyed by the awakened force of the kundalini fire released at the base of the spine and moving consistently upwards from centre to centre.

X. 1 (f) Radiation

All radiation should be regarded as the transmuting process in active operation or in other words the transference of energy from one form to another. What happens basically is that the inner positive nucleus of force or life in the atom or form reaches such an intense rate of vibration, that the negative electrons are ejected beyond the normal sphere of attraction or beyond the confining walls of the form that held them imprisoned. They are then no longer pulled back to their original polar centre but escape and have to find a new abode, becoming temporarily absorbed in the etheric or vital body surrounding each and every form. This in principle holds true not only for the atom but for all forms in all the kingdoms of nature.

The impact of a truth, or a mental concept and its recognition, is an indication that the quality of a specific sphere of radiatory activity has been recorded by the mind. This is what occurs with all so-called 'expansions of consciousness' to which the mind of man may respond: he registers a successive series of vibrations and radiations emanating from various sources of activity and as each of these is consciously registered and recognised by the mind, another brick has been built into the foundation of the developing consciousness and another rent has been torn in the imprisoning etheric web, thus leading to clearer light and deeper insight.

These spheres of radiatory activity are ever present and it is only the instrument which falls short and fails to register that which is available; the evolutionary process is therefore one of developing and refining the response apparatus, first to enable it to recognise and absorb and then to apply effectively the radiations as they are contacted from stage to stage. The mind will register these qualities, radiatory activities or emanatory impulses as impressions, ideas and revelations and the degree to which the disciple benefits from these impulses will depend on his stage of development and the firmness of his purpose and striving.

With progress along his path, the disciple becomes more efficient, not only in absorbing available energies from various sources but his own radiatory activities will also be enhanced, whether he is consciously aware of the fact or not. His sphere of influence will be commensurate with his spiritual evolution and the nature and character of his radiation will determine the quality of his surrounding aura.

One of the most potent forces that man can radiate is that dominant quality of the soul – *Love!* Provided the server's actions radiate loving understanding, they may actually be strict and even severe, without causing harm even though perhaps being the source of temporary pain.

Radiation and magnetism lie at the foundation of all group work; as the disciple gradually becomes spiritually more radiatory and magnetic and as his heart and head become consciously related, his radiation grows apace and becomes more noticeable in his environment, evoking an equal response from others. It will also attract the attention of the Master working on the same Ray on which the disciple's soul is oriented and on which he has been radiating his forces.

Different forms of esoteric healing also largely revolve around magnetic radiation and the patient can only be truly helped when the positive radiation of the healer overcomes the negative condition of the patient. Magnetic and radiatory healing comprises a full and rewarding study of its own and with increasing knowledge being acquired about the etheric body, its influence and its control, the practical application of these studies promises to play a role of growing importance in future health practices.

The dependable healer of the future should, however, not only have a sound spiritual knowledge, with control over his centres and the ability to direct and regulate his radiation and magnetism but he should at the same time have a thorough knowledge and training in ordinary medical and surgical methods. The knowledge of the medical doctor would for instance prove much more helpful in setting a broken bone, than that of the spiritual healer in the same circumstances.

X. 1 (g) **The Aura**

Every manifested form is characterised by an etheric surround or 'aura', which may be defined as the sphere of its radiatory activity. This also applies to man. Clairvoyants, favoured with etheric vision, can distinguish the human aura, usually describing it in terms of colour or light. From the esoteric point of view, however, the importance of the aura stems from its radiatory quality and its consequent sphere of influence.

The aura is a combination of radiations, energies and arranged forces, which can either attract or repel the good or the bad and it is through contacts thus effected that the whole trend of a man's life will be determined.

Similarly where groups gather, a *group aura* is created, consisting of a combination of the individual auras and the auric contribution of each group member can thus be either a hindrance or beneficial to the group's objectives. This united aura will determine the group condition, its activities, its usefulness and also its problems.

Each person looking out into the world or his immediate environment, inevitably has to look through his own surrounding aura, and the translucency of this window will define the clarity or degree of distortion of the images received. This same principle applies to all impulses and vibrations reaching him from external sources. The clarity and purity of the aura is therefore of primary importance if true definitions and impressions are to be received from or radiated to the outside world. Obscure and murky auras are one of the main reasons why the masses so often entertain distorted views and perverse attitudes, are not susceptible to reason and unconsciously reject the beauties that life has to offer. Their outlook on their environment and all that influences them is deformed; what they see is but a warped and twisted reflection of reality and they can therefore form no real concept of the good and true and beautiful, because for them everything is tainted by looking through their impure aura. The consequence is that even the most inspired and altruistic action or attitude of their fellow men, of those who may have attained to clearer views and purer objectives, are misinterpreted and treated with scorn and suspicion.

The aura of forces enveloping the human being is of a more complex nature than that belonging to forms of the lower kingdoms; man's aura is composed of radiations from the physical, emotional and mental bodies and its condition will therefore be determined by which of these vehicles are in the ascendant and also by the quality of the dominating emanations.

As the soul begins to assert itself, greater sensitivity to influences from subjective levels is automatically displayed and the individual becomes increasingly magnetic to spiritual ideas and concepts. His condition will therefore become invocative to spiritual impression and subjective ideas will be evoked into his mind without conscious effort on his part.

This magnetic aura is kindled by the first genuine contact with the soul and will grow proportionately with the frequency of such future contacts, until eventually it becomes an habitual state of consciousness and communion with the soul can be established at will and at all times. When this stage is reached, his focus will be on the mental plane and he will no longer be controlled by his emotional nature. This means that he has made a successful start with the construction of the 'bridge of light' along which impressions from higher planes may be introduced and which will increasingly serve to enhance the quality of his aura, thereby constantly improving his proficiency as a channel and instrument of service in the hands of the Masters.

The auric mechanism which every human being carries with him reflects to those with etheric vision a true picture of the stage which a man has attained in his emotional, mental and egoic evolution. A Master therefore only needs to look at the light reflected within the aura, to know exactly how far the man has progressed on his path of spiritual unfoldment.

X. 2. **The Physical Body**

The physical form, whether that of a mineral, an animal, a man or a planet, consists of millions of atoms or cells, each embodying a lesser life, each in a condition of constant activity and each preserving its individuality or identity, yet at the same time being held together in group formation by a central attractive and co-ordinating force – by Life. This Life forms part of a greater manifested Life – the Life of our planetary Deity or Logos, 'in Whom we live and move and have our being.'

A clear distinction should be drawn, however, between man as just a physical form and what is termed a comprehensive human being. The difference lies in the duality of the latter concept – a human being is regarded as a physical personality under spiritual guidance, with the soul serving as the link between spirit and matter. Although the physical body as such has its own life, this merely represents atomic life, totally lacking consciousness, and without the direction of the soul it would remain nothing more than a senseless automaton. The physical body is not considered a principle but solely a form responding automatically to the gradually unfolding consciousness. It is therefore only a medium subjected to impulses but without any innate intelligence of its own; it is a recipient body, without the ability of initiating any spontaneous form of activity.

The body of the normal physical man remains largely the victim of a capricious astral body, by which the personality is still being guided, until at a more advanced stage of development it becomes the instrument for the triumphant expression of soul energy. It can therefore be regarded as an agent reacting to the influences and directions of:

> The vital or etheric body;
> The astral or emotional vehicle;
> The lower mind, situated in the mental body;
> And finally, the Soul – the immediate spiritual guide.

One of the problems of the student is to determine the source of incentives, impulses, impressions or inspirations, which – with the vital body acting as the link, co-ordinator or transformer – sweep the physical body into activity. But more about this at a later stage.

Students are sometimes puzzled by the question of the heritability of certain characteristics of parents. In some respects children may show a remarkable resemblance to either one or the other of two parents – 'a real chip off the old block' – or they may appear to be a blended composition of the features obtained from both parents. This is as far as their outer appearance or mannerisms are concerned but their more subjective characteristics may differ so widely from those of the two parents, that it is often questioned whether a certain individual could possibly be their product. However, when once the principle of duality is understood, then these incongruities immediately become clear and readily explicable.

The physical body results from the union of two cells originating one each from the male and female parents. These cells contain the 'chromosomes' or carriers of the characteristics of each parent – but remember this only refers to their physical, emotional and mental traits. Their real character or what might be termed their spiritual qualities are produced by inner spiritual influences or soul contact. As the immortal soul is only a temporary occupant of the body, vacating it again at the termination of the life span and at no stage forming an intrinsic part of the physical body, the properties of the soul cannot be transferred by physical cells to the progeny.

The statement just made should however be qualified. During the soul's occupation of the body, it exerts a beneficial influence on the threefold complex of the personality, even though the physical man may remain totally unaware of such action or effect. This sustained influence results in the gradual refinement and upgrading of the physical, emotional and mental attributes and these improvements, when finally assimilated, will then become heritable and will be transmitted to future generations. Therefore, although the soul qualities are not directly heritable, the results of their action will nevertheless have a progressively beneficial effect on the lower vehicle of expression and these cumulative effects will then be carried forward to posterity and be manifested as the process of evolution.

Physical traits which are normally inherited are those of form, appearance, attitude, instinctive habits, appetites, desires, emotions and intelligence, which were characteristic of the parents. Whether the attributes of the male or female parent will be controlling, will depend on the relative dominance of those properties in the chromosome combinations of the male and female cells.

The problem, however, sometimes arises to distinguish between the 'higher mind' and the 'lower mind'. The simplest explanation is that all attributes which are functions of the brain, such as the reasoning capacity, intellect and power to memorise, store and convert knowledge, may be bracketed together as the 'lower mind'. These mental qualities are definitely heritable as they form an innate part or quality of the physical body. In contrast to the foregoing, there are the attributes of the Soul or Ego. This intangible or spiritual part of man which includes the 'higher mind', is responsible for the 'quality of life' and refers to the more ethereal aspects, such as the will, wisdom, consciousness, spiritual love and the intuition – these constitute the main sources of man's inspiration and guidance on the Path of Life. These spiritual qualities cannot be transferred to posterity.

For those interested in the functions of the physical human body, ample literature is available with regard to the anatomical and physical aspects, as these have been of interest to man for many centuries. A study of the terrain where the physical and etheric aspects meet and interact with the spiritual will, however, prove of far greater profit, as it is in this field that the course of human existence will be determined.

There are four great interlocking directorates which control – or fail to control – man's physical body. These are:

1. The etheric body – the medium for the reception and distribution of energies. These functions have already been dealt with.
2. The nervous system.
3. The endocrine system.
4. The blood stream.

Health problems mainly result from the lack of co-ordination between these systems. In the following pages it will be briefly indicated how these intrinsic fractions of the greater system interact and complement each other, with the result that any inadequacy in one of these links must inevitably be reflected in the whole.

X. 2 (a) **The Nervous System**

Man's physical body, the sum total of muscles, bone, blood and various other supporting systems, is correlated and co-ordinated by the nervous system and energised by what is vaguely called 'life', that vital and divine essence which will forever remain inexplicable to the Earth bound human being.

The nervous system with its complexity of nerves, nerve centres and interrelated aspects serving to co-ordinate the organism and to produce the existing sensitive response between the limbs, organs and other components of the body, all contributing towards making man aware of and reactive to his environment, has already been studied for many years by medicine. For present purposes a different approach is however indicated, placing the accent on the subjective rather than on the purely functional side.

Broadly speaking the sensory apparatus can be classified into:

1. The cerebro-spinal system.
2. The sensory nervous system.
3. The peripheral nervous system.

This co-ordinating system of communication, this sensitive network of interrelating nerves, is the symbol in man of the soul and therefore the outer semblance or expression of an inner spiritual reality of which the average man still remains blissfully unconscious.

The nervous system forms the primary plane of contact between the ethereal and physical spheres. The etheric body permeates every separate part of the physical body and its ramifications terminate in minute carriers of energy, already described as the 'nadis' and which are in contact with every single atom. It is this etheric counterpart of the nervous system which nourishes, controls and galvanises the nerves, serving as the channel or bridge between the physical and ethereal aspects of man.

Apart from the already well known nervous system, there exists a further *micro-network of nerves*, atomically reticulated, representing the direct physical counterpart of the nadi-system, of which medical science as yet remains unaware.

X. 2 (b) The Brain

Just a few lines in which to consider the brain from the esoteric point of view and thus perhaps to see its functions from a somewhat different angle from the usual exoteric approach.

The brain is the focal point of the whole nervous system. Every sensation or experience, down to the very faintest perception registered in any part of the atomically reticulated sensory system, is instantly relayed and fed into this central computer. Yes, that is actually what the brain amounts to – a beautifully designed computer which has been built into the material body of every human being; a computer conceived and constructed far beyond the imagination and comprehension of the most highly qualified and proficient physicist or technician. This wonderful instrument has been installed in the human body to serve as a link, transformer and reciprocal transmitter of impulses and perceptions of every kind, whether subjective or objective and received from both internal and external sources. It therefore serves to interrelate one part of the body with the other; it serves as the point of conscious contact between the human being and external forms of every kind, whether conscious or unconscious; and finally through 'impressions' received, it links the ephemeral, the hidden, with the dense physical. These subjective impulses may originate from several sources but for the average man who is beginning to awaken and is consciously becoming aware of some deeper spiritual existence, it may be assumed that this subjective contact usually is with the soul, the inner Christ, who is gradually and with increasing resolve bringing its influence to bear on the three vehicles of expression – the physical, emotional and mental bodies. All these contacts are effected via the brain.

This computer can be developed and refined far beyond its present performance as part of the equipment of the average man. The capacities and potentialities are built-in attributes of this instrument but they will only unfold and function in accordance with real need and will then correspond to the stage of development of the evolving etheric centres. As in the case of a computer, the brain must also be programmed and responses and reactions that may be expected can only be commensurate with the knowledge, factual data and spiritual principles which have been fed into it and subsequently classified, stored and processed by the instrument.

It could perhaps be briefly mentioned that there are three small endocrine or ductless glands which are closely associated with the brain. These are known as the **_pituitary body_**, the **_pineal gland_** and the **_carotid gland_**. They are related to and form the objective correspondences of three energy centres in the surrounding etheric body, named the **_eye (ajna)_**, **_alta major_** and the **_head centres_**. (See: X. 1 (a) – "Centres of Energy").

In primitive man these three glands are as yet unrelated, because the relative force centres are still dormant. In the spiritually developed man, on the other hand, they become closely associated through the centres which have progressively been awakened and energised and are then actively transmitting and exchanging soul energy via these glands to the brain. These are therefore the channels through which the soul begins to exert its influence over the personality and its three component bodies.

X. 2 (c) **The Endocrine Glands**
(The Ductless Glands)

In the course of human evolution and with the etheric body remaining subject to the interplay of the many sources of energy, the seven etheric centres automatically become activated. Whether still dormant or in an energised condition, they form part of the constitution of every human entity and are ready to fulfil their predestined function whenever animated by the demands of the soul.

This evolution of the centres has been proceeding quietly over the ages without any conscious effort or awareness by their beneficiaries. One of the results of this development was that the energies radiated from these seven centres were precipitated or 'condensed' in the physical body, culminating in the generation of the seven major endocrine glands, each of which being associated functionally with their corresponding etheric centres.

It should be kept in mind, however, that in addition to the seven major centres there are also many smaller centres of subsidiary importance. These secondary centres also have their counterparts, reflected as unobtrusive or even unknown glands in the physical body.

The etheric centres therefore constitute the causal source of the endocrine system, which is determined and conditioned according to the quality and source of energy flowing through the centres. The relationship is as follows:

Etheric Centre	related to	**Endocrine Gland**
1. Head centre		Pineal gland
2. Centre between eyebrows		Pituitary body and Carotid gland
3. Throat centre		Thyroid and parathyroid glands
4. Heart centre		Thymus gland
5. Solar plexus centre		Pancreas
6. Sacral centre		Gonads
7. Base of spine centre		Adrenal

The glands react to impulses received from the centres by secreting substances or '*hormones*' into the blood stream, thereby transferring the stimulus or energy to the physical system and pervading the entire physical man with its life forces. The endocrine system is therefore one of the main controlling factors in the human body, forming a direct link with the etheric energies. It is therefore one of the determinants in the general health of the individual. When the ductless glands are in perfect balance with the etheric system and are functioning correctly, there will be no diseased areas in the body.

On the physical plane man is emotionally or mentally the product of his glandular system; his physical condition thus also depends on his psychological balance. It may therefore be said that 'a man is what his glands make him' but they, in their turn depend on the energy centres, which are again influenced and animated by the soul. For medical science, therefore, to begin by treating the glands themselves is tantamount to treating symptoms instead of causes, which lie in the first instance within the etheric body and its centres. The healer should therefore focus his attention primarily on the condition and reactivity of the vital body and its controlling centres.

X. 2 (d) **The Blood Stream**

The soul has two main channels through which it informs its instrument, the physical body:

1. The Thread of Consciousness or of intelligence is anchored in the head in the region of the pineal gland and from that station of perception it directs the physical plane activities by means of the brain and the nervous system.
2. The Thread of Life is anchored in the heart, where the life principle is to be found. From this central position the life current is reticulated throughout the body by the blood circulatory system.

But the functions of the blood stream are not limited to the carrying of life energy; it is also the agent of the endocrine system, which is nourished by etheric energy transmitted through the seven centres. These glands when stimulated secrete hormones in the blood stream, which then circulates these relatively little known elements throughout the tissues of the body.

The blood stream has additional functions, such as the circulation of oxygen from the pulmonary organs, nutritive solutions from the digestive system and disposing of waste material through the kidneys. These are functions that have already been thoroughly investigated by physiologists and which do not directly concern the present approach.

Summary:

The previous pages may be summarised by drawing attention to the close interrelation between the etheric body as the transmitter of energy and the several media of transmission. Energy is distributed by four principal physiological systems, each complete as a separate performer but remaining jointly interdependent in providing the body with its co-ordinated organic life, in accordance with the point of evolution achieved and the reciprocal effect of impacting energies. The agents concerned are:

1. *The Etheric Vehicle:* This is the vital body which, with its seven major centres and numerous subsidiary focal points, serves as the medium of exchange for all incoming

and outgoing streams of energy. Its effectiveness lies in the fact that it is so intimately reticulated throughout the physical body and that by means of the myriads of 'nadis' of which it is composed, every impulse is transmitted either to or from the brain by the nervous system.

2. *The Nervous System:* This is the comparatively tangible counterpart of the etheric network which, through the instrumentality of the brain, brings the intangible inner vital energies and forces into outer expression, thus serving to condition man in accordance with the complex of outer environmental influences.

3. *The Endocrine System:* The endocrine glands may be regarded as the tangible expression of the corresponding focal centres of energy in the etheric body. The glands produce their potencies as 'hormones' which are secreted into the blood stream for reticulation throughout the physical system.

4. *The Blood Stream:* This system centred in the heart is, in the first instance, the carrier of the life principle and simultaneously also distributes the combined energies engendered or absorbed by the other bodily systems.

These four closely related but nonetheless independent agents constitute the interlocking directorate controlling the vital forces, and therefore the well-being, not only of the physical but also of the emotional and mental bodies and will therefore affect all aspects of the co-ordinated personality. They are in fact the agents through which the three divine aspects of **Life, Quality** and **Appearance** are consistently expressed with varying degrees of success. A thorough understanding of these distributory agents should lead to the realisation that they are merely four separate aspects of one vital circulatory system, responsible for the manifestation of life as it is ceaselessly affected by the surrounding and interacting streams of energy.

X. 2 (e) **The Senses**

The senses are those organs or rather media, enabling man to become aware of his surroundings. They are the means through which he investigates the dense physical plane; the means of becoming aware of and expanding his consciousness by gaining experience and learning that which he has to know. Through the senses and the associated nervous system, impulses received from the environment are flashed to the brain, where they are co-ordinated and then redirected to the vital, emotional and mental bodies to produce the reactions to the stimulus.

The five recognised senses, namely hearing, touch, sight, taste and smell, are also found in animals, where they are in some instances even more highly developed than in man, since the survival of a species may largely depend on the acute quality of specific senses. With them the reasoning faculty of the mind is, however, lacking and they are unable to correlate their perceptions; their reactions thus mainly remain instinctive and lack the discriminative faculty which qualifies man.

The first sensory attributes developed in a child are *hearing, touch* and *sight*. To begin with the young infant becomes aware of sound and will turn its head towards the source, apparently also looking that way but, in this early stage, the eyes are still vacant, not yet focussing or registering an image. The young one will also soon begin to feel and touch with little hands and fingers and it will not be long before the eyes will be focussing and awareness will develop. These are the three vital senses co-ordinating the personality. *Taste* and *smell* follow later and are of secondary importance and, should they be lacking, life can still be carried on without undue handicaps to its essential physical activities. Actually taste and smell can be regarded as an amplification of touch.

When a man is very highly evolved and has superseded life in the three worlds by attaining to full consciousness, the senses become redundant. He has reached the stage where he *knows* intuitively and the senses have become superfluous. But while still in the earlier process of evolution on the physical planes, the thinker has to avail himself of the senses to convey some aspect of the environment and by the aid of the mind he can then adjust his relationship accordingly:

Hearing gives man an idea of relative direction and enables him to locate himself in the scheme of things.

Touch gives him some idea of quantity and quality in his relation to other forms in his environment.

Sight gives him perspective and proportion, enabling him to adjust his activities to his surroundings.

Taste and *smell* help him to evaluate the innate quality of that which he contacts, to find what appeals to him and to reject or avoid the repulsive.

The senses therefore furnish the means by which the personality can evaluate various aspects and qualities of outer conditions and thus to differentiate, utilise, experience and assimilate those aspects needed for continued evolution.

The senses, as instruments of the Soul, lead the personality through graded processes of identification, utilisation, manipulation and finally to the rejection of the dense physical. The Soul registers the co-ordinated vibrations and extracts the essence of experience gained by the form in its many grades of manifestation in time and space.

X. 2 (f) **Pain**

Basically pain is a product of the senses and the nervous system. Pain is nature's way of protecting the physical body, since it warns of danger and thus induces man to avoid experiences that might cause damage to the form.

Animal and vegetable forms of life are to a greater or lesser extent also subject to pain, depending on the degree to which the consciousness has developed. As members of these lower kingdoms have no mental capacity, there is a lack of organised memory and of pre-vision; there is no capacity to relate past experience with present and thereby to create a fearful apprehension of the future. Avoidance of action or circumstances which may result in pain is therefore mainly instinctive, although in the case of the more advanced animal species it seems as though some primitive form of mental development is appearing, which also instils a fear of pain, going deeper than mere instinct.

Fear of *physical pain* is often the underlying cause of anxiety – the imaginative faculty is given free rein and tensions are built up in the emotional body. The individual visualises the painful experiences so vividly that the imaginary pain almost becomes reality to him and he suffers the agonies of foreboding, which may even lead to acute physical suffering. Minor ills or ailments which, to the phlegmatic person may be of little import, may thus be aggravated into severe suffering.

Mental pain experienced on behalf of those we love is a truly distressing experience. The capacity to identify oneself with pain which is not strictly our own, is something which all world disciples must experience, since it is the first step towards shouldering world pain and the suffering of the human family. One thus becomes 'a participant in the fellowship of Christ's sufferings and a lifter of world burdens'. We live and work in a world of pain. This suffering apparently is one of the basic requirements in man's spiritual unfolding, serving to draw him closer to his fellow man who may be struggling under heavier burdens than his own. The reason for such shared suffering is beyond the understanding of the ordinary human being but it is an incontrovertible fact that by lightening the burden of others, there is an automatic mitigation of one's own troubles.

It should be remembered that the soul has superseded all pain. When man reaches the stage where his centre of consciousness is focussed on higher levels, then pain is steadily transcended and the pairs of opposites – pleasure and pain – have no further hold on him. This refers to physical suffering but apparently something closely resembling the pain which lies hidden in compassion is experienced even on the highest spiritual levels.

Pain is the whip with which the struggling contender is driven along the Path of Life; pain is the stimulus to overcome the many obstructions impeding the way to the mountain top; pain is caused by the many frustrations before reaching the welcoming embrace of the Father. And thus pain serves many useful purposes and through the instrumentality of the suffering personality the soul is finally guided from darkness to light, from bondage to liberation and from torment to peace and concord. Pain therefore should not be evaded, because it is not the easy and passive way that leads to success and exaltation; pain is the Path leading through frustration, distress and suffering to the goal of achievement and redemption – back to the Father in whose enshrouding and consecrated love all pain and sorrow fades away.

Yes – 'great is the mystery of pain'!

X. 2 (g) Sex

Esoterically sex attraction is an expression of Life, drawing the lower self into full realisation; it is a manifestation of the relation between spirit and matter, between life and form. Physically speaking, it is the urge to unite male and female for the purpose of procreation. When this is purely an animal urge, it forms part of the dictates of nature but, with man, emotional desire has crept in and the natural function of reproduction is usually manifested as a perverted and sensuous craving for the satisfaction of desire. The result is that the life of the average individual is often dominated by sex impulses with their related problems, debasing and distorting what should be a divine quality.

Sex is one of the fundamental and primeval urges, one of the natural instincts and consequently a dominant factor in man's physical nature. It is an intimate and personal subject which, in the course of ages and during periods when man succumbed to exaggerated Puritanism, coupled with the development of secret but lustful desire, perverted a natural function into a sensual mystery. Thus it came to be regarded as unmentionable and a topic to be shunned in decent circles, instead of being seen as an instinctual and natural process, although one which should be disciplined and kept under rhythmic control.

The sex problem is a fascinating subject, which interests every normal individual because it affects each and every one separately and all of humanity collectively, owing to the permeating role it constantly fulfils in everyday life. It is also the cause of very actual, difficult and apparently unsolvable problems and tensions which are incessantly being created through its presence and influence. There are few problems which during recent years have received more public attention, and extensive literature on the subject is available. The present approach is, however, of a general nature and does not enter into details but should nonetheless be considered significant.

No immediate solutions can be offered for the many sex-related problems but the Tibetan is notwithstanding reasonably optimistic with regard to the future. He foresees great changes in human relationships and this will apply particularly to man's sex attitude and the resulting readjustments to marriage relationships. This change of attitude will of course only come about gradually and will be closely associated with the developing science of psychology. It is however essential that man should acquire a better understanding of his threefold lower nature as well as the depth of his subconscious life and this will then lead to a spontaneous change in men's attitude towards women and of women in relation to their destiny. D.K. predicts that coming generations will prove themselves well equipped to cope with these sex problems, because they will have acquired clearer vision and will think in broader and more comprehensive terms than is the case today. There will be a growing group consciousness, with more attention to intelligent thought life, greater tolerance and a spirit of loving understanding. He forecasts that in the dawning era, goodwill will be the outstanding characteristic of humanity and that selfish purpose and animal instincts in man will fade into the background. When these attitudes begin to materialise, the following three tenets will form the basis of all recognised standards of living; these will be gradually and naturally established, without the need for special legislation or control:

1. The relationship of the sexes and their approach to the marriage relationship will be regarded as a part of group life and as serving the group good; this will be the result of education in group relationships, mutual service and the law of love as understood practically and not just sentimentally.

2. True marriage and right sexual relationship should involve the marriage of all three aspects of man's nature – the physical, the emotional and the mental. For a couple to be happily married, they should complement each other in all these departments of their nature.

3. The governing principle should in the first instance be the desire to provide suitable and healthy bodies for souls awaiting incarnation. Souls will then be attracted to such couples by the strength of the parents' desire, the purity of their motives and their diligence in preparation. The majority of children born today have come either accidentally or are unwanted. Some are desired but that desire is usually based on reasons of heredity, property, family tradition or the fulfilling of some ambition.

To realise the above objectives will require careful and specific training of the public consciousness but, according to D.K., the leaders will be forthcoming when mankind is ready for these concepts. Every era in human history furnishes souls who are able to solve the dominant problems – souls delegated for that specific purpose and this will also hold for the future!

The doctrine that enforced celibacy is an indication or prerequisite for spiritual living is entirely false, as such a life would be abnormal, unnatural and therefore undesirable. There is no better training for a disciple than family life with its enforced relations, its scope for adjustments and adaptability, its demanded sacrifices and service and its opportunities for the full expression of every part of man's nature. What is required of such a man is that the higher nature should overcome the demands of the lower and that the spiritual man should refuse to be dominated by the desires of the personality and the demands of the flesh – in short to submit to self-discipline. A frustrated or abnormally suppressed sex life is definitely harmful and can lead only to physical and psychological aberrations.

X. 3. The Astral Body
(The Emotional Body)

It is of vital importance that every student should reach a clear understanding of the astral plane – by knowing its nature he can learn to stand free from it and once this freedom has been gained he will also know how to work on it when required by circumstances. When the astral plane is seen for the first time through the 'opened eye', it will give the impression of a kaleidoscopic world in a state of utter confusion and for the greater part only vaguely discernible through a foggy atmosphere, blurring the constantly changing forms and intermingled colours. This is the meeting ground of innumerable and uncontrolled forces resulting in apparently total chaos.

The astral is the plane of illusion, of glamour and of a distorted presentation of reality. Every individual in the world is to some extent working in astral matter, resulting in innumerable urges and cravings. It is the outpouring of this host of human desires into the astral cauldron, which results in the phantasmagoria of astral scenes and illusions. This conglomeration of interacting forces arising from humanity also includes numerous other forces and all these jointly act upon and influence the human being. The response to these impulses will depend on the calibre of the lower vehicles and more specifically on the condition and quality of the etheric centres.

Through this illusory labyrinth the aspirant has to find his way, snatching at every clue which promises to be of help and after many years of experience he learns to distinguish between truth and glamour, the real and the unreal. Every individual who in the course of time succeeds in liberating himself, who begins to see more clearly and who releases himself from the glamour of illusion, contributes towards the realisation of the Divine Plan.

The *pairs of opposites* meet and interact on the astral plane and this is the terrain where the potent pull of the great dualities are felt, where the interaction between the soul and the personality takes its course and also where numerous lesser dualities play their part. Light and darkness struggle for dominance and so do pleasure and pain, good and evil, poverty and riches, health and disease, heat and cold and so many more. The light which man has discovered within himself makes him more aware of the dark; through the good which attracts him, he sees the evil which is the line of least resistance; the activity leading to pain simultaneously permits him to visualise the contrasting pleasure and thus he experiences something of both hell and heaven. And so the wretched aspirant becomes aware of these dualities and is constantly pulled hither and thither between the two. The secret of eventual human liberation lies in the correct balancing of these opposing forces and in finding the narrow path between these dualities which will finally lead him to the Light. The deciding factor in this Herculean struggle is the divine Will as expressed through the soul, which so often comes into collision with the selfish personal will – but though the battle may be long and arduous, the final triumph of the soul remains inevitable. It is on the astral plane that these battles are fought which eventually will lead to the release of the imprisoned soul.

The emotional body of the average man fulfils the role of a great reflector but at the same time it is a most unreliable mirror, ever distorting the image of that which is received. It records the impulses from every kind of force and influence radiated from its environment and mixes all these colours and movements, as well as every form of desire, emotion, action and sound into a muddled conglomeration of impressions. The objective of the aspiring individual should be to bring some measure of order into this chaos and to still the agitated surface of the waters of this plane to such an extent that it can serve as a clear mirror for reflecting the qualities and impulses from the soul.

It is through the analysing mind that the astral body is brought under control. No excessive emotion should be permitted, though strong currents of love for all that breathes should be allowed to sweep through man's being. Systemic love is constructive and stabilising and does not contain the dangers hidden in sentimental or emotional love. The aspirant should rid his emotional body of all fear and worry by cultivating serenity and stability and a sense of secure dependence on Higher Powers. He should never harbour jealousy, dark depression, greed or self-pity but instead proceed calmly on the Way with quiet and joyous confidence in his heart.

Every individual constructs his own astral body from the energies of the surrounding astral plane, a body which will be responsive to his particular note and quality and limited to his specific point on the ladder of evolution. This emotional body will constitute his field of response to life experience within defined limits but it will also lend itself to tremendous expansion, development, adjustment and control, harmonising with impulses received from a growing mental body and a soul progressively asserting itself over its three bodies of expression – the physical, astral and mental.

The astral body is usually animated by forces which can be grouped under three main headings:

1. Forces of *selfish desire*. This forms an essential part of the evolutionary process, because man has to experience every phase that life in the physical has to offer, including both the good and the evil; honour and opprobrium; the pleasant and the distressful; wealth and poverty; leadership and servility; the pride and glory of position in contrast with utter humiliation. It is these desires which constitute the forces which will drive him on from life to life and from one experience to another, ever craving that which he does not possess, that which belongs to others, whether material possessions, money, power, status or knowledge. These desires will remain dominant till man is sated with all that material life has to offer; till the soul has extracted the essence from all these experiences and the higher mind takes over from the lower and the light is seen ahead.

2. The second group of forces are those engendered by *sexual attraction*. There is nothing wrong with the basic principle of physical attraction, for that is part of nature's way for the propagation of man. But man has abused this natural urge and it has deteriorated into emotional and lustful desire. However, even these hurdles will be surmounted after the necessary experience has been gained and the needed lessons have been learnt.

3. The third group of forces impelling man along the way of life is *Fear*. This illusory force is displayed daily in its many patterns, causing excruciating pain, suffering and frus-

tration, sometimes driving man to the most irresponsible action. These fears may be of a selfish nature but often they concern those who are emotionally near to us. How many torturing hours are spent in anguish on premonitions, doubts, questionings and imaginary illusions which never come to pass? These fears may assume many guises – one's own, family fears, national and racial fears, including fear of pain, of the future, of death and fear of failure. Some of these will be dealt with in greater detail under a subsequent heading.

(See: X. 3 (a) – "Fear")

The Emotions:

Emotion is the relation between feeling and thought. In other words, when feeling is encountered and is subjected to mental consideration and the reaction is radiated into the astral body, 'emotion' is generated. This process may proceed consciously and deliberately and thus with a somewhat retarded and discriminative effect, as for instance when savouring the palatability of food. The more usual occurrence, however, is that the procedure is largely automatic, with the reaction instantly flashing from the sensed area to the brain and from there to the emotional body. An example of the latter is where physical harm is suffered, followed by an immediate chain of reaction, ranging from a feeling of pain, followed perhaps by rage or fear or a combination of these effects.

Emotion may also evoke desire. When the mind recognises the feeling produced in the astral body and the resulting emotion is pleasurable, then desire for the continuance or repetition of the experience is created. If on the other hand the sensation is painful, then the mental reaction would be for desisting the causal agency.

Through the presentation of facts the mind may succeed in subduing emotions. So often the problem is how to induce the individual under emotional stress to summon his mental powers, which would enable him to assess the situation and to subject it to calm and dispassionate scrutiny.

Health conditions may be seriously affected by emotional attitudes. This is because man's vital body is still primarily governed and swept into activity by his emotional vehicle. When the latter becomes violently agitated and is for instance disturbed by excessive temper, intense worry or other continuous irritation, then a stream of emotional energy will be poured into the etheric body, galvanising such centres as the solar plexus into intense activity. This will be reflected in the endocrine and nervous systems, as well as in the blood stream, causing indigestion, biliousness, other gastric disturbances or headaches and related complaints.

Similarly bitterness, disgust, hatred or a sense of frustration, are apt to induce many of the prevalent toxic conditions of the physical system, evoking a general state of ill health. Or ideals may have exceeded accomplishments, leading to frustration and suffering. The cure for many of these conditions lies in the simple word '*acceptance*' – that is the positive attitude of accepting conditions which, notwithstanding our best efforts, seem to be unavoidable – but with the determination to bring the emotions under closer control and to do better next time.

The ideal should be to achieve '*perfect poise*' – this involves the complete curbing of the astral body and overcoming or minimising emotional upheavals. To be relieved of excessive emotional reaction must lead to considerably improved mental clarity and therefore clearer discrimination.

A closer scrutiny will now be made of some of the emotions which are daily encountered and which as a rule are so difficult to command.

X. 3 (a) **Fear**

Fear – that dark, depressing cloud which in some form or another overshadows every human life! Fear is evoked in the first instance by ignorance. Where wisdom rules, where there is real knowledge and understanding and where astral influences therefore no longer dominate, fear disappears. It is based on instinct and plays a predominating role in the animal world where instinctive fear is a prerequisite for survival, because the mental equipment to foresee impending danger is lacking. In the human being traces of this animal instinct are retained but paradoxically the power of fear is enormously aggravated by the same quality which should guard him from fear – the power of the mind. The problem is that knowledge is still incomplete and the mind is wrongly harnessed; past pain and misery are remembered and projected into the future in anticipation of what might happen, thus building an exaggerated thought-form depicting all our worst fears. By paying attention to these thought-forms they are further embroidered and magnified, for 'energy follows thought', till the individual falls a complete prey to these fears, often suffering excruciating mental pain.

Fear is a feature which all human beings suffer in common. It is the dominant astral energy and is created by the interaction of the emotional and mental planes. It ranges from the instinctive but relatively simple fears of the savage, arising from his ignorance of the laws and forces of nature and his consequent fear of the unknown, to the prevailing gamut of fears of modern man, resulting from the complexities of a more competitive existence together with the increased responsibilities and sensitivity associated with an evolving consciousness. There are the fears of loss of health and eventually of death; fear of the future, including loss of property and money, of status, popularity and friendships; fear of loneliness, of retribution, of darkness, of the unrevealed, of the great beyond … and so the list of fears may be extended, which seemingly multiply in direct proportion to man's development, until the stage is reached when understanding of the self and the soul gradually exerts mastery over the lower vehicles.

The statement that fear is an illusion is quite correct but how difficult to dismiss this illusion and to relieve the tortures of premonition, doubt and uncertainty. Undue and unreasonable fear has already withheld opportunity from many a man, so let life's activities be guided by common sense, facts and reality and not by fictitious imaginings.

Closer consideration of some aspects of fear should lead to a better understanding of its nature and therefore help in overcoming its degenerating effects.

(i) *Fear of Death:*

There are several underlying reasons for the gnawing fear of death. There is the horror of the unknown and undefinable, coupled with doubt about man's immortality and the uncertainty of what becomes of him after death. Is there a 'heaven' and what about the threat of perpetual burning in purgatory? There is also the ever present fear of the actual rending process, when the life essence is withdrawn and the spirit or soul departs from the body. People seem to forget that such sensitivity is associated with the actively functioning life in the physical body and that with the withdrawing of life all physical sense of pain will simultaneously fade away.

As will be explained in Chapter XI, 'there is no death'; it is only a question of passing from one level of awareness to another, from physical consciousness to spiritual consciousness. If man could only come to this realisation then all fears would vanish. 'Death' is not something to be feared but on the contrary, in many respects, it is a phase to be welcomed – what a wonderful thought for the older person who has been through life's treadmill and experienced its weal and woe, that he can shed the dense physical prison with all its aches and pains and fears, that he can exchange physical life with all its worries, doubts, disappointments and mental strain, for a spell of life in a spiritual body that will no longer tire and be subject to all the earthly troubles. In that new world of spirit ample work will be provided for those who would like to contribute to the redemption of humanity. Such work will be of an agreeable nature and compatible with individual character, inclination and stage of development.

As might be expected, youth's approach to these thoughts may be quite different. For them life is only commencing, with all its pleasures, experiences and challenges to be overcome. To them death is still something remote as far as their personal life is concerned – something that happens only to others. For the strong and vigorous death is something in the distant and hazy future that need not yet be contemplated, until suddenly the unexpected occurs, upsetting all preconceived plans and ideas. Suddenly the unwitting is brought face to face with the Angel of Death, starkly facing him with some of the inexorable facts of life which up to that stage had been left out of consideration. For the unprepared this will probably mean an intense shock, followed by cringing fear. This is the time when a more discerning knowledge of the facts of life will prove of immense help – a realisation that life in the physical world is merely a passing phase in an already long established cyclic pattern in the existence of the soul, alternating between periods passed either in the flesh or in the world of spirit.

What matter if an apparently promising life has unexpectedly been cut short? Although the real purpose for such a seemingly cruel fate may remain hidden to man's myopic vision, rest assured that there is good reason for such occurrences. From the human standpoint death often appears senseless and severe but remember that man can only visualise a very narrow sector of the overall Plan and his perspective must inevitably remain limited. Remember also that the earthly life which has been cut short will, after a longer or shorter spiritual sojourn, be resumed in a new physical vehicle, to continue the experiences planned by the soul.

No, those passing on should never be pitied, nor should death be feared – rejoice rather on their behalf because, for a while, they have been liberated from physical fetters and limitations. It is the immersion of the soul into the darkness of the physical form – the process man knows as 'birth' – which should be seen as entering into obscurity and a period of 'death' to the soul.

The only real sufferers caused by death are those left behind, who have suddenly been bereft of a dear one and who for a while will be deprived of the love, companionship and perhaps support of the one who has departed. However, with the right approach the survivors should soon adapt themselves, once they come to realise that the departed one is really far better off in his new surroundings and that their sorrow is mainly due to self-pity. Try to realise that it is only 'au revoir' – till we meet again!

These are broad generalisations. As among the billions of human beings no two are exactly similar, it is impossible to describe detailed conditions which will be applicable to all individuals and circumstances. Only broad principles can therefore be outlined. It must be understood that each individual life, having its own particular pattern, is adjusted and arranged around these basic principles in accordance with the position occupied in time and space by the being concerned, according to his stage of development, the rays and influences impinging upon his aura and finally according to the directives of the incarnated soul. This is another example of the relativity of all truth as far as it can be interpreted by the limited minds of men. Each individual, being a separate entity, must absorb, digest and apply, to the best of his ability, as much of the truth as he can understand and cope with at his particular stage of awakening and expanding consciousness.

(ii) *Fear of the Future:*

In contrast to 'fear of death', fear of the future really amounts to 'fear of life'.

Intelligent living necessitates a certain measure of planning for the future. This means building thought-forms of that which it is hoped to achieve. If we, however, allow ourselves to live in a constant state of fear engendered by this forward planning, then it becomes inevitable that the thought-forms constructed for this future will also be impregnated, tinted and consequently limited, by this fear complex and that it will be of a negative nature. If therefore a constructive life is envisioned, it is essential that a positive attitude towards the future must be cultivated.

A negative attitude towards the future is often the result of instinctual fears originating in man's primeval animal instinct for self-preservation. With increased mental development this characteristic may become accentuated – the forward-looking mind developing the capacity of anticipation, it uses the imaginative faculty of visualisation and unwittingly projects memories of ancient suffering and misery into the present. Thus by relating present day economic, political, social and racial conditions with the past, our mental instrument paints gruesome pictures of what might be in store for us. These conditions are often further aggravated by modern news media which daily bring tragedy, suffering and calamity throughout the world, in an exaggerated degree to man's attention. There are few who under these circumstances can retain their balance and avoid the fears which are constantly evoked. The only power which can counteract these fears of the future is the inner strength of the soul, expressed through the higher mind. Although these powers are at the disposal of every individual, there are still many who have not yet learnt to avail themselves of their inner forces.

One of the principal dangers which lie concealed in this widespread fear of the future, is that unprincipled news media, opportunists, orators and agitators may, for political or other purposes, sweep the masses into hysteria by fanning these slumbering but ever present fears into emotional and destructive eruption. Once this mass impetus has been set in motion, it usually proves difficult to control and may result in national and even international tragedies.

Man should learn to take in his stride all that life has in store for him – both the good and the unpleasant – and then fearlessly, with understanding and joy, to extract and accept the essential lessons which have been provided by destiny on his path of life.

(iii) *Fear of Physical Pain:*

Underlying many forms of fear is that of physical pain – of pain which has actually been experienced, during either the present or some previous incarnation and which has been registered in the memory. Imagination uses these memories to relive vividly such experiences, causing unnecessary tension in the nervous system. Relatively insignificant ailments may in this way be magnified and aggravated into acute suffering.

(iv) *Fear of Failure:*

There are few reasonably intelligent people who are not subject to this type of fear, which is in reality associated with 'fear of the future'. It will affect people in practically all spheres of modern competitive life, each according to his particular circumstance, environment and character. There is the fear of not being able to provide for one's dependants or for old age; the fear of losing the love or respect of those that are near and dear or even of one's fellowman in general or in other words the fear of adverse public opinion; there is the fear of not making a success of one's work, responsibilities or of life's opportunities.

A severe manifestation of this fear of failure is that of being unable to achieve the ideals imposed by the inner man – the soul. It is important not to develop an inferiority complex through under-estimating personal capacities or by being too self-critical, since this must definitely lead to inadequacy – 'as a man thinketh so is he'. Man should instead endeavour to build self-confidence, by putting his trust in the power of the soul to inspire and lead him to the fulfilment of his highest objectives.

To generalise it may thus be said that failure should be viewed as a stepping stone in the never ending process of development. We all fail at times and so we learn by experience. It is through failure that we learn to do better and so to proceed to the next step. Failure in an absolute sense therefore does not exist – only the gaining of experience on the Path of Progress!

X. 3 (b) Depression

Hardly anyone escapes periodical attacks of depression. This manifestation of emotion is liable to make its cyclic appearance from time to time, sometimes alternating with hilarity, its polar opposite. Although total elimination of depression is impossible for those still struggling towards Reality, it is important that the emotions be kept under control to avoid sinking into the depths of despondency. On the other hand it is equally important not to give full rein to the other extreme, namely hilarity.

Deep depression is a miasma enshrouding the mind with a fog, inhibiting vision and discrimination. If too long sustained it may become well-nigh unbearable with harmful psychological and physical consequences. Depression is caused by dwelling in the astral world and while man allows himself to be immersed in these emotional illusions and glamours, which distort, reverse and deceive, so will there inevitably be periods of despair, darkness, doubt, deep distress and depression. It is therefore the task of the aspirant on the path of truth to free himself as rapidly as possible of these debilitating illusions and emotions.

To attempt to drive away depression by seeking some kind of spurious happiness or by participating in various forms of emotional entertainment will lead nowhere, because such activities are all part of the astral plane and its illusions. The way to eliminate this cyclic ebb and flow of emotions is to raise life's focus from the emotional to the mental plane and, if there is sufficient spiritual stimulus, to the egoic plane – the world of the soul. This higher objective can be achieved by study, a better understanding of the self and the subjective realms, by loving service to fellow men and finally by means of meditation, the sure way of making contact with the Self – the Soul.

If the boat of life is to reach its destined harbour, then it must needs leave the protection of the sheltered port. It must sail out into the turbulent sea of experience, to brave the storms and enjoy the calms; to encounter all the ups and downs of fortune; at times wallowing in the troughs of the seas, being aware of nothing but the agitated surrounding astral waters, only to rise again to the crest of the waves, obtaining a clear view of the beckoning lighthouse on the far off coast, which will guide it towards its port of destiny. And so the dedicated server, during these cyclically occurring periods of inevitable stress, which may at times lead to despair, should never forget that the darkest night *must* be followed by the light of day; and with further sustained effort, the day will dawn which will not again be terminated by the setting sun – the day when he will abide in Eternal Light.

X. 3 (c) Hatred and Antagonism

It is sad to have to write about such a deprimating subject but attention should be drawn to the important role which hatred plays in daily life, with its detrimental effects, not only on the individual but also on humanity as a whole. As the physical, emotional and mental systems can be completely poisoned by this virulent emotion, every effort should be made either to avert or at least restrain this harmful, degrading and undisciplined passion.

Hatred and antagonism are the most vicious and destructive forces in the emotional body and it is distressing that they occur so widely, leaving very few people untouched by this scourge to harmonious existence. Because it is such a general failing of man, its tentacles embrace group life, politics, religion and all relations between races and nations.

Hatred is the opposite pole to love and stems from self-love, selfishness and separativeness, supported by envy, jealousy, spite, avarice, covetousness, intolerance, criticism, ambition, cruelty and suspicion.

Because hatred is an integral part of the astral world and its distortions, it is a powerful weapon wielded by the Forces of Darkness. By fostering that which blocks the inflow of noble and life-giving forces, they endeavour to blind mankind. They deliberately fan the fires of hate, separativeness, criticism and cruelty; they endeavour to preserve that which is familiar and of long standing, thus retarding spiritual progress and the revelations of the New Age. By feeding existing fears and hates, they incite the nations of the world to discord, strife and war, thereby delaying the forces of evolution. The individual cannot directly combat these Dark Forces but can actively contribute his small share by ensuring that every sign of hate is stifled in his own system and superseded by the opposing forces of love, goodwill and right human relationships. Hate and antagonism blind vision and warp discrimination but these *must* and *will* cease as the individual supplants them in his own life!

Hatred has been an intrinsic part of man's character ever since the emotional body began to develop as part of his standard equipment. From earliest times man has been casting the blame for adverse conditions on others and hating them for this, instead of first going in for some honest self-analysis; when things go wrong, it is far easier and more satisfactory to find scapegoats for wrong thoughts, speech or action. Every individual with any aspiration to contribute towards improved human relationships should recognise and work for the elimination of this tendency. Hatred, blame and condemnation can, however, never coexist with love and, as goodwill is planted and takes root, so will feelings of hatred wither and fade.

"Hatred ceaseth not by hatred; hatred ceaseth by love".

X. 3 (d) **Love**

Love in its true sense is a principle, a divine energy and the whole of our present world system is founded on the energy of Love-Wisdom. This means that Love is the underlying motivation for all divine activity and that the whole Universe is synthesised by this energy of Love. This concept of 'love' is therefore that of a supreme energy ranging far beyond the usual sentimental understanding of the word, which reduces it to the astral level.

A casual survey of world conditions would never lead to the conclusion that the course of events is being guided by love, much rather implying that all is based on hatred, covetousness and similar degrading qualities. It should be remembered, however, that the average human being is still surrounded and submerged by the miasmas and illusions of the emotional plane and that his views and judgements are clouded by this warped outlook. But again it is all a question of relativity, of different angles of approach to truth and of man's varying interpretations thereof. The energy of love has several aspects and the point of examination will be determined by the development of the observer and the plane from which the approach is made. Moreover the quality of love energy and its effectiveness will depend on its immediate source and adequacy.

To summarise, 'love' might be classified into:

1. *Physical love* or the natural attraction between forms for the purpose of procreation, manifested as sex life. In man this expression of love has often become perverted by astral influences.
2. *Astral or emotional love* is what in daily speech is known as 'love' and may vary between purely sensual vibrations, shallow sentimental experiences or deeply penetrating love, closely corresponding to the exalted spiritual version.
3. *Mental love* and on a still higher level, *spiritual or divine love*.

These forms of love merely indicate gradations of the basic divine energy of Love, the ruling force of our system, of which the potential power far surpasses human conception.

Where love has been referred to as the energy that will neutralise and then supersede the emotional powers of hatred, it certainly does not refer to the emotional type of love, which may even serve as an additional stimulant to aggravate these poisonous emotions. No, the antidote that will mellow, suppress and eventually displace hatred is mental or divine love and where 'love' is mentioned in these texts without further qualification, it will refer to this encompassing, supernal and motivating energy of the Universe. Therefore the principal task of those who work for the redemption of man consists in raising human consciousness from the degenerating miasmas of the astral plane. The only way in which this can eventually be effected, is by subjecting humanity to a constant stream of divine love, manifested as goodwill and loving understanding.

(See also: PART TWO – VIII. 3 (a))

X. 3 (e) Psychic Powers

In the case of psychic powers we have a somewhat similar situation to that described in the foregoing section on 'Love'. Psychic powers may either be related to egoic levels and are then associated with soul qualities or they may refer to the astral plane, in which case they will be characterised by illusion, glamour and distortion. For the sake of convenience these two aspects of psychism are referred to as 'higher' and 'lower' psychic powers.

There is the tendency among esoteric students to condemn all sensitive response to psychic phenomena as retrogressive. In many instances this is true and may well lead to a termination of the individual's spiritual development for that particular life span. On the other hand it may well be an indication of awakening spiritual sensitivity and the first expression of such development. It is only when the psychic life is uncontrolled or over emphasised that it becomes undesirable, immersing the man in illusion and glamour. What is of importance is that the investigator of psychic phenomena should be focussed at least on the mental plane but preferably he should work from the soul level.

Lower psychism is only undesirable when the experience is wrongly interpreted and applied and for this the beginner would be wise to seek the guidance of a more advanced disciple. Dreams and visions of a psychic nature, episodes of symbolic teachings and contact with thought-forms of spiritual entities, will increasingly occur in the New Era we are entering and these might well be an indication of growth and the early phases of expansion. If these experiences are, however, left undirected, unexplained, misinterpreted or ridiculed, the researcher may remain restricted to the field of lower psychism. With suitable guidance these phenomena might, however, initiate a series of graded revelations unveiling greater light and might well be regarded as the needed signposts along the Way.

With progressive development all esotericists have ultimately to become psychics, including both the higher and lower renderings. They should, however, be constantly on guard that the lower powers should not begin to manifest and dominate, until the higher faculties are functioning and well established – the lower will then be controlled and directed by the higher.

It is therefore important that esoteric students should gradually develop psychic sensitivity and a clear understanding of various psychic phenomena and what their demonstration involves. This does not mean that psychic powers must be deliberately cultivated but aspirants should maintain an attitude of guarded readiness to sensitivity and then observe and intelligently analyse any psychic phenomena that may be experienced.

The problem with lower psychics, who work purely on astral levels, is that as a rule they are absolutely convinced that their clairvoyant and clairaudient powers are indicative of advanced spiritual development, whereas it only represents the faculty of seeing or hearing on the astral plane. Apparently they are not aware that primitive races are in possession of similar qualities and even certain animals and that higher and more mentally oriented individuals often fail to register these perceptions.

It might be helpful to list some of the distinguishing qualities between:

Lower Psychism	and	Higher Psychism
Astral		Spiritual
Emotional		Mental
Uncontrolled		Controlled
Negative		Positive
Instinctual		Consciously; Intuitive
Automatic		Intelligently
Form		Life and Spirit
Trance Mediumship		Natural Sensitives
Clairvoyance		Symbols; Spiritual Vision
Clairaudience		Telepathy; Inspiration
Solar Plexus Centre		Throat and Head Centres

But remember that the greater always includes the lesser and that higher psychic unfoldment should eventually comprise the lower but to function on astral levels is certainly no indication of spirituality and may on the contrary indicate nothing more than remnants of Atlantean consciousness.

The degree to which psychic sensitivity has been developed and the different ways in which it is demonstrated, will vary within wide limits from disciple to disciple and should not be regarded as a criterion of spiritual unfoldment. The higher psychic powers are recognised by providing the disciple with growing intuition and its unerring judgement, these being the attributes of the soul.

There is evidence of a rapidly growing number of psychics. This tendency is further confirmed by ever increasing sensitivity to impression from spiritual realms, coupled with signs that aspirants throughout the world are revealing symptoms of expanding consciousness and greater awareness of the phenomena of the intangible spheres. Symbolically speaking this means that the etheric web is thinning. As a rule the world of phenomena which is being contacted is still mainly astral but at times it is being raised to mental and occasionally even to egoic levels.

This evolving awareness produces both a higher consciousness and a new state of being, serving to encourage aspirants in their spiritual endeavours but simultaneously encouraging rapid growth of various aspects of psychism and spiritualism, which are inclined to produce tensions and nervous complications. This increased impressibility of the human race is, however, also an indication of rapidly approaching developments and if judiciously handled and kept under balanced control, it augurs well for the future.

X. 4. **The Mental Body**

Over the ages man progresses steadily, at first with all his energies focussed in the physical body, then through that difficult stage where the emotional body unfolds and must gradually be brought under mental control, until serenity and stability are finally attained and all desires, greed, depression and self-pity are eliminated. This goal, however, is only reached with the development of the mental vehicle and the effective utilisation of that built-in computer, the physical brain, which has always been at man's disposal but has till now been used only in a very limited way, because the attention has largely been concentrated on satisfying physical and emotional requirements. For adequate functioning the computer should be properly programmed and therefore suitable information, facts and knowledge, should be gathered, arranged, classified and fed into this instrument, through the medium of the mental body. This will ultimately give rise to *divine wisdom*.

During the earlier stages of incarnation, with the life focus still largely centred in the physical and astral vehicles, the soul is present but remains neutral and withdrawn, since these bodies are not yet receptive to its influence and the suitable channels for effective communication are lacking. But with the development of the mental sheath the position begins to change. The mental body may be regarded as charged with positive energies, the physical body at the opposite pole is negative and the emotional vehicle is the intermediate field where the opposing forces meet and where the battle between the confronting dualities is fought, until equilibrium is finally achieved.

The soul must be regarded as the arbitrator, using its influence to guide the course of these battles and supervising the evolutionary programme towards the required balance. During this process the mental body becomes the transmitter of force currents from the Abstract Mind, via the subjective bridge known as the 'Rainbow Bridge' (or 'antahkarana') to the astral boiling pot.

The function of a disciple oriented on the mental plane is to develop a receptive mind and intuitive understanding for thoughts directed towards him from higher Entities and to transmute those thought-forms into appropriate speech or writing, thus enabling him to transmit his version of the message to his fellow men.

The intellect is an attribute of the mental body and final achievement of mental control is attained by its sound and correct application. This is implemented in three stages:

1. By means of the five senses, relayed through the computing brain, the mind receives impressions from the physical world.
2. The mind is brought into activity by these sensations but simultaneously initiates its own activities and in this function the intellect plays the dominating role. These two currents – the physical and the mental – interact and produce a third activity, where-in the *reasoning and discriminating principle* combines the information from the two informing currents and thus the 'thoughts' of the mind are formulated and registered in conjunction with those received from external sources.
3. By concentration and meditation the contents of the mind may be held 'steady in the light' of the soul. Through this technique the soul imposes its ideas and impressions upon the mind and thus becomes the channel from the spiritual worlds to the mental plane.

The mind or intellect therefore serves to co-ordinate, digest and formulate thoughts by reasoning from impressions received from the physical world, the mental plane and from the soul and subjective planes.

The main clash of forces occurs when a sound and sensitive physical body and a well equipped mentality are brought into contact. This battle is decided in the emotional body; it is only after the battle, when the mental body has reached equilibrium, that the soul can play its appropriate role. Most men still live in the world of feeling and sense perception or the emotional body and only few are as yet real thinkers oriented in the mental body, which when activated and correctly aligned, serves as the transmitter of soul energy and thus as the mediator between the soul and the lower vehicles.

X. 4 (a) **The Mind**

Every esoteric student at some stage must needs learn to understand something of his own mental processes; he must be able to form a reasonable concept of the mental tools at his disposal, how to apply them and finally what use to make of that which he learns and gains through the proper use of this mental equipment.

The mind is the faculty of logical deduction and reasoning and this rational activity distinguishes man from the animal. It is the medium through which the intelligent Will, the active Purpose and the fixed Idea of Deity finds expression through its creation – the human being. By utilising the human form, all units within its sphere of influence are driven towards the fulfilment of a set divine Purpose. The mind is the means and chan-nel through which these spiritual energies operate, whereby evolution is made feasible, understanding is achieved and activity is generated and applied.

The mind may also be regarded as a subjective organ of sense and as an instrument of discovery by means of which the consciousness systematically unfolds. Through the mind man learns to protect himself, to guard his interests and to preserve his identity; it serves purposes of discrimination and slowly builds a sense of values, which eventually enables the emphasis to be laid on the ideal and the spiritual, instead of on the material and physical.

It is the role of every thinker, even if only of limited capacity, to contribute his modest share to the pool of mental energy, which is being combined into a force of mighty power and applied towards the progressive evolution of mankind.

Right thinking is based on many aspects but for clearer understanding it may be useful to indicate the more crucial steps:

1. Sensitivity to egoic impression and intuition must be developed. This does not mean an understanding of the divine Plan but requires only the touching of the fringes of the Absolute Mind – thus intuitive ideas and thoughts are stimulated which may contribute to the furthering of the Plan.

2. Having recognised a flash of such vision, with perhaps a glimpse of its supernal beauty, the disciple has the opportunity to bring down to the mental plane that part of the Plan which he has grasped. He may find it difficult to retain anything from the first flashes experienced but in due course and with sustained efforts at apprehension, clearer contacts may be obtained and gradually certain ideas will penetrate the concrete mind. These ideas will then become concrete thoughts, which can be visualised and appropriated.

3. The next step is a period of gestation, wherein a thought-form is being built of as much of the vision as the disciple has managed to bring through into consciousness. As this vision slowly takes on definite shape, a longing will develop to share what has been received with the rest of mankind. The thought-form is thus being vitalised through the power of the will and gradually the thought-form of the vision begins to take on mental stature.

4. The disciple who can finally materialise his vision on the physical plane by word of mouth, by writing or by painting, is greatly favoured. It should be remembered, however, that such materialisation of any aspect of the vision is never the work of one man. It is only through the united work and efforts of many that it can be brought to outer manifestation and this is where the need of educating public opinion arises – it brings the many helpers to the aid of the few visionaries. This is therefore how the process works: The few intuitively sense the Plan; their thought sweeps the mental plane into activity; the thinkers of the public grasp the ideas and bring them into materialisation. This may also be expressed in terms of a mantram: "I listen, express and reveal the subtle truth that pervades my consciousness."

(See also: PART TWO – VI. 1 – "Thought")

X. 4 (b) Three Aspects of Mind

The mind may be subdivided into three aspects:

1. The *Lower Concrete Mind*, which is the reasoning principle – the receptive mind. It is the 'common-sense' and the highest aspect of the form nature.

The lower mind is the channel through which illumination and impression from spiritual sources are transferred to the three lower worlds of human existence. By too intense concentration on its own activities it may, however, retard or obstruct the downflow of inspiration from higher levels and thus dull the potential effect of soul illumination. Only when the concrete mind steadies and reaches balance and stability, will the light from higher sources percolate to the brain and be available for serving humanity.

When the lower mind activities are too frantic, these energies may dominate the personality to such an extent that barriers will be raised between the person concerned and other lives, which can only be rectified when the factor of love is introduced, mellowing and later superseding the mental faculty: 'mind separates and love attracts' – mind creates barriers which love has to break down.

The lower concrete mind stores within itself all acquired knowledge. Once it has found its balance through meditation, it becomes receptive to soul illumination and may eventually evolve into the searchlight of the soul. Through conscious creative work it eventually becomes related to the 'abstract mind'.

One of its outstanding qualities is discrimination, enabling it to distinguish between illusion and reality and between the Self and the not-self, between the spiritual and the material.

The lower mind is of a *transient nature* and dissolves into the etheric with the passing of the personality.

2. The *Son of Mind*, also known as the Ego, Soul, Solar Angel or the Christ Principle. It is the intelligence principle – the individual mind.

The Son of Mind is the aspect related to the world of ideas and therefore the pattern-building faculty or that part of the mind which works with the blueprints upon which the forms are modelled. It is the Soul itself. It summarises within itself the essence extracted from knowledge accumulated during past lives and which is then demonstrated as the light of wisdom. Through dedicated service it brings the divine Plan into activity in the three worlds of human accomplishment. It is brought into functioning activity through meditation and then controls and utilises for its own spiritual ends the consecrated personality, via the illuminated mind.

It is *eternal* in time and space.

3. The *Higher Abstract Mind*, is the custodian of ideas and the conveyor of illumination to the lower mind, once that lower mind is in alignment with the soul. Therefore – 'the illuminating mind'.

The abstract mind is the lowest aspect of the Spiritual Triad (See: X. 7 (a)). It is the transmitter of spiritual energies and reflects the innate divine nature through love, understanding and inclusiveness.

It represents the intuition or pure reason, which for man is the highest aspect of the mentality. It is the faculty which enables man to enter into contact with the Planetary Mind and grasp the first outlines of the Plan, to seize upon divine ideas or to isolate some fundamental and pure Truth. When fully developed, it summarises in itself the Purpose of Deity, thus becoming responsible for the emergence of the Plan.

The abstract mind is brought into conscious functioning through the construction of the 'Rainbow Bridge'. These three aspects of the mind are eventually united by this 'bridge of light', which is constructed through meditation, study, understanding and loving service, leading to creative work. Training of disciples should therefore aim at:

(a) Aligning mind and brain, through an understanding of the inner constitution of man and particularly of the etheric body and its centres.

(b) Construction of the bridge between brain, mind and soul, thus producing the synthesised personality, through which the indwelling soul can express itself.

(c) Building the bridge between the lower mind, soul and higher mind, to open up a channel for the effective flow of ideas and impressions from spiritual levels to the personality.

This 'bridging' process therefore consists in spanning the gaps between the integral parts of man and in providing the link between man and his environment and thus with the greater Whole. It involves constantly focussing the consciousness into the next higher vehicle or level of awareness and thereby progressively advancing along the path of spiritual evolution.

X. 5. **The Personality**

Strictly speaking the personality should be regarded as a concept rather than a true form in its accepted sense. It denotes an inclusive form composed of three separate vehicles, namely the vital, astral and mental bodies but the mere presence of these three 'bodies' does not in itself constitute what is known as a 'personality'. This designation only applies after the energies of the three relevant bodies have been perfectly blended, permitting these fused energies to function as a single co-ordinated unit. A successful integration of this nature produces a sense of individuality and self-consciousness because effective soul control can now be implemented. Where such central awareness exists, availing itself of the mental instrument which reacts through the emotional body and is energised by the vital body, the designation of 'personality' becomes justified. This sense of identity is, however, of a transient nature, only persisting during the physical existence of that particular form, as it will disintegrate and be absorbed into the etheric world at the 'death' of the form or in other words when the soul loses interest in the material vehicles and withdraws.

The average man struggles through life availing himself of the qualities provided in the three bodies which comprise his personality and as a rule they prove adequate for his requirements, relatively few changes being involved. For the man who moves on to the esoteric path, the position, however, changes. He starts with the vehicles provided but, as life develops and new subjective demands are constantly made on these bodies of expression, he must either improve the existing equipment or he must build newer and better instruments; the more advanced he is, the more this adjustment is consciously conceived. The result is that constant turmoil and frequent ill-health, so typical of the beginner in esoteric activities; he realises the need for raising his point of focus but frequently starts off on the wrong foot. The secret lies not so much in applying physical disciplines but rather in disciplining the mind, which demands control of the thought life and the transmutation of emotion to aspiration. If to this is added a simple diet of pure foods and a balanced pattern of living, then the man may succeed in building three completely new bodies after a period of seven years – bodies much better adapted to the increased spiritual demands.

It stands to reason that the characteristics leading to selfhood are basically of a selfish nature and it is this selfishness which underlies individuality. At the same time, this inherent and initially essential selfishness will prove to be one of his main handicaps when the more evolved personality strives towards synthesis with its spiritual aspects.

Some of the typical qualities associated with the fully integrated personality, are:

1. The inclination to say I am, I wish, I desire, I will.
2. The consciousness of being at the centre of one's own little world and environment.
3. The sense of responsibility often coupled with self-importance and the thought that others are dependent on one.
4. The power to use thought constructively. This definitely involves the vital, emotional and mental faculties and also leads to a capacity to co-ordinate the life, guided by will and purpose, by emotional desire and vitality.
5. The power to attract, influence and guide others by means of these personal attributes and qualities.

The potency of the qualities constituting the personality will determine the position it occupies in the community and whether the person is a server, a follower, an egoist or individualist, a group or religious leader, a political or national leader or a world leader.

It should be mentioned here that the progressive integration and development of the personality is inevitably coupled with a conscious or unconscious growth of soul awareness. The way in which this egoic influence is expressed will in the first instance depend on the degree to which the soul has identified itself with its instruments of expression and secondly, it will largely be affected by and vary with, the inherent characteristics of which each individual is composed. Egoic influence is typically demonstrated by such attributes as idealism, compassion, group service and sacrifice. At the opposite pole are to be found personalities not yet noticeably under soul influence and therefore still characterised by selfishness, dominance, ambition, pride, desire and lack of group love, with sensual love often playing an important role.

The condition of the personality will be reflected in its aura or surrounding sphere of radiation and influence. The aura is stimulated by the centres in the etheric body and it is the quality and nature of the energies being radiated which will indicate the centre mainly responsible for the stimulus and also the extent to which these centres have been awakened and activated. A study of the aura – by those who have etheric vision – will soon determine to which of the centres the vibratory effect can mainly be ascribed and this in turn will establish whether the personality is emotionally, mentally or soul controlled.

It should be recognised that perfect integration of the mind, emotional nature and physical brain, composing a balanced personality, does not necessarily imply an effective spiritual life and quite often the reverse proves to be the case. A well co-ordinated personality may well be extremely ambitious, selfish, sadistically inclined and even dedicated to evil. No, the spiritual qualities exhibited will solely depend on the extent to which the soul is influencing the personality, this process culminating in the soul taking command, with the personality being nothing more than a pure channel through which the soul can effectively contact the dense physical plane. The soul and personality will then be completely merged to function as a unit. This is what St. Paul symbolically referred to when he said that "He annulled the law with its rules and regulations, so as to create out of the two a single new humanity in himself, thereby making peace." (Eph. 2:15/16). Yet the climax of personality performance has still not been achieved. The next step is when the soul becomes absorbed in the Monad and when this representative of Spirit takes full control of the triple instrument. This stage denotes the termination of all personality life as known in the past – the outer form may be retained but henceforth it will become a purely spiritual instrument reacting to the behests of the Monad.

X. 6. **The Soul**

Each concept dealt with in this study must be considered important in its own context, since these ideas are the bricks collectively required for erection of the overall esoteric structure. The esoteric field should therefore be considered in its totality, carefully avoiding over emphasis on isolated concepts and thus obtaining an unbalanced structure. Nevertheless, in all structures there are individual bricks which could be omitted without affecting their real strength, perhaps only leaving a small scar or blemish, subsequently to be restored or rectified. There are of course certain corner or key-stones which fulfil a vital function and without which the walls cannot be erected and sustained. And such is the key role of the Soul in the esoteric edifice.

In the preceding pages repeated reference has been made to the soul and it is now time to consider this concept more closely. But what a difficult subject to deal with! The soul is something so intangible, formless and subjective, that it really lies beyond description of human words. Perhaps it is most adequately described as that inner light which at times illumines the whole being. However, no description of any kind will enable the man who has not yet contacted his own soul, to understand this inner self, this hidden observer and director.

Fortunately among normally intelligent men there are few who, consciously or unconsciously, have not at times been aware of this inner ruler. Of those who have made this contact, there are many, however, who have not consciously recognised the deeper meaning of this experience or else they have not yet reached the stage where this inner constitution of their being has become of interest to them and consequently they do not devote any serious thought to the subject. Others again are so involved in the struggle for achievement in the three worlds of human expression, by scrambling for material things, by attempting to satisfy every emotion and desire and gathering all knowledge that might serve their ambitions, that they are unwilling to devote the time to think and meditate on the deeper and spiritual side of life. Yes, this regrettably is the position and although one is inclined to be saddened by this, it should be remembered that it all forms part of the Plan of Life and that with the course of time – and incarnations – all these individuals will yet become consciously aware of the Self, the Inner Guide and the Path of Life.

The soul of each individual has reached its own specific stage of unfoldment; each soul has to endure every possible phase of experience that life in the material world can offer – the good and the bad, the bitter and the sweet and to learn from these experiences, until eventually the essence has been extracted and assimilated from all that physical life can offer and the urge to withdraw from the three worlds and to return to the Father's home becomes paramount.

X. 6 (a) Defining the Soul

The esoteric student requires some definition of the soul, so let us try to clarify this vague concept:

1. The soul is neither spirit nor matter but relates the two, serving as link between Spirit and the material instrument through which it functions. It is synonymous with the Christ-principle in man.
2. The soul is responsible for the quality and characteristics of life and represents the latent powers of expression in every human being.
3. The soul's contribution is self-consciousness and the source through which the form registers conscious awareness of its environment. The extent to which the consciousness is expanding, is therefore an indication of the progressive integration of the soul with its instrument of expression.
4. The soul represents the principles of sentiency and intelligence in man, demonstrating as mind and mental awareness and giving rise to the power to discriminate, to analyse, to distinguish and to decide.

5. The soul is immortal. When a particular life has fulfilled its purpose, the soul withdraws, the physical body 'dies' and disintegrates and the soul returns to egoic levels.
6. The immortal soul is the link between successive incarnations; it therefore provides continuity. By extracting and assimilating the essence from experience gained during each incarnation, the soul initiates the unfoldment and evolution of the consciousness

X. 6 (b) The Egoic Lotus

In esoteric literature reference is frequently made to the egoic lotus, which is but a symbolic representation of the soul, located on the third level of the mental plane.

The graphic picturing of the soul as 'the jewel in the centre or heart of the lotus', enclosed by the nine petals of the flower, is in fact very appropriate. Before the awakening of the soul the bud is still closed and the nine petals, arranged in three concentric circles or whorls of three each, tightly enfold and hide the jewel at the centre. With progressive spiritual development, step by step and from life to life, the individual petals of the lotus begin to unfold, one after another, radiating both colour and light. By the time man achieves 'perfection' in his earthly career, the nine petals have fully unfolded, displaying their beautiful colours and thereby setting off the glowing Jewel now exposed at the centre.

The Tibetan states that it is impossible to paint an adequate picture of the egoic lotus when fully unfolded, at which stage it radiates brilliant fire and constantly scintillates owing to the ceaselessly vibrating streams of energy by which it is vitalised. Every petal is sparkling with quivering points of fire and vibrating life and this vitality is reflected by the beauty of the Jewel at the centre. This glowing Jewel radiates streams of energy which may be directed towards any focal point in the system it co-ordinates.

X. 6 (c) The Causal Body

The 'causal body' is another term frequently occurring in esoteric writings and therefore needs clarifying.

This again is purely a symbolic representation of a rather obscure concept. It is the 'temple of the soul'; it is the divine storehouse where the essence of life, the good and the valuable, garnered from the experiences of many lives, is stored and accumulated. It is therefore but the figurative sheath or vehicle of the soul, which serves as a central receiving and transmitting station. The gleaned essences are retained in the causal body at the end of each incarnation and the accruing benefits are thus carried forward from life to life.

X. 6 (d) Characteristics of the Soul

It is important that attention should be drawn to some of the soul's outstanding attributes, whereby its presence may be detected. Generally speaking the soul-infused being can be identified by such qualities as idealism, group service, sacrifice, inclusiveness, willingness to share, impersonality, perseverance, compassion, steadfast love and goodwill and the calm, flexible but undeviating purpose of the divine Self. These properties may be contrasted with those of the personality when soul influences are still largely submerged, such as dominance, ambition, pride, sensuousness, selfishness, greed, hate and anger. Some of the more outstanding qualities of the soul will now be briefly surveyed:

(i) **Love and Goodwill:**

These two properties are closely associated and goodwill is merely one of the practical expressions of love. Judicious application of love and goodwill on all levels must inevitably lead to good human relations and as the improvement of human relationships is clearly one of the basic objectives of the New Age, the importance of the role of love cannot be over-stressed.

Love, like all other qualities of life, is also a very relative concept. In the personality it develops at first from an entirely selfish and sensuous emotion, until it increasingly becomes influenced by the soul, demonstrating as love of family, love of the partner in life, radiating and unfolding gradually into ever wider spheres of group love, so characteristic of the soul, until this love eventually embraces all humanity.

Love is the energy which constitutes the soul of all things and all forms; it is the principal energy of the world soul, the *anima mundi*, reaching its highest point of expression in the human soul. It may be regarded as the unifying force which serves to synthesise every form in creation into a synchronised and co-ordinated Whole. As far as the human being is concerned, it is the exalted energy responsible for all that is gracious, kind and beautiful in individual character and which serves to promote all worthy relationships between man and man, group and group and which will finally unite all nations and all races into the One Humanity.

(ii) **Intuition:**

The intuition is the faculty which will unfailingly lead the soul-infused man to right decision and action, when faced with a choice on behalf of his fellow man. This is not the emotional motivation which the astrally oriented refer to as 'intuition'. No, true intuition which will guide the advanced disciple unerringly to his destination is a characteristic of the soul and the direct product of an impression or of a spiritual flow of energy and wisdom from the Monad. The average man, still mainly centred in the personality, should recognise this and continue to base his decisions on 'common-sense' rather than to sit back in vain expectation of intuitional inspiration. Any 'intuitional' guidance such a man might receive, would probably originate from astral levels and not from the egoic plane and thus could not be relied on to lead him to his spiritual goal. Moreover the intuition relates only to group activities and never to trivial personality affairs or to satisfying selfish ambition.

Although the higher intuition is normally associated with relatively advanced spiritual contact, it will definitely also make its appearance at an earlier stage, when the disciple finds himself in extremity or when help is urgently invoked on behalf of others.

When the disciple has reached the stage where he can freely draw on the intuition with its swiftness and infallibility of decision, the use of the mind with its laborious functioning, its illusions and errors, will gradually decline, till it will eventually lapse into disuse and be superseded by the intuition.

(iii) *Light:*

Light is a symbol of the soul and the light which the disciple radiates will be commensurate with the dominance of his soul. To the disciple three main sources of light are available:

1. *The Light of Knowledge.* This is the still partly obscured light of the personality with which the aspirant may seek to dispel the various glamours which hide the truth from him. All knowledge is the product of the physical brain and will serve to illumine areas of consciousness which were previously hidden in darkness.
2. *The Light of Wisdom* is the light radiated by the soul and results from the light of long experience blended with the light of knowledge. The light of wisdom will illumine and thus reveal the subjective world of meaning or reality, which to the average man remains hidden by the outer form.
3. *The Light of Intuition* is the light of Spirit and only begins to function effectively when the soul and personality have reached complete accord. This presupposes a blending of personality and soul light with that of the Monad or Spirit and with its appearance the lesser lights will gradually be absorbed by the Spiritual Light.

(iv) *Serenity and Inner Calm:*

The soul-infused disciple is characterised by deep serenity, inner calm and an enduring patience. This is because the soul, realising its immortality, knows persistence.

Serenity should not be confused with peace, which is a relative and temporary condition in a world of constant change and evolution. To realise progress, there must and always will be disturbance. Peace refers to the world of feeling and emotion, whereas serenity is a soul quality and could be maintained even with violent disturbances in the personality worlds.

Neither should serenity ever be interpreted as insensitivity – it is in fact a reflection of intense feeling, transmuted by the soul into deep understanding. The soul-centred disciple will reach the point where nothing will disturb his inner calm and utter serenity is experienced through perfect poise and equilibrium.

(v) *Joy:*

A clear distinction can be drawn between happiness and joy. Happiness is a fine quality but it remains a personality reaction, based on the satisfaction of desire, feeling and emotion. Being founded on the unstable emotional life, it is subject to the many emotional disturbances of the environment, fluctuating between the heights of happiness and the depths of misery and depression.

Joy on the other hand is a much more stable and deeper quality and a characteristic of soul life. It arises from a close alignment of the soul with its three worlds of expression but, in contrast to emotional happiness, joy is in essence a mental experience; while happiness is produced by pleasing the personality or those associated with the personality, joy is the product of satisfying the objectives of the soul. Joy will therefore always be associated with efforts made on behalf of fellow human beings; with the consciousness of days spent in service to others; with co-operative group activities; with contributing, even if only to a limited extent, towards realisation of the Plan; or with the bringing of light to a soul in darkness. Yes, what wonderful joy it brings in being consciously instrumental in assisting a fellow worker in his struggle along the upward path. The motive inspiring action must however be selfless, non-acquisitive and altruistic – then the joy of the soul will be experienced, although the personality may simultaneously be in a state of distress and unhappiness.

Joy, being soul energy, is also qualified by strength. So learn to cultivate joy, in the certain knowledge that it is inspired by the unfailing power of the soul and will lead man unerringly along his arduous path towards divine destiny. Joy will open the portals to Light, will help to dispel glamour and misunderstanding and will bring inner serenity.

(Also see: PART TWO – IX. 3 (q))

X. 6 (e) The Problem of Duality

Unity, duality or triplicity – all facets of the same concept and merely a question of different approach and point of view and which will be determined by the unfoldment of consciousness.

From the standpoint of the awakening aspirant, all is seen as *duality* – for instance: personality and soul; matter and spirit; the Son and the Father.

Manifestation may, however, also be regarded as a *triplicity:* 'Life-Quality-Form' or expressed in different terms, as 'Spirit-Soul-Body'. But all these are merely inadequate attempts to express in words various aspects of Deity, of which man is vaguely aware but which he will never really be able to comprehend. These triplicities are therefore only facets of a Unity which man has identified under the inclusive name of GOD.

But regard the world from the standpoint of the aspirant. To him everything could be interpreted in terms of duality or opposites and these pairs of opposites meet on the emotional or astral plane, where they act and interact and where these clashes may develop into major conflicts. In reality the battle is a struggle for dominance waged between the soul and its vehicle, matter, manifested as the personality. The average man, however, remains unaware of this underlying conflict and of the issues involved; he is only concerned with the lesser or secondary activities, such as the struggle between light and darkness, good and evil, pleasure and pain, freedom and suppression, poverty and riches and many more.

Before a disciple can begin to work with world forces and problems, he first has to balance the opposites in his own system. When this equilibrium has been achieved to some extent, he has entered the Path and can become a co-worker in the wider field.

To the little evolved there are as yet no problems of duality, being unaware of anything beyond the world of matter. The aspirant, however, becomes aware of opposites and this leaves him stranded, vague and uncertain somewhere in between, being pulled hither and thither by the dual poles. The man who is thus becoming aware of the presence of the soul, realises that he is suspended between two forces – the attraction of matter and form, as opposed to that of the soul. It is this double attraction accentuating the many dualities, which brings the aspirant to recognise that his own divine will, as opposed to the selfish will of his personality, constitutes the deciding factor. Through the light he has found, he has become aware of the darkness; he sees the good as his ideal but the urge of the flesh draws him towards evil; he experiences hell on earth and thus visualises a spiritual heaven as his sanctuary.

These dual forces may be seen as two streams of energy or two paths leading in opposite directions – the one back to material, selfish desire, associated with the dreary cycle of rebirth and the other to the freedom of the world of souls.

For the aspirant who has made relatively only recent conscious contact with his inner guide, there usually follow years of severe strain and struggle. He has repeatedly to face the opposites, and decisions and choices have to be made. He comes to realise that he can no longer continue along the way of least resistance. From time to time he obtains flashes of insight and new visions appear to him, only to be engulfed again by the requirements of everyday life and the selfish desires and demands of the personality. Another consideration which may play an appreciable role, is the fear of ridicule of relations and friends who have not yet become aware of these deeper perceptions or else refuse to acknowledge these experiences. It may require very strong convictions to overcome such fears or even active opposition and to proceed calmly along the way, disregarding all disparagement and opprobrium.

Once the disciple has reached the point of decision and has turned his footsteps to the Light, he will find that active support will be forthcoming from both the soul and certain subjective Entities who are always ready and willing to reach out a helping hand. Should his resolve, however, weaken or his energies flag, then he will *temporarily* revert to the old habits and conditions of the unawakened man, with the murky clouds and glamours of the astral plane settling over him again. This only means that these same battles will have to be waged anew, until he finally succeeds in meeting these challenges.

To speak of 'final attainment' and 'final destination' is of course paradoxical, because everything in our Universe is relative and 'finality' can never be achieved in an infinite

Universe. Progress only means moving from one point of attainment to the next, from initiation to initiation, from one plane of consciousness to a higher and so for ever on and on, higher and higher, until …?!

But to return to Earth – should the aspirant's path lead him to higher levels, then this will mean new expansions of consciousness, fresh revelations, deeper understanding, a more comprehensive grasp of the realities of life and simultaneously new challenges to be surmounted. New powers and capacities will be evoked and new fields of experience and service will be disclosed to him and all this will be attended by increased responsibilities.

While embracing the inner relationships and subjective attitudes of the higher aspects of a dual life, the candidate remains faced with the fact that he is still standing in the outer physical life, with certain commitments and responsibilities which may not be lightly ignored. His problem is to stand spiritually free while surrounded by his worldly obligations; to function in subjective realms and yet to continue his activities in the world of human experience; to attain true spiritual detachment and still to render due service to his fellow men.

X. 6 (f) Alignment of Soul and Personality

Some of the characteristics of the three vehicles of human expression have been outlined. It also has been outlined that after they have been integrated, they may serve as a channel for the soul to communicate with the outer world.

When the physical body, with the brain, becomes aligned with the sentient body and subsequently with the mental body, then the lower mind can communicate freely with the physical brain, feeding its facts and ideas into this computer for further elaboration and recasting. This is how the thinkers of the world are actuated. When the causal or egoic body is also brought into line, the soul can function through these instruments and the potential is then created for the appearance of outstanding leaders of the race, who can not only sway the masses emotionally and intellectually but can also inspire them with more elevated ideals. Such alignment will also produce inspirational writers, idealists, abstract thinkers and inspired musicians and other artists.

For the beginner on the path of spiritual evolution, such alignment with the soul will only occur periodically – at first only as flashes during periods of intense aspiration or when acting in service of humanity. In due course the aspirant will find, however, that such soul contact is facilitated by abstracting the mind from the diversions produced by sensory, emotional and mental contacts; he will find that this abstraction can be implemented most effectively by suitable techniques of meditation, leading to the awakening of the abstract consciousness.

The problem of aligning the various bodies really amounts to raising the vibrations of the lower vehicles to those of the soul. This may be effected through purification of the reactions arising from the lower planes and subduing the desires and emotions. This entails endless struggle with the lower nature but persistent effort is bound to prevail. When reciprocal vibration has been attained, abstract ideas will begin to filter through to the lower mind with increasing frequency and these will eventually be followed by flashes of illumination and real intuition from the soul.

As a rule this process of alignment is not accomplished in a single incarnation but is spread over many lives of constant endeavour before the emotional body is sufficiently stilled and a mental body is constructed with the proper balance, which can act as a suitable filter and not as an impediment to the inflow of inspiration.

Alignment should, however, not be seen as limited to co-ordinating the functions of the soul and personality. Alignment will also involve contact with the spiritual realms and ultimately with the Monad, thus initiating the disciple into ever higher levels of consciousness, revelation, inspiration and service.

The various processes of alignment form part of the early stages of construction of the "Bridge of Light" which eventually will span the gap between the Monad and the material bodies. This subject will, however, be dealt with under a separate heading. (See: X. 7 (b))

X. 6 (g) **Reincarnation (Rebirth)**

For esoteric students the concept of rebirth is not an abstract belief based on theory and thus open to debate. For them it is a well established fact which has been known in Ancient Wisdom for thousands of years and has subsequently been proved over and over again in daily life. The principle is primarily based on the duality of man. Those who cannot or will not accept the fact that man is a duality, with an immortal soul which, during incarnation, inspires a material body with which it is intimately associated, are not ready for these studies – their turn will come either later during the present life or otherwise they will have to await a later incarnation.

Once the student has accepted the premise of immortality of the human soul, then logic, when unobstructed by dogma, will compel him to the conclusion that reincarnation is inevitable. If the composition of humanity is considered, with its races and nations, with their variety of colour, language, physical, emotional and mental characteristics and if in addition it is considered that there are as many characters as individuals, then some idea of its complexity is being formed.

The point to be emphasised is the disparity between individuals. Among the billions there are those who die of starvation and those who die of excess; there are those who possess nothing and do not have the wherewithal 'to hold body and soul together' and those who require large organisations to administer their possessions; there are those who still live as slaves, in comparison with those who have the power to dispose over the welfare, life and death of millions; there are the imbeciles and those gifted with brilliant minds; there are those with wasting bodies and those with radiant health. And similarly one could name many more contrasting conditions and characteristics but finally there are those interested only in their personal well-being, in contrast with those advanced disciples whose lower vehicles are already completely subject to the behests of the soul and characterised by spiritual love, living solely to serve their fellows.

Now if man were granted only one life on Earth, only a single opportunity to either succeed or fail and with all these individuals so unequally equipped for life's challenges and struggles, how could such a state of affairs possibly be justified and regarded to be equitable? How could one possibly believe in a God of love *apparently* favouring one with every conceivable advantage in life and to another nothing!... no intelligence, no worldly goods, no opportunities and no spiritual consciousness? How could two such divergent individuals be brought before the Seat of Justice and be judged on the same terms? No, impossible! No loving Father would ever countenance such anomalies, when providing only one opportunity for redemption.

Fortunately for man, we *do* have a loving Father, on whose wisdom and justice we can depend! The shortcoming lies with man himself who can neither understand nor interpret that with which he is surrounded. He can only distinguish one small facet of the Truth and of a most involved system and is therefore basing his judgement on totally inadequate evidence.

But where then has man failed in his reasoning? The answer and crux of the whole problem lies in the misleading and erroneous assumption that the evolution and redemption of the human soul must be completed in a single spell of life on Earth.

The disparate condition between both individuals and races is factual and forms part of the pattern of human existence but once the reason for this disparity is understood, there can no longer remain any doubt about the compassionate love and justice of our Divine Father. What we are observing in races and individuals, is merely the outer expression in the stages of development attained by the many components of humanity, all of whom are in a state of constant change, evolution and adaptation. Some are still at a primitive stage, whereas others are already well advanced along the Path. Man's main handicap is his lack of discernment and understanding; his myopic vision, which is accentuated and distorted by the glamour of the astral surround in which the majority still move and live.

What should be recognised, is that the personality is only the physical instrument which is *temporarily* occupied by the real, immortal, inner man – the soul. The material sheath of flesh, blood and bone, is definitely mortal and 'dies' at the end of the life span, when the soul, together with the essence of life, are withdrawn. The dead body then disintegrates into its constituent atoms but the immortal soul is transferred to one of the etheric levels, depending on the spiritual development achieved. Existence will continue 'normally' on these higher levels, except that the soul will now be free and no longer encumbered by a limiting physical outer covering. After a longer or shorter sojourn in these subjective spheres, a growing urge will develop in the soul for further physical experience.

In these writings repeated reference is made to the developing or unfolding soul. Strictly speaking this is incorrect. The soul is a reflection of the Monad or Spirit and as such is a spark or minute fraction of Deity and should therefore also be perfect. But 'perfection' is a relative concept and although our Deity, the Logos of our planet Earth, is the consummation of perfection to man, even this Deity, according to the Ageless Wisdom, remains mutable and in a perpetual state of change and evolution. For this evolution 'experience' is needed. Towards what objective the Logos is evolving will always remain beyond human conception but apparently, for the realisation of that purpose it is essential for the soul, as a fragment of the comprehensive Spirit, to sustain every possible experience which can be acquired through contact with dense matter. From these experiences the soul then gleans the 'essence', which is transmitted to the Higher Self to serve some unknown higher purpose on behalf of the Logos.

All that concerns man is the fact that the soul needs these experiences and that human bodies on Earth are required through which souls can operate.

Souls commence their age-long cycle by occupying the bodies of primitive men and the only influence exerted on these bodies at this early stage is apparently to provide them with the self-consciousness needed to distinguish them from the animal world. For innumerable incarnations, covering hundreds of thousands or even millions of years, these periodic and cyclic reincarnations are endlessly repeated, the soul gaining its requirements for gradual unfoldment but for a long time having no noticeable effect on its instrument. With the passing of ages the soul, however, becomes selective, choosing bodies that show some measure of development or refinement; at first the bodies were purely focussed on satisfying the physical aspects of existence but subsequently forms were evolved which gradually began to be oriented towards emotional living. Eventually the lower mind began to awaken, resulting in the development of the mental body. It is only with the unfoldment of the mind that the soul can begin to assert itself but real guidance by the soul only arises when the physical, astral and mental bodies become integrated and jointly function as the 'personality'.

The above digression may help to explain the wide diversity in type, quality, characteristics and development occurring among the billions of individuals of which mankind is composed. There is therefore no question of an unjust Father favouring certain races, communities or individuals and penalising others; what is observed are merely stages in the kaleidoscopic range of patterns in which souls are finding expression. Individuals and nations are to be seen in all stages of evolution, from the most primitive to the highly evolved, each and everyone undergoing those experiences needed by the indwelling soul. To man's injudicious eye some of these experiences may seem unnecessarily harsh or cruel but rest assured that, for some reason inexplicable to the limited human mind, it was exactly what the soul needed at that specific stage. We are observing the human panorama composed of millions of individuals, each guided by its own indwelling soul, each at its own particular stage of evolutionary unfoldment and in the process of gathering additional experience on its long, long journey back to the Father's home. Remember also that at whatever lowly stage of development a particular instrument may at present happen to be, all are on the same path, every soul has endured, or will be enduring, the same experiences in past, present or future lives and eventually all will attain the same temporary destination, only to proceed again still further on the interminable evolutionary path leading into the mysterious Unknown.

A few aspects of rebirth perhaps deserve some further elaboration:

1. *Intervals between Reincarnation.* Too much value should not be attached to generalisations on this subject, as wide differences occur in the rapidity with which these 'cyclic impulses' take place. Some souls linger for aeons on astral levels before deciding to return to the world of physical expression, while others rotate fairly rapidly.

It can nevertheless be said that the little evolved as a rule circulate fairly rapidly and do not dally long on subjective levels. As spiritual development proceeds, the length of these periodic withdrawals is increased, till much more time is spent 'on the other side' than in physical incarnation. However, with the path of discipleship nearing its final stages, the periods between incarnations will again begin to shorten: it is as if the soul is incited to complete its aeons of physical experience as rapidly as possible, with an urge for rounding off commitments and service obligations initiated during previous lives.

2. Normally the intent to reincarnate arises within the soul itself. When this happens, the soul, assisted by a specialised group of spiritual helpers, will select **suitable parents** who are to give birth to the physical body which must serve the soul as its next channel of expression. These parents must be selected with care, not only as to their heritable qualities but also with due consideration of the environment in which they are functioning. The soul is returning for specific purposes and for their realisation it is important that a form be provided with the required potentialities, as well as suitable surroundings for the needed experiences.

3. Souls belong to *groups* and as a rule a soul is reborn in the same period as other members of his group. The degree to which these group members will be associated during their physical life will vary. Some of these members may be born into the same family but this is only one of many possibilities. It will also occasionally happen that all group members will reincarnate in the same period or in the same region or race. When a soul returns 'home' after completing an incarnation, it will usually be welcomed back by group members 'on the other side'.

Actually group bonds and the consequent 'cyclic impulse' of groups plays a far more important role than has so far been realised by the average esoteric student. Man with his typical egotistic concern, has in the past largely been stressing the many personal implications of rebirth and development, not realising the function which the group has to fulfil or the service and sacrifice underlying group incarnation on behalf of the overall evolution of mankind. In the coming years this aspect of rebirth will receive far more consideration.

4. As far as soul life is concerned *sex* is irrelevant, since this is essentially an attribute of physical and emotional existence. For the sake of rounding off its experiences, the soul will, however, periodically be incarnated in either male or female bodies.

For similar reasons the soul will also take birth in nations and races of all colours and qualities.

5. Advanced souls who have reached the stage where they are delegated to fulfil some specific function *in service of humanity*, may be induced either to delay the termination of a particular incarnation or in other instances to expedite their return. The '*Lords of Karma*' who are mainly responsible for arranging conditions of rebirth, can therefore exert a strong influence on the trend of world affairs, by either retarding or accelerating the entry into incarnation of a suitable number of specially 'trained' souls to guide mankind in a required direction. It should also be remembered that advanced souls are no longer prompted to incarnate by a desire for achieving perfection – with them the incentive is an urge to sacrifice and a will to serve and to contribute their share towards realising the divine Plan.

X. 6 (h) The Soul and Initiation

There is a close relationship between the unfoldment of the soul and so-called 'initiation'.

Initiation is merely a symbolic way of indicating the steps which man attains during his laborious progress along the path of expansion of consciousness; it is an indication of the extent to which the spiritual man has become aware of himself as the soul, with its powers, relationships and objectives.

The stage of 'individualisation', when man passed out of the animal kingdom into the human and first became aware of himself, may really be regarded as his first initiation into consciousness. This stage of self-realisation is succeeded by aeons of gradual evolution but with the accent falling on the self and satisfying of personal physical demands. Eventually this way of life will find its culmination, leading to a crisis and new realisation, when the man suddenly becomes conscious of the duality of his existence and of the presence of the inner Self. This is sometimes known as 'the birth of the Christ-principle in the heart' and is the indication of initiation into spiritual life. Relatively few people are as yet consciously aware of the soul or that they have actually passed what in esoteric terms has become known as the *First Initiation* on the path of spiritual evolution. From now on a change in life focus will become noticeable: the self-interest of the past will decline and will increasingly be superseded by a growing interest in both the spiritual world and the needs of fellow men.

The interval between First and *Second Initiations* may stretch over many incarnations. During this lengthy period there will be a slow but steady and usually unconscious growth in soul awareness, which will begin to express itself as an unfolding altruism, demonstrated in its many facets of expression. This bridging period is also marked by gaining control over the emotions and desires and the realisation that the qualities of spiritual love, beauty, goodwill, truth and service, are of more enduring value than the momentary satisfying of emotions by pursuing pleasure and indulging the many urges of the flesh.

Meanwhile the hold of the soul on its three instruments of experience is increasing with the attention now focussed on mental unfoldment. This eventually leads to the next milestone on the path of the expanding consciousness – the **Third Initiation** or 'Transfiguration'. At this initiation the soul takes over complete control of the personality, assuming the functions of the lower mind which hitherto had been the directing force. The entire personality becomes flooded with the light of the soul and from now on the Monad also begins to take an active interest by extending more direct guidance to the soul. This interest by the Monad increases until it assumes such proportions that it fully and directly controls the personality, thus superseding the functions of the soul.

Next the phase of the **Fourth Initiation** is reached; this is known as the 'Great Renunciation' and is characterised by the recognition that the soul, the force which up till now has been inspiring and driving the human being along his path of spiritual evolution, has become superfluous and is being renounced and absorbed within the Monad. The Son has completed His work and has become one with the Father! Henceforth there will be a direct contact between spirit and matter and the personality will lose its individuality, becoming purely an instrument of service in the hands of the Monad and no longer evincing any personal inclinations or desires.

(See also: PART TWO – XIII)

X. 6 (i) **The Thread of Life**

Synonyms: The Silver Cord; Sutratma.

When considering the constitution of man, two distinct manifestations of life should be noted:

Firstly, all atoms, which in their myriads compose every form and organ, consist of primordial energy or 'life'. This might be called '*atomic life*'.

Secondly, there is the 'thread of life' representing the life of the soul, with its source in the Monad. This '*egoic life*' permeates the entire body, serving as the integrating factor within the form. When this life thread or 'silver cord' is withdrawn or ruptured, the body dies and disintegrates into its atomic constituents, in which the atomic life is retained.

In the trinity, Spirit – Soul – Matter, the soul represents the field of encounter between the two outer poles and Life is the common or uniting factor, pervading and synthesising the whole system.

The 'thread of life' therefore links and vivifies all forms into a functioning whole, embodying the will and purpose of the indwelling entity, whether plant, man or Deity. It is the stream of energy diffused throughout the form, from centre to periphery and simultaneously forming the connecting link between the spiritual source and its outer expression. It provides the fundamental source of all evolutionary unfoldment.

In man this 'thread' represents the path of the life energy flowing from the Monad via the soul to the personality, conveying this energy to its point of anchorage in the heart. From the heart as its focal point, the life energy is pervaded throughout the physical body by the blood stream and for this reason the blood is often represented as the symbol of Life.

A clear distinction should be made between the 'Life Thread', anchored in the heart and the 'Thread of Consciousness' or 'Bridge of Light', centred in the head.

(See: X. 7 (b))

X. 7. The Monad (The Presence)

The Monad (see: Diagram A) is a spiritual unit – a spark or cell in the manifested body of our Planetary Logos. As such it has already passed through cycles of previous solar systems and its expression in the physical form of a human being in the present system, is merely a step in its evolutionary development. The cycles cover such vast periods of time and the real meaning of this past history remains so obscure to the human mind, that it is meaningless to ponder too deeply on their implications. All that man can observe, and that only within narrow limits, are some of the present results – what the underlying causes are or the eventual objectives, will remain shrouded in darkness. He can but fulfil his role to the best of his ability, constantly striving to expand his consciousness, directing the light of the mind into ever wider and deeper spheres of awareness.

According to the Tibetan only certain groups of Monads have so far come into incarnation; this has occurred in different periods and there are still others to follow when interplanetary conditions are considered appropriate. During the present cycle approximately 60,000 million Monads are 'in circulation' – either incarnated in physical bodies (6 billion or say 10%) or temporarily withdrawn to etheric spheres till the time arrives for their cyclic rebirth in human bodies.

The Monad, as a minute component of the Logos, in its present stage of unfoldment needs physical experience for its evolutionary purpose. Contact with the three planes of the physical world is effected by functioning through the soul, which acts as the intermediary between Spirit and matter. Symbolically expressed, the soul, the 'Jewel in the Lotus', is the eye of the Monad, enabling the Presence, which is pure Spirit, to work, to contact, to know and to see. Because the 'Third Eye' is regarded as the window of the soul, it will therefore also serve the same purpose for the Monad.

The Monad, via the soul, is the source of Life and Light to the human personality. Through this channel the Monad serves as the organ of perception and contact for the Logos and through this mechanism the Divine Will is expressed, the Monad thus becoming the directing agent of the Logos, serving as the instrument for dispensing Will, Light and Life to the phenomenal worlds. When after the third initiation and the completion of the 'bridge of light', the personality comes into the direct sphere of influence of the

Diagram A
THE MONAD (SPIRIT)

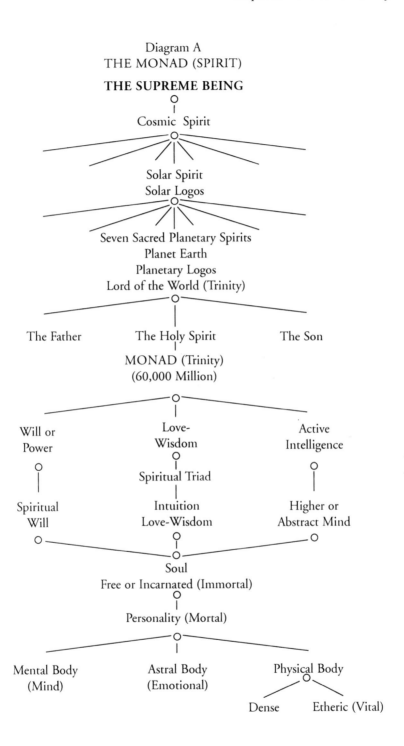

THE SUPREME BEING

Cosmic Spirit

Solar Spirit
Solar Logos

Seven Sacred Planetary Spirits
Planet Earth
Planetary Logos
Lord of the World (Trinity)

| The Father | The Holy Spirit | The Son |

MONAD (Trinity)
(60,000 Million)

| Will or Power | Love-Wisdom | Active Intelligence |

Spiritual Triad

| Spiritual Will | Intuition Love-Wisdom | Higher or Abstract Mind |

Soul
Free or Incarnated (Immortal)

Personality (Mortal)

| Mental Body (Mind) | Astral Body (Emotional) | Physical Body |

Dense   Etheric (Vital)

Monad, it will become a channel through which the Purpose and Will of God will be revealed to the world of men.

To summarise it can therefore be said that during the early spiritual development of man, the Monad delegates all contact with its reflection in the three worlds to the soul, which is related to the lower bodies by the thread of life, anchored in the heart and the thread of consciousness, seated in the brain. As the spiritual man unfolds, the soul slowly increases its control over the threefold personality. By the time the third initiation is reached, the personality is completely dominated by the soul and thus merely becomes the instrument through which the inner man functions on the physical plane. But another major change has meanwhile also occurred with regard to the relationship of the Monad. To the extent that soul activity and control over its channels of expression has increased, there has been a corresponding interest from the side of the Monad, coupled with a reciprocal reaction from lower levels. The soul-infused personality now becomes aware of the light of the Presence and an urge is born to return to the 'Father's Home' from which it has been parted for aeons. The personality finds, however, that there exists no suitable channel of contact, so it deliberately begins to construct a bridge to span this gap in consciousness – the 'Bridge of Light'. With the completion of this bridge, which only occurs after the third initiation, the Monad will be in direct contact with the threefold physical world, and the functions of the soul will thus become redundant and the soul will consequently be absorbed in the Monad.

X. 7 (a) The Spiritual Triad

The Triad is the channel through which the Monad functions and it serves very much the same purpose to the Monad as the personality does for the soul – a field for contact with the lower forms.

The three aspects of the Spiritual Triad are:

1. The Spiritual Will.
2. The Intuition or Love-Wisdom.
3. The Higher or Abstract Mind.

The Higher Mind, the lowest of the three aspects, is the interpreting agent for the Monad and can also be regarded as the connecting link with the soul; symbolically it represents the egoic or causal body, the seat of the soul.

The energies of Life, Intuition and the Higher Mind, are synthesised in the Spiritual Triad. Their correspondence in the three worlds of form are reflected in the 'life thread', the 'consciousness thread' and the 'lower mind' or principle of intelligence. Before the higher energies can, however, begin to influence the lower vehicles, these bodies must be firmly integrated into the personality, which then must become soul-infused. The final blending of the three higher energies with their lower counterparts will only be attained after the third initiation and with the bridging of the gap in consciousness between the Triad and the personality, thus creating one single field of service and activity for the initiate, under the direct guidance of the Monad.

X. 7 (b) **The Bridge of Light**

Synonyms: Lighted Way; Rainbow Bridge; Thread of Consciousness; Antahkarana.

Repeated reference has been made in previous chapters to the 'Lighted Way' but it is felt that this important subject needs some amplification.

Spiritual contact is essential to attain the unfoldment for which the aspirant yearns. For this purpose an unobstructed flow of energy must be ensured, firstly from soul levels to the three lower bodies and at a more advanced stage, from the Monad, via the Triad, to the threefold personality.

The reason why the beginner cannot contact his Higher Self and even less the Monad, is because there exists a wide gap in consciousness between each of these three centres of energy, the *Monad* – the *Soul* – and the *Personality* and these two gaps must first be bridged before there can be an effective and even flow of energy between the centres. This bridging must first be effected between the Soul and Personality and when firmly established and functioning satisfactorily, a beginning can be made with the building of the more advanced bridge between the soul-infused Personality and the Triad, the lower reflection of the Monad.

It should be kept in mind that the building of the Bridge of Light is merely a symbolic representation to simplify the understanding of a vague concept. The Bridge of Light is therefore not an actual channel between the soul and the personality or between the soul-infused personality and the Spiritual Triad but only a state of awareness – a living thought-form created by the disciple. But although this bridge may be entirely of a spiritual nature, it is nonetheless effective and will serve as a line of contact and a subjective thread along which the flow and interchange of vital energies will be conducted. The Bridge of Light will therefore finally serve to link the Monad, as the originating source of spiritual Will, Love and Intelligence, with the soul and personality, synthesising them into one vibrant whole, providing another useful and active piece of equipment for the direct contact between the Logos and Humanity. From now on this threefold personality will become purely an instrument and channel of service to the Monad and the appearance assumed by the form will depend solely on service requirements.

The Rainbow Bridge is sometimes also referred to as the 'Thread of Consciousness' in contrast to the 'Thread of Life'. An apt way to distinguish between these two vital channels of energy is to describe the 'Thread of Life' as working from above (from the Spirit) downward to the form, while the Forces of Consciousness are constructed upwards, from the world of phenomena to the world of subjective realities – the 'Path of Return'.

In the construction of the lower part of the bridge between the personality and the soul, the first essential is that the physical, emotional and mental bodies should be firmly integrated in the personality in order to establish a sound foundation for the bridge. This first span should form a clear channel of communication between the soul, via the concrete mind on the mental plane and on to the physical brain. Work on the first span should be steadily pursued until the third initiation is attained.

After the third initiation the construction of the bridge is rapidly continued and during this process the three aspects of the Spiritual Triad become perfectly linked and blended with their triple lower reflection in the personality. The world of inspiration and the field of service are thus being united into a single and efficient flow of activity on behalf of the Plan. This contact between lower and higher mind will be demonstrated in the disciple by intense devotion to that much of the Plan as can progressively be discerned and understood. The clarity with which the Plan is visualised and the extent to which it is effectively served, will depend on the efficiency with which the Lighted Way has been constructed.

During the early stages of spiritual development, the building of the Lighted Way usually takes place automatically and the aspirant remains unaware of the process. The later stages and especially the bridging of the higher gap between the personality and the Triad is an enterprise which the disciple must, however, undertake with full awareness and determination. Many disciples are subject to some form of mental lethargy and inertia and seem to sit back and wait for further development to come from outside. This, however, is the wrong approach and will result in loss of valuable time and opportunity. 'Before the man can tread the Path, he must become the Path itself'. Through meditation and concentration, deliberate efforts should be made to establish the first tenuous threads of contact with the Triad and through sustained exertion ever stronger light should be focussed on the Way, till this bridge becomes the way of least resistance and a constant and smooth interrelation and interchange of energy is ensured.

One of the most reliable techniques for erecting the supports of the Bridge of Light, is the rendering of selfless service to our fellow men. Such altruistic work will assist in esoterically 'repulsing' the hold of the personality – it is this hold by the lower worlds which must systematically be broken down to set free the impeded soul.

The completed Bridge of Light also becomes the way of escape from all forms of pain. This results from the consciousness being focussed in the Triad and no longer in the physical and emotional bodies where pain is normally registered. When the consciousness is automatically centred at these higher levels after the third initiation, pain and other negative astral sensations of the lower worlds will steadily be transcended and eventually transmuted into joy and bliss!

X. 7 (c) **Retaining of Identity**

The retention of individuality by the evolving human entity contains some apparent anomalies. On the one hand the Tibetan clearly states that 'identity ever remains' but on the other hand all esoteric study is based on the premise that each human Monad is just 'a spark of the One Life' – a spark which has been separated from the One to undergo experience in the physical world and, after being enriched with what has been gained, is returning on its way back to union with the Father.

Another approach is that each human being is but a cell in the manifested body of our Planetary Logos and that our planetary Deity in His turn represents only a minute atom of the Greater Universe, the SUPREME BEING. But although there is this merging with entities of ever increasing dimension and complexity and on ever higher spiritual level, the Ancient Wisdom teachings nevertheless maintain that identity is never lost and that each individual forever remains a separate unit of consciousness within the greater Whole.

In the course of his evolution man becomes aware of the fact that he forms an intrinsic and sentient part of a more comprehensive Entity. As his development proceeds during successive incarnations, he slowly begins to grasp something of the intent and purpose of the Whole, consciously identifies himself with that greater Purpose, swinging himself into the rhythm of that Whole of which he only forms a small part. This adaptation and merging with the greater rhythm involves the individual in the synthesised purpose and activity, resulting in enhanced experience and progressive spiritual enrichment but without detracting from self-awareness.

XI

DEATH

There is no death for man, there is but a change in consciousness, discarding a temporary garment which has been cramping the inner life's activities and restricting its expression! It involves re-entry into familiar spheres of activity from which the soul has been absent while gaining experience in an assumed body in the world of phenomena. It also means a return to group life, to the renewing of familiar relationships of age-long standing and picking up the strands of co-operative service activities which had to be interrupted during a short absence on a course of study on practical living in the physical world.

The soul now returns to its natural habitat, somewhat richer for the worldly lessons and experiences and thereby again better qualified to assist more advanced Entities in their never ending task of providing more light for those still struggling at lower levels. This means another spell of joyful work and associations in ethereal realms, until the urge arises for a further round of physical experience.

The majority of men are still under the illusion that there is but one life for the individual, that every desire should be gratified in the present short span and that all experiences contributing towards emotional satisfaction should be crowded in before this brief life ends in death. All spiritual unfoldment, however, tends towards realising the duality of physical existence and that we are dealing with a relatively unimportant and transient form which only temporarily serves the immanent spiritual being, the soul, as an instrument of expression. The developing aspirant will also recognise that death of the form is not something to be feared but rather something to be welcomed – the stage when the soul will again be liberated from the physical fetters and limitations. If there is a stage to be 'feared' in the soul's cyclic existence, it is much rather the time of birth into the physical world which, to the soul being born into the undeveloped body of an infant, is real 'death', for it will then be temporarily smothered in darkness. To the soul, release from these limitations would be rebirth into spiritual life!

Death and the return to egoic levels may, from the soul's standpoint, also be regarded as an opportunity for recapitulation and readjustment of energies in preparation for the next round of physical activity.

XI. 1. **Withdrawal of the Life Thread**

Generally speaking, ensouled man is the product of egoic will and when the purpose of the soul for that particular life has been accomplished, it loses interest and deliberately withdraws from the body and the physical vehicle dies and disintegrates.

Withdrawal of the soul is accompanied by the simultaneous retraction of the threads of life and of consciousness, both these being functions and attributes of the soul. It should be pointed out, however, that the procedure and sequence attending the recall of soul life and consciousness, does not always follow an exact pattern and will vary according to circumstances and definitely also with the stage of development attained by the disciple. Death may come suddenly and unexpectedly, as in the case of war, murder or accident, when the soul may be obliged to withdraw rapidly and without preparation; on the other hand the dying process may be extended over a period of days or even months, with the soul only emerging slowly and gradually.

The 'normal' process of dying might be divided into three stages:

During the *first stage* the life force is withdrawn from the dense physical body. This leads to the 'falling into corruption' of the material body, which refers to its disintegration during the process of releasing the 'atomic life'. The atoms, with their constituent elements, then find their way back into the surrounding scheme of nature. To those with etheric vision, the etheric body will however remain visible for some time after death.

The *second stage* is the abstraction of the life force from the etheric body, which is consequently devitalised and will fade out, being absorbed in the surrounding etheric system.

The *third stage* is the withdrawal of the life force from the astral-mental vehicles, which will then also disintegrate, with the soul life being retained in the egoic vehicle, liberated from the limitations of matter and preparing for the next incarnation.

Attention should perhaps be drawn to those exceptional instances of imbecility or senile old age, where the life and consciousness threads are not withdrawn simultaneously. In these cases the life thread, anchored in the heart, is retained but the consciousness thread is withdrawn from the brain. This results in a functioning physical body but one which is without intelligent awareness. In the case of senile decay, there may be the appearance of intelligent functioning but this as a rule is merely illusion and is due to ingrained habits and established rhythms of living. Such a soulless life has no further egoic effect but may serve some karmic purpose relating to closely associated lives.

In the case of advanced initiates, who are fully aware of the laws of abstraction, the transition can be effected consciously and in full awareness, thus preserving *continuity of consciousness* while passing on to higher levels.

XI. 2. **Life After Death**

For the unevolved savage, there is no conscious existence after death; his mind is not sufficiently awakened to react and there is no store of memory which can be relived. For these death will therefore be but a deep and dreamless sleep.

The only slightly evolved, constituting the mass of humanity, are still largely focussed on the physical and emotional aspects of life, being guided by selfish motives and gratification of sensual desire. For them the transfer to the astral world will be a condition of only semi-consciousness, of emotional and mental bewilderment and a failure to recognise their environment or circumstances – just a vague and confused dream world.

The average well-meaning man, with shortcomings typical of the normally developing human being will, during his sojourn in subjective realms, spend most of his time on the astral plane, living mainly with his memories and thoughts and carrying in his consciousness the interests and tendencies which qualified his Earth life. Many will even be unaware that they have 'passed over'. In some instances the astral sojourn will however be disturbed by a constant urge to return to Earth life – possibly caused by feelings of intense personal love for someone left behind, some unfulfilled desire or the realisation or illusion of some uncompleted task. For these there will be no rest until they return. Then there are the 'Earth-bound' – those poor souls who spent wicked, cruel and selfish lives on Earth or who lived purely material and sensuous lives and who, even after passing over, are still craving worldly goods or sensual satisfaction. For these the astral life is a time of real hell, often not realising that they have left the physical world, thus becoming extremely frustrated.

For the aspirant who has discovered the 'path of return' and has become aware of the light ahead, leading him from revelation to revelation and ever brighter light, for him death is but a release from physical restrictions and an opportunity for more effective service and expression. He will discover that, while still in the physical body, he had already initiated during his hours of sleep a field of service activities which he can now extend by giving it his undivided attention.

One of the great advantages of rapidly spreading esoteric knowledge is that the general public is becoming aware of the fact of the continuity of soul life and of the retention of consciousness after death; they are realising that there is no cause to fear death, a feeling which in the past was merely founded on ignorance and a dread of the unfamiliar and unknown. The Spiritualist movement, with its world-wide ramifications and abundant literature, has already rendered valuable service, by sweeping away many of the fears of death.

XI. 3. **Purgatory**

For the man of goodwill, life in the physical body might be regarded as purgatory; for him life in the astral 'hereafter' will be a happy release from life on Earth, with its never ending range of pain, distress, fear and friction; but he will not find that mythical 'heaven' on the other side, with its golden streets and lovely harp-playing angels flitting about. For the man of evil, the position will be different. Such a man, having first experienced 'hell on Earth', has also prepared a further bed of thorns for himself in the next life, where he will dwell in murkiness, surrounded by reflections and memories of his evil deeds and tortured by self-reproach and remorse.

One of the worst misrepresentations with which 'religions of fear' so often threaten believers is 'eternal' punishment for the misdemeanours of a moment! What a terrible alleged judgement to attribute to a God of Love! No, fortunately for us this is not the way Our Father meets out punishment to His children. There are the laws of Nature, such as the Law of Cause and Effect, which *must* run their course and in accordance with which every action inevitably calls forth a corresponding reaction. Man will consequently be rewarded or penalised for his every activity in direct proportion to its strength, quality and motivation – but this certainly must not be seen as some ruthless retribution or punishment by an unforgiving Deity.

That man should pay his dues for deeds of the past or receive commensurate reward, is fair enough. But the beauty of life, and one of the crowning gifts from Divinity, is that even the worst sinner will always be given another opportunity of rehabilitating himself – if this is not achieved in his present life, then such a chance for redemption will again be provided in some subsequent life and so, in the course of time, every individual will discover the Path of Light, the Path of Return to the Father.

XI. 4. Cremation

Throughout the ages the many races, each with their own customs, traditions, mystical and religious backgrounds, have devised numerous methods for disposing of discarded physical vehicles. These have varied from setting out the corpses to be devoured by wild animals, such as hyenas, crocodiles, tigers and vultures; burial, with the body in various postures, in graves, caves, tombs, catacombs, sepulchres and pyramids; burning on funeral pyres or other forms of cremation; and finally embalming to preserve the corpse against decomposition.

Several of these methods are still practised but burial in mother Earth is probably still the most commonly used method. This is most unhygienic because so many deaths are caused by infectious diseases and in burying these corpses, the soil becomes contaminated by the causal germs and viruses, which may remain contagious for many years. Thus the burial of millions of these infected corpses has contaminated large parts of the Earth's surface.

By far the most effective, hygienic and also the 'neatest' way of disposing of these physical remains, is by cremation. The exact technique applied and whether open fires or electrical equipment is used, is immaterial. What is important is that cremation is increasingly gaining ground over other practices and this may in future at least contribute towards purifying the soil and reducing sources of infection.

XII

HUMANITY

In preceding chapters the constitution of the human being has been dealt with, to arrive at a better understanding of the Personality – Soul – Monad complex. Care should be taken, however, not to over-accentuate the importance of the human being as an individual, ever keeping in mind his relative position as a part of a more inclusive whole. The individual will always retain his significance but this must be seen in relation to his contribution towards promoting the interests of his group, community, race and finally to the culminating whole – Humanity.

Of the seven kingdoms of nature, the Human Kingdom occupies the fourth or middle position, thus fulfilling a most important and responsible role by relating the lower to the higher kingdoms and serving as a channel for the transmission of energies from the three spiritual kingdoms to the lower three in material expression. Humanity may be regarded as the macrocosm to the microcosm of the sub-human kingdoms. As humanity evolves, a corresponding illumination is generated and this increased light is then reflected to the lower kingdoms. For instance through selection and breeding activities, man develops new strains in both the plant and animal worlds, thus bringing increased quality, beauty and effectiveness into expression and lifting these kingdoms another small step in their evolutionary progress. Similarly in the mineral kingdom the basic metals are extracted and released from ancient bonds by subjecting the natural ores to the purifying energies of fire and electricity.

Humanity is not only the spiritual light bearer, transmitting and transmuting the light of knowledge and wisdom but it also serves as the literal and physical light bearer, increasingly illuminating our planet during the hours of darkness. Think of the brilliantly lit cities, of the search and spray lights at night brightening recreational terrains and airfields, of the motor traffic lighting up the highways, of the brightly lit ships at sea and of the flashing aircraft streaking through the night skies.

Although a tendency towards closer collaboration between groups and nations is already noticeable throughout the world, the stage when the various human elements could function effectively as a synthesised unit is still far from realisation. Broadly speaking, humanity may be divided into three main groups with regard to their potential contribution towards eventual unification:

1. The vast majority, who are neither good nor bad but who plod through life without thinking and are largely guided by their desires and emotions. They are unconsciously submerged in the evolutionary tide and, although unaware of it, are working towards true self-consciousness. In the course of time this group will acquire increased light and will then be merged with the third group who have already entered the 'Path of Return'.

2. A few are really evil and consciously work for the Dark Powers. They exert a potent influence in the world, beyond all proportion to their numbers. Their power and dominance will eventually, however, be overwhelmed by the opposing Forces of Light and the universal Law of Love.

3. A number have discovered the 'Path of Return' and are the exponents of New Age ideas. This group is breaking away from the selfish approach to life, turning thoughts and activities towards selfless and altruistic living and improved human relations. The majority of these aspirants are characterised by reasonable intelligence and are encountered all over the world and in every field of human endeavour.

Humanity comprises many races, nations, colours and languages, the intelligent and the unintelligent, the spiritually developed and those who are more animal than man. Between these extremes are found many types at every stage of development. Yet they are all sons of men, belonging to the One Humanity and whether realised or not, they are jointly evolving towards a common destiny. Within this complex, one will progress much faster than his neighbour but that only means that he is increasing his responsibility and that symbolically he should link arms with those he is outstripping, thus drawing and lifting them along with himself.

The consciousness of man is rapidly awakening and with their eyes focussed on newly revealed visions, men are clamouring for spiritual guidance. It is one of the urgent tasks of the Hierarchy of Masters of Wisdom to respond to these invocative demands.

Over the ages man has progressively evolved from the animal stage, activated only by instinctive self-preservation and the urges of propagation, through the stage of concern for family or immediately surrounding group, to a feeling for tribal or national coherence and eventually to the point where he is becoming aware of his responsibilities towards the whole of mankind. He begins to realise that he is a member of the One Humanity – a vital structure characterised by the variety and quality of its constituent organs and cells, still functioning as a diffused power but nonetheless a force centre in the manifested vehicle of our Planetary Logos.

There are many negative forces separating men, groups and nations but there is also that growing subjective and mysteriously attractive force which is increasingly making itself felt on all terrains of human contact. This is evidenced by a growing idealism and a spirit of individual, group and international goodwill, sometimes coming from the most unexpected quarters. This idealistic spirit must utilise instruments which are often quite inadequate. Consequently some of the first results are immature, as for example, the United Nations. Also some newly formed governments and ideologies do not as yet express a true reflection of the motivating forces. But although this may lead to temporary debacles, delays and disappointments, it should be regarded as merely the preparatory stage following its natural development and with the knowledge that in the course of time matters are bound to improve. What is important is the existence of the right underlying spirit, consistently seeping into mankind and sustained by the divine Love-Wisdom energy systematically radiated through humanity from Higher Sources. Imbued with this spirit of the will-to-good, mankind is rapidly learning its lessons and gaining experience and this augurs well for the future. The effect of the hierarchical will-to-good is demonstrated by the emergence of a variety of idealisms, which at times may even prove of a conflicting nature. But provided these objectives are inspired by goodwill and tolerance, they will inevitably lead to greater co-operation, to security and peace and plenty for all, instead of the terror, fear and starvation of the past.

The time will come when there will no longer be individual, racial and national strife. This time no doubt still lies far ahead but the fact that we can consider it, visualise, desire and plan for it, is our guarantee that it is *not* impossible. Notwithstanding the negative attitude of many pessimists, there is no doubt whatsoever that during the past several decades humanity has already taken great strides in the right direction and that we are now well on our way towards greatly improved relations and conditions far better than the world has ever known before. This New Age that has already been entered is going to ensure a far happier humanity, bringing to an end individual and national differences and promoting a fuller and richer life for all.

These visions of a better future for mankind will naturally take many decades to materialise but it is going to be a question of decades and not centuries. There are still so many firmly established centres of self-interest, conventional and crystallised habits and ways of thought, which will have to be demolished before the foundations of the New Age can be laid. Man should therefore not become unduly upset and depressed about world affairs. These chaotic conditions must be accepted as the natural sequence of events, which must precede the general process of reconstruction. All that is now required is the fostering of a sustained spirit of *co-operative goodwill* and *loving understanding*, between both individuals and nations and this will inevitably lead to better human relations and, eventually, to the One Humanity.

Many of the older generation will adapt to this new spirit but those who will be responsible for the major changes will be the younger and coming generations. Many older people, with their relatively narrow, selfish and crystallised views, are inclined to retard this new development and will have to disappear from the scene of active participation before the new movement can blossom forth freely.

Notwithstanding superficial indications to the contrary, there is a general spiritual awakening throughout the world and people are reorienting themselves to subjective matters. This is especially true of the younger generations who, under a cloak of casualness, are urgently seeking that which lies deeper and is hidden by daily activities; it is indicated by their interest in human welfare, in their perseverance in striving towards goodwill and better human relations. This aspirational idealism is largely responsible for world unrest and chaos and evokes conditions which temporarily are most unpleasant, even leading to sacrifice of life and worldly goods by breaking down those conditions which have served their purpose and have become redundant. Out of this confusion improved conditions are rapidly being born; the eyes of mankind are opening to new visions of co-operation, sharing, mutual security and peace, which may be looked for in a united humanity. Man is discovering the joy of selfless giving and of sharing that which life so liberally offers, instead of ruthlessly grabbing, robbing and hoarding that which has been selfishly gained, while millions are roofless and starving to death.

What is true of the individual, also applies to humanity as a whole. Civilisations are born, develop and grow through experience; then they mature, become crystallised and subsequently deteriorate and perish. And thus, through the ages, humanity has grown and developed by means of civilisations that have come and gone in different parts of the world, each running its full cycle. With each reincarnation, under different circumstances and environment, new facets have been unfolded, new values stressed and new races and greater regions have been included. We have now come to the point where the wheel has turned nearly full circle, rapidly leading to a point of climax for this present round. Humanity is standing on the threshold of a New Age and a new civilisation, which this time will be all-inclusive and will be implicating the whole of humanity. Where possible races, colours, languages, distinctive customs and manners should be retained but nonetheless humanity will inevitably become united into one whole through mutual tolerance, goodwill, sharing and loving understanding.

Humanity is at present experiencing the birth-throes of this New Age but all sacrifice and suffering will be well worthwhile and gladly endured by those with the vision to picture the alluring new life and light which lies ahead.

Those who may be seen as the immediate cause of many of the appalling conditions ruling today, should not be judged too harshly. They are products of the past and victims of the present, agents of destiny and tools being utilised to bring about unpleasant but essential changes. This must necessarily lead to transitory wavering and uncertainty but this will eventually be overcome. The time needed to bring about these changes will solely depend on humanity itself and on the degree of sincerity and perseverance with which the qualities of love and understanding are applied – humanity will determine its own fate!

The basic evils opposing increased human synthesis, are:

1. Individual and national ambition, greed and rapacity.
2. Economic disparity between individuals, groups and nations.
3. Class distinctions based on racial differences and on attitudes of superiority arising from hereditary, religious, economic or political background.

People are, however, everywhere waking up and beginning to think and see for themselves. They are realising that every individual, nation and race forms an organic part of humanity and that these ancient prejudices must be ended. Fortunately these concepts are already present in the hearts of many millions and these feelings are rapidly spreading and only intelligent development and wise handling are now required to ensure improved world-wide human relations and economic stability based on sharing and supported by goodwill and tolerance between man and man, nation and nation.

The old world order has served its purpose but clearly it is now failing completely – the old building is rapidly collapsing and the present task is to clear away the rubble and lay the foundations for a completely new structure. This will mainly be the responsibility of the coming generation.

This task for the future is twofold:

First, to guide the thought and energy of the masses into the direction of improved human relations.

Second, to achieve this purpose those who lack vision and enthusiasm, thereby impeding progress, must be encouraged and educated to a better understanding of the underlying causes and future possibilities. This will be the function of outstanding world leaders – these leaders are now in embryo and will appear when and where most urgently needed. Their demand will be for new basic principles in politics, religion, education and economics and founded on the recognition of human rights and responsibilities, the need for spiritual synthesis, for material sharing and the rejection of dogmatic, crystallised and separative approaches in every field of thought.

These new attitudes are becoming **noticeable** in all countries, all races and every sphere of life and activity.

Equality of Man:

In principle all Monads are sparks of **the One Spirit**, the One Soul and as such are absolutely equal. These Monads, manifesting through individual souls are being subjected to physical experience on Earth and by means of this process are working their way back towards restored assimilation with the Father.

Men therefore belong fundamentally to the one brotherhood and are all *potentially equal;* all are consciously or unconsciously working towards the same final objective but meanwhile each individual is distinguished by his own particular level of development and his actions, reactions and characteristics will be determined by the degree to which he has become soul-infused and controlled and this in turn will determine his reaction to the dominating Rays of Energy to which he is being subjected during a particular life. Temporarily, as demonstrated in physical life on Earth, men will differ widely, depending on the degree to which their innate divinity is revealed and expressed in daily living. It should never be forgotten, however, that the divine life, the spirit of Christ, is present in every human heart and is ever struggling for expression. This struggle may at times appear futile but with the necessary experience and help from both his fellow men and from higher sources, all these challenges will be overcome and each and every one will attain the common destiny. In short there is no difference in basic individual nature but only in the degree of consciousness attained.

And the human consciousness *is* unfolding, largely due to the pressures of modern life, with its strains, mental stresses and physical terrors, all contributing to the awakening of mankind from its long dormancy. The mind of humanity is becoming aware of its true priorities, expressing itself in activities which will promote communal life and eventually leading to greater synthesis. All this is but evidence of energies and forces which are being directed towards humanity, energies of which mankind should avail itself to its utmost. Towards this objective every individual can and should contribute his modest share through a controlled thought-life, inspired ideas, a loving and understanding spirit – in short by living an invocative life that will help to evoke those energies so sorely needed for the redemption of mankind.

XIII

THE SPIRITUAL HIERARCHY

XIII. 1. Some General Considerations

Man finds it difficult enough to conceive even vaguely the nature of the Spiritual Hierarchy controlling our planetary system. Our planetary Hierarchy however only constitutes a subsidiary of the vaster solar Hierarchy and the latter is again part of an even more comprehensive cosmic constellation, reaching out to ever wider horizons beyond all imagination.

In these subjective spheres innumerable Entities conduct their activities at levels of their own evolution and in conditions which, according to the Sages, are to them far more real and vital than what they describe as our 'world of illusion'. To the man in the street reference to these etheric realms and their inhabitants may sound like pure fantasy; to him the believer in such 'unproved' nonsense, is to be regarded either with ridicule or with the sympathy reserved for the simple minded. Others hesitate to express an opinion, because who knows, in this strange world of ours 'anything is possible' and therefore there might just lurk some trace of truth in these assertions! With some a faint inner voice might also warn against too quick condemnation of these beliefs and some doubt might arise... 'would it not perhaps be advisable first to find out a little more about these claims?' But, whatever the motivation for following these thoughts, try to retain an open mind, allowing the intuition to take its course and giving the imagination free scope to roam beyond the immediate tangible environment – there lies so much, much more beyond the etheric web with which we are enshrouded, restricting our vision and discrimination. How fortunate are those who succeed in penetrating this dense curtain, to obtain even a restricted view of that which lies beyond.

There are those who believe in divine guidance, who recognise the existence of a Supreme Being or God and acknowledge Him as the Almighty Ruler of the Heavens. There are those who see God not only as the absolute but also as the *sole* Ruler, at most perhaps assisted by the Christ or Buddha or Mohammed or some other Prophet (depending on the observer's religious background) and perhaps also availing Himself of a few angels as divine messengers but no more – just the wide and empty heavens, with God the Ruler on His throne.

Diagram B
THE SPIRITUAL HIERARCHY

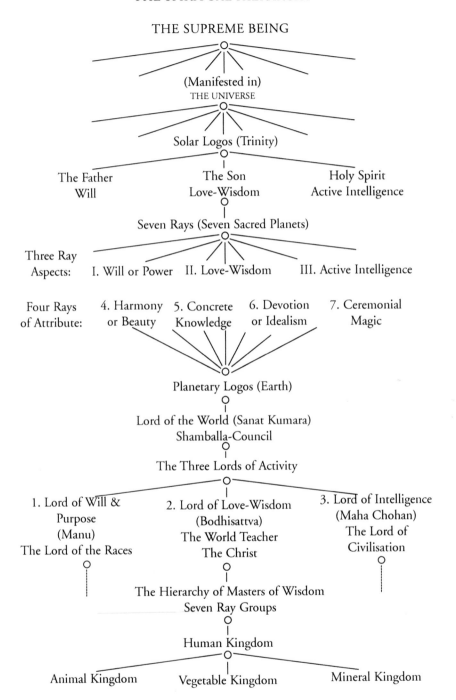

THE SUPREME BEING

(Manifested in)
THE UNIVERSE

Solar Logos (Trinity)

The Father	The Son	Holy Spirit
Will	Love-Wisdom	Active Intelligence

Seven Rays (Seven Sacred Planets)

Three Ray
Aspects: I. Will or Power   II. Love-Wisdom   III. Active Intelligence

Four Rays   4. Harmony   5. Concrete   6. Devotion   7. Ceremonial
of Attribute: or Beauty   Knowledge   or Idealism   Magic

Planetary Logos (Earth)

Lord of the World (Sanat Kumara)
Shamballa-Council

The Three Lords of Activity

1. Lord of Will &	2. Lord of Love-Wisdom	3. Lord of Intelligence
Purpose	(Bodhisattva)	(Maha Chohan)
(Manu)	The World Teacher	The Lord of
The Lord of the Races	The Christ	Civilisation

The Hierarchy of Masters of Wisdom
Seven Ray Groups

Human Kingdom

Animal Kingdom   Vegetable Kingdom   Mineral Kingdom

When it is taught that this Supreme Authority does not stand alone but has surrounded Himself with a vast executive organisation to administer and consummate His Will, Purpose and Plan, many would consider this as a form of disparagement and even as sacrilege. But when viewed without prejudice, should the existence of such an executive staff not be most logical? 'Ponder on this'!

Think back for a moment to the picture painted in an earlier chapter, in an effort to depict the immensity of the Universe, in which vast expanse our solar system disappears as the merest atom. Would it be so very farfetched and unreasonable to assume that there could or rather should be, some well organised system through which the Almighty functions and which He could use as a channel for expression and for the execution of His objectives? According to the Bible man has been created in the image of his Creator – this would surely in the first instance refer to the mental and spiritual image and likeness, rather than to any physical resemblance. One of man's most outstanding characteristics, which becomes ever more pronounced as he evolves, is his increasing power of organisation. What could be more logical than to conclude that this aptitude is also being received from spiritual planes and to presume that the subjective realms are similarly regulated and controlled by some widespread and perfect organisation under the direction of the Almighty?

Let us for a moment ignore the wider Universe and limit our attention to a closer study of our own little planet. Has the student ever visualised how every form is constructed of millions and billions of atoms, all interrelated through the etheric world? This fantastic atomic complex composed of the mineral, plant, animal and human kingdoms of nature, functions from day to day and age to age, like a perfect machine, reacting to supernal guiding forces and evolving towards some particular Purpose, which will forever remain an enigma to man. But that this development is proceeding according to a directed Plan must be obvious, otherwise the whole interrelated and interacting system between the several kingdoms would in no time collapse in chaos. The direction of this comprehensive divine Plan, with all its minutiae, must therefore surely postulate a vast and most efficient subjective organisation.

Man in his blind ignorance but nonetheless endowed with a 'free will' and dormant powers of which he is fortunately not yet fully aware, has on many occasions apparently done his best to upset this natural balance and to produce a state of confusion. Just think of the constant wars and destruction that he has provoked, of the nuclear explosions for which he has been responsible and of his wanton exploitation of the world's forests and several other natural resources and features. But notwithstanding all this and even though temporary imbalance has repeatedly been created, it is surprising how 'Nature' always succeeds in restoring some form of equilibrium. Surely this must constitute clear evidence of the amazing and widespread powers of this subjective agency, which retains an ordered control *in spite of* the many temporary disruptions caused by man's stupidities.

As a further example of the planned co-ordination issuing from hidden realms consider the flower, one of nature's 'simple' everyday products, occurring so abundantly and beautifying our world with its many variations. Think of its lovely form, colouring and perfume; consider the many fantastic ways nature has devised for fertilising and reproducing plants, each true to type and species and each a perfect specimen. The science of botany has learnt much of the plant's physiology and anatomy; with the study of genetics some of the hereditary laws to which the plant is subject have been determined but so much about the life of the plant still remains a closed book to man. It is only quite recently that science has discovered that the plant also possesses an etheric body and that reactions registered in this vital body closely resemble the emotions and consciousness as reflected in the higher kingdoms.

The Sages also teach about the Deva-evolution and that these devas are the builders responsible for the construction of every form in material expression. This deva or angel-kingdom, which includes the very actual realms of fairies, gnomes, etc., although closely associated with human activities, must however be regarded as a separate study. This subject is only mentioned here to indicate the existence of a parallel and relatively unexplored evolution, which, on different planes, is closely related to the hierarchy responsible for human evolution.

It is sometimes contended that man's spiritual and religious life should not be subjected to study and analysis, since such a mental approach might lead to a loss of the mystical and sublime. If by mysticism is understood that feeling of vagueness and uncertainty associated with the unknown, then the sooner this obscurity can be clarified by the light of the mind, the more effective will religion be in creating a better understanding and closer relationship between the aspirant and his Father. But rest assured that although study might lead to greater clarity in certain respects, man's most intensive probing will always leave ample unsolved mysteries to satisfy the needs of the most exacting mystic. It should, however, always be remembered that the characteristic of spiritual unfoldment is an ever expanding consciousness, leading from revelation to revelation, from truth to ever greater truth and from light to ever brighter light.

And why should man not be permitted to delve as deeply into the nature of his Deity as his mental capacity and consciousness will allow? Are there really those who consider that God has furnished man with a marvellous instrument of thought and mental analysis, which he is enjoined to use for the promotion of all human requirements, *except* that aspect of his being which should play the most important role in his life – the spiritual or religious world? Does such an argument not sound rather naïve? Is it not much more logical and probable that God provided man with an ever unfolding mental capacity, *not* to build more destructive weapons, *nor* to discover the secrets of 'space', thus enabling him to spy more effectively on his neighbour's strategic position but that he should better understand his own constitution and spiritual relationships?

Could those who reject the mental approach to spiritual life, only once experience the inner joy engendered with the revelation of a new facet of truth after persistent mental probing; the thrill of becoming consciously aware of the inner self, the soul; could they but realise that the focussed light of the mind leads to deeper understanding and consciousness, which must inevitably induce more effective aspiration and invocation and an increasing reverence for God. God, or Truth, basically remains immutable and invariable; what does vary and change is the undefined and ephemeral conception which each individual entertains of this spiritual Being. With growing perception this concept of Deity is ever expanding, assuming ever wider dimensions of both the Might and the Love of the Father.

A more profound appreciation of the nature of the spiritual world, its functions and organisation and a realisation of how this whole system remains subject to the Will, Purpose and Love of God, cannot but lead the aspirant increasingly to a sense of humility, respect and veneration for Deity and the intensity of this feeling will grow with the expansion of his consciousness.

Before proceeding with an analysis of the Spiritual Hierarchy, two fundamental principles should be stressed again as they may contribute to clearer recognition of concepts which many students find difficult to grasp.

Firstly, the interrelation of all forms should be thoroughly realised; the fact that every created form is linked with the rest of the manifested worlds through the etheric sphere, which not only surrounds but also interpenetrates every form and interlocks one with the other, thus synthesising all creation into one co-ordinated Whole. This holds not only for our planet but also for the unseen and spiritual, for the whole Universe and for all that IS! Cosmic and solar energies or Rays, streaming through the etheric system, constantly impinge on the Earth and on all manifestation, evoking forces which are again radiated into the etheric surround to continue the perpetual process of action and interaction. Furthermore, it may be regarded that every existing body is only a component of some larger unit, which in turn forms part of a still larger complex, thus extending into ever bigger structures, until all may eventually be seen as only elements of the ONE. The reverse of this picture is that every form may be seen as a composition of several or innumerable smaller units and these can again be broken down into still smaller constituents, until one ends at the other extreme by seeing All as Energy.

Secondly, every form must be regarded as the manifestation of a separate entity, whether reference is made to an atom, a man, a continent, a planet or a solar system. Man's personality for instance is the form through which a Monad is temporarily manifested through the soul and similarly the Sun with its planetary system is the physical manifestation of our Solar Logos. But please note that the solar system is *not* itself the Logos but only represents His physical expression and it is through the Sun that His energies are radiated to the planets – thus 'the physical Sun serves to hide the Spiritual Sun'. The physical form of expression is always of a transient nature, although in human terms this temporary period may endure for billions of years. The Inspiring Entity, on the other hand, which supplies the form with vitality, is of a spiritual nature and is immortal and everlasting.

Our planet Earth, with its kingdoms of nature, is again the physical form through which our Planetary Logos functions and man's physical body can thus be regarded as an atom in His physical form, with man's Soul or Monad a spark of the One-Soul, Oversoul, God or by whatever name this all-encompassing Spiritual Entity may be recognised. Our Planetary Logos is a subjective Entity, dwelling on the highest or Divine Plane of the Cosmic Physical Plane (of which the physical plane, of the human being is the seventh, the lowest and the most dense. Even as the human Monad is represented in the physical body by the soul, so our Planetary Logos, focussed in the higher spiritual planes, has delegated the **Lord of the World** to represent Him on the physical or rather etheric levels of the Earth. In the orient He is generally known as the 'First Kumara' or '**Sanat Kumara**' and, to prevent confusion, this name will also be retained in the present writing.

Owing to the extreme purity and high vibrations of His nature and the exigencies of His functions, Sanat Kumara has assumed an etheric rather than a dense physical vehicle. With His senior helpers – the Hierarchy of the Brothers of Light – He has established His headquarters at an **etheric centre**, which is normally referred to as **Shamballa**.

In **Diagram B** a schematic representation has been made of how the Spiritual Hierarchy is constituted. This diagram is necessarily an oversimplification but its purpose is merely to give some idea of a system which is so exalted and complicated as to be altogether beyond human conception. Only a general framework has therefore been provided, which each individual can adapt and progressively extend to accord with his particular level of consciousness.

XIII. 2. **The Supreme Being**

'*The One About Whom Naught May Be Said*'.

The concept of the **ALMIGHTY** is something totally beyond all human discernment – it is all-encompassing and remains absolutely unfathomable.

XIII. 3. **God**

'There is only ONE GOD', although He is known by many names in the many countries, the many languages and the many religions.

It may also be said that there are as many Gods as there are intelligent human beings, since each individual, guided by his own mental considerations and emotional aspiration inevitably formulates his own mental picture of the Directing Power. Each individual, irrespective of race or religion, constructs his own thought-form of the qualities and capacities of the God presented to him either through religion or as a result of his own experiences. It goes without saying that the God created in the mind of the savage, will assume quite differ-ent proportions to that of the highly developed intellectual. Similarly the attributes of the individual's God must necessarily change considerably during the course of development of a single life – from childhood to maturity. Awareness is the crucial factor, depending on an unfolding mind and increasing soul contact and attended by an expanding consciousness. The God of one man will therefore encompass an Entity of far greater format than the God as visualised by the next. The man still exclusively focussed on physical and emotional lev-els, would probably be unable to place his emotional God much higher than the astral plane, while the man functioning on mental levels would elevate his God to spiritual spheres.

So often apparently wide differences in religious views are merely due to different approaches, limitations of expression or different interpretations of the same basic prin-ciples. What the scientist may refer to as Energy, Life or Nature, is what the religious man calls God and yet both are referring to manifestations of the same Superior Power.

God manifests Himself as nature, life and energy, in every atom and form; He dwells within these forms and yet He is so much more than these manifestations of His Will and Purpose. Yet it is His Spirit which endows the forms with life and quality and is respon-sible for that vitality which perpetually spurs every form to never ending change, to that evolution which eventually must revert and transmute every atom and every dense form of matter to its basic source – to Spirit, to reintegrate with the ONE, with GOD.

XIII. 4. **The Solar Logos**

'*The Grand Man of the Heavens*' is manifested through the Sun and the seven sacred pla-nets – our Solar System.

As man merely represents a cell in the body of the Planetary Logos, so the Solar Logos fills an analogous place in a higher cosmic scheme and He in turn is but a cell or atom in the body of the Supreme Being, as reflected in the illimitable physical Universe.

As above, so below. On lower levels the human Monad, for reasons beyond human comprehension, requires experience on the physical plane for its development. This is gained through the soul manifesting in a physical body. What is taking place on the human level is, however, only a reflection or repetition of a similar occurrence on a much vaster and more exalted scale on loftier divine levels – by expression through the solar sys-tem the Solar Logos is also gaining physical experience for His further development.

Seen from the evolutionary point of view, the Solar Logos is comparatively as far advanced beyond the Planetary Logos as the latter stands above the human initiate but the Solar and Planetary Logoi are nonetheless closely linked and work towards a common objective.

It is quite natural that man, from the relatively narrow and selfish standpoint peculiar to his modest stage of development, should view the whole evolutionary process as the method devised for his personal advancement and eventual attainment of perfection. It would, however, prove to his advantage to broaden his perspective by realising that human progress is purely relative and incidental to far greater unfoldments, in which humanity only plays the role of a humble little pawn. The factor of supreme importance is the evolutionary development of the schemes of the Solar Logos. Humanity, however, happens to be in the favourable position of forming an integral part of the processes of consummation of the majestic Solar Purpose and as such must inevitably benefit from the evolution on higher levels and will thereby be lifted eventually into the overall cosmic scheme.

XIII. 5. The Planetary Logos

The '*Heavenly Man*' or the '*Silent Watcher*' manifests through a planet and, together with the other Planetary Logoi, forms part of the body of the Solar Logos.

The Earth's Planetary Logos is 'the One in Whom we live and move and have our being'. It is His Spirit that ensouls all life on Earth, His Energy, Will and Purpose which integrate all manifestation and co-ordinate every activity into the perpetually unfolding Divine Plan.

Under the Law of Synthesis, the Planetary Logos, in the course of His development, has to promote specific projects in line with the Will of the Solar Logos. On a lower step of the hierarchical order, this Law may also be seen functioning, in that Humanity is provided through His etheric representative, the Lord of the World, with cultures in which the germ of the Solar Will can also be fostered. Through such forms of relationship the required synthesis is provided throughout the solar system, thereby implementing the Divine Purpose and simultaneously providing a relating factor between Earth, Sun and Solar System or the Planetary and Solar Logos.

The Planetary Logos has the power to see into all parts, aspects and phases of His planetary vehicle and to identify Himself with the reactions and sensitivities of all that has been created and which forms part of His physical expression. The organ by means of which He effects this contact is the human Monad which, in certain respects, fulfils the same functions to the Heavenly Man, as the nervous system does to the human being.

XIII. 6. The Lord of the World

Sanat Kumara; The God of Love; The Light of the World.

Comparatively speaking, the Planetary Logos on His own plane is to Sanat Kumara what the soul of the human being is to his threefold personality. A further comparison is that the Lord of the World may be regarded as a personal disciple of the Solar Logos on supernal levels, just as a human disciple works under the guidance of a Master of Wisdom.

Just as a soul seeks incarnation in a physical body to gain experiences which should eventually lead to the realisation of a higher consciousness or initiation, so Sanat Kumara was incarnated in the physical planet Earth for His own specific purposes, which must also lead to some higher initiation on His Path of Higher Evolution.

It was during the Lemurian Age, some eighteen and a half million years ago, that the Planetary Logos incarnated and entered His physical vehicle, our planet Earth, as the Lord of the World, Sanat Kumara. Our Lord has never assumed a dense physical body but has ever since that distant past been functioning on etheric levels. 'In Him we live and move and have our being and none of us can pass beyond the radius of His aura'.

With His initial coming, Sanat Kumara was accompanied by several highly evolved Entities or 'Kumaras', Who came as His assistants, serving as focal points of planetary force, to contribute towards the unfolding of the Great Plan for the self-conscious development of all life. Of this original group six still remain with Him, functioning as members of the **Central Council** in Shamballa. Sanat Kumara, with these six supporting Kumaras, act as the seven guiding force centres, not only for transmitting energies throughout our planetary scheme but also as directing and co-ordinating agents, linking all centres and organs of life within the Earth's corporate body.

The Tibetan points out that Sanat Kumara and His Council Members, in long departed ages, all passed through human evolution, since the life principle can only be effectively blended with the reasoning intellect when expressed through a human instrument. It is only by means of this instrument that the various stages of manifested life needed for the evolution of the reasoning mind, can be consciously created. The only conclusion which can be drawn from this is that the Earth cannot be the only source of human beings and that humans also exist, or at least have existed in bygone ages, on other planets or on heavenly bodies beyond our solar system.

At the time of the incarnation of the Lord of the World, the animal kingdom was already well established on Earth, with animal-man representing its highest form of development. This fine animal had a powerful physical body, with a well co-ordinated emotional body for registering sensations and feelings but with only just the first rudiments of mind and still without self-consciousness. The lacking characteristic required for lifting animal-man into the human kingdom, was also contributed by the Planetary Logos, by providing suitable channels for the manifestation of the human Monads. The Monad, working through its Spiritual Triad (reflecting spiritual Will, Intuition or Wisdom and the Higher Mind) and subsequently through the Soul incarnating in the dense physical body, furnished this last essential for entry into the human world – the *self-consciousness*. Man, as a rational, self-conscious unit but still well down on the mental scale, could now proceed with his evolution, simultaneously providing the field of physical experience needed by the Monad.

The Lord of the World, as the direct representative of the Planetary Logos on Earth, retains in His hands the reins of government of all functional departments and is responsible for the evolutionary aspects, not only of the human race and the devas but for all of creation. Sanat Kumara also forms the direct link between the Earth and extra-planetary forces by retaining close contact with the other Planetary Logoi of our solar system. It is His task to impress the members of His Grand Council with those energies received from outer space and to reveal to Them the next phase of the unfolding Purpose, which They in turn will pass on to the Hierarchy of Masters. Sanat Kumara is therefore the One providing all men with Life and Who is carrying and guiding all of creation along its evolutionary path to its eventual consummation. With never ending patience, day after day, year after year, age after age, He continues radiating His rays of Light, Wisdom, Love and Understanding into the minds of men, thus systematically incorporating His Will and Purpose and evolving the Plan for humanity.

XIII. 6 (a) **Shamballa**

'The Father's House'

The term Shamballa sometimes implies different meanings, depending on the context in which it is being used.

Primarily it refers to the etheric seat of the Spiritual Hierarchy, the headquarters of the Lord of the World and His surround.

Based on this concept, Shamballa is also regarded as one of the seven energy centres in the etheric body of the Planetary Logos, forming a triangle with two other closely related centres, namely the Hierarchy of Masters and Humanity. It is 'the Centre where the Will of God is known' and from where the Hierarchy draws its Life.

The Shamballa Centre is activated by the First Ray of Will and Power, the major function of which is bequeathing, transmitting and circulating the fundamental principle of Life to all forms within the manifested Life of our Logos.

It is from here that the Divine Purpose is directed. It is the source from where all significant political movements originate and the point from which the destiny and progress of races and nations is determined.

In esoteric literature 'Shamballa' is often used in a comprehensive sense, as an Entity with its own life and intention and as the source of the 'Shamballa Energy and Will'. This is of course only a symbolic and inclusive reference to the powers of the Lord of the World, working through His Council and other assistants, all focussed in Shamballa and from there radiating their forces as a synthesised unit.

Shamballa is the Earth's main receptive agent for the inflow of both solar and cosmic energies and acts as the transmuting centre before transmitting the moderated energies to the human and lower kingdoms of nature.

XIII. 6 (b) Shamballa Energy

'The Will of God'.

The First Ray of Will or Power, streaming forth from Shamballa, is the most powerful force in the world today. It is demonstrated:

1. As the Will of God and therefore the *will-to-good*, guiding the affairs of men.
2. As the *destructive element* in planetary affairs. This destructive effect as a rule results from man's abuse of this force for selfish purposes, leading to domination, intolerance, hate, separativeness, war, death and destruction. It may, however, also mean the destruction of that which has become redundant or obsolete or which is obstructing the progress of the spirit of the will-to-good – whether in the field of religion, politics or human relationships and whether personal, national or international.
3. It also manifests as the *synthesising force*, binding together that which should be integrated.

For unthinking humanity it is difficult to recognise the sympathetic Will-of-God in the way this virile energy is manifested, forgetting that to produce the culture and civilisation of the New Age, those organised bodies and material forms which obstruct the free expression of the Life of God must either be removed or destroyed. But although First Ray energy may cause destruction in the early stages, it will also be the means of fusion, by blending and co-ordinating all that is good, strong and healthy, eventually proving to be the force required for achieving the objectives of the New Age.

It is the *Will of God* that certain radical changes be effected in the consciousness of man by implementing a totally new approach to life and to his concepts of the spiritual realms. Combined with the energy of the *Love of God*, these two divine energies are in the process of bringing about a tremendous crisis in the world of men, which will be demonstrated by a general awakening and expansion in consciousness of the race. This will in turn lead to a more general discovery, study and understanding of the principles of the Ancient Wisdom teachings and a consequent revelation of the many truths which for ages have remained hidden to the obscured and purblind spiritual eyes of men.

The effects of Shamballa energy certainly do not remain limited to the human being. These forces impinge upon creation as a whole, affecting all the kingdoms of nature. Their destructive effect will be marked by the removal of forms which are retarding the plans of evolution, while simultaneously stimulating forms evolving according to the prescribed pattern.

The reaction of First Ray energy on humanity itself is demonstrated in many ways, depending on the quality of the personality concerned and the point in evolution achieved. During the past few decades it has been striking how many powerful and dominating personalities have emerged into the theatre of world activity. These personalities are today making their appearance on practically every terrain and their activity and influence towards either good or bad will depend on the attributes of the individual through which the energies are functioning. The energies are of divine origin but the reaction called forth will depend on the instrument on which they impinge. They will produce leaders and directors in all fields – educational, social, financial, administrative, political and religious – guiding their followers to new heights or perhaps to their *temporary* downfall.

When spiritually immature aspirants are influenced by the Shamballa energy, the effects may be displayed as headstrongness and even cruelty, imposing their will or dictating and enforcing their often unreasonable desires. But even such unpleasant displays of power might still be a reflection of the Will of God, by bringing about changes which eventually will prove beneficial to mankind and promoting the divine Plan. So often the pain and suffering caused by implementing the will-to-good, in discarding that which is evil or redundant, may temporarily blind observers to the benefits and beauty of superseding conditions. These individual reactions may not be of great moment but, when accumulated into mass negativity, they may definitely have a detrimental effect. It is therefore important that public opinion should be correctly educated and guided.

For ages the Hierarchy has been the sole recipient of Shamballa energy, where it was transmuted and tempered before being passed on to humanity. For some time now Shamballa has, however, been experimenting with partly transmitting its energies directly to humanity, without the mediation of the Hierarchy and, according to the Sages, human response to this impact is proving satisfactory. With humanity gradually adapting itself to this First Ray force, it will also develop the power of withstanding stronger doses, which will mean the possibility of even more rapid progress.

Shamballa force may be invoked by either individual or group effort and when evoked becomes a strong inner driving force, with destructive powers when misapplied but otherwise tending towards stabilisation, clarification and creativity. When the evoked Will becomes focussed by the light of the soul and directed with love towards establishing right human relations, effective responses must inevitably follow. Correct response to the energy of Will is always characterised by a spirit of sacrifice and forgiveness; when the impulse underlying the loving Will of God is sensed and suitably interpreted, the desire will be born to participate in that Will, giving rise to a spirit of sharing and sacrifice.

The drastic impact of Shamballa energy will be mitigated when it is received in group formation and becomes evenly distributed between mutually supporting group members.

Part of the responsibility of the Hierarchy is to balance and moderate this virile energy of Will, which sometimes tends to undue destruction, by blending it with a simultaneous inflow of the Second Ray energy of Love-Wisdom – the Love of God expressed as Christ energy. These Second Ray forces of Love will provide the needed powers for reconstruction and rehabilitation. In this respect man may rest assured that his destiny lies in safe and loving hands and that he need never doubt or hesitate for a single instant, provided he contributes his share to the best of his ability.

As a rule man is so purblind that he cannot as yet recognise the evidence of the constructive activity of these creative energies. The founding of the New Age structure is, however, proceeding apace but the outlines remain unseen by the majority, since they are too occupied with selfish concerns. But the Shamballa energies, guided by hierarchical effort, are steadily achieving the objectives of the Plan. So far the vision has, however, been accorded only to the relatively few, enabling them truly to discern the beauty of the steadily emerging pattern.

XIII. 6 (c) The Divine Purpose

One of the functions of the Lord of the World is to communicate to His Grand Council in Shamballa those Divine Inspirations with which He has been impressed from solar and cosmic Sources. This Divine Will is then formulated by the Council into the unfolding phases of the Divine Purpose. The senior Lives in the Hierarchy are subsequently impressed with the Purpose, where it is also stepped down and translated into the Plan. The Plan is the blueprint which the seven Ray Groups will utilise to bring the underlying principles and ideas of the Purpose into practical expression in the three worlds of men, as well as in the lower kingdoms of nature.

The Divine Purpose emanating from Shamballa is therefore that aspect of the Will of God which is seeking expression on Earth. The Hierarchy is the channel through which this energy from Shamballa is transmitted and as the Hierarchy is characterised by the energy of Love, this divine Purpose is expressed by the Hierarchy as the will-to-good, which in human living is translated into goodwill, loving understanding and a striving towards right human relations.

But this spirit of the will-to-good, to which humanity is definitely beginning to react, is but a single aspect of the Purpose, the real esoteric meaning of which still eludes the conception of humanity. It is only with the expansion of consciousness associated with the third initiation, that the first faint light will be thrown on the deeper significance of the Will of God. Apparently it mainly concerns humanity's role in linking the spiritual and sub-human planes but this phase still lies far ahead. Humanity is meanwhile being subjected to the influence of various energies and is slowly being led and trained in the desired direction, being unconsciously exposed to every possible form of experience – good and bad, pleasant and unpleasant – all contributing to the pool of experience, which will eventually burst the floodgates of the limiting mind, allowing entrance into much vaster areas of consciousness.

According to the Ageless Wisdom, when the intent and Purpose of the Lord of the World comes nearer to fruition, a Light of supernal beauty will be revealed to those with the opened eye. Through the Light of Wisdom radiated by Shamballa, the Light of Life itself will be perceived – a concept which still remains inexplicable to the human being but which will be revealed progressively with the rupturing of the etheric veil.

XIII. 6 (d) **The Hierarchical Plan**

The Plan may be described as a pool of wisdom and consciousness, a thought reservoir established on hierarchical levels and energised by the Will of God. This reservoir becomes accessible to and may be drawn upon by those with the necessary consciousness and sensitivity. The disciple who wishes to serve his fellow man, learns to project his mind to this pool of inspired thought-forms or source of Light, where his sensitive mind will be impressed with thoughts and ideas which may subsequently be applied on behalf of mankind in the form of practical help or teachings.

The disciple need not consciously strive for the attainment of these characteristics – they will arise naturally as an expression of soul quality, which will emerge after reaching suitable alignment. Such a person will in effect become a magnet for these spiritual ideas and concepts, at first becoming aware of the general outline and later of the details of as much of the Plan as may be required for his particular service objectives. These impressions will drop into his field of consciousness because his magnetic aura has acquired the necessary sensitivity. This sensitivity is a property which unconsciously begins to develop from the earliest stages of soul control and will deepen and grow with extended and more frequent contact, till it becomes a constant and natural state of awareness – the attribute of a soul infused server. Such a disciple thus becomes an evocative channel, which can be utilised by the Hierarchy and through which relevant aspects of the Plan may be evoked for distribution and application in his particular sphere of service. Thus another small facet of the Purpose or Will of God may become implemented and materialised through a human channel, signifying another minute step forward in the progressive evolution of world affairs as envisaged by the Lord of the World.

The Plan is not concerned with individuals or separate entities in any of the kingdoms of nature but only with the overall picture, with time cycles, nations and races, with political structures, with world religions, cyclic manifestations and similar broad aspects affecting mankind in general.

Although the Plan is formulated on hierarchical planes, the Masters have to depend for its application on physical levels, on the capacities and ingenuity of man. Thoughts and ideas (brain-waves) concerning the Plan, are cast into the minds of idealists and disciples, where they are assimilated, brooded over and eventually converted into modified thought-forms, coloured by the particular mind characteristics of the thinker. As these take clearer shape, they are embodied or materialised either in speech, the written word or may be expressed in physical shape as some new invention. The stage of development of the recipient of the impression will determine the purity with which he can serve as a channel for the transfer of the impression – so often the expressed product represents such a distorted version of the original idea, that it can hardly be recognised. In these instances the Masters will have to find other and more effective avenues for conveying the ideas or principles which should be transmitted on behalf of mankind. The Masters are

Diagram C
THE DIVINE PURPOSE AND PLAN

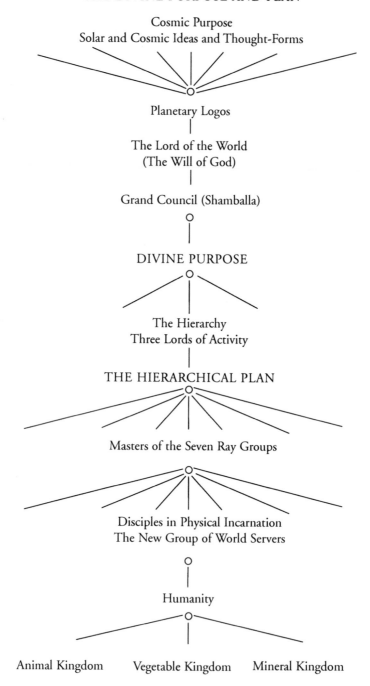

Cosmic Purpose
Solar and Cosmic Ideas and Thought-Forms

Planetary Logos

The Lord of the World
(The Will of God)

Grand Council (Shamballa)

DIVINE PURPOSE

The Hierarchy
Three Lords of Activity

THE HIERARCHICAL PLAN

Masters of the Seven Ray Groups

Disciples in Physical Incarnation
The New Group of World Servers

Humanity

Animal Kingdom   Vegetable Kingdom   Mineral Kingdom

often sorely handicapped by the unreliable quality and even failure of the instruments at their disposal.

The Great Ones do not as a rule concern themselves with the details of transforming the Plan to humanity. The disciple is imbued with a general vision indicating the potential but the stepping down and practical conversion of the higher principles into forms and details acceptable to the public, without unduly sacrificing the beauty and ideals of the original inspiration, is left to the ingenuity of the individual disciple.

In its detail the Plan will be subject to change and adaptation, to conform with the evolving requirements of mankind. In general terms it can be said, however, that one of its primary objectives is the unifying of humanity into one subjective whole; this corporate body will then not consist of homogeneous constituents but on the contrary, its beauty and effectiveness, as an instrument to serve the Divine Will and Purpose, will lie in its diversity and differentiated capacities. To attain this vision of a multiple synthesis of all nations and races, representing all colours, languages and mentalities, into one huge and efficient instrument, would require a unifying spirit of loving understanding and mutual tolerance, with constant telepathic communication and interplay of thought life and the Divine Purpose as a unifying mutual objective. This must by no means be regarded as a picture of the Plan in its totality but only as a general description of one of its principal facets, giving some faint idea of what lies in store for humanity. Man will only gain the first glimmering of real understanding of the Plan after the third initiation is achieved. Meanwhile each individual who is becoming aware of the subjective realms should constantly strive to expand his consciousness, which will eventually lead to some slight understanding of those aspects of the Plan which he is destined to serve.

Another feature of the Plan is that each disciple within a Master's group has, consciously or unconsciously, been allocated the responsibility for fulfilling a particular fraction of the Plan. Provision is made that the allotted task falls within the capacities of each individual or group. In this way all the work on behalf of humanity is carefully planned by the Hierarchy and it is expected of each disciple that he should constantly aim at expanding his consciousness and sensitivity and thus to become aware of impressions from higher levels. This will emphasise his responsibilities and spur him to become a better instrument in the hands of the Masters.

Disciples learn to work with the Plan by practical service and experience. Mistakes will of course be made and the less evolved he is the greater the number and extent of these errors. But it is only through trial and error that the aspirant will learn and in accordance with the lessons learned and experience gained will his consciousness expand and will sensitivity to new facets of the Plan increase, with a corresponding growth in his responsibilities.

It is therefore important that man should realise that the whole Universe is co-ordinated and activated according to a Universal Plan, under the direction of the Supreme Being. And, as above, so below. Our Planet Earth, with all its creation, including the human kingdom, has been manifested and evolved in accordance with such a Plan, is at present still functioning according to its blueprint and will continue to do so into the interminable future. Those aspects of the Plan which directly concern humanity, therefore consist of a relatively small part of the greater scheme but, to the average man who still sees mankind as the focal point of the Universe, this human subdivision remains of decisive importance. Man should also realise that the Plan does not in the first instance provide for his material ease, comfort and happiness – on the contrary, the purpose is that man should gain every possible experience in all phases of existence and that this experience should lead to expansion in consciousness, thus enabling each individual to discover for himself the values of spiritual life and to use his own free will to effect the needed changes. Nothing of true value to the individual will be gained by arbitrary and autocratic action on the part of the Hierarchy and man must be given the opportunity for self-determination through the expression of free will. It is towards such freedom of expression, of loving understanding and the will-to-good for all humanity, that the hierarchical Plan is progressively guiding its supporters. Man is being led towards the recognition and acceptance of the functions of the Hierarchy in its guidance of humanity and this will eventually lead to the founding of the Kingdom of God on Earth. Although the Greater Plan lies far beyond human conception, certain of its practical applications might perhaps be broadly indicated under three objectives:

1. *Political:* To develop and establish an international consciousness, by making all men aware that they collectively form part of the One Humanity, irrespective of nation, race, colour, language or the stage occupied on the evolutionary path. A spirit of international interdependence, inter-relation and co-operation should be promoted. In this respect the ruling tendency towards nationalism, racial superiority and antagonism, class hatred with its many facets and international competition for world resources, still constitute active barriers. This should make way for a brotherhood of nations based on mutual need, support, understanding, tolerance, helpfulness, goodwill and a sharing of the resources so generously provided by nature.

That there already exists a movement in this direction and that such an international spirit is awakening, is being demonstrated in several respects, of which the establishment of the United Nations is the most obvious. Although this elementary organisation has so far proved to be something of a fiasco and has in many instances been serving as a forum for the propagation of hate and rivalry rather than of goodwill and improved human relations, it is nevertheless an indication of an underlying spirit aiming at synthesis.

2. *Religious:* To establish a better world-wide understanding and consciousness of the nature of the subjective realms; of the duality of human existence; of the spiritual life and the immortality of the soul; of the presence on higher levels of the Great Ones, ranged in their many hierarchical orders. The ultimate objective is a fellowship of religions and the

gradual appearance of a world-faith, which in its broader concepts will be able to encompass all humanity.

3. *Scientific:* The workers in this field have as their objective the co-ordination of those working on the many aspects of the exact sciences and, simultaneously, a close collaboration with the rapidly expanding science of psychology. These should be further united by a joint educational programme to awaken awareness of the new concepts in process of unfoldment. At long last science has made the break-through and is becoming aware of the existence of the etheric world. There are still conservatives trying to hold back but they will find it impossible to resist the flood of evidence which is opening up new fields of research and discovery in both etheric and other spheres of science. It is expected that this will temporarily lead to a period of imbalance, with researchers vying with each other in publishing ever more fantastic claims, which will not always be substantiated by factual experiment and observation. But this will only be a passing phase and what matters is that science is now entering the New Era and that both the subjective and exact sciences will become more intimately related.

The result of these tendencies is a general movement towards better human relations and consequently greater synthesis. According to the Sages, all this is leading to a wonderful new revelation, which is to bring about radical and beneficial changes in human existence. New Light will be accorded to mankind, altering his outlook and living conditions and inaugurating the new Age.

XIII. 7. The Hierarchy of Masters

For the purpose of this treatise the description of the hierarchical complex will be reduced to a simple form, providing only sufficient detail to obtain an insight into the relationship between the three main groupings encountered on the human being's evolutionary path, namely *Humanity* – the *Hierarchy* – and *Shamballa*. Even so, most students find it difficult to conceive and accept even such a simple account, because of the abstract nature of these concepts and because the subjective Entities described remain invisible and intangible to human senses. Once a fair picture of this spiritual structure has been gained, however, then these basic ideas can progressively be amplified as wider knowledge and deeper understanding are achieved.

It has already been described how man, in the course of numerous incarnations, is step by step expanding his consciousness; how he attains the first initiation by gaining control over his physical desires, followed by the second initiation when the emotions have been reasonably curbed. Then comes that important stage of the third initiation, when after the three lower bodies, the physical, the astral and the mental, have been integrated and are jointly functioning as the 'personality', they are brought under the complete direction of the soul. This is the time when the real spiritual man takes over – when he is no longer held on leash by the attractions and urges of the flesh and when new vistas of the spiritual worlds are opening up to the inner eye. This deeper consciousness and contact with reality makes the disciple aware of new and ever greater sources of love and energy over which he can now dispose in serving his fellow man – he is becoming 'transfigured'. Up till the third initiation the disciple has been constructing, mainly unconsciously, the 'Bridge of Light', uniting the lower bodies with the soul. From now on this bridging work will be proceeded with consciously, aiming at closing the gap between the personality and the Spiritual Triad or Monad. With the completion of this final stage of the bridge, the disciple is ready for the fourth initiation – the 'Great Renunciation'. The Monad is now in direct command of the personality, which will merely mirror its threefold reflection in the physical world. The soul has thus become redundant as a mediator between Spirit and matter and is 'renounced' after aeons of service in that capacity. Although the Monad may temporarily retain the triple bodies, these are no longer required for physical experience but only serve as bodies of expression for the Monad and will therefore be solely used as instruments of service in either the human or any of the three lower kingdoms of nature.

After attaining the third initiation, the disciple may be regarded as a junior member of the Hierarchy of Masters and as such he will be incorporated into the group of one of the senior Ray Masters. He will then participate and function as part of the Hierarchy, whether incarnated in the physical world or active on subjective levels. At this stage the evolving entity is, however, not yet equal to the full responsibilities of an adept or Master – the initiate only becomes an acknowledged Master of Wisdom after reaching the fifth initiation.

The existence of a Hierarchy of Masters as an intrinsic part of the subjective hegemony, under the leadership of the Christ, was only publicly revealed by Madame Blavatsky during the last quarter of the nineteenth century or just about a hundred years ago. As was to be expected, the revelation of this hidden knowledge to the world at large was met by violent opposition from religious circles and often by ridicule from a large section of the general public. Today hundreds of thousands are accepting these principles as logical, when the evidence at man's disposal is considered without prejudice. The obstinate resistance from the orthodox is also crumbling before the persistent onslaught of reason. But there is much more to it than logic – today there are many persons of integrity who, through practical experience and conscious co-operation with higher Entities, have come to *know* about the existence of the Masters and of the help which they can afford the struggling aspirant. The intelligent seeker for Truth is no longer satisfied by the stereotyped answers provided by orthodox theologians and he prefers direct spiritual experience to doctrinal authority.

It is to be expected that time will be needed for these 'new' concepts to be generally accepted and for the principles to be established throughout the world. But there is a

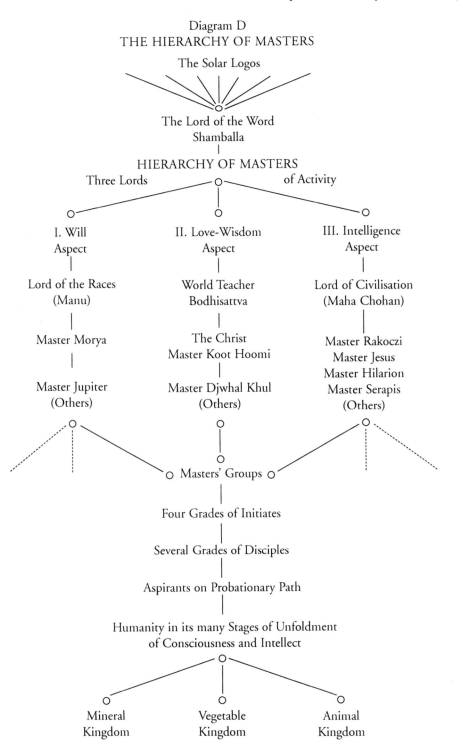

Diagram D
THE HIERARCHY OF MASTERS

The Solar Logos

The Lord of the Word
Shamballa

HIERARCHY OF MASTERS

Three Lords   of Activity

| I. Will | II. Love-Wisdom | III. Intelligence |
| Aspect | Aspect | Aspect |

| Lord of the Races | World Teacher | Lord of Civilisation |
| (Manu) | Bodhisattva | (Maha Chohan) |

Master Morya	The Christ	Master Rakoczi
	Master Koot Hoomi	Master Jesus
		Master Hilarion
Master Jupiter	Master Djwhal Khul	Master Serapis
(Others)	(Others)	(Others)

Masters' Groups

Four Grades of Initiates

Several Grades of Disciples

Aspirants on Probationary Path

Humanity in its many Stages of Unfoldment
of Consciousness and Intellect

| Mineral | Vegetable | Animal |
| Kingdom | Kingdom | Kingdom |

steady, irrepressible movement in that direction, which will inevitably result in one single world religion. Those sensitive to the incoming spiritual impacts are still very much in the minority but that is normal in the course of evolution – that which is new has to face the task of superseding what is deeply rooted and established. But that which has served its purpose in time and space and has become irrelevant, must make way for that which is vigorous, strong, healthy and the product of the times. The religion of the future will be based on love, goodwill, sharing and good human relations, not only between individuals but also between groups, communities and the nations and races of the world. This time is rapidly approaching – do not let yourself be blinded by outward discord, hate and struggle – look below the surface and see those strong and vital currents of tolerance, goodwill and consideration, which are everywhere becoming noticeable, often from the most unexpected quarters. In the not too distant future, these awakening forces will build up to such extent, that the dark and evil powers will be submerged and will largely disappear from the scene of action.

The Christ, with his adherents and disciples in the Hierarchy, have already made considerable progress with their spiritual onslaught during recent decades – the walls of opposition, built and supported by the Dark Forces, whose influence has for ages been dominating human activities, are rapidly crumbling. Now is the important time, however, when the initial success must be followed up, allowing them no respite for rallying their forces. For this purpose the Hierarchy relies upon the support of both their conscious and unconscious disciples in the world of men. On all enlightened men in the churches, political parties and the many organisations – social, economic, educational and scientific – rests the responsibility of presenting a united front based on the fundamental principles of love, goodwill and service. Thus will the path for the spiritual freedom of mankind be paved – a freedom which as yet is but a faint dream but which must and will be materialised if every capable individual fulfils his indicated role.

This spiritual inspiration which is making itself felt, comes through the Hierarchy, whose function it is to provide humanity with these energies. Humanity may therefore always rest assured of this support, which can be invoked at all times. The Hierarchy does not, however, concern itself with the petty daily problems and activities of the individual – these remain the responsibility of the personality with its free will; the interest of the Hierarchy lies with the evolution of humanity as a whole and is merely concerned with the individual when he may serve as a useful instrument to promote the general advantage. The man who, however, displays the disposition and qualifications for altruistic service, may depend upon it that these attributes will be readily utilised for the common benefit, since an urgent need exists for every suitable channel for transmitting hierarchical energies to the world of men.

As at present constituted, the Hierarchy is the product of human activity and aspiration of past ages – in other words they represent redeemed humanity. All its members are liberated human beings, who have endured worldly experience in all its diversity and phases; who have lived, suffered, failed and achieved; who have numberless times sustained the cyclic processes of death, resurrection and subsequent rebirth. Basically these Great Ones are of a similar nature to those still struggling in the flesh with all the temptations, urges, pleasures and adversities of the world of emotion and desire; they are aware of all the states of consciousness which they were able to master during the course of aeons; they overcame these conditions while participating in life in the physical worlds, thus guaranteeing to humanity the same ultimate achievement. The Hierarchy therefore wears the emblem of men sanctified by the purifying fires of daily living – they know life with all its challenges and for that reason they exhibit such unending understanding, patience and sympathy with those who are still treading the mill of life. And the Leader of this community of Spiritual Entities is the Christ, who actually was the first of earthborn humans to attain divinity; it was the Christ who embodied for man the great cosmic principle of Love and who for the first time revealed to man the nature of the Heart of God. For millions of years the Hierarchy has been guiding the destiny of men from etheric levels. Some of these functions may be briefly enumerated:

1. The Hierarchy has been serving as a protective wall between humanity and excessive evil emanating from cosmic sources. Without this protection humanity would long since have been overwhelmed and destroyed.

2. The Hierarchy works incessantly at arousing the consciousness of all forms and its subsequent effective application.

3. The Hierarchy influences and guides the trend of human affairs by impressing sensitive disciples with appropriate ideas and providing the needed revelations. In this way it directs world events but always with due consideration for man's free will which is never slighted.

4. The Hierarchy is the controlling influence behind unfolding cyclic cultures and civilisations, which provide the necessary forms and experiences for the evolving souls of men.

5. The Hierarchy acts as the transforming agency for the Will and Love of God, radiated from Shamballa. These potent energies must be moderated before being transmitted to humanity and the lower kingdoms.

6. The Hierarchy is also the agency used by the Lord of the World for eliminating redundant or inadequate cycles, civilisations or political regimes, by applying the 'Fire of God', thus opening the way for the improved systems which evolving Life demands.

7. The Hierarchy trains disciples for initiation:
   (a) By including them in a Master's group.
   (b) By providing them with opportunities for serving the Plan in accordance with their attributes and the circumstances where destiny has placed them.
   (c) By furnishing training facilities appropriate to the demands of that specific period. In each major evolutionary cycle, particular aspects of human development receive special attention and are accentuated in the instruction of disciples.

This summary only reflects a few of the varied activities for which the Hierarchy is responsible and which, as far as the ordinary man is concerned, is proceeding inconspicuously 'behind the veil'.

The Hierarchy is in reality is a great salvaging corps of dedicated, liberated 'Units of Life', working in group formation with all life, in all kingdoms – this entails much more than can be envisaged by man, because there are so many invisible and intangible forms of creation, playing an active role in nature but of which man remains blissfully unaware. The Hierarchy largely concentrates its energies on the consciousness aspect of all forms and it is at present emphasising the development of the mental life of man, according special attention to the aspirants and disciples serving as their channels of expression. The Hierarchy also avails itself of etheric thought currents, placing ideas and thoughts in the 'ether' and thus imposing hierarchical concepts on the more receptive minds of the general public. By similar means basic educational influences are inducted into the minds of the undeveloped masses of nations who thus, in the course of time, will become the more intelligent general public.

The Forces of Evil are constantly on the alert for opportunities of deviating humanity from its path towards the Light but the Hierarchy remains persistently on guard, warding off the worst attacks which otherwise might prove fatal. On the other hand it remains hierarchical policy not to avert all negative forces, since that would rob humanity of the opportunity of exerting its free will, of gaining experience and building its own inner strength by developing personal resistance. Had it not been for this partial protection, humanity would long since have been overcome by these forces of evil.

XIII. 7 (a) The Constitution of the Hierarchy
(See: Diagrams B and D)

At the head of the Hierarchy stands a triumvirate acting as the primary recipients of the Will of God, transmitted from Shamballa. These are known as the *Three Lords of Activity:*

1. The *Lord of Will and Purpose* (the 'Manu' of the Eastern races). Lord of the Races.
2. The *Lord of Love-Wisdom* (the 'Bodhisattva'). The Christ or World Teacher.
3. The *Lord of Intelligence* (the 'Mahachohan'). The Lord of Civilisation.

To avoid complicating the present study, consideration will be limited to the functions of the World Teacher. Once the student has acquired a reasonable understanding of this background, he can proceed with the filling in of further details.

The Lord of Will and Purpose has been responsible for the racial type and the destinies of the present race – the Aryan – since its inception nearly 100,000 years ago. In esoteric literature the Aryan race is known as the fifth root-race, as compared with the

Atlantean or fourth root-race and the Lemurian or third root-race. The Lord of Races is largely concerned with racial evolution – the founding, direction and dissolution of racial types and forms.

The *Lord of Intelligence* is the sum total of the intelligence aspect of the race of men. It is his task to foster and strengthen the relations between Spirit and matter, life and form, the soul and the personality and this leads to the different states of civilisation. He is also responsible for the manipulation of the forces of nature and is therefore to a considerable extent concerned with the Deva Empire.

The third of these hierarchical departments is that of the *World Teacher*. He is the Great Being known by the Christian religions as the *Christ;* in the East the same Entity is known as the *Bodhisattva* or the *Lord Maitreya* and the Moslems name him the *Imam Madhi* – all these nations or religions actually referring to the same Being and doing so with the same veneration but under a different name. It is the Christ who has been the Leader of mankind since about 600 B.C.; it is the Christ who two thousand years ago availed himself of the body in which the initiate Jesus had been incarnated a few years before and it is this Teacher of humanity who is expected to reappear among men within the near future, to lead them to redemption.

A wide range of Masters, each with their subsidiary groups, function under the guidance of the two first named Lords of Activity but these will not here be considered and where, in the following pages, reference is being made to the Hierarchy without further definition, it should be understood that the group of the World Teacher is indicated, with the Christ in command.

In the same way that each Master has a group of assistants or disciples working under his direction, so the Hierarchy of Masters may be considered as a group of disciples working under the guidance of Sanat Kumara, the Lord of the World.

The Hierarchy is sometimes regarded incorrectly as constituted solely of Masters but in fact it includes many junior members who have not yet reached this higher status. Every 'accepted disciple' falls within the periphery of influence of the Hierarchy and fulfils an intrinsic, even if only a minor, part in its activities. While these disciples are still functioning in the material worlds, they often find it a severe strain to adapt to the dual functions they have to assume – to participate in the daily activities of men and simultaneously trying to raise their consciousness to contact and include, if only briefly, something of the subjective spheres. These disciples represent an essential link between the Hierarchy and humanity and are needed to transfer hierarchical energy to the physical worlds and to transmute or step down the vibration or quality of this energy to that of the average man. They also have to translate the subjective teachings into thoughts and words which will be understandable and acceptable to their fellow men.

The Hierarchy is composed of seven main groups (or 'Ashrams' as these groups are known in the East), each corresponding to and working under the specific influence of one of the Seven Rays of Energy. Each of these main 'Ray Groups' are in turn subdivided into seven subsidiary groups, which means that the Hierarchy consists of altogether forty-nine groups, each with its special properties and appropriate functions in the hierarchical Plan. These groups are all essentially equal and there is no question of any spirit of envy, competition, controversy or criticism, as would inevitably arise in a similar organisation of ordinary men. Where there is true perception, criticism automatically fades away. These spiritual entities have reached levels where these human shortcomings have been left far behind. For the man still subject to human failings, this is of course difficult to conceive. These initiates are, one and all, inspired and held together not only by mutual love but also by an all-embracing love for humanity and a common spirit of sacrifice and service for the consummation of the Plan.

These groups have not been gathered for study or teaching or to promote individual advancement but purely for purposes of service. It stands to reason, however, that the inevitable result of self-discipline, meditation and dedicated service is that the disciple *does* learn in the process and will therefore progress on his evolutionary path.

The hierarchical groups are in a constant state of adjustment and reorganisation, to adapt their members to the ever changing pattern of planetary need. In this respect it should be remembered that hierarchical responsibilities are not limited to purely human needs but embrace all four lower kingdoms of nature, including the closely related deva-world.

Each group is under the direction of a senior Master, supported by two assisting Masters and an indefinite number of initiates and disciples in their many grades and orders. These members are bound together by karmic relationships, unity of purpose, a dedicated group enterprise and the synthesising vibration of the Master of the group. The dynamic power of a group often lies in its combination of many different elements, influenced by varying Ray qualities and functioning on different levels of development and consciousness. This interplay of many qualities and attributes enriches the group.

To gain a better understanding of their functions, Shamballa, the Hierarchy and Humanity are treated as separate units but it should be emphasised that they are merely centres of focussed energy in the manifested body of the planetary Logos. None of these centres can exist independently – they all merge and are closely interrelated and what affects one of these centres, must inevitably be reflected in the other centres.

XIII. 7 (b) **The Masters**

Esoterically an adept is not a Master of Wisdom until he has achieved the fifth initiation or, in other words, until he has entered the spiritual plane and his consciousness embraces the fifth or spiritual kingdom.

The Masters are members of that group of 'Illumined Minds' which is guided by love and understanding and by deep compassion and inclusiveness towards humanity. They are striving towards a comprehension and translation of the Divine Purpose and are illumined by knowledge of the Plan; they are also characterised by a readiness to sacrifice their own immediate spiritual progress if thereby they can assist humanity in its upward struggle.

In comparison with earth-bound human beings, who are still far behind on the evolutionary path, the Masters have attained a relatively high state of development. But, as with all else in nature, their status is only relative – in comparison with those already higher up the ladder, their own position remains humble and vast expansions of consciousness still lie ahead of them on the Path of Higher Evolution, which will eventually take them beyond planetary and solar spheres into cosmic consciousness.

On hierarchical levels there is naturally no oral communication, as the Masters do not avail themselves of physical organs. All communication on spiritual planes is telepathic. To a lesser extent this also applies to selected senior disciples on the physical plane, although effective intercourse is often limited by a lack of sensitivity on the part of aspirants.

One of the major functions of the Masters is to convey the principles of the Plan to their less evolved brothers. The usual technique employed for this purpose is impression. So far the Masters have not taught from public platforms but have mainly worked on intuitive and mental levels, by telepathically impressing ideas on the minds of their disciples. However, as more of these Masters make their appearance among men and recognition of their powers and wisdom grows, it is possible that use will also be made of oral teachings, when they might avail themselves of radio and television facilities.

Although the Masters have reached a stage of spiritual development far beyond that of man and, comparatively speaking, have achieved perfection, they should nonetheless not be considered infallible as they, at their own level, are also engaged in the never ending process of evolution.

Those occasional Masters who for purposes of service are temporarily functioning in a physical body, do not avail themselves of an emotional body, since they have complete conscious control over their feelings and emotions. For them the astral plane no longer exists, nor are they subject to any form of illusion or glamour. They are therefore completely liberated from material influences and reactions, as well as from every form of bewilderment to which the ordinary man is subject. This gives them the freedom to enter the Centre of Pure Love, the Heart of God, and from that centre to spread the spirit of love and goodwill throughout mankind.

The sphere of service of many of the Masters does not concern humanity at all, as these Entities are often fully occupied with the application of the Will of God in other extensive fields in the lower kingdoms.

XIII. 7 (c) **The Master's Body of Manifestation**

Thus far the Masters have normally functioned in etheric bodies on subjective levels. Should a Master, however, require a mechanism for contact with his disciples or the world of men, he can avail himself of any type of physical appearance which may suit his particular requirements and circumstances. He can use or 'overshadow' an existing physical body, in which case such a body would no longer remain subject to astral and emotional limitations or the mental restrictions of an ineffective brain – these he would be able to by-pass at will. Usually, however, a 'body of expression or manifestation' is instantaneously created by his spiritual Will and according to his special needs. As a rule this assumed body will resemble the human form which the adept occupied during his last initiation, although he is perfectly free to adopt any form which may suit his purpose.

Whatever type of body of expression the Master may assume, this will not encumber him with a 'personality' to curb his activities or consciousness. He retains his divine nature and the exterior through which he works is merely a created image and the product of his focussed Will and creative imagination and this may, when demanded by circumstances, also be instantly discarded or as far as the human observer is concerned, it may just fade away and disappear into nothingness. The body that he creates will therefore be of pure substance and radiant Light – it will be a perfect body, even though to outward appearances and for the purposes of the Master, it might display a deformed exterior, perhaps even covered by the rags of a beggar. Such a body is therefore not the product of the Deva-builders, as these are only summoned by desire which, being an aspect of the astral body, no longer plays any role in the life of the Master.

XIII. 7 (d) Individual Masters

So far humanity has had relatively little *conscious* contact with the various Masters, who usually function from etheric levels and therefore from beyond the conscious recognition of man. There are, however, some of these Perfected Men who have at times assumed a body of manifestation to enable them to work more effectively at their appropriate tasks among the nations of the world. These Entities of Light, although remaining unrecognised with regard to their true nature and capacities, represent focal centres for the distribution of hierarchical and divine love and wisdom and are practical outlets for certain aspects of the Plan.

Owing to their close association over the ages with the affairs of men, the names of a few of these Masters have become known as well as some details about their activities. It should always be remembered, however, that any such description given in human terms, must inevitably remain limited, since man cannot really conceive or translate that which is spiritual and sublime and for the purpose of visualisation man involuntarily lowers and reduces the exalted subjective to material terms. But even if the pictured image is somewhat warped and unreal, this may still serve to bring the aspirant mentally, and therefore consciously, another step closer to those who are ever ready to assist the human being on his wearisome path to the mountain top.

The names which immediately come to mind, are of course those of the *Christ* and the *Buddha* but since separate chapters will be devoted to these two Great Ones, attention will first of all be given to a couple of their senior assistants. Of these the three senior Masters, either acting as leaders of the main hierarchical departments or playing important supporting roles, are of primary importance. These three are the Masters *Koot Hoomi*, senior assistant to the Christ; the Master *Morya*, assistant to the Lord of Races; and the Master *Rakoczi*, the Lord of Civilisation.

(i) *Master Koot Hoomi (K.H.)*

One of the best known names in esoteric circles is probably that of the Master Koot Hoomi, often abbreviated to the initials K.H. He is alleged to appear at times in physical body in a secluded and quiet little village, *Shigatse*, hidden away in the Himalayan mountains. This village is also the physical retreat for several other Masters temporarily functioning in the human community. K.H. is described as a tall and noble man but not heavily built, fair of complexion, with deep blue eyes, pouring out love and wisdom; his hair and beard are a golden brown. He received his initiate training in a Kashmiri body but also received a sound Western education at a British university. He is controlled by the Love-Wisdom Ray and, as might consequently be expected, is deeply implicated in vitalising and proclaiming esoteric teachings. Furthermore he has been presented with the task of stimulating the latent factor of love, lying dormant in almost every human heart and also to awaken the race of men to the consciousness of their fundamental brotherhood, which must eventually lead them to the One Humanity.

K.H. is one of the senior Masters and, with his qualifications of Love and Wisdom, is being trained as the future successor to the World Teacher for, when the sixth root-race becomes established, the Christ will vacate his present office to proceed with even more advanced work on higher planes. Under the circumstances K.H. works in close association with the Christ and has also acquired the right to free entry and consultation in the 'Courts of Shamballa'. Masters of lesser degree are allowed such contact only at stated intervals.

One of the special projects on which Master K.H. is at present engaged, in close collaboration with the Masters Morya and Jesus, is to find a basis for the synthesis of Eastern and Western religious thought, with the objective of eventually developing the One World Religion, which will serve as the common bond for the unification of Humanity.

Master K.H. also has the task of reorganising world education and, partly because of this function, he is already well known in the West, where his pupils and disciples are spread far and wide. During the past several decades K.H. has, however, been engrossed to such an extent in broader world problems, watching over the destinies of prominent world figures and the handling of deeper incentives and purposes, that he no longer has the opportunity of personally dictating teachings to his disciples working in more restricted fields of activity and on subjects which can be transmitted just as efficiently by initiates of lesser degree. A number of his pupils have consequently been transferred to D.K. and other Masters for further training.

Another special mandate for which K.H. has assumed responsibility, is to collaborate with four other Masters towards initiating the steps needed to prepare humanity for the imminent reappearance of the Christ and the simultaneous externalisation of the Hierarchy.

(ii) *Master Morya (M.)*

He is the senior under-study and eventual successor to the Lord of Races. Working under the guiding energy of the First Ray of Will and Power, M. has a commanding appearance. He is tall and dark, with dark hair and beard and flashing eyes.

There is a close association between the Masters K.H. and M. and these two friends collaborate in many respects, as their work with humanity cannot be sharply delineated and a certain amount of overlapping is unavoidable. Luckily, on subjective levels competition and envy are unknown qualities and there is therefore never any danger of one group encroaching on another's terrain – they are all co-operating in their efforts to help humanity achieve its final destiny.

Being on the First Ray, the Master M. is also closely associated with Shamballa, whence the Divine Purpose is projected by the energy of Will and Power.

The Master M. is the inspirer of the world's statesmen and manipulates forces that will foster conditions for the furthering of racial evolution, thus inspiring national leaders with vision and with international ideals for greater tolerance and co-operation amongst nations and races. The initiates and disciples working in this Master's group, are consequently also primarily concerned with the expression of *synthesis* in government and the political world. The synthesis aimed at is largely of a subjective nature and will not be negated by outer differences, provided these disparities are characterised by goodwill and sound relations. This co-operative spirit must and will lead to eventual peace and understanding on Earth – a peace in which individual and national cultures will be preserved, although subordinated to the interests of humanity as a whole.

As the head and principal organiser of all esoteric schools and organisations in the world, Master Morya is also widely known and has a large number of pupils in both the East and the West. As in the case of K.H., rapidly changing world conditions are demanding his constant attention and, with the great pressure of work on his shoulders, M. has also delegated personal dictation and teachings to younger Masters and senior disciples.

(iii) *Master Rakoczi (R.)*

The Master R., often lovingly and respectfully referred to as 'The Count', is the Lord of Civilisation and in command of several groups, through which he is exerting a wide influence in world affairs. In practice he is the executive officer of the Lodge of Masters as far as the work in Europe and America is concerned, where he consummates the Plans devised by the inner executive Council of the Christ. He is consequently also known as the Regent of Europe and America, intimately influencing the destinies of governments. He is especially concerned with the future development of Europe's racial affairs and with the mental unfoldment of the American and Australian peoples.

While in physical incarnation, Count Rakoczy was an Hungarian and at one time a well known figure at the Hungarian court, even being referred to in historical records. In other incarnations he became known historically as the Comte de St. Germain and, before that in England, he first used the personality of Roger Bacon and, subsequently again that of Francis Bacon.

Although the Master R. is on the Seventh Ray, most of the pupils under his direct guidance are on the Third Ray. He works mainly through esoteric ritual and ceremonial and is vitally interested in religious ceremonial.

With the Seventh Ray of Organisation and Ceremonial now coming into prominence, Master R.'s function of synthesising all aspects of the Plan on the physical plane, is becoming more clearly defined. It is his responsibility to materialise that new civilisation for which all men are waiting. As the leader of the Third Ray department of Intelligence, it is also his function to co-ordinate the activities of the Fifth Ray groups of Concrete Science and those of the Seventh Ray of Ceremonial Order. Every effort is now being exerted to arrest the existing chaos throughout the world and out of this to produce the foundations for the ordered beauty of the future. This will inevitably be brought about but its timing will largely depend on the collaboration received from the elements of goodwill already established in various countries. The Forces of Evil are energetically opposing these efforts by sowing seeds of discord, disruption, insecurity, uncertainty and consequent fear. To counter all this is the supremely difficult task of the Count but a task for which he is well qualified. First of all the entire rhythm of international thought has to be altered, which is a slow and tedious business. Those evil personalities which have been exploiting human nature for personal, selfish and material gain and power, by promoting chaos, disruption and fear, have gradually to be ousted and replaced by those who, through the energies of love and goodwill, are in tune with the rhythm of the Seventh Ray, thus finally producing beauty out of the existing chaos.

Master R.'s task is, however, being lightened since the Seventh Ray is year by year becoming more potent and its effects are definitely becoming noticeable to those with the eyes to see. The tide has turned!

(iv) *Master Jesus (J.)*

Although the Master Jesus is an adept on the Sixth Ray of Devotion and Idealism and thus resorts under the department of the Lord of Civilisation, he has been seconded to serve under the Christ, the World Teacher, to promote the welfare of Christianity. He is at present the inspirer and director of the Christian religion throughout the world.

In collaboration with the Masters K.H. and M., the Master Jesus is deeply interested in unifying the religious thought of East and West. According to the Plan, this will lead to the One Universal Church, uniting all peoples into the One Humanity.

The Master J. is well known from biblical history, making his first appearance as Joshua the son of Nun and subsequently, two thousand years ago, as the young initiate Jesus, who surrendered his body for the use of the Christ. This culminated in his fourth initiation at the time of the crucifixion. Still later he was reincarnated as Appolonius of Tyana and took the fifth initiation to become a Master of the Wisdom. Since that time he has been moving in the world of men but beyond the public eye, continually fostering the germ of true spiritual life wherever possible, irrespective of sect or religion, by assisting theologians and churchmen to adhere to the indicated path.

Europe is his special field of endeavour and, although he has a number of pupils, his main task is to influence the masses and gradually to guide public opinion towards better relations and the recognition that all religions are invoking the help of the One God and that through tolerance and goodwill this should lead to a single World Religion. The beauty of this Universal Religion will lie in its being coloured and diversified by the many languages, characteristics and customs of the constituting nations of the world, without these factors in the least detracting from its unity of motive and objective and the close synthesis on spiritual levels.

With regard to that well known biblical era when the Christ made his fateful appearance in Palestine, man cannot yet understand that when mention is made of Jesus-Christ, this refers to two separate entities temporarily functioning as one. Firstly, there was Jesus the disciple and initiate, whose personality was born of Mother Mary and secondly, there was the Entity whom we know as the Christ and whose spirit temporarily overshadowed and took complete charge of the personality of Jesus, whose soul during that period withdrew from the body and stood aside. With the crucifixion, it was merely the physical body of Jesus that was crucified. The Spirit of Christ had departed from this body and as this corresponded with the time when Jesus took his fourth initiation (the 'Renunciation'), the body being crucified was that which had been renounced by Jesus.

The present responsibility of Master Jesus is to raise Western thought life out of the existing morass of uncertainty and fear, where mankind has landed itself through fraud, treachery, cruelty, hate and covetousness and a constant striving for dominance and power. It will be his task to bring about a change of heart. There are already many who through suffering have come to see that the old way of life cannot lead to peace and happiness, that selfish grasping should make way for selfless giving and service and that hate and fear should be superseded by loving co-operation, wisdom and compassion. All this is the responsibility of the Master J. – and what a task! But there is no doubt that progress is being made and he hopes to achieve greater success through a new approach from the Christian Churches, paving the way in both Europe and America for the return of the Christ.

Master Jesus is also striving for union between science and religion, through which he hopes to counter the extremely materialistic attitude of many people and also to break down the unreasoning, sentimental devotion to religion so distinctive of a large section.

It is forecast that the Master Jesus will yet occupy the chair of the Pope of Rome and that from that seat he will then be able to re-inspire and reorient the whole field of Christian religion, diverting it from its present political and temporal trends, towards a more spiritual approach.

(v) *Master Hilarion (H.)*

This Master is already very well known in the Christian world as Paul of Tarsus or *St. Paul*, the author of a large part of the New Testament. In more modern times he has also been responsible for a small treatise well received in esoteric circles – '*Light on the Path*'. He is also the Master stimulating all psychical research groups and it was through him and his pupils that the *Spiritualistic movement* was initiated.

Master H. assists those endeavouring to develop the intuition and also those trying to penetrate the etheric web in order to serve their fellow men. He will, however, not be concerned with those purely interested in psychic phenomena for the sake of sensation and its emotional effects. Neither will he help those who seek material or selfish advantage by contacting the astral images of those who have passed over – these individuals are literally playing with fire! He will, however, assist psychics of higher order, who seek to develop their faculties on behalf of their group or the world at large, to obtain those messages and pictures from the etheric world that will serve some constructive purpose. Such contacts with those on higher etheric levels, may actually prove of considerable benefit to mankind and will certainly contribute to dissipate the fear of death.

Master Hilarion is also relieving the Master Jesus by taking over the training of many of the Sixth Ray disciples, thus enabling Master J. to concentrate on his major work concerned with world religion.

Master H. works with the Fifth Ray of Concrete Knowledge and Science. In physical form he avails himself of a Cretan body, although much of his time is also spent in Egypt and America, where several aspects of his work are focussed. A Master may avail himself of a physical cloak for particular purposes or ready contact with his disciples but his influence will certainly not remain limited to the geographic region where he normally operates in his assumed body. Although he works through this visible and tangible channel, he may whenever required, instantly transfer both his abstract mind and his vehicle of expression, through etheric channels to function immediately anywhere else in the world where his attention or presence may be needed. This is a procedure closely paralleling telepathic communication. Thus, although Master H. might be physically focussed in Egypt, he could be of instant assistance to a disciple or group, in whatever other country they might find themselves.

Master Hilarion is also responsible for inspiring many of the modern scientific 'discoveries' which are making science and mankind aware of the etheric worlds. The veils which for aeons have obscured the vision of many outstanding thinkers and scientists, are now at long last rapidly being torn away, thus opening up vast new fields of investigation.

(vi) *Master Djwhal Khul (D.K.)*

The last of the Masters to be dealt with here is D.K., often affectionately referred to by his disciples as 'The Tibetan'. He is one of the 'youngest' of the Masters, only having attained his qualifying fifth initiation as recently as 1875. In human reckoning a century is considerably more than an average span of life but with immortal entities, no longer limited by transitory material conditions, man's concept of time falls away and the accent is merely placed on the sequence of events and their relative importance in the unfold-ment of the Plan. At any rate, in hierarchical terms D.K. is still one of the younger Masters but, as far as can be judged, he appears to be one of the very active members. This impression is probably gained because his activities are so closely concerned with human unfoldment in general and more particularly with a number of disciples at present in incarnation. There must obviously be many other hard working Masters but whose interests are focussed in other directions and whose functions consequently do not immediately strike human attention.

He acquired the epithet of 'The Tibetan', because at the time of his fifth initiation he availed himself of the body of a Tibetan abbot, which is the form he still assumes when-ever there is occasion for his physical manifestation.

D.K. functions on the Second Ray of Love-Wisdom – the teaching Ray – under the direction and inspiration of K.H., whom he still regards as his Master, although the Tibetan in his own right is already in full charge of his own group. As mentioned else-where, D.K. has taken over the training of a number of disciples from both Koot Hoomi and Morya, to relieve them for more important work.

One of the Tibetan's first major tasks as a teacher of humanity, was to inspire and guide Mme. H.P. Blavatsky, nearly a century ago, with the writing of that outstanding esoteric work, '*The Secret Doctrine*', which subsequently formed the basis of the 'Theosophic Movement'.

In 1919 he approached Alice A. Bailey (A.A.B.) and persuaded her to act as his amanuensis, for releasing to the world a later phase of his teachings. In the course of the following thirty years she put to paper, from his *telepathic dictation*, 18 volumes, con-taining nearly 10,000 pages of text. Shortly after having completed this valuable series, A.A.B. passed on in 1949.

This set of books by A.A.B. must be considered as the most comprehensive treatise on the Ageless Wisdom at present available to man and it actually contains so much knowl-edge and wisdom and of such profound nature, that no ordinary student can fully absorb and appreciate all they contain. Thus only dedicated students can effectively tackle these works, each individual extracting as much as his particular stage of development will allow. What is so fascinating about these books is that they provide a progressive source of revelation for the ever expanding consciousness; although they contain a great deal of abstract and abstruse information, only completely understandable by a third degree ini-tiate, they also contain much that will be of assistance to the aspirant in his search for

Truth. The present treatise is being written to serve as an introduction to these more comprehensive teachings and to smooth the way for the beginner.

These teachings which D.K. has put at the disposal of humanity, have in fact been produced on behalf of an inner hierarchical educational group of Masters for whom the Tibetan is acting as executive secretary.

Blavatsky's work (1875/90) may be regarded as the first phase of D.K.'s teachings and the Bailey Books (1919/49), as the second phase. According to his plans, a third and final phase will be produced early in the next century by an initiate who will again be working under the Tibetan's impression.

As will be apparent from the work produced by these secretaries, working under his telepathic impression, the Tibetan must himself be a very profound student. But apart from these academic achievements, he is also deeply interested in practical healing and, unknown and unseen, he will often stand behind doctors, surgeons and dedicated men of research in their laboratories, impressing their minds with new ideas and clearer vision or guiding their hands with the skilful handling of the scalpel. This healing work, bringing relief and solace to large numbers who are daily suffering physical, emotional and mental agony, is constantly engaging his attention. In addition he is also concerned with world-wide philanthropic movements, such as the Red Cross and other welfare groups caring for the needy. He thus supports all those who seek to heal, to relieve pain and suffering and also those who work towards goodwill and improved human relationships.

XIII. 7 (e) The Externalisation of the Hierarchy

One of the main functions of the Hierarchy is the elevation of mankind to spiritual levels. Although over the ages there has always been a small number of these Great Ones living and working unrecognised in the world of men, in bodies assumed for their particular purposes, most of these Beings have been functioning from etheric levels.

To fulfil their task of human redemption more effectively and to introduce the Spiritual Kingdom to physical levels, it was decided by the Great Council at Shamballa that the members of the Hierarchy directly concerned with the progress of man, should be 'externalised' to enable them to function in closer and conscious contact with man. Before the Brotherhood can work more openly and in full recognition among men, a considerable change must, however, first be effected in man's general attitude to life; the ruling spirit of hate should be eliminated or at least considerably tempered, as well as the exhibition of extreme selfishness, often expressed as separativeness or hidden under the cloak of nationalism. These and many other obstructing attitudes must be countered by evoking goodwill and right human relations. An unbiased consideration of world conditions, ignoring disturbances from those elements which have not yet yielded to the new energies to which humanity is now consistently being subjected, will convince the unprejudiced observer that rapid changes are already making their appearance in public opinion and attitude. A new world is rapidly coming into being!

The externalisation of the Hierarchy will be a gradual process but eventually it will restore the Ancient Wisdom teachings to their rightful position in the human community and will form an integral part of both education and the coming world religion. The whole of mankind will then, step by step, become familiar with the significance of the subjective worlds. The growing awareness of human brotherhood and the awakening tendency towards internationalism, sharing and a general spirit of goodwill, indicate that the principles of the hierarchical Plan are slowly but surely infiltrating the consciousness of humanity and are taking effect. These promising inclinations are indicative of the influence already exerted by the energies released throughout humanity by the progressive externalisation of some of the representatives of the Hierarchy.

Externalisation will demand a tremendous sacrifice on the part of those concerned. The higher evolved the particular initiate, the more refined will be the spiritual atmosphere in which he moves and to descend from those ethereal spheres to the secular conditions of men, will therefore be correspondingly difficult. Only a vast inflow of divine love will facilitate this transition; evidence of this potent energy steadily streaming into the human atmosphere is, however, becoming noticeable and is being demonstrated by ever increasing goodwill, compassion and tolerance in the undercurrents of human behaviour.

This gradual externalisation of members of the Hierarchy must be seen as the harbingers and eventual founders of the Kingdom of God on Earth and the fulfilment of the Divine Plan.

XIII. 8. **The Buddha**

In the past westerners were often inclined to regard Buddhism as heathenish, based on worship of images and statues of the Buddha. In truth the Buddha was as much a divine envoy to the peoples of the Far East as was the Christ in Palestine some six centuries later. The Buddha was the spiritual leader for the East in a similar way that the Christ fulfilled that function for the West.

Of recent years many are obtaining a clearer perspective on these matters and recognising that one of the means employed by the Lord of the World to effect man's subjective growth, is to provide humanity periodically with spiritual Envoys or 'Avatars' – divine Messengers who come as Prophets or Teachers, each bringing some special revelation, message or teaching, applicable to the needs of the people of that particular time, region and stage of development.

During the past three millennia, two of these major approaches were made to man, each enabling the human soul to express a particular aspect of the Divine:

Firstly – the manifestation of *Light*, Intelligence or Wisdom, as embodied by the **Buddha** and

Secondly – the manifestation of divine *Love*, combined with the light of reason, as displayed by the **Christ**.

The Buddha came to the East, focussing in himself the divine qualities of light, wisdom and reason – all attributes which could readily be transferred to and utilised by man. The 'Illumined One' indicated the Way and challenged humanity to tread the 'Path of Illumination' through mental understanding, wisdom and the intuition. Today the Buddha is therefore widely recognised as the 'Light Bearer'.

His teachings mainly centred on the *Four Noble Truths*:

1. Cease to identify yourselves with material living and physical desires – the cause of all misery is the misuse of desire.
2. Gain a proper sense of spiritual values.
3. Do not regard earthly possessions and existence in the physical body as of major importance.
4. Follow the *Noble Eightfold Path* of right relations to God and your fellow man, which will lead to happiness.

The eight steps on this Path are:

Right Values	Right Aspiration
Right Speech	Right Conduct
Right Modes of Living	Right Effort
Right Thinking	Right Rapture and Happiness

What better foundations could be devised for combining eventually with the Love of Christ and for those right human relations for which mankind is now striving?

When the Buddha came, he demonstrated in his own life both God Immanent and God Transcendent; man thus became conscious of the Self, the God within the heart of man and simultaneously the idea and awareness of the Universal God was evoked, present in each and every form of nature and creation.

Those sufficiently sensitive to absorb the Light of Wisdom and to allow it to flow into the mind, will evoke wisdom and discrimination. To the degree that this Light of Reason is expressed in man, to a similar extent will glamour be dissipated.

In the hierarchical system the Buddha operates as intermediary between Shamballa and the Hierarchy of Masters. He constitutes part of a Triangle of Force consisting of the Buddha, the Spirit of Peace and the Avatar of Synthesis. These three associates are jointly supporting the Christ, supplying him with the forces of Light, Love and Power so urgently required for fulfilling his responsible task as Leader of the Hierarchy and Teacher of humanity during the Aquarian Age now coming into manifestation.

On subjective levels the Buddha and the Christ are closely associated, with Buddha taking an active part in the preparations for the reappearance of the Christ in the world of men. These strong bonds between the Buddha, the Christ and Humanity, stretch back over the ages but, relatively speaking, are now climaxing. After supporting the Christ in this demanding task of re-entering life on physical levels, the Buddha will withdraw from all further direct contact with humanity, to focus his attention exclusively on higher spheres of activity, no longer directly concerning the human evolution.

XIII. 9. The Christ

(i) *Evolution of the Christ*

The Christ is the Master of the Masters, the Leader of the Hierarchy and the World Teacher and as such is man's principal source of inspiration and his guide along the evolutionary path. Christ was the first Earth-born individual to be initiated into the Kingdom of God and ever since has retained his position as the loving and loved leader and teacher of 'both men and Angels'.

Every entity, not only in the little world of men but throughout the Universe, attains momentary phases of achievement but these merely represent points of achievement on the interminable Path of Evolution. To those still on lower levels of the Path, the consciousness attained by the Christ might well appear to be the acme of perfection but this difference is entirely relative. For each developing entity there must necessarily be a process of ever changing values – a constant shifting to higher criteria. To the Christ, in his ever expanding worlds of experience and consciousness, his present position might well appear comparatively insignificant, when seen in relation to new vistas and realms of being opening up before his spiritual vision.

Some two thousand years ago the Christ set himself the task of saving humanity but, according to the Tibetan, it will require a further two millennia (the duration of the Aquarian Age) for this work to be completed. For the Christ this achievement will lead to a higher initiation which, to the ordinary human being, must remain beyond conception. Apparently such higher evolution will terminate his direct association with the affairs of men, as he will then move on to service on even more supernal levels.

(ii) *The Christ-Principle*

In modern terminology 'The Christ' is normally used to indicate the illusive but potent energy of the 'Christ-Principle'. The entity known to man as the Christ is in fact the entity within whom this principle is so strongly focussed, that he has become the living identification of this energy, exhibiting all its qualities. This Christ-principle is, however, not limited to the Christ but is universally present and an energy readily available to all human beings. It is intrinsically part of the soul which, in the undeveloped, is as yet obscured and unrecognisable because of the overwhelming physical and emotional qualities still dominating the individual.

The Christ-principle is characterised by selfless love and an inflow of this energy will evoke the development of a spirit of understanding, goodwill and co-operation. In the masses it will be expressed as an urge towards better human relationships. The world of men is at present systematically irradiated with this divine energy, embodying the Love and Light of the Christ, and its effectiveness will only depend on the receptivity of the individuals and masses.

(iii) *The Love of Christ*

Just as the Buddha was characterised by Light, so the distinguishing quality of the Christ is the principle of Love. But the Christ combined within himself not only the highest aspect of divine Love but also all that the Buddha had of Light.

Christ's life on Earth came to be seen as the emblem of love and service and one of his first precepts was that men should love one another – but how little attention was paid to this injunction during the following two millennia! So often men of religion, who claimed to expound his teachings, proved to be the worst offenders against the lofty principles of love, by actually being instigators of hate, persecution and bloodshed. Even in present times, with the New Age forces of the Christ-principle streaming into the world and impinging on all those in any way sensitive to these influences, its effects are still so often submerged by less desirable qualities. But although these effects may as yet be largely hidden by an outer cloak of materialism and even by the ruling powers of evil, a clear and strong undercurrent of love and understanding is nevertheless becoming apparent to those with perception.

Another aspect stressed by the Christ is that God, of whom he is the reflection, is a God of Love and certainly not a God of vengeance as so often represented in the Old Testament. The retribution at times overtaking man is but the inevitable result of some improper action and not a vengeful act of God – it is but a law of nature, the Law of Cause and Effect, working out to its natural conclusion.

Christ taught of the supernal Love of God and that love constitutes the whole objective of creation, forms the basic principle of all better relationships, as well as being the foundation for the divine Plan and Purpose. The Christ revealed these divine objectives, setting new ideals and values for human living but man still has far to go before these targets will be achieved. It is the hearts of men which respond to the love of Christ and once the heart is activated, a new approach to life will be inaugurated.

(iv) *The Living Christ*

When Christ withdrew from the crucified body of Jesus, two thousand years ago, it certainly did not mean that he left humanity to its fate. He did return to etheric levels, to spheres still invisible to man but this only meant retiring to a station from where he could retain close contact with the activities of man in the three worlds. He has assumed the onerous task of guiding humanity along its path of redemption and man can therefore depend on it that he will never be left in the lurch. Because his presence is so intangible, there is often the inclination to forget about him altogether or otherwise to think of him as a vague entity in some distant heavenly sphere. But actually he remains in intimate contact with all man's doings and his help is always at our disposal. The extent to which his aid is evoked will solely depend on the aspirant's attitude and dedication.

The church is inclined to emphasise the blood of Christ and his death on the cross as a sacrifice to humanity, instead of stressing his resurrection, his livingness and presence, here and now in our etheric surround. In this etheric realm he is surrounded by his disciples, the Masters of Wisdom and is accessible to all men entertaining selfless motives and with love and goodwill in their hearts.

(v) *Teachings of the Christ*

The Christ stressed that our Father is not a God of retribution; that all men are his children and therefore brothers; that man's spirit is eternal and that it is only the temporary vehicle which dies and disintegrates.

He taught that something of his own Spirit, the Christ-principle, the God within, is present in every human being, although this may often be obscured during early development by the many urges and desires; he taught that the keynote of spiritual life was loving service to fellow beings and that the Will of God must inevitably be revealed through the aspirant.

A sad disenchantment lies in store for many professing 'Christians' when the Christ returns to Earth and resumes his world-wide teachings. They will then discover that the so-called Christians are not the only children of God but under the latter are included all those truly inspired by divine spirit, no matter under what religion or ritual this may be expressed. The only decisive criterion will be the real Christ-consciousness in their hearts, expressing itself as a spirit of love and goodwill. It will then be found that other religions harbour individuals who spiritually may be even more advanced into the Kingdom of God, than many 'Christians'. Christ's task is that of the World Teacher and not the 'Christian' Teacher and one of his principal objectives will be the uniting of all nations and races into a single, closely related and mutually loving and serving humanity, held together by One World Religion.

(vi) *The Christ-Consciousness*

This alludes to that vibrant, conscious recognition of the inner Christ-principle existing in every individual. In the undeveloped this principle still lies dormant but eventually an incarnation must come when it will awaken and make itself apparent in the unfolding individual. It is this Christ-consciousness or the reaction to the behests of the inner Christ, which ultimately leads to perfection. It is this innate divinity which urges every man towards betterment, to the extraction of the good from all experience, to ever increasing revelation, to a recognition of the revealed and thus eventually to the envisioned ideal.

There is nothing which can permanently withstand this inner driving force which, during some life or other, will be evinced by every evolving soul. This upward struggle is an unfailing characteristic in the life history of every human entity and, although such progress may be retarded owing to circumstances and lessons to be learned, the eventual stepping on to the Path of Return to the Father cannot be arrested by anything on Earth. It is this inner Christ which generates the forward urge and provides the guarantee of attainment.

It is believed that within the relatively near future, the Christ will make his reappearance on Earth by assuming a physical body but, apart from his physical reappearance, his spiritual manifestation will become increasingly apparent in man's daily activities. Those with the required sensitivity will readily recognise this Christ-consciousness in their fellow men. This presence of the inner Christ is evinced by all who are becoming aware of the energy of the will-to-good, displayed as kindness, loving understanding, tolerance and goodwill. It is also clearly expressed in humanitarianism and dedication to improving human relations and conditions of existence, thus also ensuring more equitable distribution and sharing of the amenities of life. This inner spirit also engenders a resistance and revolt against the dogmatic tenets of churches, religious practices or any attempt to dominate the spiritual life and thought of the individual. Formal religion is no indication of spirituality, which can only be reflected by a display of Christ-consciousness in every phase of physical, emotional and mental living.

Christ is the messenger of liberation and the symbol of freedom. It is this aspect of his spiritual energy which is now permeating the nations of the world with an irrepressible urge. This energy is furthermore characterised by a magnetic force which draws individuals and groups together, uniting men to serve the common good. It stimulates both the group spirit and group consciousness. To the extent that humanity is becoming overshadowed by the Christ spirit will the Christ-consciousness be evidenced by a closer association of all men and women of goodwill, irrespective of colour, nationality or religion. The good which exists in all will correspondingly be recognised.

It is irrelevant to the Christ to what extent man accepts the theological interpretations of scholars and churchmen or whether the details of the Gospel story are recognised and accepted. What matters is that the search for truth and spiritual experience by the individual should be awakened and sustained and that the Christ-consciousness, which lies dormant in every human heart, should be brought to active response.

(vii) **The Reappearance of the Christ**

Early in the 1920's the Tibetan prophesied that the reappearance of Christ on astral levels (whether followed by his physical materialisation or not) would date from the time when a most potent mantram would be released to humanity. This mantram, known as '*The Great Invocation*', was actually made available in June 1945, since when it has been distributed world-wide and has also been translated into all the better known languages. This was also the date when the Christ finally decided that he would again return to Earth, to walk with men in tangible form and that this would be brought about as soon as circumstances would allow.

Many of the disciples and initiates now in incarnation have been sent to prepare humanity for this return. The majority of these workers will, however, remain unaware as to exactly when, where and how his appearance will take place. Of the rapid approach of this momentous date, there can no longer be any doubt and the etheric atmosphere is literally tingling with the energies engendered by his coming. These influences will be increasingly demonstrated by an ever wider spreading spirit of goodwill at all levels of human relationships.

The return of the Christ is being delayed by the virulent forces of hate, selfishness, greed and desire, which are as yet largely dominating relationships between men and nations. Before his coming these attitudes will have to be considerably tempered and superseded by moderation, understanding and goodwill. The possibility of such a volte-face may perhaps sound far-fetched but a closer study of world conditions, and also of narrower environments, will disclose that this metamorphosis is actually *now* in process of accomplishment. This overwhelming spirit of goodwill, streaming in from subjective levels, has such an infectious influence, that rapidly changing attitudes may often appear in the most unexpected quarters.

One of the signs that the time of his coming is approaching, will be that many of the key posts in governments and in organisations playing a leading role in local communities or world affairs, will become occupied by those who are being overshadowed and guided by the Christ principle. These men and women will in many instances be spiritually highly evolved and will be specially (even though unconsciously) prepared for their positions to lead the masses through the difficult transition stage into the New Age.

To talk about the *return* of the Christ to Earth is strictly speaking incorrect, because he has never left the Earth and for the past two millennia he has constantly been working with and for humanity. His activities, however, proceeded from etheric levels, on which planes the average man could not consciously become aware of him. In the years to come, even before his physical reappearance, those sensitive to the pervading Christ principle will increasingly become aware of his overshadowing presence and of the light and love that is being radiated to mankind. Where individual disciples are overshadowed, this will be evidenced by the effectiveness and potency of their work and service activities.

The coming of the Christ will herald an entirely new civilisation – a New Age in human existence. His coming will be preceded by the externalisation of many of his adepts and disciples and, although unrecognised by the general public, this is already taking place through the normal processes of incarnation and by the overshadowing of

186

individuals. Eventually this new Aquarian Age will be characterised by goodwill, peace and better human relations, leading to synthesis and the One Humanity, under the guidance of the Christ and the members of the Hierarchy. For the construction of this new and improved human edifice, much of that which is old, outworn, false, decadent and redundant, has in recent years already been destroyed, is now in process of being broken down, or will have to be removed in years to come. Much of this destruction was physically initiated with the wars of 1914/45 and has subsequently been continued on social, economic and political levels. This process of change, transfiguration and adaptation, is still in full swing. 'New wine cannot be put into old bottles'. One of the main features of these new tendencies, is the urge towards *freedom* – freedom of thought and of speech; political freedom, economic freedom and most important of all – *religious and spiritual freedom*. These trends are shown by men who, on an increasing scale, are beginning to think and meditate on these problems, eventually leading to the enrichment of the world of thought and the gradual transition of the human family from a relatively materialistic and emotional existence, into a period of illumined mental control.

The Coming One will not be a Hindu, a Christian or a Buddhist; he will not be a Jew, Greek or Russian; he will not belong to any particular religion, race or nation; and whether he be called the Bodhisattva, the Christ, the Maitreya or the Imam Mahdi – what does the title matter! What is important, is that he will be coming for the whole of mankind, to unite all religions into the One World Religion and to draw all nations and races into the community of the One Humanity, held together by a common bond of goodwill and mutual understanding. This does not mean that all nations should conform to some standard political ideology, language or form of government. The beauty of this world-wide confederation of nations will lie in its diversity of languages, cultures, customs, habits and characteristics, all seeking a common purpose and striving for mutual welfare and progress. This must then inevitably lead to that everlasting world of peace – the Kingdom of God.

That which will finally determine the time for the Christ's return to the world of matter, is the strength of the united invocative appeal for his help, the 'massed intent' of the world's disciples and men of goodwill. This should be kept in mind and every man must contribute his small part towards constructing this invocative force, which will eventually build up to the required potency to recall man's Saviour.

How the true Christ will be distinguished from the many *false prophets* and claim-makers, is still unknown but there is no doubt that when the time arrives he will be recognised by his many disciples throughout the world. With his previous coming, some two thousand years ago, there as yet existed no world-wide system of communication. Thus his *immediate* sphere of influence largely remained limited to 'walking distance', representing only a relatively small region in Palestine. His words and teachings were subsequently carried to every corner of the world by his disciples but that took time and, in the process of handing down the relatively simple principles of love and brotherhood, these teachings became badly distorted and complicated, resulting in the many Christian religions and sects, usually characterised by their petty theological dogmas. This confusion of words and concepts, aggravated by man's cupidity, intolerance and lust for power and possessions has, under the cloak of religion, led to some of the worst excesses of human history, characterised by bloodshed, cruelty and numerous other forms of atrocity.

When the Christ now returns, the position will be changed completely. Within a few hours of being recognised by his disciples, the news of his return will be broadcast far and wide over the whole world. By means of radio and television, millions will not only hear his spoken messages but will actually see him and witness his activities. Aerial transport will furnish direct contact with all peoples and facilitate his great task of improving human relations. This memorable day is now approaching and, whether observed from physical or subjective levels, it will be a day of jubilation eagerly awaited by millions.

It stands to reason that there will probably be a fairly large number of unfortunate individuals who will not immediately be able to appreciate his coming. There will be the undeveloped who will understand relatively little of the meaning of it all and will continue with their daily physical activities, without in the early stages displaying any marked interest. There will be others so deeply immersed in their material concerns that matters affecting their spiritual well-being will make relatively little impression on them. Then there will be those who, for some karmic reason, will not be ready for the immediate acceptance of his Presence and who may even ridicule his reappearance. This attitude need not necessarily arise from malice but might be caused by ignorance, insensitivity or spiritual blindness.

Then, regrettably, there will also be another category of men and women, working under the influence of the Dark Forces. These poor wretches, acting as the instruments of Evil, will oppose the recognition of the Christ with every malicious means at their disposal – but this will prove to be a losing battle!

There has never been any question about the Christ's eventual 'return' but for a long time uncertainty has prevailed as to whether this return might perhaps remain limited to astral levels, whence he would have radiated his influence to men in the physical world. However, in June 1945 his final decision was announced to return to mankind in physical manifestation and to resume his responsibilities for man's redemption, while in direct and personal contact with all their problems. What a sacrifice this will mean but what a gift to man! This return will take place as soon as humanity indicates its readiness and will in fact be earlier than was originally anticipated. Unfortunately relatively so few are aware of the authenticity of these tidings and are therefore willing to share in preparing for his coming!

The Christ may appear in the most unexpected way, place, time or guise; he may come as politician, scientist or artist; he might land unexpectedly at some airport in a craft of unknown origin, accompanied by some of his assistants; he might materialise unannounced at a meeting of international leaders, perhaps bringing harmony and co-operation where disagreement had been ruling. Another possibility is that he might avail himself of the body of an existing personality, which could be completely overshadowed, inspired and used by the Christ, as was done with the physical vehicle of the Master Jesus during his appearance in Palestine. But all such speculation is rather futile, as the imagination can picture any number of possibilities for this longed for occasion.

The Christ will be the embodiment of *Freedom* and the messenger of *Liberation* – not only physical liberation but in the first instance release of the mind, leading to expansion of consciousness. He will stimulate group work, group spirit and consciousness and with his magnetic energy will unite men in their striving towards the common good. His basic attributes of Love and Light will unite all men and women of goodwill throughout the world and only then will it really become apparent to what a large degree the forces of will-to-good have already infiltrated the human community. A widespread recognition of the inner good which exists in all, will also be evoked.

Although the Christ has decided to manifest in a physical body, his influence and energies will also be felt and accentuated by:

1. *His overshadowing of all disciples and initiates* in incarnation. Before his appearance this influence will already inspire his disciples to increased activity in preparing mankind for his coming and subsequently they will form part of his executive staff to spread his influence and teachings amongst men.
2. He is *also radiating a constant stream of the Christ-Energy* over the masses of mankind. The average man will not be consciously aware of this influence, although it is having a potent effect on humanity as a whole and is the source of the spirit of goodwill seeping through the world and is steadily impregnating the consciousness of man. This will lead to a more positive response when the Christ eventually does make his actual appearance.

(viii) *Christ in the Aquarian Age*

The world is now passing from the Piscean into the Aquarian Age and for the next two thousand five hundred years, mankind will remain subject to the energies released under the benevolent influences of this regime. The great gift of this Age to humanity will be the *Principle of Sharing* which will gradually permeate all aspects of human life. Firstly, there will be a physical sharing of all world resources, combined with the products of human activities; this will end the present unbalanced distribution of the products so bountifully provided by nature, combined with those ingeniously produced by the devices of man. All forms of malnutrition and starvation will therefore disappear and all will be properly housed and protected against the extremes of nature. But of even greater importance will be the sharing on emotional, mental and spiritual levels, leading eventually to an integrated human community, bound by mutual understanding and goodwill.

As Leader of the Hierarchy and as Teacher of mankind, it will be the task of the Christ to implement this New World with all its new relationships. What a formidable task but also consider the joy that will come with its achievement! In this great work the Christ will of course have the co-operation of the Hierarchy of Masters and in addition he will also be inspired by the Lord of the World, working through '*Three Associates*', a triumvirate producing a '*Triangle of Force*' for supplementing the Christ with the energies required for bringing his exacting assignment to its conclusion.

The work of the Christ will lay the emphasis on Divine Intelligence, Love-Wisdom and Will. These will be consciously developed in mankind, thus forging a closer relation between the activities of **Shamballa**, the **Hierarchy** and **Humanity**.

With increasing intelligence and greater use of the mental approach, the mystical concept of religion as a whole and of the Kingdom of God in particular, will be superseded by a more reasoned, intelligent and even scientific approach. All this will take place under the guidance of the Christ but the keynote of his mission will be to evoke a response from Humanity to spiritual influences, which will lead to the unfoldment of intuitive perception and sensitivity. Furthermore, theology will be superseded by spirituality and living experience will replace theological dissertation. As spiritual qualities emerge with increasing clarity, the form aspect will recede and become of secondary importance. The hold of the churches will steadily diminish and the living Christ will assume his rightful place in human consciousness.

XIV

PLANETARY ETHERIC ENERGY CENTRES

As previously explained man's physical body is provided with seven energy centres, located in his etheric surround. This is but a reflection of a similar arrangement applying also to the physical manifestation of a Planetary Logos – 'as above, so below'.

There exists a definite relationship between the location of a 'centre', the nature of the Ray seeking definition through it and the channel and field of its expression. As far as the Planetary Logos is concerned, a schematic representation might perhaps serve to clarify the position:

Energy Centre	Field of Expression	Ray:	Nature/Objective
Head	Shamballa	1st	Will
Heart	Hierarchy	2nd	Love
Throat or Ajna	Humanity	5th	Intuition
Throat	Animal	3rd	Intellect
Solar Plexus	Vegetable	6th	Instinct
Sacral	Deva	7th	Responsiveness
Base of Spine	Mineral	4th	Synthesis

For present purposes, only the first three of these centres are of immediate relevance:

1. The *Head Centre* is focussed in *Shamballa*, which is situated on etheric levels and is the seat of Sanat Kumara, the Lord of the World who, together with the members of his Council and other assistants, are jointly responsible for the expression of the divine *Will* and *Purpose*. This is also the source of entry and distribution of all planetary *Life*.
2. The *Heart Centre*, represented by the Hierarchy of Masters of Wisdom, briefly referred to as the '*Hierarchy*'. This is really the Kingdom of Souls, through which the energies of divine *Love* and *Wisdom* are expressed. The Hierarchy is also the agency for the formulation and execution of the divine Plan of evolution, based on the Purpose as defined by Shamballa. The Masters may function either on etheric or material levels, depending on circumstances and the demands of their service.

3. The *Throat or Ajna Centre*, for which *Humanity* serves as the channel of expression of divine *intelligence* – the energy of the active Mind. In this respect Humanity fulfils the same relative function for the three sub-human kingdoms, as the Hierarchy does for the human kingdom. Humanity could therefore be regarded as the macrocosm for the three lower kingdoms.

It is important to see these Centres in their triple relationship; the aim of the evolutionary scheme being to bring them into true alignment, through which the energies of the One Life may then be directed without undue obstruction and for the harmonious expression of the divine Purpose on every level of consciousness. Through Shamballa the Will and Purpose of God becomes known; this is then communicated to the Hierarchy, where the Purpose is sensed and embodied in the Plan. For its expression the Plan is then presented to human initiates, disciples and aspirants for practical realisation and application on physical levels as far as allowed by their recognition.

In the past all Shamballa forces were first directed through the Hierarchy for reduction before being transmitted to Humanity. With the unfoldment of Humanity, its vibrations have been sufficiently strengthened to withstand the direct impact of the potent Shamballa energies. With further reinforcing of Humanity's powers of energy resistance, free circulation will be possible between the three points of the Planetary Triangle: *Shamballa – Hierarchy – Humanity*, with forces flowing freely in reciprocal directions.

This means that Humanity is at last beginning to respond consciously to the Will of Shamballa. Although the esoteric significance of this new development is not yet fully recognised, it is actually the indication of an entirely new relationship which is unfolding, as a result of which far reaching spiritual effects will be evoked.

CITIES AS SPIRITUAL CENTRES

For the purpose of future hierarchical manifestation on the physical plane, five major spiritual centres for energy distribution have been founded, where Master's groups will, in the course of time, be located. At present these points of spiritual outlet are:

1. *London* – for countries under British influence or association.
2. *New York* – for the American continents and spheres of influence.
3. *Geneva* – for Europe, including the U.S.S.R.
4. *Tokyo* – for the Far East.
5. *Darjeeling* – for Central Asia and India.

When the time is opportune, two further centres will be added.

These five centres are closely interrelated, jointly forming a five-pointed star of inter-locking energies, associating the more important aspects of the civilisations of the modern world. Each of these centres may be regarded as a vortex of spiritual forces and will form the headquarters of a Master with his group of disciples. The Hierarchy will utilise these focal points as organised centres for the distribution of spiritual energies.

From these central points, subsidiary stations with their groups, each sponsored by a senior disciple with his helpers, will develop all over the world, to carry forward spiritual influences and educational facilities. All this work will be preparatory for the planned externalisation and appearance of the Hierarchy on Earth and will therefore take place through subjective concepts and planning.

THE AKASHIC RECORDS

The 'akashic record' is another of those rather vague concepts, relating to the intangible higher-dimensional worlds, which ordinary man, limited by the three worlds of matter, has difficulty in understanding but of which he must take note if he desires a deeper insight into the mysteries of the encompassing Whole.

The Tibetan describes this 'record' symbolically as an eternal scroll existing in spiritual spheres, whereon the greater Plan for world development is inscribed and from which World Teachers and Guides gather information and direction for certain aspects of their activities.

On this record is also registered progressively all activities of the past, thus providing a complete history of the world to those capable of reading these chronicles. Details of the past lives of every individual are recorded. The Akashic Records are thus the archives of the world but representing something incomparably more comprehensive and perfect than similar human attempts could ever hope to achieve.

A semblance of these archives is reflected on the astral plane but this image is distorted by the 'watery' astral atmosphere and is therefore untrustworthy. The picture obtained by the would-be investigator of this astral record will not only be influenced by normal astral distortions but will even be further coloured by the effects of looking through the disturbed conditions of his own aura. Claims made about reading these records, although probably made in good faith, should thus be regarded with reservation, as it will always be difficult to determine how much such observations have been affected by glamour and illusion.

DEVAS AND ELEMENTALS

Devas and elementals constitute a separate evolution to that of the human being. All evolutions or involutions are, however, intimately integrated and together compose the body of the Planetary Logos. Each of these vast systems is independently controlled by Hierarchies functioning on parallel levels and status.

The intention is not to make a close study of these other vast fields of expression but the esoteric student should at least be aware of these related evolutions, with a general idea of how they are related to and affect our own immediate system.

(a) Elementals

The elementals are sub-human forms which have not yet reached the evolutionary stage. They are in fact still in process of *involution*, on the downward arc – the stage where spirit is still being involved in matter. *Evolution*, in contrast, denotes the upward gradient, where that which has been created evolves or is being transmuted into forms on higher levels of development and thus refers to the ascent or return of Spirit to its Source, carrying with it the gains in experience of passing through matter.

Elementals are etheric forms of being, occurring on all planes and which have traditionally been known as gnomes, brownies and pixies.

They may also be classified as:

1. Earth or Physical Elementals
2. Air or Etheric Elementals

These elementals are the essence or primordial phase of all creation in both our Solar System and the Universe.

Within certain limits these elemental forces may be controlled or guided by man. They can as a rule be harnessed by particular rites and rituals but this is an entirely separate study and the uninformed are warned that it is definitely undesirable to meddle with these matters unless thoroughly understood. The present purpose is merely to point to the existence of these forces.

With more advanced spiritual development the disciple will acquire the knowledge and proficiency, based on the laws of nature, enabling him to co-operate successfully with the involutionary realms and thereby also to promote the evolutionary processes.

(b) Devas

In contrast to the elementals, the devas are already on the evolutionary path. They are the builders of the material system, in which they work in their myriads in 'serried ranks' and where they are grouped into many grades. Devas of every status are to be found, somewhat paralleling those of the human evolution and grading from ranks comparable to that of a Planetary Logos, through the many intermediate hierarchical grades, down to the lesser ranks of the building devas, who work unconsciously and automatically in large groups, building the many forms known to human evolution. These lower groups are guided only by vibration and sound.

The devas avail themselves of the elemental forces and the deva builders control these blindly working forces to perform their involutionary functions. The devas in their constructive work produce cohesion, harmony and beauty out of elemental chaos.

The lower strata of the devas, the practical builders, comparatively speaking, vary from the unthinking, automatically working labourers, rising progressively until the foreman quality is encountered, then the supervisor, eventually arriving at the controllers, the industrial executives or 'Great Building Devas', who are on a comparable level with the Masters of Wisdom.

On the physical plane man is, mostly unconsciously, in daily and constant contact with the deva world. All matter and every physical form, whether mineral, vegetable, animal or human, is constituted of the vital substance of the many lesser ranks of deva entities and these are held together by a higher ranking deva providing the coherence of form to the object. Thus every crystal, drop of water and every plant or animal, has its own controlling deva-life.

The Dark Forces have also acquired the technique of handling the elementals or involutionary forces and pervert these unwitting lesser forms of life to their evil and selfish purposes. For man the correct procedure, as practised by the Masters, is not to attempt direct control over the elementals and lower grade devas but rather to effect such control through co-operation with their senior ranks, such as the deva Lords or Angels. It is therefore not for man to *control* the deva world but to *collaborate* with them by intelligent and loving understanding of their functions.

Adepts have been taught the art of calling specific devas or elementals to serve their purpose, by the use of '*mantrams*'. By a mantram is understood arranging words or syllables in some rhythmic order, which when thus sounded, will generate the desired vibrations. These vibrations may then serve as a call-note for the required devas or elementals. Such powers will be accorded to the disciple when he is ready for their use and when his work demands it. Danger is, however, definitely provoked when the lesser devas and forces are called by the unqualified in attempts to further selfish ambitions.

As man is the custodian of the mental principle, so the deva evolution is the custodian of the life principle and therefore also of magnetism and vitality – those qualities playing such an important role in the three worlds of human manifestation. For their mutual benefit close co-operation is essential between these two evolutions, neither of which can develop effectively without the support of the other and, as far as the form is concerned, they are actually indispensable partners. On the other hand, man should increasingly orient himself towards spiritual relationships, thus striving to evolve away from dependence on form and matter.

The aspirant should recognise that it is not only his physical body which consists of deva life but also his etheric and emotional bodies and that even thoughts are nothing but deva substance. It is for this reason that the average man, still functioning on emotional levels, remains largely under the control of astral devas and his objective must therefore be to liberate himself as soon as possible from these influences, allowing the soul to dominate his life and the Spirit to become his guide.

It is perhaps interesting to know that a group of entities have been gathered from the ranks of the more advanced devas, who are serving as *'guardian angels'* over the physical bodies of the human race. Each human being has thus been furnished with his own particular guardian angel, whose function it is to remain with him night and day, warding off unfavourable energies which might constitute a menace to the physical well-being of the protégé. These guardian angels must not be confused with those spiritual helpers, who on etheric levels stand by the disciple providing him with Spiritual support when needed and invoked. The guarding devas have much to give to humanity but their own attainment also lies in this kind of service.

On hierarchical levels there is close collaboration between human and deva evolutions. Evolved devas may be recognised on etheric levels as great *Angels* and according to the Sages, at least four groups of these Angels are assembled around the Christ, pledged to his service and that of humanity. One of the responsibilities with which the Christ has charged them, is to make men aware of certain concepts or conditions which today may still seem far-fetched:

1. Humanity must be taught to see etherically. This the devas will achieve through heightening human vibration by devic interaction.
2. Man must be taught the use of colour and sound for healing certain diseases. Violet light, for instance, seems to be particularly effective for treating disturbances originating in the etheric body.
3. Materialistic thinkers must be convinced of the existence of the etheric worlds, where the 'spirit' of both men and angels may be contacted.
4. Men must be made aware of *'super-human physics'* – how to eliminate gravitation and

attain weightlessness and how to eliminate fatigue by moving without resistance and with the rapidity of thought. These 'impossible' conditions will only be accomplished by gaining control over the etheric vehicle.

5. Humanity will be taught how to nourish the body by drawing sustenance from etheric energy. This will mean that life activities will increasingly have to be focussed on etheric existence, with a simultaneous withdrawing of active attention from physical functions, allowing the latter to become largely automatic.

6. To encompass the above will involve penetrating and eventually destroying the 'etheric web', which today still separates the physical world of human existence so effectively from the invisible etheric spheres.

To the ordinary human being these conceptions may seem fantastic and even beyond all consideration and many will consequently ridicule these visions. But just think how impossible many of our present day scientific inventions, such as television, computers, electronics, nuclear power, spacecraft, etc. would have sounded if prophesied to our forbears of only a hundred years ago. Nobody at that time would have taken any notice of such utter nonsense!

Those with an open mind and unbiased outlook must already be aware of the steadily spreading influence of these Deva Angels, which is slowly but surely permeating human life, affecting its many activities and fields of consciousness.

Everywhere there are signs of increasing psychic awareness; science is rapidly discovering and accepting several aspects of 'extra-sensory-perception' (E.S.P.) and these are now receiving widespread attention. At long last science has ascertained the existence of the etheric world (or at least certain aspects thereof), although the scientific approach is being wrapped up in such complicated technical terminology, that it becomes nearly unrecognisable to the esoteric student.

The existence of telepathic faculties of communication is also being recognised and with growing human sensitivity it is expected that there will be a corresponding increase in the practical application of these powers.

The fulfilment of some of these prophecies must therefore be regarded as imminent and it is merely a question of time before a more refined sensitivity will be developed for recognising the surrounding etheric world, with its many active Entities and influences. This will again lead to further expansion of consciousness and a deeper comprehension of the reality of the inner worlds.

Yes! – the Great Angels are hard at work accomplishing the Christ's mandates and Humanity is beginning to react favourably to the stimulus!

PART TWO

Man on the Path of Life

I

ESOTERIC STUDIES

I. 1. The Nature of Esotericism

In its essence esotericism is the art of consciously recognising that all existence, manifested in its myriad variations of form and quality, is fundamentally based on energy. Not only are all forms of creation composed of energy but every form of activity also arises from streams of energy activated by that all encompassing Law of Nature – the Law of Cause and Effect.

The function of the esotericist is to take cognisance of these energies and, as far as his mental and spiritual evolution allows, to learn how these energies may best be guided and controlled to the maximum advantage of humanity, thus implementing the precepts of the Divine Plan. In the early stages of his conscious development as an esotericist, the aspirant will only be aware of a limited range of these energies impinging on his system but with growing sensitivity the observed range will increase, thus progressively expanding his consciousness and consequently his capacities for effective service.

The beginner will at first be lost in a maze of interlocking and interacting energies. In due course he will, however, begin to distinguish between:

1. Purely physical energy, consisting of energy and forces which have been transmuted and engendered in his physical system.
2. Emotional forces and mental powers evoked by energies focussed through the etheric body to these two planes.
3. The impelling energies sent forth by the soul and therefore emanating from the higher mental and spiritual levels.

The esotericist must also learn to recognise the energies which determine the nature of his environment. He must come to the realisation that all happenings and circumstances, and every physical manifestation of whatever nature, are but the symbols or reflections of events and activities occurring within the etheric worlds. These inner realms are the worlds of reality and it is the task of the esotericist to penetrate the separating veils, to familiarise himself with the newly discovered conditions and then to qualify himself for fresh fields of activity.

The field of esoteric study should not remain limited to considering only those energies which are directly affecting the individual or his immediate environment. It will be of even greater significance to consider the more comprehensive energies affecting for instance national and international politics and world events. Each disciple should endeavour to understand the nature of these forces, enabling him to contribute his part, whether large or small, towards promoting favourable world conditions.

It should always be kept in mind that all creation is but spirit in manifestation and therefore every form of energy, whether it concerns the individual, the group or the nation and whether in the field of religion, science, economics or of a political nature, has its spiritual aspect and stands to gain by correct spiritual approach. Thus wars for example are caused by energies which have accumulated till a point of saturation is reached and these pent up forces are then both literally and figuratively released explosively. The time will come when it will be possible to determine the incentive esoteric causes of such wars, thus enabling them to be either avoided or eliminated.

Esotericism therefore concerns itself with the many energies of the soul and aims towards free access to and functioning in the subjective worlds. It serves as the mediating principle between life and substance but is oriented to the spiritual rather than to the physical aspects. To attain these ideals, the disciple must have a reasonably well developed intelligence and must definitely be mentally oriented, because it is essential that, while contacting and moving amongst these inner realities, he should be able to draw his own logical conclusions and arrive at a clear understanding of that which his consciousness may register.

Increased light, leading to illumination, is the inevitable result of all true esoteric activity and, under the guidance of the soul, this in turn intensifies the inherent light of all substance brought under the influence of the work. The soul-infused and dedicated esoteric student may therefore continue on his chosen way with confidence and with the knowledge that as he proceeds, overcoming all obstacles on his ascending path, this path will be irradiated by ever brighter light. And as each disciple, through his own efforts, is endowed with greater light, it will become part of his responsibility to develop into a light-bearer in his own right, dispersing this light amongst his fellow men who, although still largely unknowingly, are yearning for this light to brighten the darkness by which they are surrounded.

I. 2. The Mystic and the Esotericist

The esotericist is consciously aware of the world of energies and forces and it is part of his functions to determine the extent to which he can control and direct them. This approach is largely mental.

The mystic, however, mainly works from the emotional level and his life is charac-

201

terised by a deep and sincere aspiration towards contact with some vague concept of Deity, which he may name the Father, God, the Christ, Buddha, the Beloved or any other name, signifying a hungering of the soul for synthesis with the spiritual, the Monad.

The mystic way is as a rule the first approach to esotericism, leading the aspirant to the 'first initiation'. Having attained this initial milestone, mysticism is then renounced and the attention becomes focussed on the 'lighted way' of esotericism, which will inevitably lead the disciple to the higher states of consciousness and therefore to greater Light.

Aspirants with a highly developed mystical consciousness are often inclined to resent the mental and even technical considerations of the esotericist, whose approach is most-ly stripped of emotionalism. The mystic senses something of the truth but is not inter-ested in having these truths intellectually presented and clearly defined. There is, how-ever, no reason whatsoever why a clearer definition of all that is encompassed by the truth should in any way detract from the beauty and grandeur of that which becomes revealed on the higher planes by esoteric means. On the contrary, these 'discoveries' should pro-vide a deeper awareness of the majesty of all that is included in the concept of Deity. The recognition of the existence of ever greater mysteries and the comparative insignificance of human capacities can merely increase humility, with a corresponding deference for those exalted aspects of Divinity which are gradually revealed to the mind's eye.

It should also be recognised that opposition to the esoteric approach is often engen-dered by mental laziness – a form of mystical inertia. It demands far less mental exertion to express one's aspiration and love to God by various forms of devotional ritual, than by a careful mental analysis of all the facts at the disciple's disposal, supported by studies that will lead to deeper penetration and understanding of the arcana of the subjective worlds.

The esotericist should at the same time be on his guard that his approach should not become so objective that he loses contact with or suppresses his natural '*mystical percep-tion*' – that quality inherent in every human being and indicative of the presence of the soul. It is a power that constantly urges each individual forward, striving for something lofty and undefined but which seems to remain beyond reach.

The Tibetan prophesies that the men of the Aquarian Age, now coming into incarna-tion, will be distinguished by a widespread recognition of this 'mystical perception'. This will lead to intuitive understanding of the nature of energies and a consequent rapid increase in spiritual development of the race.

The path of the esotericist is that of reason, intellect and knowledge and therefore of the head, in contrast to the path of the heart as expressed by the aspiration of the mys-tic. True understanding should therefore be the product and wise blending of intellect, love and devotion. Both the mystic and the esotericist should follow the balanced path of wisdom. The mystic will eventually find that his devotion must be guided by the intel-lect and this will lead him to the path of the esotericist. The latter will, however, also fail to achieve his goal without retaining or recovering his mystic sense.

Another way of expressing the above is to state that the esotericist is but a mystic who has lifted his functions from the emotional to the mental plane. Individuals exhibiting these qualities in their daily activities usually rise to the top of their professions, showing outstanding creative ability in their particular field of service; they also radiate personal magnetism and have the knack of gathering and uniting people under their influence. These are also the attributes which will qualify future world leaders.

I. 3. Esoteric Training

The basic aim of esoteric training is not so much to provide the student with knowledge but rather to train him in the use of energy and thought. A conglomeration of ill-assorted facts will be of relatively little help to him and will only lead to confusion.

During the early stages of esoteric study, it is important that the student should progressively grasp and assimilate the various aspects of truth which he is taught.

Before esoteric studies can really become effective, the mind and brain of the student, or his lower self, should become aware of the existence of the higher self – the Soul. It is only with soul stimulus that sufficient mental interest will be generated to provide the impetus for continued study and training. It is also soul incentive which will provide the persistence needed to overcome the many obstacles and reverses which will inevitably be encountered. These obstructions will serve the purpose of testing the aspirant as to his motives, strength of character and perseverance and those approaching these studies just as a pastime, out of curiosity or because of the fascination of the unknown, will soon lose interest and drop out, while those who are really soul inspired will finally persist.

Some people are under the impression that esoteric training consists of breathing exercises and certain forms of ritual, whereas these are merely incidentals; of far greater significance is effective thought and mind control. A purely intellectual investigation of the Ancient Wisdom might bring a glimmering of light but the purely mental approach will also end in a blind alley unless supported by the qualities of the soul. Therefore all intellectual study will remain of relatively little avail, unless earnest endeavours are made to apply the principles of the teachings to daily life.

The candidate can hardly be expected to achieve immediate mastery of the visualised ideals because, with complete accomplishment of the final objectives, perfection will have been achieved, thus obviating the need for further reincarnation. No, all that is expected of the aspirant is **right motive** and that he should sincerely apply himself to the **endeavour** to walk the Path towards the Light to the best of his ability. That he will at times wander off the track is only to be expected and such temporary failures need not upset the devoted student unduly, provided he has the courage to acknowledge his shortcomings and once again to apply himself to walking the narrow and difficult path. Such defaults should moreover provide the lessons to serve as warnings about the snags which may be expected and which should be avoided in future.

A great deal of unnecessary remorse is caused by the commonly held idea that there is only a single path leading to final salvation, from which none may deviate. This path is of course that specifically prescribed by the many religious sects, each being convinced that only their particular path represents the correct way! There *are* of course certain basic ethical standards of behaviour, such as norms of honesty, decency and attitudes towards our fellow men, to which every individual should conform to fit him for participating in communal life. These norms are, however, well known to the average civilised man. Awareness of these principles is in fact the first intimation that the soul is beginning to assert itself. For the rest, each individual must find his own path towards the common destiny and this path must be broken, cleared and paved by himself with the equipment at his disposal. There are no two individuals who have been furnished with exactly similar characteristics and capacities and consequently each man must use the tools and conditions at his disposal, in his own way and to best advantage. Provided man carefully attends to the dictates of his soul, he may rest assured that he will never swerve far from the prescribed path.

One of the principal objectives of esoteric training is to develop sensitive instruments which will be available to the Masters as suitable channels for the effective transmission of energies and forces, thoughts and ideas, to the rest of humanity. Such training is tedious, proceeds slowly and several lives will normally be required before the qualities of the disciple have been sufficiently developed for him to serve as a proficient instrument in the hands of a Master.

The student is reminded that all such training will follow a cyclic pattern of ebb and flow – periods of intense activity and spiritual experience, being inevitably followed by periods of inactivity and relative quiet. These alternations are but demonstrations of the Law of Periodicity and students should always be prepared for these rhythmic pulsations of life. This law does not only apply to the human being but to all manifestations. The student should regard these cyclic periods of rest and apparent dormancy as periods which will be succeeded by spurts of even greater effort on the task which lies ahead, leading to ever greater achievement. Particular attention is drawn to these fluctuating periods, because students are apt to become discouraged when stages of lower activity set in and performance does not achieve the expected objective.

Aspirants who have decided to walk the esoteric path should ensure that their motives are unselfish. In the early stages it is only to be expected that the aspirant will be motivated by self-improvement but he should soon realise that such self-improvement can only be justified if supported by altruistic objectives. If the striving towards improvement should only be for personal gain, then it is at fault and might readily deteriorate to evil. The urge towards improvement should therefore be solely motivated by a striving to become a better equipped instrument in the hands of the Masters for serving humanity and fulfilling the Plan.

Those who feel inclined to enter the path of esoteric training should carefully weigh the cost. Final rewards will be considerable but heavy demands will be made on the aspirant. It is oft a lonely path, obstructed by many unexpected and obscure dangers which the struggler will have to overcome by his own efforts. For a long time there may also be no apparent rewards, until eventually, with expanding consciousness, the aspirant becomes aware of the more exalted objectives which he is achieving.

In olden days esoteric training could only be accomplished by direct instruction under the supervision of a living Master or at least a senior initiate. The past century has, however, been marked by notable changes in this respect and today, with the available literature, a distinctive reorientation is taking place with regard to procedures that are being followed. The approach of aspirants has become of a less devotional nature and intelligence and mental analysis is playing an increasingly important role. Considerable progress can now be made by students working all alone and without any *apparent* outside help. Under such circumstances the chances of successful training will, however, be improved by joining efforts with other seekers after truth and then working together as a group. Where at all practicable such group work is always recommended since the combined invocative appeal from such a group must obviously be much more effective than the outgoing energy from an individual and it stands to reason that the energies evoked by the group should also be commensurate. Group work will also complement individual effort and will thus lead to better results. Another advantage of group training is that the members learn greater adaptability, tolerance and mutual consideration, thus promoting collaboration and group effectiveness.

All dedicated training, whether undertaken alone or as a group, will eventually, after achieving progress, lead to contact with a Master, who will then take the disciple under his wing for more advanced work. Such contact may take place during the hours of sleep, leaving the aspirant consciously unaware of the help accorded; such support may nonetheless be most effective. The Master's interest is not primarily in the disciple's personal progress but he recognises those who are motivated by selfless service and who therefore provide potential material for shaping into instruments for ultimate service on higher levels. The Master's real objective is therefore preparing disciples for progressive initiation, thus qualifying them for more responsible duties and eventual incorporation into the ranks of the Masters.

I. 4. **The Tibetan's Teachings**

Djwhal Khul's teachings cover such a wide field that it is impossible to do justice to their scope by trying to describe their range in a few brief paragraphs. Actually this whole treatise is based on his work but nonetheless represents only a rather superficial survey of his ideas, omitting much of his more profound but oft abstruse concepts. To become better acquainted with the esoteric truths taught by the Tibetan, the only way open to the dedicated student is to turn to a personal study of the original books.

Broadly speaking he had two main objectives:

First: To explain the need for certain great fusions, including:

(a) Those fusions in man's nature which lead to the emergence of what is esoterically known as the 'personality' – that is the integration of the physical, emotional and mental manifestations of man, producing a powerful, self-controlled human being, which can be more effectively subjected to soul control.
(b) The next step is the fusion of personality and soul, which will entail that the personality subjects itself consciously and willingly to the dictates of the soul. The inner Christ-consciousness now becoming apparent.
(c) Several more integrations will eventually lead to the present great objective for humanity – the externalisation of the Hierarchy, under the leadership of the Christ and its ultimate fusion with humanity and consummation in the Kingdom of God on Earth.

Second: Instilling certain procedures in the human consciousness, whereby man's qualities will be affected and which will bring about the new relationships required for the designed fusions. These will then lead to the appearance of new cultures and civilisations and eventually to the anticipated Divine Kingdom.

There are some further outstanding aspects emerging from D.K.'s teachings, which should perhaps be stressed:

1. The existence of the *Hierarchy of Masters*, with the Christ as Master of all Masters. The Hierarchy is in close touch with humanity and all its activities, forming the link between Humanity and Shamballa, the seat of the Lord of the World.
2. The existence on Earth of the *New Group of World Servers*. The members of this group, already closely united on the subjective front, are mostly unknown to each other on the physical plane. This group is constituted of all those individuals motivated by goodwill and love and working for better human relations. Although many of them may not yet be consciously aware of their group functions and the role they are playing, each in his own way is contributing towards the redemption of humanity. As a group they are already the effective intermediaries between Humanity and the Spiritual Hierarchy and this function will progressively become more significant.
3. The rapidly approaching time for the *Reappearance of the Christ*, when he will probably again walk amongst the sons of men in physical manifestation. This time his advent will be marked by the presence of some of his senior disciples or Masters, who will accompany him to assist with the arduous task of promoting love and understan-

ding throughout the world. D.K. stresses that humanity must first be prepared for this reappearance, which will have to be delayed until the spate of hate, greed, envy, revenge and selfish desire has been somewhat dissipated and transmuted into goodwill. This preparatory work is the function of the New Group of World Servers.

Another point with regard to the 'Reappearance' to which D.K. draws attention, may seem of minor concern but can in fact not be over-emphasised. People love the idea of a *World Saviour* by whom they may be saved without self exertion – they are, however, under a misapprehension and that is why the preaching about the symbolic death of the Christ on the cross has in so many respects remained ineffective. The accent should be on the Christ as the *World Teacher* and it is primarily in this capacity that his coming should be seen. It is only *through their own efforts that men can be saved* and the final responsibility therefore rests on their own shoulders and will depend on their response to the Christ's teachings of the past and the supplementary precepts now being provided by the Tibetan. Man's reactions are, however, guided by his own free will and the benefits derived from the furnished opportunities will therefore solely depend on himself – his ultimate saviour must be his own Soul.

'THE OLD COMMENTARY'

In his writings the Tibetan quite often refers to or gives extracts from the 'Old Commentary'. The origin of this ancient text book of the Sages fades into the dim and unknown past but it forms part of the 'etheric library' of the Adepts and is one of their principal sources of knowledge and wisdom. As a point of interest, it could be explained that these old records are not books in the ordinary sense, containing printed words – which are but symbols which man has devised for expressing certain meanings. Instead of printed letters or words, these scriptures are pictorially illustrated and these illustrations then convey to the initiated the embodied ideas. They are therefore not read in the conventional way but the meaning of a complicated subject will be instantly disclosed to the Adept merely by looking at one of these ancient pictures.

I. 5. Esoteric Teachings

The world is at present being flooded with a spate of esoteric, semi-esoteric and devotional literature, in the form of books, magazines and papers of many qualities and originating from all kinds of sources. There are inspired or pseudo-inspired writings, telepathic dictations and psychic communications of varying quality; there are products of students and thinkers, mainly with an intellectual approach; there are the many communications from religious spheres of influence, varying from rational and carefully considered themes by mentally oriented theologians, to purely devotional writings by those who hope to arouse the spiritual sense of the masses through emotion, often supported by the spectre of fear. Some of these writings are of the highest order and obviously the inspired work of advanced disciples; these are of considerable spiritual value, contributing towards spreading subjective teachings to the evolving masses. Simultaneously a great deal of literature is also published, which appears to be of only a mediocre and ineffective nature.

All these communications, of whatever description, are a clear indication of a worldwide spiritual awakening and a general need and search for Truth. One disadvantage of these profuse publications, each with its own concepts, ideas and ways of approach, is that they are inclined to be confusing to the earnest seeker. In this respect the 'faithful' members of religious sects and institutions who limit their devotional reading (and thinking!) to some prescribed literature, are relatively better off, because they have accepted certain dogmatic teachings which may never be questioned. Where this attitude fails, is that it must inevitably also limit vision, expansion of consciousness and consequently spiritual growth.

These teachings, in their diversity, have all arisen from the One Source and are all derivatives of the One Truth, which in its immensity is, however, far beyond the limited understanding of the minds of men. What the individual considers to be the Truth is but a facsimile or distorted version of the Universal Truth, which in descending through many stations and channels, is already badly distorted by the time it is ultimately registered in the mind of man. It is for this reason that each individual has his own version of the truth and it is in these many divergent interpretations that the source must be sought for so much of the existing discord between men. If people could but learn to be more tolerant, allowing each man to entertain his own convictions in accordance with his particular stage of unfoldment and the circumstances determining his existence. Furthermore, man's interpretation of the Truth will constantly remain subject to adjustment in accordance with his ever developing mind, which will be expanded by the absorption of increased knowledge and the gaining of fresh life experiences. Thus ever new facets of the Truth will be revealed to the evolving individual.

So often students are concerned about the actual source of teachings, with differences of opinion readily leading to discord. It should be recognised that the supposed source is relatively unimportant but that it is the content and quality of the teachings which is of real moment. What does the identity of the teacher really matter? – he is in any case but the channel for such teachings. It is the purity and quality of that which is being taught which matters and for a verdict of this one can only rely on the intuition, the faculty of the soul. Teachings which will suit the needs of one individual may prove totally inadequate or unsuitable for the next, depending on stage of development, environment, circumstances and Ray influences. The sole criterion should remain the teaching and not the teacher and let the soul be the ultimate judge.

It should also be remembered that the quality of teaching evoked by a student, and even more so by a group of aspirants, will be commensurate with their aspiration or invocation. The attitude should, however, always be assumed that teachings are not provided for personal benefit but to equip the recipient for better service. When all efforts are thus dedicated to altruistic service, then the soul will gain an ever increasing hold over its instrument and these endeavours *must* and *will* inevitably evoke personal growth and expansion of consciousness.

The ideal attitude of the teacher is that of the onlooker. He should acquire that inner detachment through which life may be seen in true perspective, undistorted by surrounding happenings. He should not allow himself to be disturbed by events on the physical and emotional planes, allowing the mind to become a perfect reflector of the truth. When the vehicles of perception have become serene, the truth will be perceived clearly and intuitively and may then be presented with a minimum of distortion.

Teaching is something that evolves from stage to stage. Esotericists cannot develop from within themselves the thoughts that will lead to deeper recognitions of the truth – these ideas are inspired by entities from higher levels. Our Guides in their turn must receive their concepts from still higher sources and thus the ladder of knowledge reaches ever higher – from man to the hierarchical Adepts and then onward to include our Planetary Logos, next to the outer spheres of the Solar Logos, then on to Cosmic Sources and eventually to the Ultimate Source. Teachings which today may be regarded as highly selective by those responsible for educating the race, will tomorrow be assimilated into the instructions and articles of faith of their successors, eventually to be incorporated in the religious beliefs of the masses. As these truths are brought down to ever lower levels of comprehension, they necessarily have to be simplified and adapted to make them acceptable to lower degrees of intelligence and thus they must also lose in clarity, quality and potency. This deterioration will be further accentuated by the fact that teachings have to be translated into many languages or presented in symbolic form.

I. 6. Ritual and Ceremony

Ritual is the process whereby the attractive and expressive qualities of energies may be organised and related and whereby their action is canalised and directed to become more potent and effective. In practice ritual is but the imposition of a regular form of rhythm to a specific procedure.

Every form of manifestation, whether on Earth or anywhere else in the surrounding cosmos, is based on energy and as energy constantly moves, vibrates, vivifies, acts and interacts in an unremitting series of rhythmic waves, all of creation remains correspondingly subject to the rhythms of nature and therefore to some form of ritual. All of Earth's existence is typified by great ritual processes: the rising and setting of the sun; the coming and going of the seasons; the waxing and waning of the moon; the ebb and flow of the tides of the oceans. If other life processes are carefully considered, it will be found that both individual and communal activities similarly conform to ritual of some nature; there are man's heartbeats and his breathing, his alternating periods of waking and sleeping, of work and rest, of birth, death and rebirth. All organised society is also based on the regimentation of time and action – time is divided into years, months, weeks, days and hours and man's actions are largely scheduled to conform to more or less ritualistic programs and therefore to ceremonial living. This ritualistic existence is mainly performed unconsciously and even instinctively, constituting part of the blending disciplines of life.

Psychology, the science of human reactions, which is so rapidly gaining pre-eminence, could well be described as the science of rituals and rhythms – or the study of the effects of the disturbance of these rhythms. The motivating forces disturbing rhythmic impulses may originate either from the self, from the environment or from circumstances. They then impinge upon and influence the regulated actions and reactions of the physical, emotional and mental bodies, which constitute the mechanism through which the soul has to function and may therefore be seen as the direct cause of the many disorders to which the human system is so apt to be subjected.

When rhythm is applied to the life of an individual, it is known as discipline. Where groups of all kinds have to perform communal functions, whether of a religious, military or any other nature, the only way to prevent chaotic conditions and to ensure unified and orderly conduct, is to organise such a group by the simultaneous and rhythmic performance of prearranged activities or ceremonies, whether vocal or of some other nature. Ceremonial procedure to ensure uniformity of action therefore remains essential to all kinds of group work. Instances occur, however, where older, traditional institutions still practice certain physical rituals and ceremonies, sometimes attended by great pomp and the glitter of paraphernalia but where the meaning or purpose of such ritual is unrealised and often has been entirely lost. Under such circumstances the ritual has grown obsolete and is merely burlesque, perhaps only serving to provide a sense of drama to impress the masses.

There are forms of ceremonial ritual which contribute to harnessing planetary forces to the service of the race. They may for instance be the means of directing the energies which favourably influence the work of the deva world, the builders of matter. The lower forms of these devas largely function unconsciously but can definitely be guided to fulfil required work by subjecting them to suitable forms of ritual. It must be considered as part of the functions of the trained esotericist to harness natural energies whenever possible by the judicious application of ritual processes, if he can thereby serve to thin or tear away the obstructing etheric veil hiding the subjective realms from the eyes of men.

I. 7. **Breathing Exercises**

Breathing exercises may have vital effects upon the physical body as a result of the oxygenation of the blood stream but their real potency and subtlety lies in the exercising of thought control during the acts of prescribed breathing. It is a method whereby energy may be controlled and utilised for the expansion of consciousness and for establishing desired relationships between man and his environment.

The purpose of this brief study is mainly to warn unwary disciples not to dabble with forces and systems which are relatively unknown to them. Breathing exercises may without doubt lead to striking results if correctly prescribed and implemented, regularly performed and undertaken with a spirit of idealism. As with the generation of all esoteric forces, required results may be produced under controlled conditions and may be utilised either for good or bad, depending on the motivation. If through ignorance, incompetence or inadequacy, forces should however be released without proper control, then the individual concerned is looking for serious trouble, irrespective of how admirable his original motives might have been.

Under the circumstances aspirants wishing to expand their subjective consciousness or sensitivity, are advised to forget all about breathing exercises and rather to proceed with the acknowledged and normal methods of dedicated study, loving service and meditation, to achieve these objectives. If these methods are faithfully pursued, the student will in due course be led to those circumstances and experiences which will be appropriate to his stage of unfoldment and which will be required to prepare him for his next step of progress. Every deserving aspirant may rest assured that he is never overlooked or forgotten by the subjective entities, that he is constantly kept under observation and that the requirements for the next step will be put in his way. The expedients which will be provided might be in the form of suitable material, resources or circumstances for the successful continuation of his studies; opportunities for special service may be created; or his footsteps might even be led towards direct contact with his designated Teacher. All that will be required from his side, will be the right motives and ideals and the exertion of his free will to provide the necessary effort, stamina and perseverance.

Too much irresponsible publicity has already been accorded to the 'science of breath' and many false claims have been made by those wishing to exploit the unready commercially. It has been found that emotional types and particularly women, are inclined to be victimised by so-called esoteric teachers who offer to communicate their accomplishments to enthusiastic but too gullible aspirants (at a price!). Each person must decide for himself what esoteric books or other literature he wishes or can afford to buy through normal trade channels but treat with misgiving any projects where esoteric knowledge has to be 'bought' from individuals or organisations! Profit making schemes are often camouflaged by membership subscriptions or by emotional extortion of contributions. From some source or another and sometimes most unexpectedly, esoteric knowledge will always be freely available to the correctly motivated aspirant and nobody will ever be retarded in his destined spiritual progress because he cannot afford to participate in some expensive course of study.

Courses on breathing instruction offered 'for sale' are fortunately mostly inaccurate and therefore fairly innocuous. In addition aspirants joining such courses will usually also lack the determination and persistence to make these exercises really effective and therefore potentially dangerous. There are also so-called esoteric groups who in order to surround themselves with an atmosphere of mystery or to keep their adherents occupied, may in their ignorance also impose inappropriate breathing exercises on their members. On the whole these injudicious practices are rather harmless but in principle they should definitely be discouraged.

The factor underlying the effectiveness of breathing exercises, is that the aspirant should be trained to direct the intent and purpose of thought – 'energy follows thought'. Unless the disciple clearly appreciates what he hopes to achieve, these practices will be a sheer waste of time and effort and may even prove dangerous. Effective results can only be produced when there is a close alliance between the breathing and the thoughts and this co-ordination must then be concluded by directing the thoughts towards their consummation by means of the spiritual Will. The purpose therefore is to control the etheric centres by the directed Will, using the organised rhythmic breath as its agent. Therefore when the disciple has some dominating idea or purpose in his mind, this is sent forth simultaneously with the breath and the Will towards its implementation.

When the disciple is truly motivated by idealism and when his studies, service and meditation have brought him to a stage where the right teacher will appear to guide him along his path, then the suitable breathing exercises will also be provided.

II

EDUCATION AND RELIGION

Because the study and consideration of religious concepts should form a significant part of all education, these two subjects are closely related and are being
dealt with in one chapter. Education is the more comprehensive subject, basically
including the science of all human relationships in its many ramifications and therefore also religion, which more specifically refers to man's relations with the spiritual
world – with Deity.

These themes, so vital to man, have led to the writing of sufficient books and treatis-
es to fill several libraries; it is therefore not intended to supplement these voluminous
records with a further exhaustive dissertation. An attempt will merely be made to consider briefly some of the salient points advocated by that outstanding pedagogue, psychologist, humanist, teacher and Sage – *Djwhal Khul*, the 'Tibetan'. It is realised that justice
cannot possibly be done in such a summarised review to the depth and comprehensive-
ness of his work but pointers can at least be given to some of the ideas and ideals that he
has been promoting in preparing mankind for the New Age which is already in genesis.

II. 1. EDUCATION

There are so many aspects of education, that within the scope of this discussion the spot-
light can only be briefly focussed on a few particular points of interest:

1. As a rule the concept of education is associated with children or young people and although the accent should primarily lie in this quarter, because of the need of preparing
them for life's experiences, the wise man will recognise that his education can never be
regarded as fully completed. *The deeper truths of life can in fact only be learned after
reaching maturity* and after gaining some measure of life experience based on earlier education. The endeavour should therefore be made to keep the mind viable and keen, even
though over the years a certain amount of deterioration in the physical vehicle might
become noticeable. Therefore, how fortunate the man who manages to keep on expan-

ding his consciousness right up to the end of his present spell in the material body and who can then pass over to the spiritual world with full retention of consciousness.

2. When considering the mass of knowledge and all the facts of life which every unfolding personality must step by step accumulate and then assimilate in his brain, one often marvels at the complexity and efficiency of that wonderful computer with which man has been equipped. All this knowledge is of great importance and will play a distinct role in his future development, provided always that all this information is considered with a sense of balance and that certain essential life values are retained.

One of the most fundamental principles which should be recognised, is surely the *value of the individual,* the fact that he forms an integral part of that one whole – Humanity – and the consequent responsibility which rests upon each individual to contribute his full share towards the promotion of *good relationships* within that overall community. And the fair share to be subscribed by the individual will not be calculated in accordance with the mathematical fraction which his life constitutes as a small part of the whole of humanity – no, his share of the responsibilities will be determined by and will increase in direct ratio to the amount of spiritual light with which he has been endowed.

3. In its broader aspects education might be considered as consisting of three steps:

First: The process of *acquiring facts* from all spheres of life, both past and present. The effectiveness of this procedure will be subject to several factors, of which some of the more significant are: The inborn intelligence of the individual and the efficiency of the computer with which he has been equipped; his natural inclinations as determined by the several 'Rays of Energy' to which his life is subjected; the setting in which destiny has placed him, such as the quality and sex of the vehicle which the soul has assumed, the nationality in which he has been born and the nature of his environment and circumstances. The candidate must then learn how to apply the information and knowledge that is gradually gathered, to maximum advantage under the circumstances where he finds himself.

Second: The process of gradually *transmuting the acquired knowledge to wisdom* and the persistent attempt to grasp and understand something of the meaning and nature of the subjective realms which are closely related to and support the outer facts and appearances. This implies the power to apply knowledge to produce sane and balanced living conditions and the development of intelligent techniques of conduct to qualify the candidate to occupy a suitable position in his community and to contribute his share towards promoting right human relations. This will also involve training for specialised activities, commensurate with his inborn and ruling qualities and tendencies.

Third: Effective education should lead to a sense of synthesis and of recognition of the bonds and relations stretching beyond family ties, to include the local community, then the nation and eventually encompassing world relationships and thus all of humanity. This training should begin by suitable preparation for parenthood and good citizenship but should not end before the pupil has been brought to an evaluation of the position and responsibilities he carries in relation to the rest of the world of men. This training would basically be psychological and should convey a reasonable understanding of man's own constitution and functioning and how this relationship stretches beyond the self, eventually becoming all-inclusive. He should also be made aware that the main causes of disharmony are based on selfishness, possessiveness, intolerance, separativeness and the lack of love. These objectionable qualities should first be eradicated in the pupil and this will then gradually lead to better relations between individuals and subsequently will follow a similar pattern with regard to group, national and international relations.

4. One of the first educational objectives should be to eliminate the **competitive spirit** and its substitution with a spirit of loving co-operation. Competition is definitely not a **sine qua non** for reaching high levels of attainment. What is needed is to surround the child with an atmosphere which will foster a sense of responsibility and which will set him free from the inhibitions generated by a perpetual sense of fear of life and which then becomes the stimulus for competition. These qualities of responsibility and goodwill will be encouraged by stressing a new approach in the child's education:

(a) Surrounding him with an **atmosphere of love and trust**, which will suppress the causes of timidity and will largely contribute to cast out fear. This love must be based on true and deep compassion and tenderness and not on emotional demonstrations. It should lead to courteous treatment of the child and the expectation of equal courtesy to others. Loving compassion and a true understanding of the difficulties and complexities produced by the necessary adaptations to daily circumstances and the demands of life, must inevitably bring forth the best that is in the child. Such reaction could be further stimulated by displaying sensitivity to a child's normal affectionate response.

(b) An **atmosphere of patience** will contribute considerably towards engendering the rudiments of responsibility. It will require patience but the parents and teachers should persist with the effort of increasingly shouldering the youngsters with small duties and responsibilities, thus making them aware of their fundamental usefulness in the community and inculcating self-confidence.

(c) For the developing child an **atmosphere of understanding** is absolutely essential. So often older people, by their negative approach, are apt to foster, even from very early years, a sense of wrong-doing with children. The emphasis is constantly laid on petty little things, which may be annoying but are not basically wrong. To the child they are, however, being blown up and represented out of all proportion. Psychologically this must have an adverse effect on the child's character, developing a warped sense of values and an attitude of defensive resistance towards its elders. Instead of a purely negative attitude, one should reason with a child, explaining relative values and the reasons for the state of affairs and the natural consequence of actions. In this way the elementary principles of the Law of Cause and Effect should also be introduced and it will be found that such explanations will inevitably evoke response and build self-respect, confidence and responsibility.

Many of the so-called wrong actions of a child are prompted by a thwarted, inquiring spirit or by an impulse to retaliate for that which the child, because of lack of understanding, regards as injustices. Other irresponsible reactions from the child may also be caused by an urge to attract attention or by frustration because of an inability to employ time correctly and usefully, either with play or with small responsibilities. It should also be recognised by the educator that the developing standards of children must inevitably be influenced by daily observing the evil which is constantly being perpetrated both in their direct surroundings as well as in the wider world. Quite often such evil is committed before their very eyes and in their own homes but if not, modern news media will quickly ensure that everybody is made aware of all that is unwholesome in the world. As a rule the same procedure is being followed in everyday conversation, the accent usually being put on that which is wrong and ugly, instead of focussing the attention on that which is good and uplifting. With lack of understanding, love and patience and with unreasonable demands being made on them, such children will be apt to become anti-social and uncooperative.

5. Every youngster should from an early age be taught the principles of *discipline* and that a certain measure of discipline in one's attitude towards others is an essential in any decent and law-abiding community, where the human and moral rights of fellow citizens must be respected. But of equal consequence for the building of character is that children should be taught the principles of self-discipline, that emotions and appetites should be controlled and that this could save them from considerable distress and misery in later life.

6. Education therefore consists in the training of youth to enable them to deal intelligently and sanely with their environment and the circumstances of life which they are bound to encounter and to be able to adapt themselves to the unexpected. It should equip them to play the role of *worthwhile citizens*, not only in their own community but also as subjects of their nation and as members of the greater human family.

7. In the New Age which man has entered, youth will increasingly be trained in the '*Art of Right Human Relations*' and the improving of social organisation. This does not imply changing the existing curriculum but rather the use of quite a different approach. It is man's objectives and motivations which must be redirected. The accent must be changed from self-interest to communal benefits, from competitive concerns to co-operation, from the needs of the individual to those of the group or nation and from individual effort to team or group work. To achieve this altered approach, it is essential that he must be made aware of the inner Self, recognising that it is the soul which is now taking charge and bringing a new outlook to the personality.

The child must be taught the value of apparent barriers on his way of progress and that these should be regarded as challenges and their overcoming as opportunities for better qualifying himself in service of fellow human beings. He must be taught that all life's problems will fade when approached with altruistic motives and with goodwill and loving understanding.

8. The principles of goodwill and right human relations must also be extended to include the development of the *creative ability* in every human being, according to temperament, natural talents, qualifications and capacities. This should cover all fields of human activity and thought, including both the arts and sciences. Man should be induced to contribute his share to all that is beautiful in the world or if his bent is more of a technical or scientific nature, then let him contribute something towards making the world a better place to live in by creating or producing something on the physical side that will be of common benefit. The main underlying principle is that man should be taught to relinquish the purely selfish attitude and to develop the altruistic outlook, which is a soul quality and therefore lies dormant in each and every man and only needs awakening.

9. What all the above really amounts to, is that *various soul qualities in man should be developed from as early an age as possible*. Many have not reached the stage where they can consciously be made aware of the existence and functioning of the soul, whilst others will readily accept this and will do their best to adapt their lives accordingly. The teaching of the constitution of man, definitely including a description of those most significant aspects, the *etheric body* and the *soul*, should form part of every educational curriculum and could be adapted to each required level of teaching. The next step should be to indicate the intrinsic position occupied by man and the purpose which he should fulfil in the general scheme or Plan of Life. Such education should awaken human interest, human potential and achievement. In other words sound subjective motives for living will be supplied, leading to spiritual idealism, which should contribute towards the transmutation of the present selfish pursuits for gain and possessions, for power and status, at all cost and without consideration of the fellow man.

Therefore train man to realise that *if he allows his soul to rule his daily activities, all will be well!*

II. 2. Religion

Religion refers to man's relationships with the subjective worlds; it concerns his invocative approach to Deity for guidance and support with his daily problems and the response evoked by these calls of distress.

217

In the above definition reference is made to man's appeal for assistance, because this is so typical of the human being – while his concerns are prospering, he is independent and well able to manage his own affairs without any outside help! But inevitably the day will dawn when matters no longer run smoothly and in accordance with human plans and schemes, particularly where such plans are aimed at selfish gain and aggrandisement. For each individual the time will come when everything and every circumstance will seem to fail him and will apparently turn against him; in desperation he will then realise that his own powers are inadequate to cope with circumstances and in anguish he will turn towards subjective sources for help. Fortunate those who under those circumstances know where to turn and are aware of the One Source which will unfailingly provide relief and soothing salve for the wounded heart.

The Ancient Wisdom teachings indicate the broad principles and laws underlying religion. They indicate man's relation to the Source and the way man should act and live to make contact with and to evoke the cooperative forces and energies emanating from On High, instead of trying to be self-sufficient and to negate all subjective relationships. If man could only gain a fairly clear concept of his position as a minute link in the greater Whole, then he would soon recognise the physical impossibility of a selfish, separative existence. Such an attitude may be maintained for a shorter or longer while, yielding perhaps great material success but if this is achieved at the sacrifice of spiritual life, then it is doomed to failure as far as attainment of joy and happiness is concerned. How often is it not seen that power and riches go hand in hand with the utmost misery and disenchantment – how people have acquired possessions but in the process have lost their souls. How true that old adage that happiness cannot be bought with money! No, joy is something intangible and of the spirit and can only be earned when activated by the soul!

The Ageless Wisdom must, however, not be regarded as a religion. It is but a philosophy, a search for Truth, an analytic study and consideration of the underlying forces affecting and controlling the life of man and relating him to his environment and to the rest of the Universe. All religions are based on the same fundamental concepts as the Ancient Wisdom but instead of allowing man's unfolding mind free play in its ever expanding search for Truth, religious leaders and theologians have been trying to limit the thought-life of their members to dogmatic and fossilised doctrines. Notwithstanding constantly changing world conditions and human relationships, notwithstanding ever growing mental development of individuals, groups and nations, the theologians are desperately clinging to tenets, conventions and practices which were instituted centuries ago when circumstances, human relations and especially human concepts, were in many respects so totally different from what they are today.

Basic truths of course remain immutable but as already pointed out, what man considers to be the truth are but facets and human versions of the greater divine verities, which are beyond human conception. Therefore, although the basic nature of these truths will forever remain unaltered, their human interpretations will definitely be subject to different rendering and expression and will therefore have to be adapted from time to time to changing human circumstances and outlook and in some instances undoubtedly also to more profound discernment.

By laying down dogmatic tenets to which members of a religion are supposed to abide, the religious leaders are attempting to limit free and objective thinking and discrimination and thus to lead their flock along a narrow track which they seem to consider the only right way. But in practice there are actually hundreds of different sects and religions in existence, each disposing over the 'one and only correct way to salvation'. These leaders in their ignorance largely succeed not only in limiting both the mental and spiritual development of their members but also their own. The trouble is that to a large extent they are parrot-like repeating prescribed doctrines, instead of thinking out these problems for themselves. One is involuntarily left with the impression that many of these theologians are afraid to think or afraid to carry their arguments to a logical conclusion, as such deductions might conflict with their tenets and might lead to doubt and uncertainty and an undermining of their established beliefs.

The logical conclusion is that there cannot possibly be only one absolute way to salvation. Neither will there be only several hundred ways as prescribed by as many religions or sects. No! – there are billions of paths leading to the mountain top – in fact as many paths as there are struggling human souls, because each individual soul must find his own way back to the Father's house, each according to his own characteristics, circumstances and stage of development and as stimulated by the many varying motives and forces, either driving men forward or retarding them on their long and difficult way to the ultimate Destination. But one fact should be clearly understood – none of these paths are easily followed; all are narrow, arduous and full of obstructions; some of the pilgrims allow their attention to be diverted and instead of following the shortest route available under the circumstances, they will first wander off exploring some by-paths, thus losing time before they continue their upward struggle. Others again are still half asleep and with myopic vision blunder into obstructions, thus hurting themselves badly until they have learned their lessons and with clearer vision succeed in surmounting obstacles and by-passing pitfalls.

All these paths, even though they may vary in route and detail, will nevertheless lead to the One Destination, the One God. The inherent sense of divinity present in every human heart, must ultimately lead each individual soul to synthesis with the ONE.

The great religions of the past have been founded on the teachings imparted by some outstanding spiritual personality or Teacher who, centuries ago, appeared to a particular race or region. The influence of these Lives and their words have persisted, although often badly distorted, in the religions which have developed around their original precepts. These Teachers were all delegated from On High to give spiritual guidance and aid to races of men occupying particular regions during specific ages. Their virginal teachings were clothed in language and symbol suited to the understanding and circumstances of the people of that age. In later years many of the original teachings were adapted by religious leaders to conform to their own concepts, often with the purpose of securing power over their community or else to maintain such influence.

Whether a man today belongs to one religion or another, is largely determined by the family, community or religion into which he was born. Basically these various religions differ relatively little from each other and existing differences are mainly man-made, concerning non-essential human interpretations of the Truth, of various dogmas or of ceremonial rituals, which are all of human origin.

II. 2 (a) Churches, Theology and Dogma

The world is passing through a temporary state of chaos in many respects but also in particular as far as the various churches, their religious dogma and theological doctrines are concerned. Men, and especially the younger generations, are coming into revolt against the traditional power, authority and domination which some of these institutions have been wielding for centuries. Systems of scientific investigation, analysis, comparison and deduction are taking root in the minds of men and are being applied to all fields of thought and therefore also to religion. The result is that men are beginning to question and to reject the traditional authority of these old institutions. There is a gradual awakening of the awareness of the soul and its powers and, combined with a more mental approach, this is leading to a disowning and supplanting of the power of the churches.

The origin and history of religions and the foundation of their doctrines is being investigated anew and many of the old established conceptions as to the nature of man, his destiny and his soul, as well as of the nature of Divinity, are being reconsidered and even rejected. This leads to endless disputes, confusion and uncertainty and new schools of thought are consequently arising by the day. Out of all this melodrama little that is new has however developed.

From this medley of thoughts, ideas, ideals, speculations and theories, sprouting from the many youth movements, schools of thought, churches, religions and sects, two main lines of thought may, however, be formulated:

Firstly, there are those clinging to their *traditional religion* in its many forms and who do not want to see any changes effected. They usually belong to the older generation and prefer obedience to ancient recognised theological or religious authority, rather than obedience to the guidance of a consciously recognised soul. This group is often distinguished by their devotional attitude, which may take on fanatic proportions, spurred by intolerance. Their strict consciences are sometimes distorted, being biased by dogmatic concepts and not by logical reasoning by an enlightened mind. The divine intelligence with which they have been endowed is neglected – this may be applied to every other phase of God-given life but not to their religion. These traditionalists are therefore paragons of fossilisation in the field of religion and, being unable to adapt themselves to the progressively unfolding world of new ideas, new vision and *spiritual development*, the standpoints they entertain, in common with their churches and institutions, are doomed to extinction and must inevitably disappear from future active religious participation.

Secondly, there is a small embryonic *group of esotericists* which as yet only forms a small minority but which is rapidly growing to larger dimensions. This group however, is not composed of those who have revolted against the religious establishment; many of these are only unruly youths who are rebelling against authority and tradition and often have nothing substantial in mind which they would substitute for that which they are breaking down. These rebels, however, also include mystics, idealists and potential thinkers, who eventually, after reaching intellectual maturity, will regain their balance and may then swell the ranks of the second group.

Those who really constitute the second group are deeply spiritually orientated and might be called *intellectual mystics*, because their devotion is mentally focussed and not purely emotionally guided. Their approach to religion is through the mind and is carefully and deeply considered. They do not belong to any organised group or nation or to any race, colour or creed – their only bond is that they speak the same spiritual language. They recognise each other by having the same thoughtlife, entertaining the same nucleus of beliefs, without these being dogmatically circumscribed and rejecting the same non-essentials. They also recognise the role played by historical spiritual leaders of the world, together with the Scriptures arising from these teachings, which have largely been responsible for shaping the world pattern of spiritual beliefs.

This small group may be regarded as members of the Church Universal and they are building the subjective background, the spiritual nucleus of the coming *New World Religion*, which will finally encompass the peoples of the whole world into a single spiritual unit.

Today a common cry of distress is reverberating through the religious world, to the effect that man is turning away from the churches. This is so but not because of a lack of spiritual awareness – on the contrary there is a very meaningful spiritual awakening throughout the world, with an urgent searching for Truth, and man has never before been so spiritually inclined and in need of spiritual values, revaluations and recognitions. Men are searching for Light but where to find it? Orthodox churches with their leaders certainly do not provide the wherewithal; they are either limited by their narrow theological interpretations of the Scriptures, which the masses are no longer prepared to accept or they go to the other extreme and are inclined to be too materially or politically oriented.

In the past all religions, including Buddhism, Hinduism, Islam and Christianity, have produced outstanding minds, thinkers and leaders, who have in all sincerity formulated their ideas as to God and the meaning of the Scriptures into doctrines and these have in the course of time been dogmatically accepted by the religious and foisted on to the unthinking and ignorant masses. But the younger generations have had enough of this procedure; the stage has been reached where they are no longer satisfied with prescriptions dictating what they should believe or disbelieve – they want to reason things out for themselves and reach their own conclusions. They want freedom in all respects but most of all *freedom of mind*.

These explorers of the New Age want to be supplied with the basic facts and truths as far as these may be available but then it must be left to them to decide which of these truths, facts, ideas or views they may find acceptable. It will then be for them to incorporate in their creeds what their reason or intuition allows them to believe, either tentatively or absolutely and then to draw their own conclusions and reach their final decisions. Provided these searchers are honestly and sincerely motivated, their spiritual unfoldment is assured and will take its due course. Man can never be saved by theological tenets but only by awakening and expanding the Christ-consciousness in the heart.

Attention has been drawn to the limiting and retarding effect that the narrow outlook of many churchmen exerts on the spiritual development of their flocks. At the same time it should be pointed out, however, that these church servers are mostly well meaning and spiritual men, who are working to their best ability and in accordance with the light at their disposal but that in the ministry of their ecclesiastic duties they have been propagating dogmatic tenets, instead of allowing themselves to be pure channels for expressing the immanent Christ spirit by which they should be controlled. If these preachers could only become men of God in the true sense, rather than church-men, and allow the immanent God to speak from their soul-infused minds, then all would be well and they would then become the true spiritual leaders of the future. These same men would then realise that there is only One Religion and only One Church – God's Church – and that the same God works through the many faiths, the many races and colours of mankind and the many religious agencies and that the fullness of the Truth will only be realised through the final synthesis of all these into the Universal Church and the One World Religion.

II. 2 (b) The New World Religion

All nations, with their many religions, have one bond in common and that is their belief in a Supreme Being. This Deity is designated by many names and venerated by many different ceremonies and rituals, without the masses being aware of the fact that in all these instances they are actually invoking the powers of the same Entity. Once the peoples of the Earth can arrive at the recognition that they have One Father in common, it will indicate the awakening realisation of the brotherhood of man and that we all form part of one great family, the One Humanity. Out of this recognition will then be born the One Church and the New World Religion, which will gradually emerge as a mutual tie to unite men with closer bonds.

This great objective of eventually gathering all peoples of the world into the one great Universal Church, is the task of the Masters Koot Hoomi and Morya, assisted by the Master Jesus.

The world is at present increasingly coming under the influence of the energies of the Seventh Ray of Ceremonial Law and Order and out of the present chaos the New Age is in actual process of being born. A new rhythm will gradually be imposed on the present disorganised condition of humanity and this will step by step lead to new social orders and relationships. These changes are now in active manifestation and are expressed on all fronts of human activity – social, economic, scientific, political and religious. It is out of the present religious turbulence that the New World Church is eventually going to evolve. These great changes must inevitably take time but will come sooner than is generally expected.

The devotional approach of the New Church will be mentally oriented and will largely rest on the scientific recognition of the subjective worlds and the appreciation of certain aspects of scientific ceremonial. Many members of the scientific world will prove to be disciples and even initiates on the Path of Light and the present scepticism will begin to fade away. The danger will then arise that the intellectual approach might become so overbearing, that the devotional and mystic aspects might be relegated too far into the background, thus allowing a temporary foothold to the Dark Forces. The development of such a condition, when foreseen, can however be guarded against.

Concepts of the Truth are ever evolving and can never come to a conclusion. Because of the intellectual and mental awakening of the past two centuries, a corresponding spiritual adaptation is now taking its natural course, with man incessantly searching for fresh interpretations of ancient spiritual principles. He is no longer satisfied to have prescribed to him what to believe or to reject. He is searching for new light on his path and he is going to find this light; he is becoming aware of his personal contact with his Father and that this can be achieved without the mediation and the authority of a church, the dogmatic creeds of a minister or some approved ritual. Once he has become conscious of his own soul, no imposed religion will in future be able to restrain his spiritual unfoldment. With the discovery of ancient but so far relatively hidden truths, the ordinary man can now make his own interpretations of the available knowledge, formulate his own ideas as to the nature of the subjective worlds and of Deity and arrive at his own conclusions as to his future attitude and procedure to be followed on his path of spiritual development.

The spiritually minded men of the future will largely be guided by these underlying attitudes towards religion and these men are now beginning to lay the first foundations of the New World Religion and the Universal Church. This New Age religion will not be founded on dogmatic doctrines but on a few simple principles, which may perhaps be summarised as:

(a) *Spiritual freedom* and therefore *freedom of thought*, each man having to work out his own salvation, in his own way, as guided by the direction of his own soul.

(b) *Spiritual love towards fellow man*, leading to universal *goodwill*, the *brotherhood of man* and *right human relationships*, expressed and demonstrated by *selfless sharing* and *mutual service*.

All religion will then be regarded as emanating from One single spiritual Source and this will gradually draw mankind together to be united in the One World Religion. Such a One Humanity will not imply a single homogeneous group in which all races have been physically, socially and politically amalgamated. On the contrary: the beauty of such a synthesised Humanity would lie in its variety and differentiation into the many races, colours, languages and cultures, with its varying customs but bound together by common religious principles and mutual understanding.

This New World Religion is not merely some imaginary fiction of a vague dream but is something which is *now* in actual process of taking shape! It is prophesied that as soon as man has finally prepared the way and is ready for it, another great *Revelation* is await-ing him. The nature of this coming Revelation is unknown and man can only seek to develop his intuitive perception and to live in expectation of the new Light to be revealed. Let him attempt to evince increased spiritual recognition and to become aware of the 'rain cloud of knowable things' perpetually hovering over humanity!

One aspect which will come to the fore in the New Age is the development of the brotherhood of man into a real and accepted fact. In the past so much has already been written and talked about this and so little has been achieved in practice. It is in fact as if relationships between nation and nation and race and race have even deteriorated and have gone from bad to worse. Regarded superficially, this is so. But man should not allow himself to be totally overwhelmed and blinded by all the noise, bluster and dust that is being raised by this fighting and struggling on the surface. It must be acknowledged that outer conditions are bad enough and certainly most disturbing and every attempt should therefore be made to calm down ruffled tempers and help these storms to abate, thus per-mitting increasing numbers to *see* what is happening underneath this disturbed surface, to *hear* those quiet but insistent and penetrating voices calling for attention and intuitive-ly to *feel* the vibrations of the new energies issuing forth from the ethers and coursing through every sphere of human life. The immanent and transcendent power of God, the Christ spirit which has so incessantly and insistently been invoked by spiritual men and groups throughout the world, is now having pronounced effect. The evoked energies of love, tolerance and goodwill, are being poured into the world of men, while increased and more permanent reactions are becoming apparent from day to day.

The tide has turned, the change towards a better and happier world has actually set in and no power of evil can any longer prevent the coming of the New World! Open your eyes and you will see this! Open your ears to the beautiful tones of goodwill systematical-ly penetrating the relationships between men and nations and robbing the harsh voices of hate of their erstwhile effectiveness and dominance! Can you not intuitively sense the beauty of that which is in process of being manifested and established and which is step by step leading to improved human relations and finally to the Kingdom of God on Earth? All these things are already there and it merely remains for the human being to become consciously aware of them, to accept, accentuate and reveal them by displaying them in one's own life and by helping to calm and silence the outer tumult of squabbling and fighting, by suppressing selfish and separative urges and tendencies and by contributing one's personal share of genuine goodwill.

These visions and promises of a new and beautiful existence for humanity, **must** inevitably be recognised. But nothing in life, even if predestined, can be acquired without it being deserved and although the above prospects will in due course be meted out to man, he nonetheless still has to earn all that he is to receive. Therefore the rate at which this New World will be realised and brought into living practice, lies entirely in the hands of man himself. It is for him to exert himself to the utmost to achieve the ideals designed by the inner self, the soul; if he is to sit back and relax, nothing constructive will occur and matters may even temporarily deteriorate, till he wakes up again and begins anew to strain and struggle forward and upward with inspired new force to the goal that has been set. This holds for the individual, the group and the race. In fact right at this moment each and every individual is surrounded by these energies which are ready to carry him onwards in the required direction and the only provision is that he must open himself and become receptive to these forces.

And how can this sensitivity and receptivity be acquired? ... By expressing loving goodwill to **all** and by promoting the common good to one's best ability under prevailing circumstances.

How this **service** to our fellow man is expressed is not of primary importance, neither whether it may seem insignificant, nor whether it is something that might draw public attention. The **nature** of the service will in fact depend on many factors and will be determined by the individual's capacities and characteristics, as well as by his environment and circumstances. What does matter, however, is the **motive** inspiring the action and whether such service is performed with a loving heart. Furthermore service is something more than just an act of momentary nature. To perform an act of service and then to sit back and smugly contemplate the sacrificial deed, will probably prove largely ineffective. No, the beauty of constructive service lies in the fact that it will merely prove a stimulant and therefore but a step to ever more effective and sustained service, in the end demanding the use of all the powers and capacities over which the server may dispose. What others may regard as a **sacrifice**, to him becomes a gift offered with sheer joy, because he gives, shares and serves with love springing from his heart!

A number of people from all over the world and from the many religions, are beginning to recognise that all these religions really emanate from the one great spiritual Source. They are becoming aware that all the hate and fighting over the ages, between man and man, group and group, nation and nation and worst of all, between religion and religion, has to some extent been founded on limited vision and understanding but mainly on such egotistical properties as self-righteousness, urge for power, envy and desire in its many forms. They are coming to the realisation that we all belong to the One Humanity and are worshipping the One Father.

Talking of a 'new world religion' is but a relative expression. Fundamentally the same age-old truths are being dealt with, the same Ancient Wisdom but with this difference that a *new approach* to these old verities will be followed. Some of these essential truths will be particularly accentuated:

1. *The Fact of God Immanent:* During past centuries the stress has been on God Transcendent, the Father in Heaven, who from his throne somewhere in outer spheres, has been ruling the destinies of man. Today it is increasingly recognised that each human being and every created form, is also pervaded by the immanent spirit of God.
2. *The Fact of Immortality and Eternal Persistence:* In the coming religion particular emphasis will be placed on the eternal life of the soul, that it progresses from life to life, experience to experience, revelation to revelation, on its Path of Evolution, unfolding steadily and displaying progressively the divine attributes which have been attained.
   Closely integrated with this principle of the unfolding soul, are of course the Laws of Rebirth and of Cause and Effect. In these coming teachings the accent will specifically fall on these important principles, emphasising that old but so readily forgotten truth, that man shall reap what he has sown.
   It is the innate divinity in the heart of every man, which constantly urges him towards betterment and towards that faint vision of which he may not at first be consciously aware. During the early stages his striving is purely instinctive but as time and lives go by, the vision clarifies and his striving becomes consciously directed and ever more purposeful.
3. *The Christ and the Hierarchy:* Until such time as the Christ will make his appearance on Earth, to walk again visibly among men, the fact will be emphasised that even though still invisible and moving in etheric spheres, the *living Christ* is nonetheless constantly and actually present with humanity and that his loving support can at all times be depended upon by those who need him. It will also be stressed that he stands at the head of a group of Adepts, the Hierarchy of Masters, who have all been through the trials of human existence on Earth and, through the experiences thus gained over the aeons, have evolved to their present position. It will furthermore be accentuated that one of the principal functions of this exalted group, headed by the Christ, is to guide those still subject to physical incarnation and glamoured by the astral world of illusion, to their higher destiny.
4. *The Brotherhood of Man:* And then it will be emphasised that all human beings are manifestations of small fractions of the Spiritual One, who have taken on physical form to gain experience on Earth. These experiences are apparently essential for eventual achievement of spiritual perfection. It should therefore be realised that all human beings are closely related brothers but brothers in different outer garb and each and every one finding himself at his own particular stage of development on the difficult

Path stretching before all. It will be stressed that life on Earth could be turned into something so much more beautiful, pleasant and bearable to all, if each individual would only contribute his small part towards sharing the amenities of life, showing greater tolerance and consideration in so many possible respects and a greater display of love and goodwill in daily associations and interrelations.

The world is at present being flooded by these new and potent energies and although the results are still somewhat obscured by the effects of well established older influences, such as selfish desire, greed and hate, the reactions resulting from the ever spreading and deeper penetrating energies of universal love and goodwill are becoming noticeable and these must and will eventually gain the upper hand, dominating all human relationships.

5. *The Divine Approaches:* One of the greatest truths, of which man in the past has been insufficiently aware, is the divine relationship between man, humanity as a whole and its Creator. In the Scriptures the presence of some vague transcendent God is described but so far religions have largely left the impression of a rather one-sided approach by cringing human beings imploring a stern God for his favours. Could it but be recognised that the position is in fact so totally different. There is only a God of Love, who entertains a loving interest in his children who are experiencing the physical phase of life on Earth. Once a deeper and more general consciousness is developed of the immanent God, of whom each individual is an integral part, then it will also be realised that there exists a reciprocal attraction and approach – that of the Father towards his children and of the children to the Father. It is for this reason that future religion will accentuate the invocative approach from man to divinity and the response which will consequently be evoked. Greater attention will therefore in future be given to the art or *Science of Invocation* and the powers which will thereby be evoked.

The vast possibilities of *Group Work* and the increased power which can be generated by concerted invocative activities, will be emphasised. This will lead to the observance of world-wide sacred festivals, when humanity as a whole will direct its united petition to God, thus inevitably evoking far more potent results.

The realisation of these visualised changes will take time and it stands to reason that mistakes will be made, causing delays, but meanwhile humanity has already set its feet on the Path towards its sanctified destination. Attainment of this ultimate goal can no longer be prevented by any adverse powers but the rapidity of accomplishing these ideals will depend on the consecration and persistence with which man is going to apply himself to this most demanding task.

III

Science, Economics And Politics

This book covers such a wide range of the field of life, that it is merely possible to allow the thoughts to skim lightly over the whole, only here and there touching some of the more salient facets, to indicate how the many features are all related and interrelated to form the intricate pattern which constitutes the beautifully organised Whole. When considering the following pages it should therefore be kept in mind that this study does not profess to deal authoritatively with any single subject but merely denotes the existing relationship between the component parts.

III. I. Science

All scientific work is in essence spiritual and although scientific workers and inventors will mostly be unaware of the fact, their work is inspired from subjective realms. Even though these workers may for the time being vigorously deny such spiritual contact, regarding their own intelligence as the true source of their creativity, these scientists, who in one form or another are manipulating the forces from the world of energies should in reality be recognised as true esotericists.

It is true that many scientists, being naturally rather self-confident and aware of their prowess, will be either contemptuous or indignant about such assertions. They do not yet realise that their scientific training has merely served to make them intellectually better qualified and more sensitive instruments for the perception and transmission of ideas with which they will be impressed or inspired from etheric spheres. Sometimes an individual scientist with special qualifications or working in a particular environment or under favourable circumstances, will be selected by the Masters for the revelation of some new scientific 'discovery' and the relative ideas will then be 'impressed' upon his mind as inspired thought.

At other times scientific ideas will be 'broadcast' into the ethers by the Entities concerned, thus making them accessible to the mental antennae of many scientists. This may then lead to the more or less simultaneous discovery of the same scientific principle by more than one scientist, working in localities often situated in widely separated parts of the world and who have had no conscious contact with each other. In such instances it may happen that although two scientists have contacted the same principle, their translation and understanding of the received impression will be so dissimilar, owing to differences in the quality of their instruments of reception, that by the time the ideas have been transposed into material form or words, they will hardly be recognisable as originating from the identical thought-form.

Although many scientists are spiritually guided and will primarily work for the benefit of humanity, there are also the exceptions. There are those who are solely interested in the financial potentialities of their intellectual product and how their ideas may be commercialised or even translated into power over the fortunes of their fellow men. Such an attitude might easily land such workers in the hands of the Dark Forces, with the result that inventions which were intended for beneficial purposes may at least temporarily be applied to man's detriment. A typical example of this is the discovery of nuclear power, with its wide range of possibilities for service to humanity but which, in contrast, was primarily used for strategic purposes and the destruction of man.

Generally speaking scientists in the past have entertained a very sceptical or even disdainful attitude towards all that is spiritual, because these subjective worlds contain so much that is invisible, intangible and immeasurable, and the existence of which can consequently not be 'proved scientifically'.

During the first half of the present century the Tibetan prophesied that a change in this scornful attitude was in the offing. This New Era has now dawned, **the tide has turned** and throughout the world a rapidly growing interest by science in subjective matters is becoming noticeable. There still remain many die-hards who, as might be expected, largely belong to the older generation, who rigidly resist, refusing to concede the existence of the etheric worlds. They strongly resent the 'unscientific views' of members of their fraternity who are moving away from the sound and well beaten track of the past.

One of the first break-throughs was the tentative interest which a few pioneers displayed in 'extra sensory perception' (ESP). For a considerable while there have also been somewhat vague and unconfirmed stories in circulation of individuals claiming to have photographed etheric bodies. At first these claims were mostly rejected, often even with contumely and accusations of deceit. But the practicability of such photography has subsequently been thoroughly tested and has now been proved beyond all argument. Better and more effective equipment for this purpose is now rapidly being developed.

The **spiritualist movement**, which has been active throughout the world for many years has, with its wide membership and consistent emphasis on the existence of the etheric, astral and spiritual worlds, been responsible for a notable contribution in preparing the general public for a more ready acceptance of the reality of these hidden worlds.

Exhaustive and scientifically controlled tests with regard to **telepathy** have further substantiated the existence of the etheric surround. Irrefutable evidence has now been established to confirm the existence of various forms of telepathic contact, which may be produced under many circumstances. Investigators have also determined that such telepathic contact is not limited to the human kingdom but is unconsciously or instinctively also registered by animals and even plants. As might be expected, the possibility of utilising telepathy for strategic purposes is also being investigated.

Scientists are therefore rapidly being convinced of the existence of the etheric and spiritual spheres but the problem is that the human being lacks the natural equipment and his sensitivity is still too undeveloped for registering these subjective worlds. One of the outstanding human characteristics is, however, the persistence displayed when once the mind has been provoked by certain challenges. Now that interest in these hidden spheres has been awakened, it may be safely predicted that resourcefulness (stimulated and supported by hierarchical impression of thoughts and ideas!) will soon devise the technical equipment for compensating the shortcomings of the human senses.

All this will probably result in a wide new field of scientific research, which must inevitably lead to a considerable broadening of the public outlook and a clearer recognition of the persistence of the human spirit and soul. This awareness, supported by scientific evidence must also lead to a better understanding between science and religion. This closer association will be further reinforced because the emotional and mystical orientation which characterised religious practice of the past, is now rapidly being superseded by a more sober and mental approach.

It is regrettable that the Dark Forces have also to be considered with these new developments. These powers will, however, do their utmost to misconstrue new findings and to sow distrust regarding the authenticity of results which may become available. It stands to reason that the forces of evil will use fair means and foul to promote their own negative purposes and to oppose beneficial effects which promise to accrue to humanity from these new fields of exploration.

Under the circumstances investigators should therefore keep a constant guard on the motives inspiring them towards this deeper probing. Should their objectives be altruistic and aimed at serving humanity, then both these workers themselves, as well as their fellow men will profit by these efforts. Should they, however, be motivated by selfish gain, then the results might lead to endless suffering for all.

In his writings D.K. has prophesied that in the New Age which man has now entered, a group of disciples will emerge whose efforts will lay the foundations for a new civilisation, which eventually will be characterised by *true freedom*. This will be an era when man will be relieved of the present day responsibilities of labour, allowing him the time to think freely, to establish new cultural interests and with the opportunity of unfolding his higher abstract mind. These changes will be brought about because scientific development will be of such a nature that all phases of man's physical needs will be furnished to such an extent by science, that present concepts of 'labour' will be practically abolished. This prophecy may now appear chimerical but with closer consideration and taking into account recent developments in electronics and automation, it no longer sounds quite so absurd!

III. 2. **Medical Science**

Academically and technically considered medical science with its diagnostic, surgical and other skills, is today far advanced. The knowledge of the human body and its reactions to both internal and external physical stimuli and disturbances, is outstanding. In one most important aspect medical science has so far unconsciously been badly handicapped. It has remained unaware of the existence of the etheric body, which forms the intangible framework on which the physical body is constructed and which therefore plays an important role in the maintenance of its health. No wonder that physicians, notwithstanding their extensive knowledge of the physical aspects, have in the past so often been sorely puzzled by inexplicable features of diseases and by the unaccountable reactions of their patients who for no explainable reasons might show either improvement or deterioration. Little did they realise that the real underlying cause for many complaints was to be found in the inharmonious condition of the etheric vehicle.

With the existence of the etheric body now becoming an accepted fact, medicine is standing on the verge of a totally new approach to disease and its treatment. As yet there are, however, only few who fully recognise the extent of the implications of this so-called 'electromagnetic field' and that it constitutes the mainstay of all physical existence, not only surrounding but also minutely interpenetrating and supporting the tangible body. Neither is it realised that the individual etheric body is but a small component of the overall etheric system, with which it is therefore intimately associated.

The pioneers in this new field of research, however, still need more corroborative evidence, not only for strengthening their own convictions but also to convince the rest of the medical profession of the important role played by this subtle body. It must be recognised that this electrical surround not only serves as the conductor of all incoming energies from external sources but also acts as the channel for the distribution of the forces which have been generated and transmuted within the personality complex and are being radiated to the environment.

Future medical science will therefore be largely concentrated on a study and better understanding of the etheric body and even more particularly of the etheric centres which it contains. As already pointed out in a previous section, there is a close relationship between the etheric centres and the endocrine system. The result is that the endocrinologist, when he becomes aware of the relationship between the etheric vehicle, the endocrine system and the blood stream, will also obtain a much clearer insight into many of his inexplicable problems of the past.

As far as the purely physical aspects are concerned, medical science is actually nearing the limits of what man can accomplish. But fortunately unfoldment and achievement are never ending and wonderful new vistas are now opening up before the healer of the future. He is now on the point of advancing on to a fresh terrain, which up to now has largely remained hidden to science. With the advent of greater light, illumining all spheres of human activity and with man's increasing perceptivity, the intangible realms will be opened up to him. This will prove of great advantage to medical science, allowing the dedicated and altruistic practitioner to draw closer to the world of causes.

All the efforts of medical science are today concentrated on prolonging the life in the form. The time is not far distant, however, when it will be realised that the form life is relatively of only secondary importance. Man's attitude will undergo a radical change when once it is recognised that the physical body is merely a channel through which the soul may gain certain experiences and is only its instrument of expression in the world of matter. Future medical science will therefore focus its main efforts on prevention of disease, thus keeping the instrument sound and efficient. Furthermore, when nature has run its course and when the soul has accomplished the task for which it came into incarnation, it demands liberation. This stage should be recognised by the healer and he should then know when to stand aside, leaving nature to fulfil its purpose without attempting to retain the life artificially in the form.

III. 2 (a) **Psychology**

The present century has seen the birth of the new science of Psychology, which is still essentially in its juvenile stage. Some profound thinkers have originated this field of thought, on the one hand through sound reasoning but mainly through intuitive recognition of the existence of some form of higher consciousness, which has been vaguely described in varying terms, by several schools of thought.

Psychology is rapidly gaining increased public attention but psychiatrists are still treading dangerous terrain. The presence of hidden forces controlling man's being is acknowledged but the knowledge of how to deal with these little known powers is still hopelessly inadequate, with the consequence that in their ignorance serious mistakes are being committed, often with harmful results to their patients. Mistakes of the past should, however, not be rated too heavily against this young profession, which is still largely groping in the dark – on the whole their motivation has been admirable and it is only their ignorance that has been to blame. The time has now, however, arrived for a new approach to be implemented.

The break-through effected during the past few decades, in which the existence of the etheric spheres has been brought pertinently to the attention of the scientific world, should be regarded as inaugurating the long expected New Era. The 'discovery' of these subjective worlds should provide psychologists with a totally revised perspective, opening up new fields of study and bringing past knowledge into new relation. Much which in the past was wrapped in obscurity, should now be clarified and seen in a new light. The facts about the existence of the etheric realms have actually been available for many years but this information was slighted and ignored by the men of science, because no 'scientific proofs' could be provided for substantiating these assertions. Fortunately conclusive proofs are now forthcoming and the sceptics are rapidly being convinced.

Merely to accept the facts about the etheric spheres is, however, of little direct benefit. The next step for the scientists concerned, should be to make a profound study of these new findings to determine their full implications and to what extent this knowledge of the subjective may be co-ordinated with existing material knowledge. For this new approach to the world of thought scientists are in the fortunate position that a suitable range of literature is already to hand for becoming acquainted with the subject. Among these the authoritative work of the Tibetan should take precedence. Even though investigators might be unwilling to accept all of D.K.'s teachings, these writings could at least serve as a most useful guide for practical investigation, which would mean the saving of valuable time.

Knowledge of the vital body and its close interrelation with the rest of the etheric world, is going to disclose vast new possibilities to the world of science and particularly to psychology. To appreciate the impact which a deeper awareness of the world of energies is going to have on future psychology, the relationship between the material, etheric and spiritual worlds must first be acknowledged and understood. These are the relationships which esoteric studies endeavour to clarify. It is of primary importance that psychologists should arrive at a better understanding of the nature and constitution of man, recognising that an imbalance in one of the composing bodies must inevitably be reflected in other directly or indirectly related parts. It will then be found that because the physical body is based on the vital body, the cause of physical complaints should in the first instance be sought in that subtle body. This will also apply particularly to mental disorders.

For the general well-being of man, psychology is the obvious science of the future, once it can be liberated from the many prejudices which restricted its early development. Psychologists will not be able to make real progress till the existence of the soul is definitely accepted and until they recognise the role it fulfils in co-ordinating spirit and matter. It must also be recognised that man's well-being will ultimately be determined by the extent of his soul contact and its consequent influence on the personality.

The psychologists of the future will become aware that their studies should be principally concerned with the control and direction of forces and energies and that the condition of the physical vehicle is primarily determined by the vitality of the seven energy centres found within the vital body. They will also find that the whole etheric system is controlled by the *Seven Rays of Energy* and that each individual reacts to his own particular set of five Rays, manifesting as his:

1. Soul Ray
2. Personality Ray
   (a) Mental Ray
   (b) Emotional Ray
   (c) Physical Ray

It is the combined effect of these five interacting Rays which will decide the character of each individual and his reaction towards his environment.

The dilemma of the psychologist is that he cannot arrive at a true understanding of man until he has become aware of and accepted the *Law of Rebirth*. This law pictures man as the product of a long preceding range of lives, filled with experiences of every possible nature, from which the soul has garnered the cumulative essence, to bring it to its present stage of development. Next there is the closely associated *Law of Cause and Effect (Karma)*, which decrees that each action inevitably results in a corresponding reaction or, as applied to man, that each individual will be rewarded or penalised in like measure for his deeds of the past. This balancing process must obviously exert a marked influence on his psychic and therefore also health condition and it will be the function of the psychologist to take the effect of these two Laws carefully into consideration before deciding on his treatment.

Once the psychological nature of many physical disturbances is acknowledged by the orthodox physician, the surgeon and the priest, who are all working for man's physical, psychic, mental and spiritual well-being, then they can all collaborate to promote the principles of '*preventive medicine*'.

III. 2 (b) Healing

Disease denotes an imbalance in the combined functions of the human system. With the exception of systemic disorders caused by wars and accidents or by virulent epidemics, whose origins are of a planetary nature and have been induced by defaults of humanity as a whole, all physical disturbances must first be sought in adverse influences emanating from the etheric centres. These vital focal points of energy influence the activity of the 'nadis', those minute links between the subjective and the material underlying the nervous system, which in turn affect the endocrine glands and the blood stream, all jointly regulating man's condition of health.

One of the principal healing techniques of the future will require that the healer should learn how to direct chosen energies towards specific objectives. He should thus learn to gain some measure of control on etheric levels, enabling him to heal physical disorders by influencing the supporting etheric structure.

Healing therefore need not primarily be of a physical nature. In most instances psychic restoration will automatically result in physical recovery.

The true esoteric healer will reach the stage where he becomes aware of the subjective condition of his patients. Through increased sensitivity he becomes subtly perceptive of the needs and conditions of his patient. When under such circumstances his reactions become automatic and intuitive, they will also be more reliable. The ideal healer should not depend solely on either his esoteric or his exoteric attributes. Basically he should be a qualified orthodox medical practitioner, with the scientific and technical knowledge of modern science at his disposal; but simultaneously he should also be a good psychologist, as well as a spiritual healer, knowing how to avail himself of the energies of the etheric world.

As the several qualifications mentioned above are rarely combined in a single individual, it will therefore be advisable for healers of different bent and training to combine their service efforts and to collaborate in groups in which physical, psychic and mental healers will be able to merge their efforts to the advantage of the patient. The aim should be to co-ordinate the following specialised functions:

(a) The orthodox and academic physician, endocrinologist and surgeon.
(b) Psychologists, neurologists and psychiatrists.
(c) Mental healers of various quality – often classified as 'New Thought' workers.
(d) Trained esoteric workers who endeavour to reach the souls of men.

It is predicted that the time will arrive when hospitals will be available where these various phases of medical treatment will be provided with perfect co-operation.

When considering the Seven Rays of Energy, both the Second and Seventh Rays are recognised 'healing Rays'; of these two it is the Second Ray which plays the most eminent role. It is for this reason that natural healers will as a rule be found to be Second Ray souls, although the success of their work will largely depend on their dedication in training themselves for the purpose. It is only by such consecration that natural aptitude will be brought to effective practical expression.

Every initiate automatically becomes a spiritual healer, because he is learning to direct energies – the underlying principle is that 'energy follows thought'. The more advanced he is, the less will he consciously concern himself with the intricacies of the centres and the direction of energies and forces; he will sense these intuitively and will learn to perform the correct functions automatically.

Although in the early stages expertness may be lacking, it may nevertheless be said that every individual who is prompted by the urge to serve, who has achieved effective mental control and who is inspired by an impersonal love of his fellow man, can in due course become a healer. Productive work will be enhanced by joining a healing group and gaining experience under the guidance of a qualified leader. In addition the joint efforts of a group must inevitably generate energies which should be considerably more potent than those available to single workers.

The work of a healer in the New Age will actually be much simpler than that of the present day physician. One essential for the healer is that he must be abundantly provided with the *Energy of Love*, which can be radiated to his patients. The potent healing qualities of Love Energy so often remain unrecognised and consequently neglected. The healer's approach and contact with the patient must therefore primarily be through love and goodwill, which will then act as a channel for further healing energies.

The future healer will require less detailed academic and technical knowledge, as his qualifications will be of a more fundamental nature. He will be concerned with energies and their points of distribution, the seven etheric centres and not so much with the physical details of the diseased organs. His functions will therefore be largely intuitive and soul inspired, rather than the product of academic training.

III. 3. Astrology

As with most of the other subjects that have been dealt with, an attempt will merely be made to explain briefly what the term 'astrology' embraces and how this theme is related to the Ageless Wisdom studies.

Astronomy is the inclusive study of all that relates to the heavenly bodies contained within the Universe. In recent years these studies have been extended considerably, because rapid strides have been made with the improvement of technical equipment. These have increased the sensitivity of human observation beyond all expectation and have permitted the discovery and registration of vast new regions in the infinite sidereal expanses. *Astrology* on the other hand is limited to a narrower but nonetheless most complicated field of study which concerns the influences exerted by the energies emanating from these celestial bodies. Astrology could therefore be regarded as only a subdivision of astronomy.

Many scientists hold astrology in contempt as being a fictitious instrument in the hands of fortune tellers. This attitude is typical of those who as yet have been deprived of closer contact with the esoteric approach. In some respects they demonstrate almost total ignorance of available facts and on the other hand misrepresentations are often made by the uninformed or, what is worse, by those who do know something of the subject but who for personal purposes use distorted versions for deluding the public.

Those who have already been introduced to esoteric principles, will realise that all celestial bodies are interrelated by constant streams of energy passing through the ethers and by whose action the quality and character of all manifestation is established – including the attributes of the personality aspects of the human being.

The one extra-terrestrial energy which man can readily observe and register, is that emanating from the Sun and which provides the Earth with light and heat. It is also generally accepted that the Moon radiates or reflects energies which exert magnetic and other influences on earthly forms. There are, however, always those who for some or other reason try to disparage these effects. But that the Earth as a whole and human beings in particular, are subject to potent energies issuing from other planets or constellations from beyond the boundaries of our solar system, is a concept which relatively few people have ever seriously considered and which many will question.

The problem is that so few realise that 'all is energy' and that all manifestation is in constant movement or vibration and that all existence is consistently influenced by the most bizarre complex of interrelated and interacting streams of energy, issuing from countless sources. Most of these energies, however, impinge on their objectives, including man, without conscious recognition of their presence and, because they are so imperceptible, their existence is oft disclaimed. Man does not realise that his whole being, his physical, emotional and mental reactions, his character and all his comings and goings, are determined by these energies and forces which are constantly acting on his personality and environment.

Although the 'primordial energy' originates from the Unfathomable, as far as man is concerned, it may be assumed that his primary sources of energy arise from the many stars, systems and constellations of the firmament. Very few are consciously aware of the fact that the human system is subjected to constant streams of energy which are directly or indirectly emerging from these celestial fountain-heads and that these energies incessantly affect all his being and doing. The Sun only represents one of these sources of energy.

Astrology is in fact one of the most ancient human sciences and if the profound knowledge exhibited by the ancients is studied without prejudice and with due consideration of the limited and primitive equipment at their disposal for observing the heavens, then one can only conclude that a considerable part of this knowledge could not have been derived from their own technical observations but must have been imparted to them from super-human sources. Whether this superior knowledge has subsequently been judiciously applied is of course a different matter.

Trained astrologers claim that when they are provided with the date of birth and preferably also the exact hour of an individual's birth, this date can be related to the planets, stars and constellations which were in the ascendant at that time and which are purported to influence the whole course of such a life. From this data diagrams and plans – known as '*horoscopes*' – are computed which profess to give an analysis of the individual's character and wherein the main events of his life are forecast.

In practice horoscopes have frequently proved quite accurate for the unevolved and in those instances where the soul is still dormant and not yet asserting itself. The horoscope may therefore present an effective picture of the destiny of the personality, but the soul, which is an expression of spirit, is not subject to these astrological influences and is guided by either free or divine will.

Therefore, as soon as the soul begins to awaken and to influence the unfolding spiritual life, the applicability of the horoscope will diminish correspondingly. As man develops he will therefore gradually lose interest in his personal horoscope, he will display less concern in his own expansion and increased interest will be generated in the universal picture, in the materialisation of the Plan and the role he should fulfil as an integral part of this greater whole.

III. 4. Spiritualism

The modern Spiritualist Movement was inspired by the Master Hilarion as a contribution towards stripping the veil still largely hiding the subjective worlds from the materially blinded vision of man. Through his disciples Master H. provided the energy for stimulating the development of Psychic Research groups in many parts of the world. He is also maintaining a watchful eye over the more advanced psychics, assisting them with the development of powers to be used on behalf of their groups and therefore to the advantage of humanity.

Although spiritualism is a movement that has been reawakened during the past century, it is a human interest which dates back to the time of old Atlantis. In those days humanity as a whole was astrally focussed and the religion practised by the masses was principally founded on spiritualistic contact with the astral world. Even today the masses are still emotionally oriented and therefore Atlantean in consciousness and the emergence of the mental approach to life – or Aryan consciousness – is still far from becoming dominant. It is for this reason that the lower aspects of spiritualism find such a ready response and so many adherents. They include those who are mostly occupied with the form side of life and interested in phenomena and the satisfaction of desire.

Spiritualism may therefore be practised on several levels and its merit will consequently depend on the level of approach. Generally speaking spiritualism includes all efforts to determine the true nature of death and of what the hereafter holds in store for man. For this purpose he avails himself of the help of psychic mediums who are able to contact the subjective worlds, either with or without retention of consciousness.

The vast majority of these contacts occur on astral levels and it is only in exceptional instances that contacts are raised to mental levels and even more rarely to intuitive or buddhic planes.

The medium goes into trance by temporarily withdrawing the conscious mind and surrendering the physical vehicle as an instrument for the use of disembodied entities, who through this channel are then enabled to come into touch again with the world of matter. As far as the medium is concerned, this must be regarded as a dangerous practice, because he temporarily renounces all control of his vehicle and stands aside, allowing any astral entity to avail itself of this material instrument without any guarantee that the body will again be vacated to the original occupant. It therefore does happen occasionally that the astral occupant abuses this privilege by retaining possession for a prolonged time or even for the duration of that life, resulting in a 'possessed' personality.

Most of the disembodied 'spirits' contacted through the ordinary trance medium, are inhabitants of the astral world. As a rule they are the undeveloped who can contribute little or nothing at all towards the intelligent understanding of conditions on their side of the curtain. They themselves may not even fully realise their own illusionary condition. Some of them are still earth-bound and not even aware of the fact that they have already passed over.

Natural clairvoyants or clairaudients function under much safer conditions than trance mediums, because they retain full mental control during all phases of their work.

There are at present an increasing number of individuals with the gift of etheric vision and hearing and who are thus able to contact entities in the subjective spheres. This is no indication at all of spiritual development, because this characteristic also occurs quite commonly with the underdeveloped races and may even be regarded as a relic from the Atlantean Age, when this was a normal attribute.

The factor which has often been responsible for discrediting spiritualists, was that this system readily lends itself to sensational and sometimes even dishonest practices. Furthermore as commonly pursued, it contributes little towards the spiritual upliftment of those taking part, nor towards helping those who on the other side of the separating veil are in a state of bewilderment.

Fortunately a strong and definite movement has become noticeable in spiritualistic circles, to move away from the purely phenomenal and emotional approach and to emphasise the higher motives and to strive for better understanding of spiritual occurrences. One of the important functions of spiritualism is to bring the general public to intelligent recognition of the existence of the worlds beyond the etheric veil. Once this concept of the continuation of life is mentally grasped, the fear of death will fade away. The aim should therefore be the training of intelligent psychics, to whom the astral plane will be but an intermediate stage on their way to the mental and intuitional planes, where contact will be made with the more advanced spiritual guides and Masters.

D.K. has made the prophecy that, within the relatively near future, spiritualism will make a discovery which will considerably facilitate contact with those who are out of incarnation. He also states that selected mediums will serve as intermediaries between scientists who have passed over to the inner side of the veil and those who are still functioning on the material side, assisting the latter with new ideas for the advancement of their activities.

As in the case of other movements and schools of thought, all that really matters is the *motive* inspiring these psychic mediums and the *quality* of the teachings which they are transmitting – the apparent source of these teachings is of small significance.

III. 5. **Schools of Thought**

With the growing mental development of humanity, new 'schools of thought' will constantly make their appearance to keep pace with the ideas which are progressively being impressed on the human mind from subjective spheres. Actually these ideas contain nothing new, as they all form part of the age-old wisdom teachings but quite often they represent modern versions of old truths, now furnished with a new garb on a somewhat higher level, to guide those human beings in whom the urge has been awakened, to achieve loftier objectives.

The ideas, which have been hierarchically released in the ethers to impinge on receptive minds, are fundamental and it is only because of imperfect instruments and consequent faulty reception and interpretation, that so many versions of the basic truths find their way into the many nations, communities and schools of thought. If this principle could only be recognised, it would lead to greater tolerance and understanding, not only between individuals but also between groups, nations and races.

At any rate, today there exists a great variety of schools of thought, each of which has its own special facet to contribute to the overall pattern of world thought. If man could but reach the stage where he could appreciate the next man's point of view, instead of constantly criticising and condemning every opinion which differs from his own. Could it but be appreciated that none of the 'bright ideas' which may be entertained, no divine revelation which may be expressed, no thought that has emerged after deep pondering, no product of the mind of any nature, can ever represent perfection or the full and pristine Truth. As spiritual truths penetrate the spheres of matter, they unavoidably become distorted, like a beam of light passing through a crystal. So the absolute Truth will never be known to man on Earth and all he can do is to garner and distil that much of the truth as can be discerned and then to live and act accordingly. But simultaneously grant your neighbour the same privilege of drawing his own conclusions and living his life in accordance with his particular ideas, without interference from you, even though your opinions may not coincide.

The first and main criterion should, however, remain the *motive* underlying thoughts and actions. Any action which is mentally formulated and not merely inspired by emotion or tradition, which is selflessly undertaken and is motivated by love and goodwill, must eventually lead to a favourable conclusion. And that which holds for the individual is just as valid for the group, so there should ever be tolerance and even co-operation with other groups or schools of thought, when the common objective is human betterment, especially if it concerns the unfoldment of spiritual life. Attempts should also be made to retain an open mind to new ideas and points of view and not to adhere blindly to traditional and dogmatic tenets, especially where these are coupled with devotion to personalities. Yes, a sense of balance and of proportion should always be retained and it is surprising how a proper sense of humour will contribute towards such equilibrium.

It is regrettable that there are several so-called spiritual movements which have gained considerable public support by emotionally inciting the under-developed masses and the gullible. A fluent orator may easily influence large crowds, especially by stressing sentiment and working on the emotions, but these are mere astral and personality incitements and do not indicate spiritual awakening. Such techniques of sweeping up the emotions may indeed cause more harm than good and may lead selfish and even sadistic temperaments to irresponsible action under the cloak of religious fervour.

Other idealistic schools of thought have founded their system on the unsound principle that final liberation from natural and material limitations may be instantly achieved by the use of *affirmations*. They tend to ignore the time element required for spiritual evolution, nor is the point of development of the person concerned taken into consideration. All physical limitations may eventually be overcome by faith but only when such faith is matched by conforming to the loftier principles or by living a life of redemption. It is only when the soul of the individual takes over and fully controls the lower self and when the physical body reacts to the behests of the soul, eliminating all selfish desire and emotional reaction, that physical limitations will disappear, provided this is in line with the monadic purpose for that life.

It should always be remembered that any permanent progress must be *earned* by persistent struggle and dedication to the vision and cannot be suddenly acquired by wishful thinking, affirmations or the innate selfish desire for comfort and peace. Intense auto-suggestion may sometimes lead to *apparent* rapid changes but these will only prove to be of a temporary nature and the original condition, which was provided in the individual's life for some sound karmic reason, will return at a later stage and will remain effective until the person has learnt the lesson for which the condition was originally provided. Permanent and worthwhile changes will only occur when these are effected with the full and conscious cooperation of the soul.

Several of the so-called mental sciences have lost sight of the nature and purpose of life on Earth, regarding it as man's right as a son of God to have all the good things that life may offer. These misguided individuals have been brought under the impression that the graces of life may be selfishly claimed, disregarding the stern fact that the soul is reincarnating life after life to gain experience the hard way and thus to learn life's lessons which are needed for spiritual unfoldment. These explorers of the way should rather be taught to forget about self-advancement and to evoke the life expression required by the soul, by focussing their attention on service to humanity.

III. 6. **Economics and Finance**

Future economic relationships between the nations of the world must eventually be based on the *Principle of Sharing*. The natural resources and energies of the Earth belong to humanity as a whole and not to individual nations who happen to exert temporary political control over regions where such resources can be favourably exploited. An equitable basis will have to be devised which will enable every section of humanity to benefit proportionately and rationally according to their circumstances and needs. These are matters

241

which can never be solved by fighting, by power-politics or selfish grabbing and holding by the strongest or by those who have the advantage of some favourable strategic situation. There will only be one way of solving these knotty problems and that will be through tolerance, understanding, discussion and mutual goodwill. Until this attitude is adopted, further fighting, with its attendant miseries and injustices, will remain inevitable.

The principle of sharing not only holds for the world's mineral wealth, its oil and the riches of the seas which are increasingly being developed but is just as valid for the product of the fields. There are the productive regions of the world which, owing to favourable environmental conditions, are enabled to produce an abundance of food, often far in excess of local requirements. Simultaneously there are marginal regions where under existing climatic conditions, crop failures frequently occur, resulting in severe food shortages. A fair basis for apportioning the world's seasonal food supplies must therefore be found to ensure that every individual will at all times have sufficient to eat to sustain normal health.

Whatever the detailed reasons, the position at present remains that the distribution of the essential commodities which man needs for the maintenance of life and a reasonable degree of comfort is inequitable and totally inadequate. While food is rotting and surpluses are dumped and destroyed in certain regions, thousands may be starving to death in other parts. No argument can be advanced to justify such disparities!

Comparable conditions prevail in all larger communities, where the unfair allotment of worldly goods remains such a striking fact – on the one hand there are found those who live in palatial residences, wallowing in every imaginable form of luxury, while nearby may be found those living in abject squalor and privation, often literally starving.

No! – such a state of affairs cannot persist in the New Age we are entering and must be one of the first conditions to be rectified to achieve improved human relationships. It must be acknowledged that several meaningful changes in this direction have already been effected but only enough to make the awakening consciousness aware of so much more that needs rectifying. And these are not matters which can be postponed indefinitely, because they are the direct incentives to discontent, revolution and war and must therefore be adjusted as soon as possible if man is to live in peace.

It is recognised that solutions are not always readily available but this is no reason for remaining inactive. Provided man is motivated by the will-to-good and active steps are taken to achieve something constructive, then the worker – whether an individual or a nation – can depend on it that the necessary help and inspiration will be forthcoming to guide him on his path of service.

Differences in standards of living of the leaders, entrepreneurs and intelligentsia, as compared with the lower executives, workers and labourers, are always bound to occur. Then there are those who for some or other reason are incapable of earning their own living or are simply too lazy to work. Similar differences will be found between communities, countries and races. Broadly speaking these unbalanced conditions may largely be ascribed to selfish grasping and hoarding by those who have had the advantage of being better equipped for the exigencies of life than their brothers and this privilege they have abused by retaining an inordinate share of the *mutual earnings* for their personal use. But mankind is no longer prepared to tolerate these blatant extremes so emblematic of the past. Levelling processes have already been set in motion but it will always be difficult to find a fair basis for partitioning the earnings and profits of an enterprise between the members functioning at various mental, physical and technical levels. The only principles which will ultimately provide the solutions will be reasonableness, understanding and goodwill. As the future scene unfolds, however, it will be found that with spiritual development man's *sense of values* is also radically transformed – he will no longer want to be encumbered with material possessions which he cannot apply to communal service.

With regard to the stragglers of mankind – and this again holds for both individuals as well as communities – it should always be remembered that the reason for their dropping out must primarily be sought in some form of lack or disease in their physical, psychic or mental condition. Such a diseased state is often the direct consequence of inadequate or unbalanced nourishment during the past or detrimental environmental conditions. Attempts should therefore be made to help and uplift these people and they should certainly not be cast aside and left to their fate. The provision of the needed food and shelter for the less privileged masses of humanity will lead to a new and constructive approach to life, which in turn will introduce a new era of peace and plenty. These steps will, however, demand careful planning and discrimination.

Up to the present the resources and riches of the world have mainly been usurped by a limited number of selfish and grasping individuals or institutions, who are still desperately endeavouring to retain their hold and striving to acquire an even greater share of the world's riches and power. The time has arrived, however, where drastic changes are being implemented in the world's economic structure and after the necessary adjustments have been effected (with hierarchical assistance!), a new international economic order will make its appearance. This new order will be based on goodwill and world wide-sharing of the fundamental necessities of life and the wise pooling of all resources – both material, scientific and technical – for the benefit of everybody, plus a wise system of distribution. It will take time for this new spirit to become established throughout the world but the die has already been cast and there is nothing that will be able to stem the tide that is now rapidly building up!

III. 6 (a) **Money**

To effect some of the envisaged changes in the world economic system will require a totally new approach with regard to the application of world funds. The billions that are being wasted annually on armed conflict and competitive rearmament, on the search for excitement and self-escape, on useless luxuries of every kind – all these billions should be deflected to more fruitful purposes, to achieve some of the essential aspects of the new economic world order and to educate the masses to a better understanding and awareness of the required spiritual approach. A great deal of money will be needed for these objectives but the money is available and it is only a question of its reorientation and application to more constructive purposes.

A wider appreciation must be engendered for the esoteric value of money used in service of humanity. The spiritual significance of money is as yet only rarely appreciated but in future the position which the aspirant occupies on the spiritual path, will often be determined by his attitude towards and handling of money – that valuable potential energy which the masses still abuse for gratifying their desires.

The true server solicits nothing for himself, except that which he lacks for keeping the physical instrument in efficient working condition and which will better equip him for the work to be accomplished on behalf of his fellow man. To him money is an energy to be used creatively for others and for fulfilling that much of the hierarchical Plan as he can sense and appraise. Those who strive to enrich themselves and that as a rule at the cost of their neighbour, will eventually find that this brings only discontent, sorrow and distress, while those who desire nothing for themselves will inherit the riches of the soul, with all the joy that this will occasion.

The time has arrived when mankind should begin to recognise the *spiritual value of money*. Money is nothing but manifested energy and, as is the case with all energy, it can be exercised either for good or bad. So far its use has been tainted, like everything else in human living, by selfish individual or communal objectives. It should now be diverted to new objectives and in the first instance to awaken the spiritual consciousness of the masses and to impress the urgent need for improved human relations. This means training the public in the principles of world citizenship, based on mutual goodwill and the correct application of their money energy for expressing these aims.

And who should take the responsibility for reorienting world opinion and its values and for deflecting money into avenues of constructive service? The answer is simple – the appropriate movement is already in full swing and has been initiated by thousands of individuals throughout the world, who are working either singly or in groups. They have been and still are inspired by energies, thoughts and ideas that have been impressed upon their minds or are being projected as specific thoughtforms into the mental ethers, by the Hierarchy. These ideas are therefore not only exhibited by some prominent leaders but are now in effect being implemented by the thousands of men and women of goodwill present in all countries. All these disciples are diverting the smaller or larger sums of money at their disposal towards these new objectives and it is expected that this money, as yet only a small trickle, will rapidly assume larger proportions and will wax into a mighty stream of creative energy and power, which will be used to improve human relationships and towards the redemption of man.

(See also: X. 4)

III. 6 (b) Capitalism and Labour

Broadly considered and viewed from the economic and social standpoints, the world can today be divided into two strong and opposing factions – the **Capitalists** and the **Labour Movement** – with the average consumer caught up somewhere between these contending forces.

From the point of view of the general public, both these systems have their advantages and drawbacks, which in different ways have proved either beneficial or detrimental to humanity. Both these systems, however, also have one characteristic in common which seriously discredits them – their *selfish greed*.

There fortunately are exceptions but on the whole both capitalism and labour, as constituted today, represent two great factions fighting each other to obtain as big a share as possible of the world's goods and wealth for selfish enrichment and the wielding of power.

Both of these combinations are immured by a spirit of greed but their approach for achieving their objectives differs widely. To revert again to the dangerous practice of using generalisations, it might be said that in their fight for dominance, the capitalists, who are numerically far outweighed by labour, have the great advantage of both the powerful backing of money and also of the better innate and trained brain capacity, available from a large part of the supporting intelligentsia as well as from a number of interested scientists. It is, however, noticeable that many belonging to the latter two groups are maintaining a somewhat neutral position between the two main contending factions, with probably a stronger inclination towards the capitalist side.

Labour has the great advantage of numbers and also that they form an absolute *sine qua non* of the production machine of the capitalists. This is consequently the most powerful weapon over which they dispose and which they have learnt to apply most effectively as organised '*strikes*', implemented through their Labour Unions. The use of strikes, which in the early days of the labour movement was a most useful and justifiable tool to achieve their immediate purpose of alleviating deplorable labour conditions, has subsequently degenerated into a tool of tyranny in the hands of the unscrupulous and self-seeking. With growing power the whole labour movement has changed in essence. With accumulating funds these organisations have themselves assumed many of the adverse qualities of capitalism. With their increasing strength labour has in many instances become a dictatorship, using threat, fear and force to attain ends which are often not justifiable and are selfishly motivated.

In the earlier stages of their fight, labour as a rule is not sufficiently aware of the fact that in their attempts to destroy and eradicate capitalism, they are also to a large extent destroying the machine producing so many of their conveniences. When at a later stage they are to some extent gaining the upper hand over traditional capitalism, labour sometimes becomes conscious of certain of the valuable functions of capital for the maintenance of production of commodities demanded by modern standards of living. Out of all these circumstances various forms of labour-socialist-capitalist combinations have developed but so far they are all suffering from the same disadvantage, which has proved that the resulting productive machine is on the whole not functioning as effectively as used to be the case with the original capitalistic system.

To the student of economy or the social sciences, a study of all these tendencies would prove most interesting but to the esotericist these conditions are merely transitional phases through which long suffering humanity is struggling on its laborious way to greater light. Man apparently needs all these experiences to awaken his consciousness and to bring him to the recognition that his happiness and peace are not to be found in the acquisition of a maximum quantity of goods, commodities and power but in acquiring a peaceful mind and conscience and the maintenance of the right spirit of fellowship with his neighbour.

What has so far been lacking in the case of both capitalism and the labour movements, are the right motives and objectives and as long as their main striving remains selfish acquisition, they are both doomed to failure and eventually will have to make way for the all-engulfing, all-embracing and rapidly awakening and spreading New Movement of the Aquarian Age – the movement of World Goodwill!

This Spirit of Love expressed as service to the Whole, is applicable to every phase of life and is at present being actively introduced into the spheres of capitalism, business, industry and labour. Throughout the world men of thought are applying their intellects (supported by soul intuition and hierarchical inspiration!) towards the working out of new systems wherein the money of the capitalist, the technical proficiency of the scientist and industrialist, the administrative ability of the trained and experienced executive and the dexterity, skill and aptitude of the labourer, may be combined in a production machine that should prove of mutual benefit to all included within this co-operative group. The essential synthesising factor on which these undertakings *must* be based if they are to entertain any hope of success, is **right human relations**, characterised by mutual trust, goodwill, tolerance and sharing. Without these criteria, applied to all levels of the organisation, it will be doomed to failure.

This **symbiotic synthesis of capital and labour** is the only possible solution for the future well-being of man. In the beginning the problem will remain to find and attract correctly motivated individuals. These men, however, do exist and there is something in the 'atmosphere' which *is* bringing them together and which is also going to lead them to success. Mistakes and disappointments are bound to occur in the early stages and some wrong elements will unavoidably be incorporated, which in due course will again have to be eliminated but these schemes, after tentative trials to find the right way, are going to prove a huge success and are going to play an intrinsic role in introducing the New Age.

In industry this tendency towards collaboration between the various levels of production will give rise to the development of '**Production Groups**'. If these groups are correctly motivated by a genuine spirit of goodwill, which essentially must pervade the whole organisation and which cannot be limited exclusively to their internal activities, then this energy will also find expression in influences which the group will radiate to its environment and to the world at large. Therefore another attribute of these groups will be their striving to be of service to humanity as a whole and this spirit will also be reflected in the superior quality of their products, which will be offered at prices which will only make provision for a minimum margin of profit.

These co-operative and altruistic principles, based primarily on goodwill, are already being brought into practice on a limited scale but it is expected that they will rapidly attract wider attention. Improved systems will progressively be devised and established in all countries and as the success of these new systems becomes apparent, they will increasingly supersede the old competitive and acquisitive methods. Yes, *the tide has turned!* Sense the vital vibrations now pervading the world atmosphere and influencing all man's activities! The men of goodwill who are prepared to give their selfless service to humanity already exist in large numbers and their numbers will rapidly keep on growing; they are discovering each other and are becoming consciously aware of the power to good which is increasingly placed at their disposal and also of the mighty force which could be generated by uniting their energies and wielding this concerted force to the advantage and in service of humanity!

III. 7. Nationalism, Racialism and Politics

Each and every individual starts off by being influenced by national or racial glamour, which often becomes excessive and unbalanced when stimulated by emotional public speakers or politically motivated news media. The overcoming of this trait will be facilitated considerably once the person becomes aware of the fact of reincarnation with its many implications; when he comes to the recognition that it is merely the personality which is concerned with the race or nation into which he has been born for this particular life; that he may have been born into this race only for this one life and that in previous lives he probably has belonged to many of the other existing races.

As group consciousness gradually assumes control over the disciple; as the principle of coherence and synthesis takes root; as he increasingly becomes aware of the oneness of humanity and the underlying solidarity of all existence; as the outline of the hierarchical Plan is steadily revealed to his expanding consciousness; so will his concepts broaden and will his erstwhile traditional and narrow views on nationalism and racialism begin to fade.

The disciple should train himself to become consciously aware that the real self is seated in the soul, which only temporarily occupies a personality placed within a particular environment to gain certain experiences and that he should therefore feel no undue pride or shame because of the race in which that personality happens to function during this life. Once the disciple has reached this awareness and this concept has become firmly

247

established and really meaningful to him, then he will automatically disassociate himself from the narrow delimitations of nationalism, becoming aware of his membership of the **One Humanity**, irrespective of the position and environment which he happens to occupy for the moment and where he probably has some specific mission to fulfil. The disciple should therefore learn to stand free from environmental limitations but meanwhile to radiate love and goodwill to all with whom he happens to be associated. This should, however, be effected with relative detachment and no undue emotion.

National characteristics are often largely determined by the principles advocated by the leaders. Because man in the past was mainly motivated by ambition, acquisitiveness and greed, the nations of the world were also similarly qualified. With more pronounced recognition of man's responsibility towards the whole, this same awareness will be demonstrated by the leaders of the nations, who will introduce this spirit of altruism and goodwill into national and international relationships. This tendency is already becoming noticeable in the world of international activity but for the time being it is still submerged by the powerful retarding influences of those who have not yet advanced to this stage and who are still adhering to the old systems of aggressiveness, greed and hate. The change has, however, set in and it is only a question of time before the forces of evil will succumb and be submerged by the energies of light and love now being radiated over humanity. The impeding agencies will during this process either be converted to the principles of goodwill or otherwise their continued resistance will lead to self-destruction and elimination by the same evil forces which they are now directing towards others.

The realisation of the One Humanity does not entail the sacrifice of national identity. On the contrary, differences of language and culture will and should always remain, as these differences can only contribute to enhance the beauty of the tapestry constituted by these many coloured facets of human living. The hope of the world therefore lies in the retention of identity of the many nations, each with their attributes of varying colour, language and culture but simultaneously in their closer collaboration and maintenance of right relationships, economic sharing and interchange on a mutually beneficial basis, as exemplified by unselfish international policies, free from pride, greed, ambition or interference and founded on goodwill.

The Spiritual Hierarchy is not interested in the ideological or political leanings of the individual or his community, neither is it affected by the religious practices which may be supported. All it is concerned with is that Humanity as a whole should avail itself of the spiritual opportunity which, more compellingly than ever before, is becoming available to mankind.

IV

GLAMOUR AND ILLUSION

No clear distinction can be drawn between glamour and illusion, as they are both concerned with mental deception. Where glamour however alludes to deception on the astral plane, illusion refers to a similar condition on the mental plane.

Glamour therefore concerns the condition when the *mind* becomes veiled by emotional impulses generated on astral levels and preventing the mind's eye from clearly distinguishing reality. This condition may readily be aggravated by desire.

Illusion is a state of the *soul*. The soul, using the glamoured mind as its instrument, obtains a distorted picture of the phenomenal world. Because of these misrepresentations the soul fails to see with clarity and reality is only discerned with the course of time and experience, after learning to pour its light into the mind, thus illuminating the brain and bringing ideas and thought-forms into proper perspective.

IV. 1. Glamour

The majority of men still live on the astral plane or the world of emotion and glamour. It is only when man consciously shifts his awareness to the mental plane that he learns to eliminate the glamour that has kept him enthralled for many lives but probably only to be ensnared again by illusion on the higher level.

One of the tasks of the disciple is to assist the Masters in making his fellow men aware of this world of glamour by which they are surrounded and which holds them in a state of semi-blindness, only allowing a distorted image of what can but vaguely be distinguished through the astral haze. Men must be taught to think and thus to understand the condition under which they are living; by understanding the nature of glamour, it may eventually be transmuted and dispelled by the mind. Glamour cannot survive the light of truth and when the light of the mind becomes focussed on it, it must inevitably fade and disappear.

The objective of the disciple must be to keep his emotions under control and to cultivate an attitude of 'divine indifference', which will ultimately eliminate glamour through attrition. With restrained emotions glamour cannot be aroused and it must then inevitably vanish. Should emotions, however, occasionally gain the upper hand, this must not be regarded as failure but merely as a warning not to relax unduly and to fall under the glamour of *self-assurance*. Failure is only indicated when the disciple identifies himself again completely with the astral life from which he has temporarily escaped and reverts to the old rhythms.

To the aspirant endeavouring to tread the Path of Truth, glamour and illusion are probably the worst enemies, particularly during the early stages of his conscious training. This training releases several potent energies and because as yet he does not know how to handle these forces effectively, they are inclined to overwhelm him and to create fresh glamours. The trouble with glamour is that it is so illusive, knowing how subtly to masquerade as the truth.

There are innumerable conditions in the daily life of the disciple which will encourage states of glamour and it is difficult to isolate the worst offenders in this respect. It may, however, prove helpful if the attention is drawn to some attitudes of mind which the aspirant will readily be able to identify within himself, because to enable glamour to be dissipated, it is first of all essential that its presence should be recognised:

1. *Self-pity:* This is one of the most insidious of glamours to which every disciple is at times subjected and every effort should be made to eliminate it. It is a deluding force which exaggerates and dramatises all events and conditions and tends to isolate the individual in his own life, bringing him under the impression that the adversities of life are specifically aimed at him and inspired for his personal detriment. Basically it must be regarded as a perverted form of self-interest, which if demonstrated to a marked degree will shut out the light of the soul and will lead to a feeling of persecution and deep unhappiness. (See: VIII. 2 (a) (ii))

2. *Criticism:* Is there a single person who can honestly regard himself as redeemed of this most persistent of glamours and which has already been the cause of so many disturbed relationships? If so, then this individual must be nearing the final stages of perfection. By criticising one's fellow man a thought-form is created which is usually false or badly exaggerated and which adversely surrounds the individual concerned. The consequence is that the man is never seen as he really is; a distorted image is always obtained of him because he is seen through the false surround of the thought-form, which is perverting the reality of his being. Instead of criticism, rather try to project thoughts of goodwill and kindness and allow these attitudes to become an automatic part of one's conduct to others – not only will this effect a total change in one's own life but it will also prove of incalculable value to others and will contribute to augment the world reservoir of love and goodwill.

3. *Suspicion:* That sordid weakness which so often poisons and undermines not only our own lives but also that of others. And how often such suspicion proves baseless

and unjustified but meanwhile this poison has been spread and has also been used to infect the minds of others. The effect of such defamation, even if not expressed in words, can never be perfectly eliminated. (See: VIII. 2 (b))

4. *Self-righteousness:* It is a glamour to which all fields of thought are exposed but which is evinced particularly by religious fraternities, politicians and even by scientists. These self-righteous thoughts so often portray antiquated ideas, presented emotionally as traditions which cannot be allowed to be superseded or substituted by modern concepts. Advocates of this attitude usually function under astral glamour, recognising only their own narrow and stereotyped point of view and unable to concede that certain crystallised and outworn ideas of the past must eventually be adapted or even superseded by more advanced thought. The only way of dissipating this glamour is to free the mind from all restrictions engendered by fossilised convictions and doctrines, only allowing it to be directed by love and goodwill as dictated by the soul. With freedom of thought leading to views that are only restrained by the humility of the man who acknowledges his limitations in terms of the greater whole, self-righteousness can never be sustained.

   The problem of the aspirant is that after some progress on the Path of Light, he at times obtains flashes of clear vision into the future but these are only of short duration, after which the astral fogs of glamour again settle over him, obliterating the light which for a while had set him free. This often leads to severe distress and self-disgust, when seeing everything again in its warped appearance, giving rise to frustration at his impotence and inability to penetrate the veiled reality which he knows lies beyond. During these periods of dejection, the aspirant should assume an attitude of 'acceptance'.

5. *Fear:* Although of a negative nature, fear remains one of the principal elements governing human activity and relationships. Fear is one of the most distinctive features of the astral world and consequently also one of the most fruitful sources of glamour. The sense of fear will, however, be dispelled to the same extent that the light of the mind brings deeper understanding and discrimination.
   (See: PART ONE – X. 3 (a))

6. *Materiality:* A glamour by which all evolving human beings are held in thrall and the main cause of the world's varied economic problems. Down the ages materiality has been one of man's normal characteristics and in modern life it is expressed by his enslavement to money and possessions and the power which these provide. Only with the liberation of the soul is it discovered that merely those possessions are needed which can provide a healthy and complete life, in which the qualities of the soul may be effectively expressed. Possessions exceeding these needs may be acquired and held only by sacrificing the deeper and subjective values of life.

   The material necessities of life will vary according to the stage of evolution that has been attained by the individual. Each soul in its gradual development must, during some life, experience the effects of large possessions, of riches and abundance and the powers and responsibilities which are coupled with them, to enable him to arrive at the eventual recognition of their uselessness and even of the harm that such chattels may cause when solely used for personal and selfish gratification, instead of applying them to the service of humanity.

It is the unconscious identifying with glamour and its disturbing effects, which at times may overwhelm the aspirant, causing deep depression and profound inferiority complexes, which in extreme cases may even lead to suicide.

Dissipating Glamour:

Individuals who emotionally and mentally are still quite undeveloped, are not yet subject to glamour – they are still complete realists, seeing life baldly and in its bare outlines. The very highly evolved are similarly liberated but in this instance because reality is now viewed from the opposing pole of life, lying beyond the astral spheres. The great bulk of humanity, however, live in the emotional world, where they are surrounded by distorting miasmas of glamour but of this they are unaware, not realising the cause of all their pain and suffering. It is only as man begins to think and enters the mental life, that he recognises the glamour that surrounds him and from that moment of discovery he starts on the lengthy struggle of overcoming this emotional handicap. A growing power of discrimination then emerges, which will slowly change his sense of values and will become his major weapon for dispelling both glamour and illusion. The old and established values of the emotional and physical world of phenomena are step by step relegated to the background of his consciousness and his centre of attention becomes focussed in the subjective world of intangible realities, the world of the mind, of ideas and causes. Once these principles are grasped and man begins to live accordingly, the glamours by which he has been enthralled will fade away.

In all attempts at dispelling glamour the disciple must necessarily be patient and must work with pure faith and love. Astral glamours are of very ancient origin and although there may exist good intention and a sound grasp of the required techniques, it cannot be expected that these phantasms can instantly be dispelled by the waving of some magic wand. The aspirant should therefore proceed slowly and with care, as this process may easily lead to emotional disturbances and even to temporary instability. Brief periods of liberation may be followed by long periods of depressing defeat and bewilderment. Provided the cause of these disorders is intelligently acknowledged and receives no undue attention, no harm will ensue. With perseverance the dominance of these glamours will ultimately be offset by the strength of the soul, resulting in a state of balance during which the disciple will at least be partly liberated from astral control.

It is also said that glamour is dispelled by the light of truth, which is but another way of referring to the light of the soul. In its early stages this disappearance of glamour is as a rule only of a temporary nature, because few aspirants are as yet ready to face the truth, as this would involve the abandonment of certain glamours to which they are still devoted, as well as the acknowledgement of past error. In this respect it will again be found that *humility* will prove to be one of the most effective ways of releasing the illuminating power of the mind, which serves as the transmitter and reflector of soul light. By facing the facts of life calmly and dispassionately, illumination will be facilitated, with the consequent dispelling of glamour and thereby preparing the disciple for more extended and effective service.

It is at this stage that the mental control should be supported by the practice of meditation, which will allow the blending of the light of the soul with the inherent light of the mental body. With sustained meditation this blended light may be steadily intensified, until glamour vanishes in the light of truth by which it is being superseded. When both glamour and illusion have been overcome, the existence of the astral body will through attrition fade from the consciousness.

Every bit of glamour that is dissipated by individual disciples contributes towards the dispelling of world glamour and will thereby help to clear the path for those who follow. In this way each inspired individual subscribes towards the fulfilment of the divine Plan.

For the initiate the time will arrive when the astral will no longer exist and when he will therefore stand free from glamour. But when he has released himself from this realm of fog and delusion and stands in the 'clear cold light' of the intuitional plane, he will come to the conclusion that his work in the world of mists has not yet been completed and that he will have to return. But from now on the astral vapours will no longer engulf him, as he will function from the clear light of the intuitional plane which hovers above the astral, thus enabling him to introduce divine light into the darkness of the emotional plane in aid of his fellow man.

IV. 2. **Illusion**

The aspirant is oft imprisoned on the mental plane by man-made thought-forms, by illusion which temporarily bars all escape to the higher subjective realms and also prevents him from according that loving service to his fellow man which his soul demands. It is only by developing the *intuition* that these fetters of illusion may be broken. Through the intuition a faint concept may be gained of the divine Purpose and of the immanence of God.

To develop the intuition, the first essential remains mental training and the unfoldment of the mind. Actually this is the whole purpose of esoteric training – the liberation of the aspirant from ancient rhythms of thought and deep-seated habits and convictions. The aura must steadily be clarified, to enable light to penetrate to the mind. So often well-meaning, idealistic people are found but with their minds so obscured and crystallised that light seems unable to penetrate their consciousness and to permit clear thought and a vision of reality.

The first problem for the aspirant is to recognise that glamour and illusion exist – the majority of men as yet cannot realise this and consequently these illusory forces cannot be opposed or broken down as they progressively arise. The dilemma is that a principle of truth may sometimes be clearly grasped but no sooner has this happened than the mind immediately begins to surround this truth again with readily forming illusions, thus temporarily neutralising the advance that has been made towards the light. With persistence this effect will, however, not last and by gathering further facets of truth, the cumulative effect of the penetrating light will finally supervene.

Most of the thought-forms crowding the mental plane draw their life from the desire nature of the lower mind and are the product of the masses of men and women still functioning on astral levels. These thought-forms really originate from the realm of ideas but owing to the deforming effect of the swirling currents and mists of the emotional world, they have been twisted to serve the selfish purposes of men. These distorted ideas have been converted into the thought-forms which crowd and intensify the world of illusion and there are consequently but few who escape their influence and remain free from deception.

One of the principal disadvantages of illusion is that it may dominate the mind to such an extent that the entry of further ideas is precluded. The mental ability of the man therefore becomes limited and cramped by the illusion and his progress is retarded, because the deluded aspirant remains devoted and enslaved to only a partial conception or a warped expression of an idea or ideal, while the complete truth escapes him.

In those rare instances where the idea is grasped in its completeness, there remains no room for illusion. Recognising the Truth in its fullness will, however, make such an overwhelming impression on the disciple, that he will be reduced to humility and this will save him from any inclination towards arrogance and presumption. It is illusion which gives rise to fanaticism, impracticable idealism, revolting application of distorted ideas and cramped versions by narrow minded men and women who want to enforce **their** biased vision on their fellow men and who will not allow even the possibility of the existence of other points of view.

It is the birth of these perverted ideas in the minds of strong but deluded personalities which have already caused so much misery and suffering in the world. When these distorted ideas are imposed by the leaders as ideologies, their effects may prove catastrophic.

Although illusion is a phase that eventually has to be overcome, it must be regarded as a natural condition in man's process of unfoldment, forming part of the normal procedure of testing and training which appears to be essential for shaping mind and character and for developing the powers of discrimination.

All men in the course of their spiritual development, unavoidably have to pass through the state of the 'Great Illusion', which means the misinterpretation of the world of phenomena by the mind. In man's development he progresses from the life of instinct to mental reasoning, from understanding to illumination and then finally to identification with Reality and the liberation from the Great Illusion. While the phenomenal world and the life of desire predominate, the individual remains under the restrictions of the Great Illusion and he only starts breaking away from this influence when he becomes aware of the existence of the subjective world of Reality and step by step escapes from the snares of glamour and laboriously starts on the Path of Return.

Dispelling of Illusion:

Illusion can only be effectively dispelled by the intuition or to put it in other words, 'by holding the mind steady in the light of the soul'. To do so the disciple has to develop the art of living simultaneously and consciously in two worlds – the world of practical and mundane activity and at the same time becoming intensely and consciously aware of the underlying world of spiritual being. To do justice to both these realms of existence will demand great patience and persistence and at times particular discretion and inspired discernment.

It is taught that with the overcoming of both glamour and illusion, the astral plane will vanish for that individual, because the life of desire has disappeared and with it the emotional world. This is a phase which cannot really be understood by the disciple until he has personally reached that stage and experienced its meaning. As he progresses he will, however, experience fleeting moments of such recognition, which may give him an inkling of that which lies in store for him.

To enable the intuition or the light of the soul to dispel first glamour and subsequently the illusionary thought-forms, the mind must systematically be subjected to this light. This is effected by the processes of concentration, meditation and contemplation. These techniques will receive more specific attention in a later chapter.

V

LIGHT

The theme of Light is fundamental to man's whole existence. During the early stages of his development he is unconscious of this light but as lives go by he gradually becomes aware of the various forms of light which affect his being. In the first instance there is the light of the Sun, providing all kingdoms of nature not only with the light of day but also with warmth. As man develops he displays an ever growing demand for more light, which amongst others is demonstrated by the provision he is making for artificial illumination during the dark hours of the night. He is simultaneously also exhibiting an increasing need for the more subtle forms of light – for the light of knowledge. This is reflected by the many schools of learning, encompassing ever extending fields of interest and reaching an ever larger proportion of the human race. All these aspects are contributing towards the awakening and final recognition of the light in the head and the guiding of humanity as a whole towards this consciousness.

With the evolution of man the *One Light* is finally attained after progressively advancing through four stages:

(a) The *Light of Instinct*, which is normally associated with the animal stage and is the guiding force before the light of reason supersedes.

(b) By means of the *Light of Knowledge* the glamours of the astral plane are dispelled by the *light of the mind*.

(c) The *Light of Wisdom* is the *light of the soul*, which is blended with the light of knowledge to carry the aspirant another step forward on the Path of Light.

(d) The *Light of Intuition* is the instrument of the initiate. This is a blending of all lesser lights and leads to *illumination*.

It should be remembered, however, that these stages are not clearly demarcated. They merge and overlap and are merely used symbolically to illustrate the progressive spiritual unfoldment of the disciple. With each of these steps new spiritual environments will be revealed and closer contact will be effected with the soul. Each step will lead to further expansions and increased competence and capacities.

Attainment of more Light will automatically also increase man's responsibilities, for it will exact from its recipients that such light should be effectively applied to the benefit and service of mankind.

Once the aspirant has distinguished the first glimmering of light in the head, the inner darkness becomes accentuated. In the beginning this may lead to despair and the depths of depression but this stage must be endured, until the dark shadows are eventually dispersed by the pure light of the soul – then will life be brightened by the sun in the head, diffusing its light in all its glory. This light in the head will lead the aspirant to soul consciousness and the Path of Light. By entering this Path he himself becomes a light and may then function as a lamp, carrying illumination to others and thus lighting their way for them. The radiance of this light may be intensified by concentrating attention on the inner life by means of consciously directed love and meditation. As the disciple advances along the Path he progressively acquires the ability to utilise stronger light, thus becoming aware of fresh revelations.

Students sometimes become conscious of a diffused light or glow in the head – this is the light of the physical atoms composing the brain. When later they see something like a sun in their heads, this indicates a recognition of the combined etheric light plus the physical atomic light. The semblance of an intensely bright electric light would probably denote a merging of the etheric and atomic lights with that of the soul.

The recording of these light phenomena must not be regarded as essential criteria for evaluating the stage of spiritual development. There are disciples who have already achieved an advanced stage of spiritual development, without becoming aware of the brain radiances described above. Disciples should therefore not be disturbed if they fail to discern these lights in the head.

In the field of science one point of light after another are systematically being revealed, gradually serving to tie up the relationship which exists between its numerous branches and the subjective world of energies. With new discoveries now rapidly succeeding each other, previous findings are being supported and amplified and these separate points of light are now being associated and co-ordinated, thus synthesising the original single strands of light into one comprehensive beam of radiance, which will herald the New Era and will revolutionise practically all basic scientific concepts.

This new light to which science is being subjected, largely concerns the etheric spheres, better known in scientific terminology as the field of electromagnetism, which sustains and interpenetrates every substantial form in nature and which serves as the common link uniting every phenomenal manifestation into the One Whole. In this connection it should also be kept in mind that 'light and matter are fundamentally synonymous terms'. The present scientific interest is largely focussed on the many aspects of radiation, their direction, control, reception, action, interaction and relationships with the mineral, vegetable, animal, human and finally the spiritual kingdoms. At the same time this new 'light' is definitely leading science to the recognition and acknowledgement of the soul and of Spirit.

Divine Light:

On his evolutionary path in the physical world, the disciple has made contact with the light of matter, the light of mind and the light of the soul and intuition. These will serve to sustain him till perfection on Earth is achieved and therefore till such time when there will be no further need for his return to phenomenal life for the sake of experience. When the radiant life of the soul is blended with the magnetic light of the vital body, it stimulates the atoms of the physical body, till each atom in turn becomes a small radiant centre. Therefore, when the man is under control of the soul, there eventuates the shining forth of the Light throughout the body. This is the radiance emanating from the bodies of sages and saints, encircling them with Light. The initiate will now enter the Supernal Light, the Light Divine, emanating from the Logos and channelled through the Spiritual Triad. This greater Light will reveal to him undreamed of new horizons, which are beyond the description and comprehension of the limited human mind.

> "From the point of Light within the Mind of God
> Let Light stream forth into the minds of men;
> Let Light and Love and Power restore the Plan on Earth."

V. 1. Instinct

Instinct is that God-given and mysterious attribute which guides all manifested forms on their ordained path through life, until the stage is reached which esoterically is known as 'individualisation'. This is the stage when purely instinctive action is for the first time superseded by the awakening incentives of reason, engendered by the mind – the first expression of 'self-consciousness'.

Much of the emotional life is governed by instinct, which functions below the level of consciousness and serves as a natural protection against adverse influences occurring within the environment. Instinct is also responsible for the development of the habits and characteristics which distinguish an organism and ensure procreation and propagation of all species in nature.

The instinctual nature which is so characteristic of the animal kingdom, must therefore be seen as the immature principle which stage by stage will develop into ultimate consciousness. It is that capacity which becomes aware of the environment and spontaneously reacts to certain component factors of that environment and which will finally lead to the building of certain patterns of instinctual behaviour. A type of unconscious memory is established which will function and lead to specific reaction without conscious recollections; a typical illustration of this is the instinct of self-preservation displayed in numerous ways in both the animal and human kingdoms. Another striking example is found in the protective mother-instinct which females of many species exhibit when their young are threatened.

V. 2. **Knowledge**

Knowledge is that which is acquired by learning and may be regarded as the sum total of human experience and observance – that which he has registered in the brain by means of his five senses and which has subsequently been correlated, classified and stored for future reference and programming in the human computer. It is the compendium of all that man has extracted from life experiences and because it is concerned with what has been observed by the senses and emotions, it therefore mainly remains limited to the material aspects of human living.

Memory is closely associated with knowledge and is a reflection of the clarity with which facts have been registered in the brain. The quality of the intellect may be seriously limited by shortcomings of the memory. In other instances there may be an excellent memory but when combined with only a mediocre brain, which cannot fully avail itself of the prime qualities of the memory, only indifferent results can be expected.

Gains in knowledge increase *responsibility*. If knowledge acquired through the many possible channels is not applied with discrimination and given expression in some appropriate way, it will cause stagnation and obstruction, which will be demonstrated as some emotional or physical disorder of the system. It will literally cause intellectual indigestion. A principle which the aspirant should assimilate at an early stage, is that knowledge should be shared with the fellow man – it is not acquired to be used for selfish advantage but should be applied to the benefit and service of a needy world.

All knowledge does not, however, purely concern material things. There is also knowledge concerning the subjective life – esoteric knowledge. This knowledge concerns energies and forces as distinct from that dealing with the manifested world. The average man, however, still lacks the necessary equipment for effective registration of subjective phenomena, which mostly remain outside the range of normal consciousness. The vast majority of men are only fully aware of the physical plane but perfect knowledge will not be achieved until man also becomes consciously aware on the buddhic plane – the plane of the soul.

Knowledge may be classified under three categories:

(a) *Theoretical Knowledge:* This may also be called 'book knowledge'. Man is not in the position personally to verify all so-called facts and experiences of life and its many branches of learning and he also lacks the necessary training and equipment for such versatility. So the greater part of knowledge acquired by man is founded on what he believes to be authoritative sources provided by either writers or speakers. He accepts these statements largely on trust as originating from experienced workers in the many and varied fields of thought. In many respects his views will therefore be influenced by others. A great deal of man's so-called knowledge is therefore not factual information but merely represents beliefs which have been transmitted to him and have been accepted, and much of this can definitely not be supported by 'scientific proof'. These same people will, however, quite often loudly protest against the acceptance of new ideas, especially when these concern the subjective world, because no 'material' proofs can be provided.

(b) *Discriminative Knowledge:* Here the concrete mind is brought into play and a number of facts are rationally considered and weighed against other known information, thus attempting to arrive at an intelligent conclusion. As far as possible that which appears unsound, unreasonable, unverifiable or non-essential is eliminated or rejected and every endeavour is made to penetrate to the core of the matter by logic or scientific means. This is therefore the approach of the thinker and of the scientific mind and entails concentration and meditation. It is through these latter processes that many scientists unknowingly set foot on esoteric terrain, because during such meditation their minds become receptive to some of the eternal verities from the higher worlds. These ideas are subsequently transferred to their brains and thus give rise to the brilliant 'discoveries' of science!

(c) *Intuitive Knowledge:* This step follows logically on the phase described in the previous paragraph. On the buddhic or intuitive plane there are many truths which have always existed there but which have not yet been recognised and accepted by the world of men. It is only the occasional individual, with a mind trained in clear thinking, who can penetrate these planes by focussed meditation and who with their receptive minds, can bring down to the physical brain some of the ideas encountered on these higher levels.

To the above classification could perhaps be added a fourth category, which might be called '*Spiritual Knowledge*'. This is the inner knowledge of the disciple, which could be associated with his spiritual development and which may be encouraged in three ways:

1. By systematic expansion of consciousness he successively becomes aware of the next step ahead and the next objective to be mastered.

2. The new truths that have been sensed must become more clearly defined, absorbed and then manifested through meditation, practical experience and service. This is often a lengthy procedure because these new ideas or principles must be thoroughly assimilated, until they form an intimate part of the disciple's very self.

3. With increasing knowledge the time will arrive when the disciple has gathered sufficient to be able to transfer or impart some of this knowledge to others. Through teaching, the teacher's own knowledge will be further amplified, because to enable him to impart facts, these must first be clearly defined in his own mind and during this process of crystallising and rounding off his subject, his knowledge will be further augmented.

Although acquired knowledge must be shared, newly gained information should be given the opportunity to be assimilated, to mature and to be co-ordinated with existing knowledge or otherwise it might be found that a little or only 'half-baked' knowledge might readily lead to confusion. In sharing knowledge, care should also be taken never to become presumptuous, conceited or arrogant about it and never to force one's views on others when these ideas are not welcome.

V. 3. **Wisdom**

Whereas knowledge concerns the material side of life, wisdom refers to the progress of spirit through the three vehicles of human expression and with the coinciding expansions of consciousness. It deals with the life side of being and therefore with the essence of things and not with matter itself. It is that innate perception which enables man to distinguish between the real and the unreal, between truth and deception.

Wisdom is an outgrowth of knowledge and is the interpretation and understanding of the inner meaning which lies behind the imparted facts. It therefore implies the power to apply knowledge sanely and understandingly, not only to individual but also to the common benefit. It is the product of blending the light of the soul with the light of knowledge. It is the sublimation of both the higher and lower minds as reflected in the intellect and expressed as loving understanding in the affairs of men. Such expression will not always take the form of speech but at times may involve a beneficial silence or perhaps be combined with kindly action, which might actually carry far greater effect than a spate of words.

The inner world of meaning, normally hidden by the outer veil of matter and ignorance, becomes revealed by the powers of the light of wisdom. It will throw light on the causes producing the outer forms and this will evoke understanding. Wisdom therefore is synonymous to understanding.

V. 4. **Understanding**

Although classified separately, understanding is really an integral quality of wisdom and forms the link between Knowledge and Wisdom. It is the faculty which the Thinker applies to transmute knowledge into wisdom. Where knowledge is concerned with observing and experiencing the material side of life and wisdom reflects the spiritual effects, understanding is the relation between these two opposite poles, as brought about by the intervention of the soul, the Thinker. It does not only relate the form life to the subjective spheres but also serves as the channel whereby inspiration from the higher levels is translated into appropriate form to the intellect.

The main constituent of understanding is the soul quality of love and it is therefore only through understanding that identification with other individuals or groups will be achieved. It is this quality which will prove essential for every form of identification, on all levels and which eventually will lead to man's final objective of synthesis with all forms of divine expression or in other words right human relationships.

It is only through *loving understanding* that one's fellow men may be recognised for what they are in truth, with all their shortcomings and all their virtues, with their pettiness and their outstanding qualities and perfections. It will need understanding not to condemn them for their false steps and errors and to accept them lovingly for the good to be found in every individual and where possible to assist them to find their way on to the Path of Light.

Although loving understanding should be applied world-wide with regard to all human relationships, there is surely no other single field of activity where its application will yield such immediate and positive results as with the *education of children*. So much needless sorrow is caused by misunderstanding of the child by grown-ups who should know better. So many of the errors of a child are merely committed on momentary impulse, to attract attention or maybe prompted by a thwarted, inquiring spirit. At other times it may have been an impulse to retaliate against what the child regards as an injustice. So many of these difficulties will be eliminated by an understanding approach and will largely contribute to guide these youngsters to become worthwhile citizens of the world.

Goodwill, love, wisdom and understanding are all team mates and constitute the basic qualities on which right human relationships should be founded and will finally prove to be the only effective agents for negotiating world peace.

The Law of Loving Understanding is also one of the qualifying characteristics of the Aquarian Age which is now coming into manifestation and will eventually become the guiding spirit of human relations and will be demonstrated on every level of human association – individual, group, communal, racial, national and international. The superficial observer is still blinded by the many and crude demonstrations of hate, greed and selfish acquisition but to those who are sensitive to the under currents which will finally determine relationships, the influence of the inpouring energies of love, goodwill, understanding and tolerance, can already be clearly felt. It will not be long now before their effect will become obvious throughout the world. Let each contribute his small share of loving understanding to hasten the coming of these joyful days for which all men yearn!

V. 5. The Intuition

Intuition is an expression of the light of the soul. It is the awareness by the mind of some aspects of truth, inspired by the soul and emanating from the world of ideas. These truths are always present on the higher spheres but remain unrecognised by the average man, beglamoured by the worlds of emotion, desire and physical manifestation. It is only when the disciple moves on to mental levels and the mind becomes trained, grows in sensitivity and is focussed on buddhic levels, that these ideas may be registered and revealed. These truths are first recognised, later understood, then gradually absorbed and finally adjusted to the disciple's needs and circumstances in accordance with the demands of time and place.

The final step achieved in the development of consciousness, is that the disciple functions through the intuition instead of through the lower or concrete mind, which will gradually be superseded.

Most of the advanced thinkers, active in the world's many fields of learning, avail themselves of the intuition but without being consciously aware of the process. Gradually large numbers are, however, becoming conscious of the subjective worlds and are being trained to qualify themselves for effective contact with the plane of the intuition.

When correctly used, the intuition enables man to become clearly aware of reality, without being obstructed any longer by the glamours and illusions of the three lower worlds. With the intuition functioning, the human being is enabled to take correct action in accordance with the demands of the Plan, because he is no longer dealing with distorted vision and ideas. He sees both life and all forms in true perspective and he is consequently pervaded by a proper sense of values, leading to a balanced outlook.

It is only as the disciple becomes intuitive that he is of real value in a Master's group. When the intuition is unfolding, the disciple may therefore be promoted from the probationary stage to that of acceptance in the Master's group. Every disciple should therefore strive to rid himself of his glamours and to live and function in the light of the intuition. This primarily means growing in sensitivity and an inner response to the soul. It is, however, a slow and gradual process and care should be taken not to hurry it unduly – in the life of the soul the time factor, reckoned in human terms, is not very important.

The great advantage of intuitive perception is its infallibility and swiftness in arriving at correct conclusions, in comparison with the slow and laborious working of the mind, coupled with its deviousness, inaccuracies, illusions and many other shortcomings.

Students are often inclined to confuse a clear analytical mind and an aptitude for rapid summing up of conditions and arriving at sound decisions, with the presence of the intuition. Such an individual may in fact still have a long way to go before intuitive perception will be at his disposal.

There are three basic attributes which qualify the intuition. These are:

(a) An *illumined mind* which will light the disciple's way and will guide him on his path of service.

(b) Perfect and spontaneous *understanding* in his dealings with his fellow man. This will be demonstrated by a steady love for all beings but also coupled with emotional detachment, which will ensure an objective and balanced approach to all problems.

(c)   The constant presence of *soul love*, demonstrated as that inclusive grasp of the inner needs of all beings and the ability to react positively to the relief of such need. This will lead to the breaking down of all barriers and the negating of hurtful criticism.

While glamour and illusion still dominate the life of the aspirant, the intuition cannot function. During his upward struggle he may, however, on rare occasions experience a flash of intuitive understanding, which might prove an additional spur to urge him along his adopted Path. It is only the intuition which will finally liberate the disciple from all illusion.

Although the unfolding disciple may during times of stress be guided by flashes of intuitive inspiration, the normal exercise of the true intuition will only become possible after the Third Initiation has been attained and when the concrete mind is being super-seded by the higher mind of the Spiritual Triad. At that stage the intuition will operate as normally as the mind principle in the case of an intelligent individual.

The intuition may be regarded as the channel of *revelation*. It is through the intuition that man progressively becomes aware of the subjective worlds, obtains the first inkling and insight into divine wisdom and the divine Plan, becomes conscious of the inner Christ and obtains a clearer concept of both the transcendent and immanent Deity.

It should always be kept in mind that the intuition is an impersonal energy which will not work effectively to obtain self-centred personality benefits. The individual will only be favoured by intuitive inspiration when his personal gain happens to be coincident with that of the group, commune or humanity as a whole. New truths and revelations are imparted with the purpose that these should be used to the advantage of the race and not to the perverted and glamoured desires of the individual. In many instances such new ideas however do fall into wrong hands and may then temporarily be abused and distort-ed to personal advantage, before they are finally retrieved and applied correctly to fulfil their original purpose of promoting communal interests.

V. 6. Illumination

Illumination is the condition of divine inspiration enabling man to recognise the Whole of which he forms a minute part. It is a form of super-human consciousness, functioning through the soul, which floods all human energy centres with light and links the con-scious mind through these illumined centres with the corresponding divine Whole.

In the past, illumination was associated with religion and mysticism but the position is changing and in the future the accent will rather fall on the intellectual approach and the light received from the mind as a reflection of soul light – intellectual illumination.

As the disciple progresses along his path of spiritual development, he may at first receive only an occasional flash of illumination, revealed through some rents which are appearing in the etheric web still separating the lower physical consciousness from the inner planes of being. As the years or lives go by and the disciple persists with his efforts at self-purification, study, meditation and loving service, these rents in the web will become more distinct and the illuminating flashes will recur with increasing frequency, until ultimately the Third Initiation is attained. At this stage the initiate is finally admitted into the World of Light of the soul and in the world of men 'he becomes a burning and shining light, radiating forth a light which burns from within.'

VI

THE SCIENCE OF CONTACT AND COMMUNICATION

VI. 1. Thought

(See also: PART ONE – X. 4. – "The Mental Body")

Man is today moving into a New Era; an era wherein the mind is going to play a dominating role; an era wherein human desire and emotion will be subverted to intellectual considerations and where improved human relations, based on loving understanding, will supervene. It will be an era wherein the power of thought will become the guiding principle of man's activities, in contrast to the past when man's actions were largely determined by physical and emotional considerations.

Under the circumstances a better understanding of the laws of thought must be regarded as essential. In the distant future the time will come when even concrete thought will be superseded by the intuition and when the lower mind will merely fulfil the functions of a transmitter – but that time is not yet. The attention should therefore first of all be focussed on the period of transition which is now being entered – the mental age, commanded by the realms of thought.

It should be pointed out that there are many grades of thought, when origin and consequent quality are taken into consideration. The mentally developed man will produce thoughts of totally different calibre from those of the man whose life is still largely focussed on the physical and emotional planes and who hardly ever touches the mental level. But there is also the other extreme of the advanced spiritual man leading a dual existence, manifesting in his material body in the physical world of men but simultaneously spending a considerable part of his thought life in contact with the intuitional plane of the soul.

Thoughts of an elevated nature which do not in the first instance concern the self but cover a wider interest, affecting the group, the community or the race as a whole, have their source from higher spiritual levels. The disciple is inspired with these subjective ideas to enable him to bring them down to mental levels and depending on their nature, subsequently to materialise them on the physical plane. These ideas, with their wide diversity, are intended to serve humanity's extensive needs during its never ending process of evolution.

Most of the thought-forms encountered on astral levels are, however, of quite a different quality. These are the thought-forms produced by the little evolved, who constitute the bulk of humanity. Many of these forms, which as yet hardly deserve the name of 'thoughts' originate from the solar plexus region as a result of emotional impulses, principally motivated by various forms of desire. They are mostly of a selfish nature, highly emotional and with only a minimum of mental inspiration. These thought-forms are as a rule rather vague, incomplete, of low vitality and are produced in such myriads that they hang like a heavy, slow vibrating fog or dense cloud, closely surrounding and partly smothering the greater part of the minds of the human family. This dark 'smog' deprives man of the light and energy with which mankind is being irradiated from On High and is responsible for much of the evil, crime and mental lethargy with which humanity is afflicted. Only those who after aeons of experience and suffering and after determined effort have managed to extricate themselves at least partly from this sapping atmosphere, can begin to benefit from the more refined energies so copiously available to those who are consciously becoming aware of their presence.

But for those who after persistent striving have found the Light, there is still no rest. On the contrary, their responsibility has now been increased and their next task is to forget all about further self-salvation and to throw in every ounce of their weight to help with the saving and up-lifting of their brothers who have been left behind and are still blindly struggling in the suffocating vapours of glamour and illusion. The one means of introducing light into these obscure layers is to concentrate on the right techniques for contacting the ideas constantly being inspired from higher planes, and how to translate these into suitable and vital thought-forms which can penetrate the layers of darkness and eventually disperse them.

The intelligent individual working from mental levels, consciously or unconsciously becomes a creator through the manipulation of the powers of thought. In the early stages this is a purely mental process but it should be remembered that all physical creation must primarily be either emotionally or mentally stimulated.

Thoughts are the product of the mind. To obtain a clear picture of these abstract concepts, a brief recapitulation might be useful:

Remember that the mind has three aspects:

(a) The Higher Mind – this is the spiritual aspect of the mind and constitutes part of the Spiritual Triad (Monad).
(b) The Son of Mind – the Soul.
(c) The lower or concrete mind of the personality.

Revelations from the Hierarchy are brought to man through the Higher Mind, which by means of the intuition passes ideas on to the soul, from where the lower mind is again inspired. The concrete mind formulates these ideas into thoughts and thought-forms, which are then reflected to the physical brain.

The present theme is concerned with the formulation of these thoughts and how they are brought into creative expression. It should first of all be realised that 'thoughts are things' and although of a most ephemeral nature, they nonetheless consist of substance, are in fact created entities and depending on the potency with which they are imbued, even dispose of creative powers. What man creates through the mind may be either commendable or harmful, depending on the motivating desire or purpose – the thoughtform being characterised by the nature of the infusing thought or spoken word.

The bulk of the human race have, however, not yet reached this creative stage, as they are still mostly emotionally activated and do not yet know how to handle matter on the mental plane. These human beings may be regarded as wax in the hands of the more advanced thinkers, until the stage arrives when they also begin to develop independent thought and are gradually transferred into the ranks of the creators.

It might be mentioned that the Tibetan has forecast that the New Age now being entered, will be characterised by tremendous mental unfoldment in the human race and it is fascinating to observe how this prophecy is actually in process of being verified. The relatively undeveloped, who in the past led a more or less passive existence and whose destinies were mainly dominated by the activities of the more advanced, are now mentally waking up. They refuse to be governed any longer by the laws of others and are coming into revolt. In the initial striving to realise their sometimes rather crude concepts of freedom and in exercising their new-found power, they are inclined to begin by smashing everything within reach; this often includes not only breaking the bonds which confined them but in their lust to exercise their power, they may also strike out wildly and injudiciously, hurting their own environment and the group to which they belong. Although sometimes most painful and expensive, such unbridled expression must fortunately only be regarded as a difficult phase of transition which will be outgrown with experience. The exuberant activities of these communities or nations will after a while calm down again and balance will be somewhat restored. As these people mentally develop, grow in sensitivity and become aware of higher vibrations, a growing consciousness will also develop of their destiny and the function they have to fulfil in the divine Plan. They will then begin to awaken to the beauty of the Plan and under the influence of the energy of the will-to-good, the urge will develop to submerge their own selfish concerns by promoting the interests of the greater human race. Their creative power will thus be sacrificed and merged with that of the greater encompassing energy and the smaller plans and ideas will be included in the greater Plan.

The above evolutionary unfoldment is similar whether applied to individuals, groups or nations and examples of those actively functioning on each of these levels and at the various stages of their development, may be observed all over the world.

Man himself is today directly or indirectly responsible for the distressing nature of human affairs. With some rare exceptions the majority of the race are distinguished by their selfish and sordid motives and prompt response to evil impulses. Subject to the Law of Cause and Effect, such attitude inevitably must lead to retributive effects and consequent world-wide suffering. Not only does man experience the harmful results of past undesirable physical activities but probably even worse is the fact that the etheric world has been poisoned by evil thoughts, energised by desire, greed and other injurious expressions of the promptings of the lower nature which have been accumulating over the ages. This giant thought-form of man's own making, hovers over and continually threatens the human race and it is going to be man's responsibility in the coming age, to break down and dissipate this menacing cloud of evil. This can and finally will be effected by the co-ordinated efforts of all men of goodwill under the active guidance and support of the Great Ones but it certainly will need time and unrelenting effort. Meanwhile every endeavour should be made to oppose all activities which might serve to increase the already fearsome dimensions of this threatening thought-form and to this every disciple who finds his way on to the Lighted Path can contribute his small share.

Although only few are yet consciously aware of it, one of the main functions of the Masters of the Wisdom is to guide and train man to become aware of his destiny as a creator within the divine Plan. In this respect it will be his responsibility to learn to work with and direct energy from the mental plane for creative purposes, in accordance with the ideas and plans which will from time to time be revealed to him. The needed inspiration will be acquired by sustained study, meditation and service.

Constructive thinkers will already have encountered the existing wall of antagonism which opposes the stream of energy they are directing for the construction of vital thought-forms intended to relieve suffering humanity. With the help of the Hierarchy all such opposition will be overcome:

(a) By imposing new, purer and more potent rhythms of thought and by raising these to a higher level.
(b) By contributing towards the dissipation of the murky clouds of vague and only partly vitalised thought-forms which clutter up the atmosphere surrounding mankind and which obstruct the constructive and vital thought-forms from higher mental levels.
(c) By awakening within increasing numbers of disciples the power of clear thought, teaching them how to energise these thought-forms to greater vitality and how these should be directed to achieve the desired objectives and maximum results on the physical plane.

To materialise these aims will require a clear comprehension by workers in the science of thought-construction of the power of thought; the directing of thought currents; the manipulation of mental matter and the process of thought manifestation and vitalisation. Above all it should be realised that no disciple will become of real assistance to the

269

Masters on behalf of humanity, until he has consciously directed his thought energy to some particular channel of service, with full understanding of the implications and sacrifices that will be involved.

For the building and materialisation of superior thought-forms some essential considerations must be fulfilled:

1. For achieving clear esoteric vision, to become aware of group needs and to serve world interests, the disciple must purify himself of lower desires and selfish obsessions.
2. The mind must be brought under control through concentration and esoteric meditation, to enable him to obtain the necessary inspiration from higher levels and thus to become aware of some of the basic principles of the divine Plan and to determine what his contribution should be towards realising the Plan.
3. The disciple will have to acquire the correct technique for directing the newly constructed thought-form on its mission and to supply and vitalise it with sufficient and suitable energy until the objective is attained and fulfilled.

VI. 1 (a) **Power of Thought**

Could man but be convinced of the fantastic powers at his command when thoughts are correctly motivated and controlled! God has provided his children with the divine spark of mind but how few there are who realise that the divine prerogative of creative power has been coupled with this sublime grant. Men are mostly totally unaware of these powers which are at their disposal or these faculties are slighted and neglected either through ignorance or indolence. With the right motivation and the correct techniques of thought manipulation, man is literally able to 'move mountains'.

The creating entity generates energy in direct proportion to the intensity of his thinking and its quality will be determined by the theme of the thought. Directly or indirectly all conscious thought is of divine origin, although in its process of descent it may become badly distorted and degenerated.

All of creation, the whole Universe with all its manifested forms of life and appearance, is the product of Divine Thought. The Supreme Creator has partly delegated these powers of conscious creation by thought to entities of an ever descending range of power and quality, till in our solar system the lowest point in this sequence has been reached by entrusting the human being with these creative forces which can be consciously wielded.

The truism that 'Energy follows Thought' is but another way of expressing the statement by the Christ that 'As a man thinketh in his heart, so is he'. Both these sayings indicate that these facts have been known from time immemorial – what a pity that man does not take sufficient notice of this law of nature by keeping a constant watch on his thought-life. To produce salutary effects, this potent and creative mind organism should, as far as possible, be kept under close control, with the purpose of guiding it only into positive and constructive channels. Instead of this the mind is usually allowed to wander arbitrarily and to jump about ineffectively from one thought to another, not focussing clearly and long enough on one subject to be able to give it form and to put it on its way to realisation. In a way this probably is just as well, because so many of man's casual thoughts are not only of a negative nature but are degrading, vindictive and most undesirable in some or other respect and would definitely have been harmful to the individual himself or to others, if they had been given sufficient form and potency and if purposefully directed.

The statement that thought is a product of the mind is, however, not quite correct – thoughts are elaborations or recastings of ideas, which originate from spiritual levels, and the mind is but the instrument by which these ideas are transmuted into thoughts. The mind is furthermore the agent for the direction of the thought and guides the energies needed for this purpose.

VI. 1 (b) Thought control

The Tibetan has summarised the problems of thought control in a number of rules, the gist of which have been set out below. Some of these may appear unduly simple to the self-assured, others are couched in symbolic terms and still others cover more than will be apparent to the casual student. He gives the assurance, however, that they will serve as a safe guide to effective thought control, which will then lead to Truth.

1. Consider the world of thought and try to separate the false from the true.
2. Become aware of the fact of illusion and search for the purity of the underlying truth.
3. Emotions should be controlled, because the disturbance they cause precludes the light of truth and brings all plans to failure.
4. Become aware of the dual purposes of the mind.
5. Learn to concentrate the thought-life and to gain control over the mind.
6. Learn that the thinker, the instrument through which the thought is passed, is not the origin of the thought.
7. Learn to make positive use of thought and not to debase it for purposes of desire.
8. The energy of thought should not be used for selfish purposes but should be applied on behalf of humanity and to promote the realisation of the Plan.
9. Before constructing a thought-form make sure of its true purpose and that it is soundly motivated.
10. The aspirant has not yet reached the stage where he can consciously construct creative thought-forms. His task, to begin with, is to clear his thought aura of undesirable elements, by excluding all thoughts of hate and pain, of fear, jealousy and desire.
11. Speech is a reflection of the thoughts, therefore mark your words.
12. There are three kinds of speech:
    (a) If idle words are used, these should be of a kind nature. If vindictive, the price will have to be paid for their harmful effect.

(b) Selfish words cause separation which may be difficult to rectify. Before speaking attend to your motives – seek to use words which will blend your life with the divine Plan.

(c) Words of hate and poisonous gossip must harm those whom they concern but at the same time they will smother the soul impulses and destroy the spiritual life of those who send them forth. If they are uttered to hurt and harm, these energies must in due course inevitably recoil on the sender with equal strength and with their full adverse effects.

13. Forget about the self with all its personal desires, emotions and ambitions; forget to pity the self for all the apparent reverses of life. This self-focus prevents contact with the soul. Think of others and how and where help can be rendered. Strive for greater subjective sensitivity and for more effective service of the Plan.

VI. 1 (c) Speech

A great deal of talk is heard that is mostly ineffective, denoting only inane babbling, representative of the crowded, superficial thoughts flitting through the etheric world and originating from the lower astral spheres – talk that merely concerns the many aspects of the personality and the life of desire and emotion. Such talk will have little positive influence on the affairs of men and merely contributes towards increasing the dense fogs of glamour and of indeterminate thought-forms by which man is surrounded, thus limiting his consciousness and outer vision.

Speech is the purveyor of thought. As a man progresses along his evolutionary path and his thoughts and consciousness are elevated to higher levels, his speech becomes correspondingly more meaningful and the disciple should begin to take greater care of the way he expresses himself. On still higher levels, the role of speech will again begin to decrease, because the stage will eventually be reached where communication between fellow workers will principally be based on intuitive perception and telepathic interplay of thought, making speech to some extent superfluous. However, for the average man this is still something for the distant future.

In ordinary social relationships man is judged by his speech, by what he says and the opinions he expresses, by his fair analysis and summing up of his fellow human beings or his unjust and harsh criticism. The man is judged by his conversation – both by the thoughts he expresses and by what he leaves unsaid. His words disclose what is going on in his mind and therefore give a reflection of his ethical standards and the levels attained in his mental and spiritual development.

In the modern world with its ever improving communication systems and news media, represented by widely distributed newspapers and radio and television networks, written and spoken words are becoming of increasing importance and the power which such speech may exert in shaping public opinion, can hardly be over stressed. The masses who themselves have but limited reasoning powers, are readily swayed by the smooth orator gifted with the effective use of words and knowing the art of just slightly distorting facts to gain the required effects, meanwhile retaining the semblance of speaking the truth. Such men also know how to abuse inherent racial differences and feelings and how to fan race and class hatreds and thus to turn the balance of unthinking public opinion in their favour. If wrongly used, as so often happens, such agitators may cause incalculable harm with their gift of speech and may easily retard the development of whole nations for decades.

So far these news media have as a rule been controlled by self-seeking men with selfish financial or political motives. But changes are becoming noticeable and as the thought-life of mankind is being lifted to higher mental levels and as new ideas and patterns of thought are being introduced by the Hierarchy, these same powers of speech will gradually be transferred into the hands (and words) of trained intuitives and thinkers. These men of goodwill and high mental calibre will prove to be well equipped for their purposes; they will be free of personal ambition and will be inspired by altruism and love of humanity; by their powers of speech they will exert enormous influences to guide the masses towards the Lighted Way and the creation of a better world.

VI. 1 (d) Ideas

Ideas are the single bricks from which the divine Plan is constructed. Occasionally and for some specific purpose, a Master may by mental telepathy bring a particular idea to the attention of a disciple but usually it is left to the initiative of the thinker to penetrate the intuitive levels by means of the focussed mind and there, by his own powers, to recognise those specific ideas which are required for the purposes of his life.

The plane of the intuition contains that inexhaustible hoard of ideas, comprising every conceivable subject on all spheres of human activity, which may be needed either for the present or for the ultimate development of man. These ideas have been gathered there by Spiritual Entities to serve the needs of humanity and in their totality they constitute the divine Plan. In esoteric literature this world of ideas is also known under the descriptive name of the '*Raincloud of Knowable Things*' – an expression derived from the writings of an ancient Sage, Patanjali. It is this 'raincloud' which serves as the revelatory storehouse and the source of inspiration for all human development.

Without being aware of it, this raincloud is the fountain head from which philosophers, scientists, inventors, visionaries and the thinkers of the world obtain their ideas, impressions, brain waves or promptings, oft under the illusion that these ideas are their own brain-children and the direct product of their own intelligence. The fact of the matter is that through their training or inherent intelligence, they have merely been qualified to act as suitable instruments for registering existing ideas on the plane of the intuition and for bringing them 'down to Earth'.

Esotericists on the other hand are being trained to contact the raincloud by means of conscious meditation and thus to tap these intuitive sources of ideas, which are then brought down to mental levels to be incorporated in their plans of service for humanity.

All esoteric themes are subject to qualification depending on the point of approach and because it is rarely possible to cover a topic completely owing to the numerous facets every subject contains, many of which will only be revealed with increasing light and expansion of consciousness. This also applies to the assertions made above with regard to the manifestation of ideas. There are for instance ideas which do not need to be laboriously abstracted from the 'raincloud' by thinkers of the race but which the Hierarchy *nolens volens impose* on the racial mind. Notwithstanding man's *free will*, he cannot escape being influenced by these imposed ideas and in this respect he certainly is no free agent. Once these ideas have, however, been cognised and translated into ideals, then he is again free to either accept or reject them. The rate of man's progress will largely be determined by the effective use being made of these divine presentations.

The ideas which will be contacted in the early stages will be faint and nebulous and difficult to bring down to mental levels but with sustained efforts results will improve and the ideas will become more clearly defined for registering on the concrete mind. It is only after reaching the mind that these ideas are formulated into distinguishable thoughts.

A period of gestation will follow during which the newly born thought-form will slowly begin to take on more definite shape. As this child of the mind develops, an urge is sensed to bring this thought to Earth and to materialise it, so that it may serve its purpose and can be shared by others. The thinker then begins to vitalise it by means of the power of his will and slowly the thought-form is clothed in mental and astral matter.

From this stage the final materialisation of the vision on the physical plane rarely remains the work of one man. The thought is communicated to many and only after several workers have contributed their share towards its vivification, can their united efforts bring the form into physical manifestation. Successful cultivation of public opinion may under such circumstances prove of considerable value to obtain sufficient helpers to bring the form into actual appearance.

Every creation or manifestation in the three worlds of human expression must be regarded as the materialisation or reflection of some subjective idea or complex of ideas. The idea must, however, first exist on spiritual levels before it can take on the qualities of a thought and can subsequently be translated into material form.

The rate of revelation as reflected in human development, will depend on the number and quality of the available thinkers, how soon the ideas can be recognised and abstracted from the 'raincloud' and the efficiency with which these ideas are nurtured and finally materialised and put at the disposal of mankind. It is of course of the greatest importance that this translation of the idea be effected with the minimum of distortion. If the idea becomes too badly mutilated, it may become worthless or its effects may even over-balance and prove to be harmful and work out to the detriment of man. It should always be remembered that every idea has both its positive and negative pole and its final influence will depend on man's approach and handling of the forces that are put at his disposal.

The history of the world is but the recording of the results that have accrued from the ideas which have over the ages progressively been revealed to man through various channels. It reflects the extent to which these ideas have either been beneficially applied to the common benefit or abused by applying them for the satisfaction of selfish desire in some of its many facets.

Illusion may be regarded as the reaction of the undisciplined mind to the newly contacted world of ideas. A basically excellent or sound idea may readily be distorted into a useless or adverse illusion. One of the main objectives of the disciple should therefore be to qualify and train himself to lift the mind to the plane of the intuition and there to work and live in the world of ideas; to learn to recognise and distinguish them clearly and then to bring them down to Earth with a minimum of distortion for the service of humanity. No idea that may be contacted is ever complete or perfect in itself. Every idea is merely a fragment of the greater Whole and the endeavour of the disciple should therefore be to bring down as much of the Plan as lies within his capacity.

In the early stages of his development the aspirant, the scientist or thinker may be inclined to appropriate ideas as their own and to regard them as the product of their own fertile brains, little realising that they have but served as a channel for its manifestation and that no ideas ever can belong or should be retained by an individual for selfish purposes. Ideas should be regarded as a universal gift to mankind as a whole and the channel or instrument should recognise that he has had the honour to have been selected to serve its purpose. There is therefore no such thing as a man-made idea, since all basic and true ideas are of divine origin. Those ideas which are considered to be man-made, are merely thought-forms which are greater or lesser perversions of some original idea derived from the plane of the intuition.

Moreover, no ordinary human being can ever hope to encompass the full extent of an idea, which is always so much bigger than the idealist who may be favoured to contact it. Such recognition must inevitably lead to an attitude of humility and no great mind can ever be anything but humble, thus being protected against narrowness of outlook and interpretation.

VI. 1 (e) Dreams

Man has been interested in his dream-life since the earliest days of his conscious existence. Dreams largely concern the astral life and during Atlantean times, when man was basically astral in consciousness, a complete science was built on dreams. With the passing ages and especially with the decline and subsequent final destruction of the Atlantean civilisation, this science was lost. It is only now being revived to some extent by individual psychologists, who are trying to establish the link between dream life and the condition of their patients.

During these intervening ages interest in dreams, however, never faded and every period of civilisation produced its quota of magicians, prophets, soothsayers and psychics, who served as explainers of dreams to royalty, the intelligentsia and to the man in the street.

Until recently the analysis of dreams has generally been approached from the astral aspect, instead of considering it mentally. The consequence has been that during the course of the ages there probably have been very few who have fully realised the extreme complexity of the subject. Those who are interested in dreams and more particularly those psychologists who make a penetrating study of this theme, might find useful guidelines in the Tibetan's exposition on pages 493-510 of *Esoteric Psychology* (Vol. II).

Briefly summarised, there are ten principal sources of dreams:

1. *Dreams based upon brain activity*. In these cases the subject is sleeping too lightly and his thread of consciousness is not as completely withdrawn as in deep sleep. He therefore remains in a state of daze or semi-sleep but without a clear recognition or interpretation of his normal thought life. No importance need be attached to this type of 'dream', which in fact is not dreaming at all. This condition indicates a state of physical nervousness which should be attended to. It is one of the demands of nature that all forms of manifestation should at times go through periods of rest or 'sleep' for physical recuperation.

2. *Dreams of astral remembrance*. These dreams are a pictorial recovery of the sights and sounds experienced upon the astral plane during the hours of sleep. This is the plane where the consciousness usually dwells when temporarily separated from the body. All such dreams concerned with the astral world, are evidently subject to glamour and illusion. They may relate to personal participation in astral activities or else they may merely refer to the registration of impressions of the sleeper while he acted as an astral onlooker at sights and performances of people within the astral environment.

3. *Dreams which are recollections of true activity*. This is the capacity to continue man's normal waking activities on the astral plane during the hours of sleep. The dreams will then simply be the record on the physical brain of the recognised astral experiences and may thus prove to be of direct help. The value of such dreams will, however, have to be carefully considered, as they might be affected by glamour and illusion, as well as the impressions of other beings which may have been contacted during such astral excursions.

4. *Dreams of a mental nature*. In contrast with the majority of dreams which are of a purely astral nature, these have their origin on the mental plane and indicate a considerable degree of mind control. These dreams are fundamentally of three kinds:

(a) Those based on contact with the world of thought-forms. They may comprise both the realms of ancient and modern thought but they remain of purely human origin and will consist of every possible theme of thought.
(b) Dreams of a geometrical nature, in which the subject becomes aware of symbolic patterns and forms, sometimes of a strange and totally unexpected and inexplicable nature. These are concerned with the evolutionary process of the man and the symbols of his unfolding consciousness.
(c) During the hours of sleep disciples often undergo mental instruction on the astral plane by subjective entities. These teachings are unconsciously registered by the mind and may sometimes be reflected in dream by some symbolic representation.

5. *Dreams of astral activities.* During their hours of sleep many aspirants are constructively employed on a variety of activities, in accordance with their qualifications and characteristics. This work may be selfishly performed or of an altruistic nature, depending on the stage of development and attributes of the dreamer. The clarity with which such activities are reflected in the dreams, will depend on the continuity of the unfolding consciousness.

6. *Telepathic dreams.* During moments of crisis real events are sometimes telepathically communicated from one person to another. This the mind often registers unconsciously, only reflecting it as a dream during sleep. Happenings to other people which may have been telepathically recorded, can subsequently be interpreted by the dreamer as being his own experiences. There are four types of dreams which may be associated with individuals who are establishing closer and conscious, soul contact. Their *experiences on soul levels* are registered in the mind, from where they are transferred to the brain and this impression may then be reflected in the individual's dreams.

7. *Dreams which are dramatisations by the soul.* This is a symbolic performance by the soul to give instruction, warning or command to its instrument, the physically conscious man.

8. *Dreams concerned with group work.* In this type of dream the soul trains its instrument for group activities. Many mystical writings of the past, intended for the guidance of group members, are the recordings of dream experiences of this nature.

9. *Dreams which are records of instructions.* This concerns teachings given by the Master to his disciple but communicated to the soul. The soul then impresses them on the mind, where they are formulated into thought-forms for reflection on the brain. The disciple's response will then depend on his mental development, which will determine the correctness of his interpretation of the teachings.

10. ***Dreams connected with the divine Plan.*** In certain instances a Master may communicate teachings to an advanced disciple during his dream-life and on awakening the server will recognise this 'dream' as a spiritual message or inspiration and therefore of deep significance. This is another illustration of the direct line of communication between soul and brain.

In the foregoing summary the various types of dreams have been set out very sketchily, merely with the object of providing an idea of the complexity of the subject and to indicate a few of the many facets which should be considered when attempts are made at analysing and explaining the world of dreams.

VI. 2. Consciousness

The basic concepts of the Ageless Wisdom all revolve around the principle of consciousness, its awakening and its evolutionary progress through the world of physical expression. Consciousness and Light are largely synonymous – consciousness merely representing the manifestation of Light as expressed through God's creations on Earth.

Consciousness is that intangible product of the relationship between Spirit and Matter. This same description can actually be applied for defining the soul and a close similarity therefore exists between these two concepts. The difference will be recognised when it is stated that consciousness is the main characteristic of the soul. This also denotes the inseparable trilogy of:

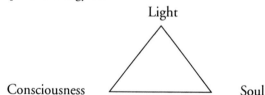

Light

Consciousness   Soul

Consciousness also implies ***understanding*** – understanding of the relationship between that which man knows as physical manifestation or appearance and the subjective, intangible world of Reality. May man ever strive for deeper and more complete understanding!

Individualisation or the lifting of man from the animal to the human kingdom, was achieved with the first manifestation of *self-consciousness*. The whole object of man's subsequent existence is the progressive unfoldment of this consciousness and it is taught that when man finally achieves consciousness on all planes, then the present solar system will have served its purpose.

Progressive evolution of consciousness will lead to successive points of attainment, which in esoteric terminology are known as ***initiations***. With individualisation there is therefore firstly initiation into conscious existence and, after aeons of development, this subsequently leads to initiation into spiritual existence or group identification.

The concept of consciousness as a rule denotes the self-consciousness as exhibited by man but it should be pointed out again that every form in manifestation, whether this refers to an atom of a mineral, a plant or an animal, contains life of some sort and will therefore also exhibit some degree of consciousness, which is reflected as reaction to external stimuli. With improved equipment, science is now discovering that both plant and animal life dispose of a much more refined and sensitive consciousness than man ever dreamt of. These new scientific explorations are only in the initial stages of unveiling a vast new realm of research, which is now rapidly being revealed as a result of man's inspired mental probing. The Aquarian Age is now definitely being entered and man is availing himself of the new stream of Light-energy to which the Hierarchy is subjecting humanity, which must inevitably lead to a clearer recognition of the veiled subjective worlds and also to a better understanding of the consciousness of the lower kingdoms of nature.

One of the results of these new disclosures will be that many old and established concepts and laws of science will be shaken to their very foundations and will have to be drastically revised and adapted. It will, however, prove to be a golden age for science and will ultimately lead to a point where both science and religion will meet on the same plane and where a relatively close co-operation will develop between them.

A point that should be clearly understood is that man is not only conscious while he is in physical incarnation. Because his consciousness is associated with the soul, it does not matter whether the soul happens to be in or out of incarnation – the consciousness remains unaltered. The consciousness can in fact evolve with greater ease when not restricted by the limitations of the physical brain.

All forms of creation, all lives, whether mineral, plant, animal, human or spirit, are intimately related to each other through the planetary etheric body which integrates them all and through which the One Life is poured. The only meaningful difference which distinguishes the many and various forms, is the degree of consciousness they exhibit. It may be said that the unfoldment of consciousness is the goal of all the evolutionary processes on our planet. All forms are constantly vitalised by perpetual streams of circulating energies which simultaneously promote the unfolding consciousness. The state of consciousness attained by any form at any particular time, is reflected in its *etheric aura*, which can thus be evaluated at a glance by those who dispose of etheric vision.

As far as the human being is concerned, his phenomenal appearance is controlled by two principles – *Life* and *Consciousness*. While man is in incarnation, the consciousness principle is located within the brain and the nervous system is used as its sensory instrument. The heart on the other hand, acts as the central organ for the life principle, with the bloodstream as its medium of control.

A clear distinction must therefore be made between the Life Thread (or 'sutratma') and the Consciousness Thread (the 'bridge of light' or 'antahkarana'):

The *Life Thread* links and vivifies all forms into one functioning whole and embodies in itself the Will and Purpose of the expressing Entity by Life. In the human being the thread of Life reaches from the Monad to the personality, via the soul and finally becomes anchored in the heart.

The *Consciousness Thread* is the ever extending channel, connecting the consciousness within the form to an expanding range of contacts within the surrounding whole. It is the result of the union of Life and substance or the reaction of Life on the physical form.

The Life Thread therefore operates from the Monad downwards into physical manifestation, in contrast to the Consciousness Thread which is evolved by the primary creation of Life and then unfolds from below – from the form upwards, with the object of reuniting with the Monad. This is the 'Path of Return'.

VI. 2 (a) Expansion of Consciousness

The evolution of spiritual man by means of physical incarnation, is simply a process of progressive recognition of new facets of the Truth, each recognition leading to fresh expansions of consciousness. Experience gained in the material world, signifies that the point of view becomes enlarged, which must inevitably lead to unfoldment of consciousness. This in turn, if carried forward, produces a changing appreciation of the qualities of the environment, leading to fresh experiences, further phenomena and ever new stages of being. And thus will the spiral of life experience and expansion of consciousness continue, reaching to ever higher levels.

The rate of development will vary from life to life, as well as during the course of individual lives. Periods of apparent spiritual stagnation will alternate with periods of rapid unfoldment of awareness but the tendency will ever be upwards. Once the disciple has entered the Path of Return, he can never again be really static; he will never rest and will constantly have to adjust himself to new conditions and make new adaptations, until his consciousness is stabilised in the Self.

In the early stages of his development, the disciple identifies the soul with the form and regards his physical appearance as the Self, considering this form as all there is. The next stage is the recognition of *duality*, when the indwelling self becomes aware of Itself and begins to distinguish between the Higher Self or Soul and the form or not-self. He then realises that the human being is constituted of the soul and the threefold personality, through which it functions and gains experience in the world of physical expression.

This awareness of the duality of being may continue for a long period, often stretching over several lives, with the consciousness still predominantly focussed in the form and with only a periodic faint recognition of the presence of the soul. This balance will, however, gradually change with a growing realisation of the pressure that the soul is beginning to exert on life attitudes and decisions. This will lead to a period of vacillation and uncertainty but little by little the soul will acquire greater dominance, till finally the disciple comes to the realisation that there is nothing but the soul working through an instrument perfectly responding to its behests.

As the disciple progresses along the Path, every expansion of consciousness increases his capacities and therefore his responsibilities, and this also denotes an ever growing scope for effective service of his fellow man. In the early stages there remains some degree of selfishness in his striving for unfoldment but in the course of time this attitude will pass; the will-to-good will begin to supervene and all personality concerns will fade into the background. The striving for greater expansion of consciousness and for more Light on the Path, now indicates the intent to become a more effective channel for the flow of soul energies and thus a more efficient instrument of service.

An aspect which should be recognised, is that in his progress the disciple does not necessarily move onwards towards new environments. The process is literally that of an expanding consciousness and thereby recognising that '*all that IS, is ever present*'. What it amounts to is that purblind man is surrounded by the distorting fogs of the astral world and with the etheric web separating him from subjective realms, is prevented from seeing that which eternally exists. These astral miasmas and the obstructing veil can only be dispelled by focussing the light of the mind and soul on the obscured regions. Meanwhile the portals giving access to fertile realms of investigation, of discovery and subsequent expansions in consciousness, stand wide open and it is but for the explorer to avail himself of the opportunities.

VI. 2 (b)   Continuity of Consciousness

The advanced disciple should strive towards continuity of consciousness. This is the capacity to preserve a constant and sequential recollection and awareness of both the physical and astral worlds – the outer and the inner life. As the energies of light of both the mind and the soul progressively dissolve the etheric web separating the two worlds, he will consciously become aware of and will be enabled to participate in the activities of the astral spheres. He will then be fully aware, for twenty-four hours a day, of the happenings on both these spheres of man's being.

The majority of disciples in training are actively engaged in some sphere of service in the astral realm during their hours of sleep but, as yet, they remain unaware of this in their physical memory. With the destruction of the etheric web, these activities will, however, also be registered by the brain and the disciple will thus achieve constant contact with the astral world.

Continuity of consciousness will of course dispel all fear of death and when the time for transition arrives, this will be effected without any break in conscious awareness. As far as his consciousness is concerned, the man who has 'passed over' will know himself to be exactly what he was before, with only this difference that he will no longer be encumbered and restricted by the physical vehicle.

Sustained esoteric meditation is the surest method for promoting the bridging of the gap in consciousness, firstly between the soul and the lower bodies and subsequently between the soul-infused personality and the Higher Mind. Such persistent work on the construction of this 'Bridge of Light' will ensure that continuity of consciousness is eventually achieved.

VI. 3. The Science of Impression

All modes of communication between the physical and spiritual worlds are founded on the laws of impression. The constant unfoldment and evolution of all that is manifested on the physical plane is but a reflection of parallel processes proceeding on subjective levels. As above, so below! For this higher evolution to be maintained, it stands to reason that there must exist still more exalted planetary or cosmic sources of knowledge for satisfying the growing demands of the superior Entities. This lofty information is apparently also provided by means of impression but these are matters of interest which do not directly concern us at this stage and the present context will therefore be limited to a consideration of those impressions which affect the activities of man.

The classification to be used in the succeeding pages is largely artificial, as the subject matter interflows and overlaps. The sub-divisions which have been adopted are merely intended to stress particular facets of 'impression'.

VI. 3 (a) Impression

Impressions guiding the disciple towards his next objective on his evolutionary path, may arise from several sources:
(a) From his own *Soul*, after alignment with the personality has been established. This is the silent but insistent inner voice which so often remains unheeded. It may also reveal itself as the **intuition** which will guide him unerringly if correctly interpreted and obeyed. The aspirant, when registering his first clear impressions, often has the erroneous idea that these must emanate directly from some elevated source, not yet acknowledging the inherent powers of his own divine soul, which in the past has been suppressed or negated, with little opportunity of exerting its influence. Only after the gap between the soul and the lower mind has been bridged, will the soul be able to play its effective and destined role, and this role should never be slighted.
(b) From the *Master* by direct telepathic impression after the necessary sensitivity has been developed.
(c) Through the *disciple's group* and the interplay of mental and spiritual energy which results from the co-operative rendering of service to humanity. This group refers not only to those with whom he is collaborating in the flesh but also to those very active

members who are out of incarnation and with whom he is consciously or unconsciously co-operating. These members, working from subjective levels, may exert a considerable influence on his activities.

(d) At a later stage, after completion of the 'Bridge of Light' and when contact has been effected with the Spiritual Triad, personality activities will come under direct ***monadic control.***

In addition to the above, some lesser sources of impression can also be mentioned, such as mental or telepathic impression originating from the multitude of thinkers in the world. On a somewhat lower plane emotional impression also occurs, often evoked by aspiration, but this astral product will be mainly of a selfish and individual nature.

Aspirants are mostly still polarised in their astral nature and their problem is how to withdraw their attention from the astral aura and to swing the focus of their efforts to the mental sphere. This can only be slowly achieved and will demand the persistent and concentrated efforts of the disciple.

The etheric body is the vital link between the subjective and tangible worlds. It not only serves as the connecting medium for conducting energies but also as the extremely sensitive receiver of impressions and impulses from external sources. These impressions are passed through the relative etheric centre and are then finally registered in the human consciousness, where they become the incentives for the shaping of thought-forms which will eventually initiate some form of conscious activity.

These motivating energies, under the comprehensive name of 'impressions', are also known by several other synonyms such as inspirations, impulses, guidance, incentives, influences, potencies, desires and aspirations and they all convey the same general idea of a vibrant and stimulating energy or force.

The primary task of the beginner is to develop sensitivity to impulses from higher sources and this can be effected by purifying the mind and cultivating selflessness and harmlessness. Such practices will lead to emotional control, a serene aura and a responsive spiritual sense, which will be receptive to impression and will subsequently become adjusted to correct interpretation of the impressions.

As the disciple acquires greater freedom of thought and develops sensitivity to impressions from the abstract mind (monadic impression), as well as from the several other sources, he accumulates within himself a *'reservoir of thought' or wisdom*, which will be at his disposal whenever required for the helping of his fellow man or for the requirements of his growing responsibilities towards world service. A 'fount of knowledge' is thus being provided on which he may draw at will when material may be needed for the teaching of others.

The point that should be stressed is that sensitivity to impression is a normal and natural unfoldment and is evoked by engendering a magnetic aura upon which impressions from elevated sources may be registered. This unfolding aura naturally and spontaneously evokes into his field of consciousness the broad outlines and later some details, of the hierarchical Plan and eventually also some concept of the divine Purpose. There is no need for him laboriously to search these impressions – they are inevitably attracted to him because he is ready and they have been spiritually invoked. With the course of time and increasing contacts this 'spiritual sense' will become an habitual state of consciousness and will be an indication of the successful completion of the 'Bridge of Light' between the soul and the personality and that the second span between the soul-infused personality and the Spiritual Triad is under construction.

Sensitivity to hierarchical impression will, however, not exempt the disciple from simultaneous sensitivity in his astral nature to emotional appeals from his fellow human beings – to be of real service to humanity the disciple must at all times be prepared to live the dual life and to function in both the spiritual and physical worlds of activity.

It is also important that the disciple should train himself to improve his capacity for *correct interpretation* of recorded impressions. All recorded truths are subject to several interpretations and as the server progresses on his path of enlightenment, new facets of these truths will be revealed to him with increasing clarity. In this respect it is important that impressions, from whatever source, should descend directly from mental levels to the brain, avoiding all contact with the astral body. It is the astral consciousness which is fallible and which distorts all thought-forms passing through its murky atmosphere.

VI. 3 (b) Inspiration

When esoteric literature refers to inspiration, it specifically alludes to impressions emanating from higher levels. In these instances the inspired messages are transmitted directly from the mind to the brain, without any danger of distortion by the astral consciousness. Once the disciple has succeeded in lifting himself out of the astral world of glamour and illusion and has eliminated all fear, doubt and worry, his sources of inspiration will increase surprisingly.

Only the well advanced disciple is ever favoured with genuine inspiration, for it involves egoic consciousness. Because these inspired ideas originate from the pure sources of the soul or from higher planes, they may always be reacted to with confidence.

Inspiration may be transmitted:

(a) By telepathically radiating thoughts into the brain of the designated channel.

(b) By direct overshadowing or occupation of the disciple's physical body, while the latter consciously and willingly stands aside in his etheric and astral bodies.

(c) By a temporary fusing on mental levels of the inspiring entity with the inspired instrument.

The disciple is often unaware of the source of his inspiration but provided his motives are pure and his efforts are directed towards serving humanity, this ignorance will not matter and his thoughts will continue to be inspired, provided that there exists effective alignment with his soul and that the suitable channels of contact are maintained by meditation.

Inspired thoughts are responsible for the writings which in the past have resulted in the world's Scriptures and in more recent years in other inspired writings, as well as the illumined utterances of inspired speakers. Inspiration is also reflected in the several forms of art which under favourable circumstances are the expressions of soul-infused personalities, who act as co-operative channels for forces and ideas originating from higher planes.

VI. 3 (c) Sensitivity

In every disciple spiritual development automatically results in a growing refinement of the vehicles and consequent increased sensitivity. This produces a capacity for ready response to incentives but simultaneously exposes the individual to increased pain and suffering on the emotional level. The latter disadvantage will, however, be far outweighed by the spiritual gains.

Undue attention to the cultivation of sensitivity may easily lead to harmful emotional disturbances. This quality should therefore be allowed to unfold normally and as a natural sequence to spiritual evolution. When the disciple is correctly oriented, completely dedicated and is becoming less self-centred, then the needed perceptivity will follow automatically.

The Hierarchy, in their search for disciples who might serve as channels of communication, are mainly interested in men who display the basic qualities of sensitivity. These qualities will allow the consciousness to expand to ever wider ranges of contact. Such workers should be vitally alert and quick to recognise and then to react to the physical, emotional and mental needs of their fellow men. The required sensitivity should not be confused with petulance, super-sensitivity or self-centredness, with a proneness to depression and self-pity or touchiness to slights and misunderstandings. These only cause bewilderment. It is *spiritual sensitivity* that is required, which will be distinguished by alertness to soul impression and reactivity to the inner voice of the Teacher, plus susceptibility to the impact of new ideas and intuitional impulses.

As a rule man is innately sensitive but this sensitivity to subjective influences is largely nullified by preoccupation with material concerns and objective living – man is so occupied with his daily physical and emotional activities and reactions, that he does not allow himself a quiet moment to think beyond his material requirements and desires or to sense the impressions playing on his mental aura. There are many, however, who are ready for this subjective impression, if they can only dim the loud claims of the personality and allow the voice from the soul to penetrate their mental consciousness.

The mind of the advanced disciple may be compared with a sensitive receiving plate, on which impulses and impressions are telepathically registered. These impressions originate from thoughts produced from his human environment, from the intuitional plane and inspired by the soul and finally from hierarchical levels.

Although man, while still functioning in the physical world, needs *emotional sensitivity* for his daily activities and relationships, this astral response should be kept under close control. Astral sensitivity is fallible and the resulting interpretations are frequently glamoured and erroneous. What the disciple needs is *mental sensitivity* to impulses emanating from intuitive and higher planes – when these are correctly registered, recognised and interpreted, they will prove infallible and will lead to perfectly rendered service.

The human race is showing a growing perceptivity, which is in the first instance demonstrated on astral levels, as evidenced by the world-wide growth of both spiritualism and other aspects of the psychic sciences. It is also evinced by increased nervous tension and related neurotic conditions and mental diseases. These disrupting influences, although temporarily unsettling and disturbing, should be welcomed as heralds of the New Age. Conditions will begin to improve when more of the world's sensitives raise their perceptivity from astral to mental levels and when recognition of and alignment with, the world of souls is becoming more general.

The sensitive disciple can become a power station for his environment, working in close association with the Hierarchy. He can become a focal point for the reception and distribution of energies which have been evoked by humanity and thus he may become a beacon of Light for the spiritual illumination of the minds of his fellow men.

VI. 3 (d) Guidance

As man becomes spiritually oriented and more clearly aware of inner realms, there will be a simultaneous recognition of the presence of various forms of subjective guidance.

To subject oneself blindly and submissively to external guiding forces of whatever nature, would eventually reduce man to a purely negative and impressionable automaton. Man should therefore make an effort to determine the source and quality of guidance, thus gaining a better understanding of the forces to which he is being subjected and with which he should endeavour to co-operate.

There are many mystic groups, schools and movements in existence, who stress the need for guidance but few of them seem to have any real understanding of the subject. On the whole their approach is sentimental, negatively introspective and astrally oriented, with very little or no mental substantiation at all. Many of the voices giving guidance or impulses which they claim are divinely inspired, are merely the products of auto-suggestion and are of a purely emotional nature. These practices will yield very little spiritual progress and might even have harmful physical and psychological effects.

The theme of guidance is extensive and complicated and will provide the student with a fertile field for deeper exploration in an endeavour to reach a clearer understanding of its many implications. For this purpose a few notes on the variety of forms of so-called guidance might prove useful:

1. Guidance or instruction from teachers on the physical plane will either be of a mental or emotional nature and may be of widely varying quality, depending on the qualifications and experience of the teacher.

2. The introverted approach of the mystic may bring to the surface his subconscious 'wish life' and this may be exhibited as immature religious activities. The man himself may, however, be convinced that this subconscious state is an expression of divine guidance.

3. The recovery of old spiritual aspirations and tendencies, coming from a previous life or lives, may be brought to the surface by group stimulation. To the performer they appear as utterly new, phenomenal and of divine origin.

4. The 'guidance' received might be of an astral nature and due to sensitivity to the voices of well-meaning beings on their path of return into incarnation. These 'spirits' are oft contacted unconsciously as they hover on the borderland of outer living, awaiting their time to be re-born.

5. As many aspirants are still mainly focussed on the astral plane, their so-called guidance will be of an emotional nature and based on glamour and illusion. This will be the result of weak mental orientation and consequent astral excursions. These emotional impulses may be of a sweet, harmless and well-intentioned nature but they will certainly lack divine inspiration and may tend to develop hysteria, fanaticism or ambition.

6. Those who are mentally focussed may unconsciously tune in telepathically upon the mind or minds of others. Such 'guidance' from other human minds is usually imparted unconsciously and will be of varying quality depending on the source of contact.

7. Thought-forms produced by humanity as a whole occur on both the mental and astral planes and may be picked up by man on either of these levels. The thought-form content of the mental plane will be further augmented by thoughts which have been placed there by the Hierarchy for human guidance. The quality of the thought-forms contained in the mental plane will therefore vary within wide limits and thoughts derived from this source should consequently be used with discrimination.

8. Guidance can therefore come from incarnate or discarnate beings of many kinds and may range in character from superior to trivial or even unwholesome. One thing

should be kept in mind, however and that is that no true initiate or guide ever seeks to dominate any person, nor will he ever give him a positive command to take any particular action. Furthermore, many of the impressions or teachings which are telepathically recorded, may either be received in a perverted or very vague form or may be wrongly interpreted by the mind. Where a line of guidance is picked up by several individuals, each furnishing it with his own interpretation and each convinced of the correctness of his particular version, misunderstandings are bound to occur.

9. So-called guidance may also be the product of a man's own powerful and integrated personality. His ambitions, desires and prideful planning will therefore be mainly astrally inspired and may work down from the mental body and impress the brain but leaving the man under the impression that these impulses originate from extraneous sources as guidance. This may leave him in a badly glamoured state.

10. *The most important source of real divine guidance is a man's own soul.* Through self-discipline, study, meditation and service to his fellow men, the 'Bridge of Light' between the soul and brain will gradually be established via the mind. When this alignment is clear and unobstructed, true guidance will flow through from the divine Self, the Inner Christ. With a developed mind and a purified character, no longer ruled by the emotions and desires of an astrally dominated personality, the inner voice will be truly interpreted and will provide the disciple with infallible guidance.
   After soul guidance has been firmly established and has become a normal part of the functioning of the mind, revelation can proceed systematically and without undue restraint. Because the individual soul forms part of the One Soul, true soul-consciousness will eventually lead to All-consciousness. It is through the soul that the Master, as part of the Hierarchy, will be able to impart the rudiments of the Plan, which will lead the disciple to revelation after revelation, until ultimately he becomes aware of the Light Supernal.

VI. 3 (e) Telepathy

'Telepathy' refers to various phases of mental contact and thought exchange, without the use of either written or spoken words or instruments – therefore, *wordless thought transference over the ethers*.

Once the concept of the etheric system is accepted and understood, then the basic principles which govern the functioning of telepathy can also be readily grasped. Because this vital energy vehicle interpenetrates and interrelates *all* that exist on our planet – and the Universe – impulses that are sent forth on etheric waves will vibrate and circulate throughout the entire etheric world. All that is needed for some desired reaction is a suitable receptive instrument to record the nature of the impulse that has been sent forth, plus the capacity to translate the registered vibrations into their correct meaning. The process is directly comparable with radio transmitting and receiving.

Although only few are aware of the fact, the human mind, when suitably developed, can serve as a perfect instrument for both transmitting and receiving etheric impulses. The mind interprets these impulses and then passes them on to the physical brain, which in turn transposes the thoughts into words.

All men have the same inherent potentiality of mind but all minds differ in their degree of development and efficiency. With the average man the greater part of the potential of the mind instrument still lies in cold storage. For the mind to function effectively, these stored parts must be brought forth, one element at a time and then properly adjusted and fitted into the instrument. The mind's capacity will thus be developed progressively, increasing its efficiency, until the stage is reached when it will consciously and deliberately be able to radiate thought-forms to other individuals or conversely to tune in to the thoughts of another. This reciprocal process is known as *mental telepathy*.

Mental telepathy should be clearly distinguished from its primitive counterpart, which may be called *instinctive telepathy*. Quite undeveloped human beings, who are not at all mentally inclined, often display telepathic propensities. In these instances the reactions are of an emotional nature and are registered through the solar plexus centre instead of through the mind-brain complex. A typical example of this form of telepathy is that which exists between a mother and her child, where the mother may instinctively realise that an absent child is in serious danger or has experienced a bad accident. By availing themselves of sensitive electroencephalographs, scientists have now determined beyond any doubt, that similar instinctual telepathic reactions also occur in the case of animals.

There is still a third type of telepathic contact – intuitional telepathy. The distinction is that this form of telepathy takes place on the intuitional plane – the communication is no longer between mind and mind but between soul and soul and it is on this level that the Masters communicate with their disciples.

Effective telepathic work is mainly dependent on three types of energy:

1. The *energy of love* will provide the needed material with which the idea, thought or concept which is to be transmitted, may be clothed or formed. For telepathy to work smoothly, this force of love should be reciprocal and should go out from both the transmitter and receiver. The love referred to is that of the soul and should not be confused with emotional or astral love. *The force of love is essential for successful telepathic work* and will remove all barriers. That is why an attitude of criticism from either pole will immediately neutralise or cut off telepathic radiation.

2. The *force of mind* is the illuminating energy which will 'light the way' for the idea to be transmitted. Remember that Light is an ethereal substance and that mental energy can materialise on a beam of light, thus enabling the mental beam of light to carry and transmit the thought-form to its objective.

3. The *etheric energy* of the vital body is the medium of despatch and reception on which the previous two forces are dependent for successful functioning.

There is a growing sensitivity or *telepathic rapport* between all disciples. This is often indicated by an instinctive recognition of fellow workers when meeting each other for the first time in the course of their activities. Such occasions are as a rule characterised by an immediate flashing forth and a reciprocal interplay of light and an awareness of a similarity of vision and objective and the recognising of opportunities for collaboration in the One Work in which each individual has been allotted his own particular task.

Even though the task of working disciples may outwardly differ widely, all such work is spiritually founded and represents but facets of the One Work. All disciples, whether in or out of incarnation, are in fact fellow workers, subjectively united into a single active group – the White Brotherhood – who are all telepathically interrelated. The conscious awareness of these telepathic bonds may temporarily fade during physical incarnation and as a result of the veiling by the etheric web, but etheric contact will again be restored and the darkness lifted, as soon as this web is ruptured – which may either occur during physical existence or else after 'passing over'.

One great advantage of telepathy is that it does not entail any language limitations and in the world of thought a Greek and a German will understand each other just as readily as when exchanging thoughts with their own countrymen.

Today ideas are still communicated to the fellow man by means of either the spoken or written word. Humanity is now rapidly nearing the stage, however, where telepathy is going to play an increasing role in human communication and the Sages prophesy that our present system will gradually be superseded by the wider use of telepathy. This condition will, however, take time to be generally manifested but meanwhile the development of radio and television systems may be regarded as the preliminary and symbolic indications of what is still to come.

According to D.K. it will take about another five hundred years for the intelligentsia of mankind to become consciously and functionally telepathic. Imagine what it will be like when your neighbour can freely read your thoughts and when there will no longer be a secret thought-life. Man will then definitely have to keep a closer guard on his thoughts than is the case at present and the mind will have to be cleared of many of the unsavoury aspects which can now still be kept safely hidden from all outsiders – but not from the inner judge, the soul!

VII

INVOCATION AND EVOCATION

Strictly speaking this chapter is but a continuation of the previous one – the 'Science of Contact and Communication'. The Science of Impression, dealt with under the preceding heading, is the process for establishing the relationship between the many units of which Life in its several realms is constituted. 'Invocation and Evocation' on the other hand may be regarded as the technique or method whereby this relationship is brought about. This is then followed by creative work, for the manifestation of the former processes.

VII. 1. The Law of Cause and Effect (Karma)

In the course of this writing, brief reference has in several instances been made to the Law of Cause and Effect, perhaps better known under its Eastern designation of 'Karma'. The whole of human existence and evolution is so intimately concerned with several aspects of this Law, that it is considered advisable that the student should become better acquainted with some of its details, as these principles play a commanding role in the shaping of man's daily life.

Individual karma is the cumulative result of all of man's actions and thoughts, not only of his present life but also of his innumerable earlier existences. This individual karma is in itself a most complicated matter and difficult to comprehend in its totality. But the position is even far more involved, because in addition to the result of man's own activities, his life is also subject to several other types of karma over which he has no direct control and as a result of which he may be considered as merely a puppet or an insignificant atom in the cosmic destinies. He is, for instance, also subject to Universal or Cosmic karma, to world karma, as well as to the karma of humanity, the race, nation, group and family – to mention only a few. All these different types of karma are intermingled and are interacting in such an inconceivable and inextricable manner, that the total complex is far beyond human conception.

The complexity of karma has been pointed out because students are sometimes inclined to over-simplify the position. Every human being is governed by forces far beyond his consciousness, sweeping him, his associates and environment into incomprehensible circumstances from which there is no escape and which he must learn to accept.

Notwithstanding this relatively sombre picture, man still retains his *free will* with which he, within certain limits, can control his own destiny, or in other words – 'man can make or break his own life'. He can initiate action which will definitely produce recognisable results and he thus can, to a large extent, be the architect of his own future and guide his own affairs. He will certainly be the meeting place of many forces which lie outside his control but many of these forces he can manipulate and turn to his own purposes according to circumstances and environment.

In the course of man's development there ever comes a life wherein he becomes consciously aware of the practical working of the Law of Cause and Effect. From that stage he learns to recognise karma in life's happenings and to evaluate events with a questioning consideration and consequently with greater understanding. He begins to study the radiatory quality of his life and the possible karmic effects of his actions and thus consciously he begins to build and shape his own destiny and future. From now on his reactions to life's circumstances cease to be purely emotional – he consciously and mentally begins to study and analyse the possible causes responsible for occurrences that have been evoked. A totally new approach and outlook on life is engendered as he comes to the recognition that karma is the source of all events and circumstances and that it is the instrument employed by the soul for shaping evolutionary development.

The one dilemma by which the exploring disciple is so often confronted, is that many karmic events will have their origin from activities in previous incarnations of which he has no conscious recollection and which therefore cannot be correlated with present day conditions. This is even further complicated by karmic conditions arising from extraneous sources, altogether beyond his ken or comprehension.

The Law of Cause and Effect teaches that every action is registered in the etheric field and must unavoidably be followed by some reaction of comparable potency. From this it should, however, not be concluded that the vibrations set in motion by the causative action have been cancelled or neutralised by the reaction. No vibration can ever be finally effaced – it can merely be transmuted to a higher or lower vibration or deflected into a new direction. Strictly speaking, *no new action can ever be initiated* – it is merely a question of diverting existing energy into other channels and thus giving rise to the manifestation of changed vibrations and consequently a different sequence of events. The whole phantasmagoria of phenomena into which man is *nolens volens* caught up, must be regarded as a most involved pattern of an interwoven and interacting system of chain-reactions – each action leading to some reaction and this again to a further reaction ... a simply never ending series of actions and reactions!

And notwithstanding all this apparent and impossible confusion, there still remains a systematic Purpose and Plan underlying it all and leading to some planned Destiny – but a destiny which, as far as man is concerned, disappears into the infinite and forever keeps on disappearing notwithstanding the ever expanding vision and the detection of constantly widening horizons.

Although many of these thoughts may appear to be paradoxical, the fact remains that man retains a considerable degree of free will and the capacity to guide to a large extent the course of his own life and destiny; he has even been granted the power of neutralising or wiping out certain bad karma accrued in the past, by initiating the correct redemptive action in the present life. One of the most effective means of realising this, is by leading a life of sacrifice and of dedicated and loving service of the fellow man – 'What man has made he can unmake'. Man was never intended to be the helpless victim of circumstance – for life after life the soul returns, utilising a physical instrument to gain experience and training this tool to become the intelligent arbiter of its own fate and a conscious exponent of the indwelling divinity.

In the past, when discussing the Law of Karma, there has been the inclination to put too much accent on the negative aspect of karma. It should therefore be emphasised that there is as much good karma as bad, all depending on the focus of man's activities. As the disciple advances on the Path, there will be a corresponding change in his motivation and objectives and his accumulated store of unfavourable karma will systematically be worked off and dwindle and will be superseded by a commensurate stock of good karma.

VII. 2. Invocation and Evocation

The beauty of human existence is that within each and every human being, no matter what his stage of development, there slumbers the spark of divinity. During the primitive stages this spark may be obscured by a coarse outer appearance and cruel, selfish and sensual action but nonetheless it will be present, perhaps only expressing itself at rare intervals by involuntary acts of kindness or some crude demonstration of love towards dependants. As the ages progressively roll by and innumerable lives are experienced through recurring incarnations, the innate divinity of the slumbering soul will, however, come more and more to the fore to make its presence felt. This inner power will exhibit itself as an ever growing impulse to love and to go out towards that which lies beyond the self; as a capacity to sense the unknown, combined with an instinctive knowledge of a Divine Presence; as an urge to seek that which cannot be proven and to reveal that which is hidden. It is this inner divinity which gives birth to the power to recognise the good, the true and the beautiful in life and which also comes to expression in the creative arts. It is this recognition of an affinity for the immanent divinity, the Self, the Source from which it has sprung, which eventually gives rise to an irrepressible urge towards reunion and synthesis – the *invocative spirit*.

This attraction of the inner Self towards the Higher is present in every single individual. In one it will be more apparent than in the next; some will be conscious of this feeling, whilst with others it will be unconscious and purely instinctive; there will be those who will try to negate and suppress this inner voice; with others some religious orientation or practice may tend to guide its expression along a particular channel; still others will be so strenuously busy satisfying their carnal desires, that for the time being these inner urges will be impatiently shoved aside and will temporarily remain unattended. It is this urge, either instinctive or recognised, that will give rise to the invocative spirit. This spirit may for a while perhaps be suppressed or negated but ultimately it will be expressed as invocative living or will consciously and purposefully find expression in invocative appeals to Divinity. With the masses it will be demonstrated as some form of religious aspiration.

The human race is entering a New Age and as far as religion is concerned, the Sages prophesy a New World Religion in which all nations and races will participate. It will be founded on the principles of the One Humanity consisting of the many races and nations, as differentiated by colour, language, characteristics and their various stages of development but all synthesised into the Brotherhood of Man by a common source of origin and a common final destination – the One Father, the One God.

This World Religion will also be founded on the intelligent application of the principles of Invocation and Evocation and the recognition of the tremendous potency of unified and consciously directed appeal.

Man will become increasingly aware of his invocative powers and that these powers may be accentuated by the intelligent organisation of the spiritual energies of the masses for the realisation of common objectives. This will in fact consist of focussing the combined forces of love, thereby evoking a corresponding response from hierarchical levels.

Three kinds of Invocation may be distinguished:

(a) There is the inchoate, *voiceless appeal of the masses* in times of crisis, which is wrung from the hearts of suffering men living in some area of disaster. Such an invocative cry will go forth ceaselessly from the sufferers and will be vaguely directed towards some extraneous Power which they hope might bring some relief in their condition of extremity.

(b) There is also the *invocative spirit evidenced by sincere individuals* practising the rituals of their particular religion, through single or united prayer or worship, thus laying their supplications before God. These belong to the many religions, churches and denominations of the many nations and races throughout the world.

(c) Finally there is the *invocation by trained disciples* who have some knowledge of the energies with which they are working and how these may be controlled and guided more effectively in the right direction. They may also succeed in focussing the invocative appeal of the previous two groups more effectively.

This latter group may be regarded as already forming the core of the New World Religion. Still mostly unaware of each other, functioning under various disciplines and disguised under different schools of thought, groups of these disciples are forming throughout the world. The time is, however, rapidly approaching when they will begin to recognise each other for what they are and will realise that the many individuals and groups, each in their own time and place, are striving towards the same objective. This will lead to a gradual drawing together, each group retaining its own individuality, character and colour but learning to collaborate in focussing their invocative powers into united and therefore more potent appeals to the Most High. This must inevitably evoke a response from the waiting Hierarchy and its Leader, the Christ, which will be commensurate with the potency of the invocative cry. The growing recognition by the masses of the effectiveness of such invocation will help to transmute their trust and belief into conviction and thus large numbers will be transformed and spiritualised. This in turn will lead to the general redemption of Humanity, its merging with the Hierarchy and finally to the true manifestation of the Kingdom of God on Earth.

One of the ways to ensure joint and world-wide invocative action, will be the organising of simultaneous *religious festivals* during prearranged periods of *Full Moon*. It has been found that there exists a fluctuating rhythm in the potency of energy fields and that this is closely correlated with the monthly phases of the Moon. During the full-moon periods the energies reach their highest potency, so these are the most effective stages for observing the invocative festivals.

The focussed aspiration and prayers of the millions of average men and women from all nations, who unselfishly struggle to serve to their best ability and who for this purpose invoke the help of Higher Entities (under whatever name), are wielding invocative powers which have fantastic possibilities if suitably co-ordinated and directed. A composite stream of energy of unrealised potency could thus be created, representing Humanity as a whole and serving to forge a close link between Humanity and the Hierarchy.

It is with the purpose of strengthening these bonds that the *Great Invocation* was put at man's disposal. With the concerted use of this World Prayer by the masses, even though the majority might not be fully aware of its deeper and spiritual significance, a most potent invocative force will be built up, which should evoke responses which could prove of considerable advantage to Humanity. But more about this under a separate heading. The power of massed thought and aspiration is fantastic and will in future, under the auspices of the New World Religion be utilised more effectively to human advantage.

The *power of thought* constitutes the basis of invocation. Thought energy is telepathically directed towards its destination and the larger the number of these separate energies that can be combined, the stronger will be the synthesised outgoing stream of energy. This stream will telepathically reach those Spiritual Beings who are sensitive and responsive to these impacts and will evoke their response. This response will be directed and returned as spiritual energy, which on human mental levels will be stepped down into thought energy and thought-forms which will be impressed on the minds of men, bringing new inspiration and revelation.

In the past religion had an entirely emotional appeal but through intelligent invocation and direction of thought energy, this appeal will be lifted to the mental field and will be a further demonstration of the growing tendency of the human race towards increased mental polarisation.

The Tibetan has stated that when the invocative spirit is present, resultant effects are inevitable and that man will always succeed in evoking that which has been intelligently invoked. When this knowledge is scientifically applied, it will prove to be one of man's great liberating forces.

What are the implications of these words? Does it mean that every casual thought or wish that may momentarily flash through the mind will at some stage or other be realised? No, fortunately not! For thoughts to take on the defined lines of thought-forms and to lift these from the murky hazes of the astral plane into the brighter light of the mental plane, needs clear thinking thus charging and clothing the thought with energy. If these thought-forms are to materialise, they need still further energising and must be directed with understanding and purpose towards higher levels – this then becomes 'invocation' and it is these clearly defined and purposeful invocative calls which inevitably must and will evoke responses from On High.

There are those who quite unconsciously have learned the technique of invocation but generally speaking it will take time, study, self-discipline, concentrated and conscious application on meditation and above all the *right motives* to develop the required technique for effective invocation and subsequently the perceptivity for recognising the evoked response. Once these capacities have been acquired there is, however, no end to what man may accomplish. The attainment of these powers will be one of the main objectives of the New World Religion.

One fact should, however, always be remembered and that is that *these powers will not be accorded to man for selfish gain or for material control or influence over the minds of other human beings.*

The ability to invoke will be steadily developed as the disciple progresses along the Path of Light. In the earlier stages it might be prefaced by a certain degree of confusion but this will be overcome when general purification of the personality and gaining of experience and sensitivity to impression, lead to greater clarity of mind. This will be but another instance of learning by trial and error.

As the disciple becomes more proficient in these techniques, fundamental changes will be effected in his life and particularly in his consciousness and orientation and he will develop into *an invocative and evocative centre of energy*. The powers that have been evoked in him will become a potent factor for evoking a fresh flood of ever higher impressions. He will also become evocative upon the physical plane, his magnetic aura becoming increasingly sensitive and receptive to inflowing spiritual impressions and by its radiation he will evoke noticeable effects on all and everything constituting his environment.

'Invocation and Evocation' is the science underlying all evolutionary development of man. It is the science of bridging, producing right relationships by mutual invocation, which in turn evokes magnetic response. It is the science responsible for the awakening of all etheric centres and their interrelation, leading finally to the rapport between man and man, group and group and eventually between nation and nation. It is these evoked energies which first relate soul and personality and subsequently also the Monad. It is finally the science through which the bridges are built, leading to a closer union and understanding between Humanity, the Hierarchy and the Spiritual Powers of Shamballa.

VII. 2 (a) **Invocative Living**

With his strenuous struggle along the Path of Life, man slowly comes to recognise the futility of striving purely for self-advancement. There is a growing awareness of his responsibilities as his 'brother's keeper' and that it is part of his function not merely to strain ahead on his own single path but that he should also look back and take notice of those who have been left behind. He will then realise that he should forget about his own further progress and that he should rather turn back to reach a helping hand to the less favoured ones still mired in the depths of the astral world; he now recognises that he must share the Light he has found with those who are still living in the dark of ignorance. He discovers that peace of mind, contentment, spiritual prosperity and progress cannot be fully achieved without it being shared by his brother. This altruistic approach to life may be called invocative living.

As with all else, these principles which apply to the individual, are also relevant to the group, the community and the race of which the individual only forms a part. That is why there is also a very noticeable change in outlook by the leading classes in all nations concerning their responsibilities towards the welfare and upliftment of all less favoured men, communities and nations. This is being reflected in the numerous groups, clubs, organisations and movements, who do not only concern themselves with the physical welfare of the less privileged but also with educational, economic and cultural improvements and how to better human relationships on all levels. Although these influences are radiating their effects into ever wider circles, the most vital problem remains the suppressing of man's still dominating inclinations towards selfishness. The basic concepts of universal brotherhood are, however, steadily gaining ground, coupled with the principle of sharing and that it is of greater value to give than to receive.

Every man who has stepped on to the Path of Light, inevitably evokes an effect on those who surround him and also contributes his small part towards improving world conditions as a whole. He may remain totally unaware of the influence he is emanating but that will not diminish its effect. By sharing that which he has, he will receive; by living a life of redemption, he will be blessed with the joys of the soul; by giving all, he will reap the gifts of the heavens.

VII. 2 (b) **The Great Invocation**

> From the point of Light within the Mind of God
> Let light stream forth into the minds of men.
> Let Light descend on Earth.

> From the point of Love within the Heart of God
> Let love stream forth into the hearts of men.
> May Christ return to Earth.

> From the centre where the Will of God is known
> Let purpose guide the little wills of men –
> The Purpose which the Masters know and serve.

> From the centre which we call the race of men
> Let the Plan of Love and Light work out
> And may it seal the door where evil dwells.

> Let Light and Love and Power restore the Plan on Earth.

This ancient spiritual prayer was given to the world by the Christ and was released in 1945 by the Tibetan through Alice A. Bailey. It belongs to no group or religious denomination but to all Humanity and may thus be used by anyone, no matter what his religion or beliefs. If said with mental concentration and dedicated purpose, it has a most potent invocative appeal. It has been expressed in terms which are understandable and familiar to the average individual, although the meaning that the masses will attach to it will differ considerably from that of the esotericist.

One of the primary objectives of the Invocation is to serve as a spiritual bond and to provide an element of synthesis in human thinking. Because it is a prayer that can be used at all levels of human development and by all nations and races, it will serve as a common denominator which will contribute to draw people closer together and thus improve human relationships. This will certainly not be immediately noticeable but as the Invocation reaches wider distribution and is being *regularly* and *purposefully* used by ever increasing numbers, it is bound to evoke effects.

As it is, the Invocation has already been translated into all the better known languages and is being faithfully used by men and women in every country throughout the world. It should be realised that each additional individual who regularly uses this prayer, adds his contribution of spiritual power to the ever waxing potency of the invocative energies directed towards the House of the Father and this in due course *must* evoke a commensurate response.

It is therefore imperative that continued efforts be made towards mobilising the powers of growing numbers of individuals throughout the world for the daily use of the Great Invocation. Endeavours should be made to obtain the collaboration of all available agencies of communication, such as the press, radio and television, to propagate the use of the Invocation by as many as possible of the public who support the practice of goodwill. Few realise what a large percentage of the average public already resort under this category. It does not matter at all if the majority are not fully aware of the implications of the Invocation, perhaps only regarding it as a suitable prayer to promote love and goodwill. The effect that will be reached can hardly as yet be imagined. By means of the Invocation barriers can be broken down which separate individuals and nations. The spirit of loving understanding and peace can be introduced, leading to increased activities in promoting better human relationships.

The general public will regard it as a prayer to God and will send it forth with the hope for light and love and peace for which they have longed without cease.

The use of the Great Invocation is destined to bring about three great events:

(a) An outpouring of the spirit of *Love* and *Light* upon mankind from Shamballa.
(b) The physical *reappearance of the Christ* amongst men, supported by members of the Hierarchy; this will lead to the uplifting of man and the establishment of the Kingdom of God on Earth.
(c) The establishing and working out of the *Divine Plan* on Earth (the Will of God), by Humanity's own efforts and collaboration and founded on goodwill and understanding.

It should always be remembered that both the divine Light and Love invoked are active energies and when evoked and effectively applied, are carriers of illumination and goodwill which must lead to improved human relationships. 'Energy follows thought' and it will be the function of each recipient to redirect these energies to their fellow men.

Anyone regularly using this Invocation or prayer, asking for illumination and love on behalf of humanity, is bound to become personally influenced by its potencies. 'As a man thinketh in his heart, so is he' and if a man's mind is constantly turned towards these thoughts, his life must be altered as a result of a spiritual outlook which is steadily being lifted to ever higher altitudes. Many will, however, largely use it with selfish intent, even though they may remain unaware of this. The public should therefore be taught some of its deeper meanings and that the spiritual potency of the appeal is intended to serve mankind as a whole without any bias and not the narrow selfish interests of the individual.

This Invocation which is being used by Humanity is but a version of the invocation used regularly and telepathically by members of the Hierarchy and even by the Christ himself. Basically it remains the same invocation but it stands to reason that with every higher level to which it is lifted, it will also take on new dimensions and will acquire ever deeper spiritual meaning.

VII. 3. **Meditation**

Because man is incomplete within himself, only forming a small fragment of a greater whole, there is always a conscious or unconscious urge within him to seek closer co-ordination and union with that which is greater but which as yet only assumes a vague and undefined form. This attraction is the driving force inciting him to seek the centre of his being and which leads him on to the Path of Return to the All-Self. It is merely the Prodigal Son being inspired with that irresistible urge to return to the Father's home; but this Path is long and arduous and the many obstacles will only be surmounted with the expending of great effort and after brave and persistent struggling for every step that is advanced.

The surest way of overcoming these subjective obstacles is by means of meditation. This practice is also known as the **Science of Bridging** – the bridging between various states of consciousness. It aims at producing sensitivity to impression from higher Sources and for this purpose it must primarily ensure the construction of the **Bridge of Light** ('antahkarana') between the personality and the Soul, followed subsequently by that which also links up with the Higher Mind and Intuition of the Triad.

Actually meditation forms the foundation for all spiritual growth. By dint of certain techniques and strenuous and persistent invocative efforts of concentration, the aspirant learns to become aware of his real inner Self; he learns consciously to interpret the wishes evoked by the Soul and to carry out its plans as far as these are comprehended at various stages of realisation. Technically this means bringing the lower instrument into a state of receptivity and vibratory response that will correspond with that of the Soul. A vibration must therefore go out from the mind and brain of man to meet a reciprocal vibration emanating from the Soul. When these vibrations have been successfully aligned and synchronised, a rhythmic interplay and flow of energy will be effected and a clear impression of ideas from egoic levels can then take place.

This contact of mind and brain with the soul may be achieved by suitable techniques of meditation but may also be brought about by living a life of inner mental reflection, by disciplining the lower nature, by expressing goodwill and self-forgetfulness and by rendering dedicated service to fellow human beings. Where permanent alignment between the soul and its instrument has been established, meditation may be shifted to a higher level and then serve to construct the 'bridge of light' connecting the personality with the Spiritual Triad and thus allowing the intuition to come into play.

So often the one aim of the aspirant is only to effect contact with his Master, little realising that his first and most important guide is his own soul and that the Master can only be contacted through the mediation of the soul.

The steps to be followed by the aspiring meditator are firstly to practise certain physical disciplines and to purify his system. The second step will be to obtain reasonable control over the emotions and thirdly he should aim at some measure of control over the wild horses of the mind.

For present purposes, only the general principles affecting meditation will be considered, giving no attention to various systems and techniques which might be followed. Meditation is something personal and the method and detail will vary from individual to individual, depending on the student's soul and personality rays, his stage of spiritual evolution, his karmic condition and demands, as well as the needs of his environment, of the group with which he is associated and the contribution he can make towards improving human relationships and world conditions in general. In other words it will depend on the service that the soul has planned for that particular incarnation.

How fortunate the man who has a knowledgeable and experienced teacher to guide him and who will be able to prescribe and adapt differentiated techniques for the aspirant's particular requirements. As a rule, however, aspirants have to make a beginning without any reliable guidance and for them it is advisable to adhere to standard practices which carry in them the elements of safety and universality.

Students who have incorporated meditation as a regular part of their daily routine, should learn to avail themselves fully of the increased opportunities for contact which become available during the time of the *full Moon*. During these monthly recurring periods it is as if a door is being opened which normally stands closed. This door may then be entered, providing access to energies otherwise not available and thereby improving the possibility of approaches to the Masters. This period of stimulated activity stretches over about five days – two days prior to the full Moon, the peak of the forces on the day of the full Moon and the two subsequent days of shrinking activity.

When after due consideration of all the facts at his disposal, man decides to tread the Path of Light, trying to release the indwelling soul life from its fetters and to disperse the mists and veils which have kept it hidden, he should apply his efforts mainly in three directions:

(a) By means of *study* he should acquire as much knowledge and understanding about man's constitution and of the Ageless Wisdom in general, as his circumstances will allow.

(b) His subjective life should be expanded as far as possible by *esoteric meditation*, applied to the best of his ability. This should, however, always be undertaken with the full realisation that he is 'playing with fire' – the fire of mind and spirit, which may literally burn and badly damage the mental body if unduly stimulated and allowed to develop beyond control. The secret is to see to it that balance is retained by undertaking all steps with discrimination.

(c) Should any subjective development occur, this must be allowed to find objective expression in some *field of service* to the fellow man. Without such an outlet the unfoldment achieved will be obscured by the generated energies. Providing he is serving to the best of his ability and is inspired by altruistic motives, then the nature of expression of such service is immaterial and will vary with the individual, the rays under which he is functioning and which determine his character, as well as the environmental circumstances.

The student undertaking meditation without the guidance of a well qualified teacher, should be warned that he is submitting himself to several dangers against which he should guard. If such virtues as aspiration, concentration and persistence are used indiscriminately and without proper consideration of the evolutionary stage that has been reached, then the aspirant is looking for trouble, because it may readily lead to a disturbance of the balance and co-ordination of the personality. It is therefore of the greatest importance that the student should retain a sober and sensible approach, coupled with a sound sense of proportion. Meditation is particularly dangerous to the man whose character still remains unpurified, because the released energies could readily exert a stimulating influence on his shortcomings.

If the meditation technique that is followed leads to mental fatigue, then do not persist with it and rather try a different approach. Correct procedure should gradually lead to co-ordination and alignment of the physical, emotional and mental vehicles with the soul and to a subsequent rounding out and symmetrical development that will make the man of real use to the Master for serving humanity.

Aspirants are as a rule mainly focussed in their emotional bodies and as this body is most difficult to bring under control, it plays a dominating role in meditation. It should always be kept in mind that before the spirit can function through the lower forms, all vibrations of desire must be eliminated and selfish inclinations must be transmuted into spiritual aspiration. For the average man this will mean years of sustained and painstaking effort. Without such dedication and sacrifice very little will, however, be attained. Relatively large numbers will usually join esoteric study groups with great enthusiasm but as a rule their numbers will rapidly dwindle, because only few have the perseverance to proceed when the usual difficulties and disappointments begin to make their appearance.

The emotional body can really only be effectively controlled from the mental plane and it is only when this has been attained through meditation and intensity of purpose and will, that the emotional plane becomes quiescent and receptive. To ensure the achievement of a well balanced condition the student should always strive to retain *conscious control*, even during moments of highest vibration and contact.

Meditation is the mental power 'to hold the mind steady in the light' of the soul and in that light to become aware of particular elements of the Plan and the 'raincloud of knowable things' from which ideas may be tapped to fertilise the field of human living. The disciple should learn to avail himself of meditation to gain spiritual independence; he must learn to effect his own higher contacts and thus to obtain personal inspiration for the work and service for which he is assuming responsibility. Meditation helps to purify the mind and to transform material and emotional desire into spiritual will and thus becomes the dispeller of glamour and illusion. It is the primary creative instrument which has been placed at man's disposal; it is the main factor by means of which the individual mind may be consciously fused and blended with the Divine Mind to which it belongs. It aligns instinct, intellect and intuition and becomes the agent for both invocation and evocation. When meditation is introduced into the ordered rhythm of daily living, it will gradually develop into a meditative existence and a one-pointed life of service to humanity; the lower man will slowly but surely become submerged and controlled by the energies of the spiritual man.

Subjective training and spiritual development cannot be bought. All the money in the world will prove useless and may to the contrary even prove an added obstruction to the man who hopes for spiritual expansion. No, such progress may only be achieved by an inner awakening, an urge towards satisfying some indescribable heart-hunger and a subsequent persistent striving for the fulfilment of that undefined objective by harnessing all internal qualities and mental powers at the disposal of the aspirant.

As a general principle students are therefore warned against joining so-called esoteric schools or meditation courses (no matter by what attractive name they may advertise themselves) when tuition and admission to membership may only be acquired at a special fee. Such institutions betraying commercial motivations, should preferably be avoided, notwithstanding plausible arguments which may be used to justify any mercenary approach. Students who are genuinely interested in the field of esotericism will always find schools who will be willing to supply all information free of charge. Those who have the initiative for self-study, either individually or in groups, will be able to go a long way by means of knowledge which these days may readily be acquired from a number of suitable books and other literature.

The time is rapidly approaching, however, when schools under qualified supervision will be established in different parts of the world for the careful training of the right pupils. These schools will be supported by voluntary contributions and tuition will be given free of any charges. There will be both preparatory schools as well as schools for more advanced training. These courses of instruction will be principally founded on meditation for developing the intuition and acquiring the necessary sensitivity to impression. Special opportunities will also be afforded for preparing every student for world service in its many facets.

VII. 4. **Revelation**

All revelation is dependent on *recognition* and *understanding*. Understanding is the essential quality needed to achieve identification with any form of divine expression and nothing can therefore be revealed without understanding. The whole object of esoteric training is to lead the disciple to clearer discernment and sensitivity of that which is eternally present but which only becomes revealed when the disciple is ready for its recognition. To the esoteric student the theoretic knowledge of many hidden aspects is of relatively little value if not coupled with deeper vision; what he needs is to gain sufficient inner light through personal experience and consequent spiritual unfoldment and thus to become *consciously* aware of that which so far has been veiled.

Intelligent recognition of that which is revealed means a growing awareness of reality and therefore demands emergence from the world of glamour to allow clearer perception of the new vision. Old and well known truths are then seen from a new point of view and are subjected to brighter light, thus altogether changing their previous significance and bringing the Plan and Purpose of the Logos into fresh perspective.

Whenever a disciple arrives at the stage of recognition of fresh revelation, his inner light increases and he involuntarily diffuses some of this light to his environment, thus contributing towards the dissipation of the glamour still blinding the mass of men. This also means that he, in his small way, is also instrumental in implementing the divine Plan and that he is beginning to serve as an outpost of the Hierarchy and is becoming an Agent of Light.

The development of the sincere disciple is in fact nothing but the recognition of a series of revelations or enlightenments. One revelation supplies the material which, when correctly applied, will provide the key to the door giving access to the next revelation, thus serving as another step in his progress to the mountain top. Each fresh revelation will mean another break-through for the ever expanding consciousness. It will signify the partial shattering of the boundaries which have constituted the ring-pass-not of the disciple's vision and field of activity. This breaching of the enclosing walls does not, however, mean perfect freedom but merely the expansion of vision to wider horizons, the obtaining of brighter light and an ever growing capacity for more efficient service over an ever widening terrain. The extended vision will, however, again be circumscribed by the boundaries of a new ring-pass-not, which will confront him and which cannot be exceeded until the disciple has consolidated within himself that which has been gained, and has learnt to dispose of it in service of his fellow man. When this stage has been fulfilled, he prepares himself for the succeeding revelation. The whole evolutionary process may therefore be regarded as nothing but an orderly sequence of revelations; evolution and revelation are therefore closely correlated.

Revelation is the comprehensive medium through which the Hierarchy implements, impulses and motivates its activities in the realm of human experience. Through these revelations the disciple is made aware of the tasks that have been assigned to him and once he recognises that which has been revealed to him, he will become aware of the next step that is expected of him. One of the Master's main tasks, therefore, is to prepare and train his disciples towards ever increasing sensitivity to ensure the recognition of every subsequent revelation. True revelation is the unfolding of the glory of divinity in some field of expression.

The Hierarchy has to discover those who are sensitive to impression and whose minds are trained to serve as reasonably accurate channels for the transfer of the truths to be revealed to the world at large. As it is, all revelation during the process of transmission into words, inevitably loses something of its divine purity, clarity and power and to some extent is subject to distortion. All basic revelations have in the past been presented to man in simple form and yet have become warped into complicated dogma and veiled by glamour through the complexity of the human mind still functioning under astral influence.

It may often prove an exhaustive experience, first to recognise a revelation and then to hold it long enough for the consciousness to incorporate it completely, thus allowing its potentialities to be exploited. The process of recognition will vary with the revelation concerned, with the individual and the circumstances but may develop more or less along the following pattern:

With the first recognition a state approaching ecstasy is reached; this is succeeded by a period of utter darkness, which may lead the disciple almost to despair, during which the revelation fades away and cannot be recaptured – the disciple knows that he has experienced this revelation but he has lost contact with it and has to continue on his way without its stimulation. The final stage comes when the disciple, while proceeding with and engrossed in his current service and while helping others towards achieving *their* next revelation, forgets about his own experience, till he suddenly discovers that he is fully conversant with the lost revelation and that unconsciously it has been assimilated and immersed in his mind to form part of his future vision, capacity and store of knowledge and wisdom. This may then be drawn upon at any time and at will, when it is required to serve his selfless efforts on behalf of mankind.

Progressive spiritual development, leading to initiation is essentially founded on revelation and no initiation is possible without such a preceding experience. These two themes, revelation and initiation, are therefore complementary and also inseparably united in a progressive and never ending spiral – self-engendered revelation resulting in initiation and such initiation in turn evoking further revelation.

The hope of the world lies in the development and conscious training of the *intuitive capacity* of man. Every individual who has discovered the Path of Light is in the position to contribute his humble share or faint ray of light to strengthen the greater beam of divine Light. Some thought might drop into his mind which may prove of revealing potency and of great help to many; he might suddenly receive new light allowing an unexpected new perspective on some old established 'truth', thus releasing such truth from some of the trammels of orthodoxy and glamour. Light is the cause, with revelation as the effect. As the developing disciple progressively subjects his intuitive sensitivity to divine impression, he will be allowed to play an increasingly important role in serving humanity, provided such revelation is never selfishly retained and is applied towards promoting the common weal.

It should always be remembered that revelation is not limited to the realms of mysticism and religion. Revelation occurs in every field of human endeavour and the fundamental *revelations of science* must be considered to be just as divine as those of religion. The pity is that so many of these revelations have in the past been prostituted for personal gain as a result of selfish greed and desire. As a rule the revelations of science, although they may be canalised through an individual, will be the result of group endeavour. All these separate revelations in every field of human activity, constitute but a part of the majestic panorama of the total unified revelation which is progressively being unfolded before the eyes of humanity and which is slowly but surely leading to that greater revelation – the Kingdom of God on Earth.

VIII

HUMAN RELATIONSHIPS

VIII. 1. General

The nature of human relationships will be mainly determined by the extent to which soul energy is allowed to flood and control all parts of the system – the physical, emotional and mental aspects. This applies in all instances, whether man is considered individually or collectively. The soul is the source of the inner light, of love and goodwill, the characteristics which tend towards synthesis and coherence and which will evoke altruism and determine the quality of relationships.

While the soul influence remains obstructed and the animal instincts of the physical body or the astral qualities of lust and selfish desire predominate, life is characterised by separativeness, hatred, envy, greed, etc. – 'every man for himself and the devil take the hindmost'.

When the focus of living tends more towards the mental plane, some improvement will be effected because man then begins to recognise that better relationships with his neighbour will make life somewhat easier or more convenient and therefore that such conditions will be to his advantage. But his motivations remain unaltered and are still purely selfish and whenever it suits his convenience he will have no compunction in disrupting existing harmonious arrangements. If present day world conditions are considered, it is obvious that the masses of humanity have until recent years been functioning on this basis – each individual, group or nation being only concerned with their own interests and quite prepared to sacrifice the rest of humanity if considered profitable.

But at long last a change has set in – *the tide has turned!* There has always been a small percentage of human beings who, to a greater or less extent, have been guided by their souls and although they have definitely exerted a beneficial influence on mankind, this effect has on the whole been overwhelmed by the opposing selfish attitudes. The percentage of well disposed people in the world is in fact appreciably higher than would be expected, when considering the general unfavourable state of world affairs, but their influence for good is unorganised and diffused and therefore mostly ineffective. The Hierarchy, under leadership of the Christ has, however, consistently been subjecting humanity to a stream of the energy of love and this is now beginning to take effect and here and there improving human relationships are now becoming apparent in some aspects of world politics, as well as in several other spheres of human association and activity. A total reversal cannot be expected to be demonstrated overnight but the change is definitely present and once some momentum has been gained and the soul-infused personalities obtain a stronger hold on leadership positions, progress in the right direction should be rapid, because mankind is ready for this spiritual revolution.

Live 'To' Let Live:

What a beautiful theme and ideal to strive for! Yes, to live in the first instance not for personal gain but to serve and benefit the fellow man! A life of love, goodwill, tolerance, understanding, sacrifice and service – these are going to be the accepted life principles of humanity and that in the not so very distant future. But why not make a beginning by applying these ideals right now in present day living? It can be done and there are those who are already practising this way of life with great success, joy and happiness. Why not throw in your weight with this group of servers? Why not give the soul the opportunity of guiding activities? Humanity has entered the New Age and increasing numbers are joining the ranks of those striving to fulfil these ideals of altruism.

The expression 'live *and* let live' is a typical relic of the past, still reflecting something of man's selfish attitude – to grasp everything that life has to offer for personal benefit but as a gesture of kindness, to pass on that which is not needed to the next man. Although this approach remains largely self-centred, it does at least indicate the first signs of awakening soul awareness and a disposition towards sharing. But the next step is to change the wording of the older theme to: '*live TO let live*', thereby completely altering its meaning, the accent no longer being on self-indulgence but reversed to emphasise the principles of *sharing* and *service*. The objective now becomes the suppressing and superseding of all egotism, self-complacency and intolerance and to concentrate all energies on helping others – to share all one has, whether material or spiritual, with the rest of mankind. Surely this must represent the acme of all human endeavour!

It should be realised, however, that this exhorted new life should not be regarded as an unperturbed life of ease and comfort. On the contrary, it will be most exacting and will demand the exertion of all the physical, emotional, mental and spiritual powers at the disposal of the aspiring server and the offering of these on the altar of sacrifice. But it is in this giving, sharing and serving that the consummation of joy will be found. Therefore as far as in you lies endeavour to – *live TO let live!*

VIII. 2. Human Shortcomings

(For a short discussion on certain imperfections, such as 'Fear', 'Depression' and 'Hatred and Antagonism', see PART ONE: X. 3 – 'The Astral Body'; see also: PART TWO: IV. 1 – 'Glamour').

To overcome his defects, man should first become aware of what he lacks and these defects should then be clearly distinguished when they do occur, to enable them to be squarely faced. Steps may then be taken either to eliminate these failings or to transmute them to their opposites. This will result in right relations with both the soul and the environment.

The human being is subject to many imperfections and it is in the overcoming of these that spiritual growth may be recognised. Man should not be unduly appalled at the discovery of the many ways in which he is lacking – to become aware of and acknowledge these shortcomings already indicates progress. But once these defects are understood then the aspirant must assume the responsibility for overcoming them as soon as possible.

These failings are not always clearly differentiated, as they often demonstrate simultaneously, merge or are closely integrated. Attention will, however, be drawn to some of their more outstanding facets, as this may assist the disciple in recognising them. He can then either try to avoid further contact with such influences or otherwise endeavour to eradicate them altogether from his system. In this respect, the two main culprits which should be guarded against, are *selfishness* and *desire*, both of which may be manifested in a variety of unpleasant forms, some of the more troublesome of which will be briefly indicated.

VIII. 2 (a) Selfishness

This is one of the most distinctive traits of the average human being, and those who have managed to eradicate every trace of this characteristic from their system, must surely be close to attaining perfection.

Selfishness is one of the earliest attributes of man and was divinely inspired to allow man to become 'self'-conscious. It also fulfilled an essential function in providing self-protection, which was particularly important to ensure physical survival during man's primitive existence.

Selfishness is therefore a natural stage of unfoldment in man and a phase that has been with him for many lives and which he is slow in outgrowing. In the past it served a useful purpose and was an essential quality for self-realisation. But as man matures and is learning to tread the Path of Light, he should become more consciously aware that he forms an intrinsic part of the greater Whole and he should therefore increasingly forget about exclusively serving the 'self'. Synthesis with inner groups and service to his environment should now become his objective, no longer heeding the personality with all its inclinations towards separative existence.

It is through selfishness that the door is kept open for the entry of evil into human living. It is through the many aspects of this human failing that evil obtains the opportunity of expressing itself. So if evil is to be combated and if the door of its entry is to be closed, the first task will be to limit and eventually to eradicate all selfishness from the human system. To effect this, man must first become aware in which respects he is falling short, and the attention will therefore be briefly focussed on some of these characteristics which the disciple should strive to conquer.

(i) *Self-centredness:*

This is the characteristic leading to separativeness. It often makes its appearance after man has been through deep waters and badly buffeted by the storms of life. Through these adversities he has learnt to become self-dependent and to walk alone. Although self-reliance is a commendable attribute up to a point man should, however, be on his guard not to become overbalanced in this respect, by regarding himself as the focal point of his little world. This will be an indication of selfishness and will be distinguished by a lack of consideration and interest in his fellow human beings.

Such an attitude may only be rectified by reverting to a life of sacrificial service; to become out-going and self-forgetting by relinquishing and self-surrendering; by striving to serve as a soul – possessing nothing and asking nothing for the separated self.

This same shortcoming is a typical stage in the development of nations; the majority of nations in fact still maintain the selfish attitude of considering only the interests of their own particular country, this invariably leading to clashes with other countries maintaining similar narrow and self-centred approaches. The only solution, which might lead to eventual world peace, is for all nations to recognise their interdependence on other nations and countries; that no nation (or individual) can in the long run conduct a separative existence; that life can only proceed with happiness and peace where there is sharing, co-operation and mutual goodwill; and finally that all men and all nations form part of the One Humanity and the One World!

(ii) *Self-Pity:*

Self-pity is a wretched plight founded on a deluding condition which exaggerates every adverse circumstance and dramatises situations evoked in the mind, thereby isolating the individual in his own life.

Every human being will experience phases of self-commiseration, especially during periods of depression which are of normal occurrence in man's cyclic progression through life. These milder forms of self-pity are usually not serious, although its total elimination should be aimed at.

Extreme cases of self-pity, however, quite often occur and these may develop into really distressful afflictions, with individuals losing practically all self-control. Such dramatic self-pity must be regarded as but another form of selfishness or self-centredness. The person's attention is focussed far too much on himself. In his self-concern he cannot see life's adversities in their broader application and effect but only regards these harmful agencies as concentrated and aimed at him personally, so as to cause *him* personal pain and suffering; he does not realise that others experience these same vicissitudes and that these are but the buffetings of life, which man has to surmount and in the process of which his character is being built and strengthened. These poor individuals really only love themselves.

The best cure for this largely self-induced suffering is to break out of this piteous condition by concentrating all the powers of the personality towards the helping of others. With efforts focussed on such service, the disciple will discover that he is not the only one experiencing reverses and that there are others who are suffering even worse misfortunes and that in comparison he is still well off. He will also find that compassionate interest and dynamic service to others bring joy and self-forgetfulness.

The victim should also cultivate an attitude of acceptance and spiritual indifference, paying no undue attention to the well being of the physical body or to the moods, feelings or mental illusions. These personality interests should be superseded by external interests and activities – by serving the needs and demands of relations, friends and the community.

(iii) *Material Desire:*

Probably one of the most potent channels through which selfishness and therefore also evil, finds expression, is through material desire. It has its origin in the desire for satisfying the fundamental needs for physical existence – for food, clothing and protection. Over the ages, with man's emotional and mental growth and the development of communal living, his basic demands have also grown but these have often been far exceeded by the exigencies of the desire life. Selfishness as expressed by greed or the selfish desire for an ever larger and disproportionate share of worldly goods, coupled with a craving for power which usually attends such urges for acquisition, has proved to be one of the main causes of contention between men and therefore also between nations. As long as this desire is allowed free rein, no peace and happiness will ever be found on Earth.

This desire must therefore be seen as one of the fundamental weaknesses of humanity. *Money* is its symbol and the well known proverb states quite rightly that 'the love of money is the root of all evil'. Human thinking, and relations at practically every level of modern social existence, is mainly controlled and dominated by the power of money. Money is but the physical manifestation of man's desire for possessions, for material comfort and for the equipment which forms the basis for further production of goods and weapons for mutual menace and destruction. This selfish desire for possessions and power has a strangling effect on human relationships and is pulling man into the abyss of self-destruction.

But fortunately all this must be regarded only as a phase through which every human being, every nation and also humanity as a whole must pass, until all are eventually brought to the recognition that happiness is not to be found in material possessions, in riches or power. Luckily there are already large numbers of human beings whose lives are no longer ruled by the love of money and who are realising that there are higher objectives to strive for. These men and women have discovered that it is the spiritual life which really matters and that the physical body in which the soul temporarily happens to be incarnated is but of passing importance and merely serves the purpose of gaining some particular experience or else that there is some special duty that should be fulfilled.

Though these men do not love money, they will still need it for the work that has to be done; they have been caught up in a system where money has become the symbol of creative energy and has thus become an essential part of existence. So they too will have to earn sufficient to pay for their needs and above that for the work that has to be accomplished on behalf of humanity. But they will not cherish the desire for more money or possessions over and above their minimum requirements – they abhor money for power or to pamper artificial needs of luxury; money to waste on voluptuous and sensual pleasures, whilst their brothers are dying of misery and starvation! What the world needs is a total reassessment of values.

When considering the history of human development, it becomes obvious, however, that desire should not be regarded purely from its negative aspects. It is desire in its many facets of expression which has served to drive man along his evolutionary path, constantly shifting from one planned satisfaction to the next, until the stage is reached when the desire for the material is transmuted into aspiration and a yearning for the spiritual life and for serving his fellow man.

(iv) *Personal Ambition:*

Ever remain on watch for inclinations towards personal ambition – the striving for public recognition and self-glorification, which is an inherent quality of every developing human being. Ambition for power, position and status is but another expression of self-centredness and is closely related to arrogance. It must unavoidably lead to competition with others displaying similar tendencies and invariably results in all kinds of unsavoury practices to outwit and get the better of all opposition. It causes strife on various levels and as a rule only ends in disappointment and frustration. Ambitious striving is essentially based on glamour and illusion, so often leading to disenchantment when the contender eventually achieves his objective, only to find his attainment to be an empty shell.

As a rule the striver will continue on his path of conquest until he becomes aware of the futility of all attainments which only gratify the desires of the personality and that ultimately all that matters are those spiritual aspects giving expression to the presence of the soul. The recognition of these lessons may, however, be delayed till later incarnations. For each and every individual the life must inevitably dawn when he will become aware of the existence of higher values, thus gaining his first vision of the Path of Light.

Even the well intentioned disciple is sometimes caught up in the snares of ambition; in his aspiration to serve, potent forces may be generated and in some instances these may serve to fan into flame latent seeds of ambition, which may then beglamour him and temporarily divert him from the path he intended following. The true server should take his eyes off his own accomplishments, except perhaps to use them as stepping stones to even greater achievements in his service of humanity and the Plan.

In fulfilling his part in the greater work, whether large or small, the disciple should therefore forget about himself as the personality, only striving to encompass to the best of his ability what is demanded of him under the circumstances in which he has been placed. During this process he should ever retain his humility and sense of proportion, irrespective of the results that are achieved.

(v) *Pride:*

Often even well advanced disciples have to fight against an exhibition of self-satisfaction and the glamour of pride when some task has been satisfactorily completed or a difficult objective has been attained. He should always remain on the lookout not to be serving himself instead of humanity. In this respect he might be able to mislead others but never his own soul!

(vi) *Crime:*

Acts of crime are basically aspects of psychological disturbances, where various forms of selfishness find expression in distorted activities against society. It may be the product of several weaknesses, such as lack of respect for the rights and property of others or the result of selfish greed for possessions, sometimes combined with a craving for power. Some crimes also originate from deemed past injustices and the consequent development of anti-social attitudes. Other crimes may be founded on political motives and in some instances simply on laziness. Then there are what may be called *'emotional crimes'* – offences which have been instigated by feelings of frustration, grudge, hate, envy or jealousy, sometimes also combined with a distorted spirit of adventure. But the main underlying cause of crime, which to some extent comprises all the above considerations, remains a deeply seated *inherent selfishness*, finding its expression in the many nuances of transgression against the social establishment.

Dramatic penalties to prevent or suppress crime have consequently so far proved relatively abortive. The only really effective way of combating crime is that the originating causes should be removed or treated. Future generations will therefore largely succeed in eliminating crime by psychological approaches – not so much by treating the criminals but by *preventing crime* through improved environmental conditions and by more effective educational systems for the youth.

(vii) *Separativeness:*

A great deal of harm is occasioned in the world by that most reprehensible human trait commonly known as 'separativeness'. It is one of man's most outstanding weaknesses and has already been responsible for untold misery and suffering and for much of the disturbed human relationships on all levels. It is this negative attitude which so often serves as the source of a whole range of human transgressions. Separativeness generally originates from selfish motives, interests or opinions, which are inclined to set brother against brother, group against group and nation against nation. It engenders a sense of superiority and causes conflict and destruction between opposing interests, whether represented by individuals, groups or nations; it may exert major influences in economic, political, scientific and religious fields and has in many instances been the principal cause of cruel and destructive wars. Separativeness emphasises the importance of material possessions and therefore encourages acquisition in many of its unsavoury aspects; it also breeds hatred and distrust between individuals and in international relationships.

(viii)   **War:**

At the first glance one would not be inclined to ascribe selfishness as one of the main underlying causes of both war and pacifism. But that is exactly the case and the majority of wars have their origin, directly or indirectly, from some form of selfishness, displayed as desire or greed of some nature or as separativeness.

War is the explosion of energies which have been accumulating on etheric levels through man's instrumentality and his badly conducted human relationships. The tensions built up can always be psychologically released if one or both of the contending parties could but be persuaded to relinquish unreasonable and selfish claims. The trouble, however, is that, when emotional stresses build up to certain levels, emotions seem to overwhelm all mental capacity and the reasoning mind becomes obscured by astral hazes.

Every person of goodwill is averse to war and all it stands for and will take all reasonable steps within his means to avoid it. War is evil and ugly but occasions may arise when no man of integrity and rectitude can escape its clutches and when he should be willing to defend and fight for those concepts and ideals which he considers are right and decent. He is not expected to lie down placidly and to be ruthlessly trampled under foot by the intruder who is working to implement the wishes of the Dark Forces.

The attitude to be adopted towards war all depends on the underlying *motives*. War is always wrong but at times man can be forced to choose between the lesser of two evils. When the motive is wrong, then war is mass murder but with the right motive war may assume the form of a sacrificial action. When an attacker is killed in the course of protecting the innocent and defenceless, this is not murder but a justified action if not a moral obligation.

(ix)   **Pacifism:**

At least two interpretations may be attached to 'pacifism'. If it is meant that war should be avoided as far as reasonably possible and that every fair means of love, goodwill and understanding should be employed to effect this and to encourage good relationships, then pacifism should be supported to the utmost.

313

On the other hand if by pacifism is understood an attitude of pusillanimity and 'laissez faire', where forces of evil are allowed to ride rough shod over that which is good and decent, because the man is not expected to show resistance or the mettle to stand up and fight for that which he considers right and proper or to defend with all his might his dependants, community or mankind as a whole, then such pacifism itself is considered a product of evil. If analysed it will often be found that this type of pacifism originates from basic selfishness, which may be somewhat camouflaged by apparently altruistic sentiments but which is in fact founded on averseness to disturbing a convenient *status quo* or the man's physical comfort or on fear of exposing the physical body to pain, with even the possibility of death by fighting.

It must, however, also be acknowledged that there are some pacifists with whom it is an attitude of deep inner conviction. They regard any form of partisanship as an infringement of the laws of universal brotherhood and in their enthusiasm and unilateral but myopic outlook, they become fanatical and are prepared to sacrifice the good of humanity as a whole to a sentimental and emotionally distorted interpretation of the basically sound principle to 'love all men'. This attitude is therefore not based on real spiritual love and it must be remembered that man should act according to well considered mental reasoning and the inspirations of his soul and not allow himself to be guided by pure sentiment. When man is faced with a clear choice between good and evil, he cannot try to maintain neutrality by hiding behind emotional expressions – this would be shirking his responsibilities. As the Christ said – 'he who is not with me is against me'.

VIII. 2 (b)   Criticism and Suspicion

'As one knows more, one judges less'. The wise man is not quick in expressing his opinion; he recognises that the objective appearance of a subject or that which is expressed or explained in words, is so often deceptive, emotionally distorted and not at all a true reflection of what the inner vision would reveal.

Criticism is a faculty of the lower mind, is always destructive and is capable of inflicting pain and wounds. It should be realised that no true disciple can make any headway on the Path as long as others are thus deliberately being hurt.

There should be close collaboration between disciples, yet at the same time man should retain his own individuality, pursue his own way and leave his brother to work out his own salvation. It is only human to consider one's own point of view to be the correct one and this is exactly where the trouble lies. If others do not conform to our way of thinking, then the inclination is to start criticising and negating their attitude and actions. It should be remembered, however, that man can never really grasp the complete truth and that what he observes is merely one of the facets of a greater whole, and it is quite possible that when his neighbour deals with the same fundamental truth, he will approach it from a somewhat different angle and may consequently become aware of quite another version and with just as much justification. Under such circumstances the two interpretations may differ radically but meanwhile both may represent correct versions of the same truth – or both may even be incorrect or at least distorted. Disciples should learn to recognise the many ways, the many methods and the widely differing techniques, all aiming towards the same goal.

Therefore, cultivate an attitude of non-interference and a refusal to criticise and correct your fellow worker. Carry on with your own responsibilities and let your co-worker find his own way – but with your full help and support where you can do so constructively and without interference. This may sound contradictory but the true disciple will be able to understand and practise the finer distinction.

Although a strong standpoint should be taken against any form of destructive criticism, a clear distinction should nonetheless be drawn between criticism and the ability to retain a proper sense of balance and proportion and to subject circumstances to *analysis* according to their merits, based on all the facts that are at one's disposal. Elimination of criticism will therefore not mean a lack of discrimination and an inability to see error or failure where it does occur. No! – falsity, impurity, insincerity and weaknesses of whatever nature, should be recognised for what they are but the subsequent reaction should not be one of condemnation – on the contrary, it should merely serve to evoke a spirit of loving helpfulness. A clear distinction should therefore be drawn between true analytical insight and criticism which is often based on a sense of personal superiority and a love of fault finding. True insight and loving criticism will on the other hand be supported by understanding and constructive aid.

A critical spirit is always conducive to glamour and there are but few who are immune to this danger. The most effective procedure to counter this natural inclination, is to mould all thoughts, words and actions of the daily life on goodwill and kindness. This may sound a simple precept but to succeed will require consecrated attention and should be practised all day and every day, until it becomes a habit and is applied automatically.

People are seldom seen as they really are, because we are inclined only to see them through the field of illusion with which our criticism has surrounded them and which will inevitably distort their true appearance.

Suspicion is merely a perverted form of criticism and represents that ugly and poisonous glamour where criticism has been directed at another without its being founded on sufficient evidence.

The power wielded by suspicion may be curtailed and then eliminated by correct mental training:

(a) Assume the attitude of the 'onlooker', regarding life and its happenings without displaying undue emotion, with acceptance and with 'divine indifference'. Observe all men and their activities through the eyes of the soul – that is, with love and impartiality.

(b) Give every individual all possible support by contributing love and understanding

315

but otherwise leave him free to live his own life, to shoulder his own responsibilities and thus to gain his own experiences, which will allow his soul to develop and advance on the Path of Life.

(c)   The aspirant should concentrate his energies on his own life of service. If this is done effectively, it will leave no time to blight the lives of others by vile and often unfounded suspicion. *Live TO let live!*

So often criticism and suspicion are nothing but a reflection of our own shortcomings. By focussing our unconsciously troubled thoughts on these defects, we end up by visualising them in others, suspecting them of being motivated by these failings. This may be cured by subjecting the personality to careful self-analysis – by standing apart from the personality and observing its motivations through the clear and unprejudiced light of the soul.

Leaders of men, whether of groups, communities or nations, are particularly subject to criticism by those they are leading and serving. This refers to the genuine leaders whose primary objective it is to serve the interests of those they represent or those who have been placed under their charge. Such leaders should constantly be supported by the energy of 'loving understanding' but instead they are so often badly handicapped by criticism accentuating all their imperfections. Such criticism oft results in seriously crippling the leader's effective service.

So often this criticism is rooted in jealousy, thwarted ambition or pride of intellect. It is so easy to sit in judgement of the leader and to criticise him with regard to action or non-action for which the critic does not carry the responsibility and neither is he, as a rule, fully aware of all the relevant facts and their implications. Such destructive criticism is harmful to both the critic and the criticised leader.

Group leaders are often subjected to streams of poisonous thought, to idle gossip of a destructive nature and to jealousies, hates and frustrated ambitions of members who would like to see the leader superseded. As may be expected this must have an adverse effect on the leader and might produce both physical and emotional effects; the more evolved the leader the greater will be his sensitivity and the more acute will be the pain and suffering that is inflicted. All the leader can do in such circumstances, is to withdraw within himself, to guard against all signs of bitterness and self-pity which will be inclined to arise and with loving understanding to wait for the time when the members will come to their senses, arrive at clearer insight and will learn to co-operate with a spirit of goodwill.

Group members should also realise that criticism of any kind can only create disturbed relationships within the ranks of the group, thereby undermining the effectiveness of the group as a whole, delaying the progress of the work and enervating its quality.

VIII. 2 (c)   Irritation

A moment's thought will bring the student to the recognition that irritation is purely a reaction of the emotional body – evoked by friction of some kind. The degree to which the disciple still exhibits irritability will therefore be an indication of the extent to which the astral body still retains control.

Irritability is exemplified by explosive tempers, hasty words and actions, by criticism and misunderstandings, and every effort should therefore be made to gain control over the emotions – without such control very little progress can be made along the Path. It must also be obvious that irritation must have a decidedly adverse influence on man's relationships and will automatically disqualify him for harmonious group work, as irritability also has a contagious or reciprocal effect. Such a man is therefore also irresponsible and cannot yet be used as a dependable instrument in the hands of the Masters.

This disease – for that is what irritability amounts to – can only be ended by a close guard over the emotions and by focussing the life in the head and heart.

A clear distinction should be drawn between irritability and *mental sensitivity*. Where irritability refers to emotional reaction, mental sensitivity refers to the reactions of the mind and more particularly to subjective impressions and influences as registered through the etheric vehicle. Consequently, as the disciple evolves, so his irritability will decrease, to be replaced by a corresponding increase in sensitivity to impressions from higher spheres.

VIII. 2 (d) **Fanaticism**

Disciples in training should always guard against any trend towards fanaticism, which indicates imbalance and is therefore most undesirable in whatever form it is evinced.

Although the fanatic may not be aware of it, he usually is a bewildered man entertaining some potent idea but not yet knowing where and how to integrate it into its correct relation to other life circumstances. The mind of man is constantly subjected to a phantasmagoria of thought-forms and to retain some sense of reality and discrimination it is essential that a proper sense of balance and perspective be preserved. The outlook should never be allowed to become limited and warped by focussing the attention too rigidly on only a single narrow line of thought and leaving the many related aspects out of consideration. Therefore ever remain open to new visions and ideas and be prepared to try fresh approaches. When brighter light has been procured and after all relevant facts have been duly considered, do not hesitate to discard that which has served its purpose and become redundant and then to supersede and amplify it with something better and more comprehensive.

A devoted fanatic may cherish high ideals but owing to his unbalanced and narrow outlook, which often leads to irresponsible and intolerant action and separativeness, such a man cannot be used by the Masters as a dependable instrument for service. A fanatical approach to any subject, whether basically considered good or bad, is always dangerous, for such a person can only see one side of a question and finds it impossible to appreciate other points of view. Although originally the fanatic might have been motivated by high ideals, his approach lacks realism and discrimination by rushing after some half-formed version of the truth.

Many of the reactionary groups which are so typical of present day world conditions, have founded their premises on principles of the highest integrity but, owing to their limited vision, they have degenerated into merely idealistic fanaticists who may end by doing more harm than good.

VIII. 3. **Human Virtues**

(Additional aspects of 'virtue' will be dealt with in the following chapter, under the heading 'Attributes of the Disciple'. See – IX. 3).

Certain divine qualities exist in every human being. These are the inherent attributes of the soul or the Inner Christ, which largely remain hidden and dormant in the undeveloped individual. It is only after the course of aeons and after sufficient experience has been gained during numerous incarnations, that the soul potentialities gradually begin to unfold, acquiring greater dominance over the selfish and separative inclinations of the personality.

It is a difficult task to express in words the nature of the subjective concepts of Love and Goodwill. The finer nuances of these thoughts will be more readily sensed by those who are already receptive and attuned to the subjective approach, than by men and women who, as yet, are purely intellectually focussed and who therefore have to depend on elaborate explanations. A well balanced mental approach is nonetheless regarded as essential. To those who are, however, not yet ready to absorb these thoughts and impressions, this writing will remain meaningless and will represent only the idle and inane ramblings of the sentimentalist or mysticist.

VIII. 3 (a) **Love**

(See also: PART ONE - X. 3 (d))

The outstanding characteristic of the soul is Love, finding expression in various ways and known under such terms as goodwill, kindness, harmlessness, understanding, forgiveness, sacrifice, humility, compassion, serenity, selflessness and several more. All these are but variations of the energy of Love, with the accent focussed on one or other of its many facets.

The love which is here considered is not the physical or sentimental quality that the man in the street would associate with this term and which is responsible for physical attraction between individuals and also for the manifestation of sexual urges. The love under discussion is that divine principle which is the driving force underlying all evolutionary activity; it is the energy which carries everything on to expression and completion and it therefore also includes that indeterminate force which urges man along till he finds the Path, first to self-realisation and subsequently to closer synthesis with THAT of which he forms a part.

Man, in his innocence, regards himself to be familiar with love but there are very few who are fully aware of the potency of this energy which lies ready to hand, only waiting for direction and implementation by the combined powers of the mind and heart. If correctly applied, there literally is no limit to the possibilities of this salving and creative energy. But 'familiarity breeds contempt' and man just does not recognise the power-to-good which readily lies at his disposal. Those who exhibit an awakening interest in the principles of the Ageless Wisdom, are willing to spend considerable effort to acquire what they consider to be intriguing information about the after life, on initiation, or on details about the Masters but if they are taught to apply *one of the most effective esoteric laws by persistently living a life of loving kindness*, many will take only scant notice of this most significant injunction and pass it off as a mere platitude. They do not realise that such a life, where love-energy is consciously, intelligently and correctly directed, *must* inevitably lead to spiritual realisation and finally to liberation.

But it is not self-liberation that really matters; as the disciple progresses along the Path, he discovers that the helping and serving of others, of those who are struggling along the same difficult Way with him but who have perhaps been temporarily retarded and are lagging somewhat behind, is of even greater importance than his personal salvation. He will also find that the brighter the light of love burns within his own heart, the more light will he have at his disposal with which to irradiate the Way for others.

All human relationships are ultimately determined by Love – by its absence, its presence and most important of all – by its conscious manipulation and direction. It cannot be sufficiently stressed that not only the disciple's *actions* but in the first place *his thoughts* should consistently be guarded and guided only by love. There is no other way to counter or eradicate pernicious and usually well entrenched habits of hate, suspicion and criticism. Therefore persistently endeavour to see each other only in the light of love, and in due course all negative and detractive thoughts will fade and be superseded by goodwill.

Love is a difficult quality to cultivate and maintain, because to express true love man's inherent selfish nature must first be submerged. To apply this love under all circumstances will not only mean sacrificing many of the personality dispositions but also practising a strong command over the emotions.

For effective group work love is the essential requisite – it fosters that inclusive, non-critical and magnetic attitude which will preserve group integrity and synthesis and which will prevent undue personality friction and disturbances. Where there is an absence of the uniting energy of love, groups are doomed to failure but when the hearts are filled with love and actions are guided by the highest wisdom available to the disciple, then the man can proceed fearlessly, knowing that the results of his work can only lead to mutual benefit. Genuine love recognises no barriers – it is exemplified by deep understanding, which ignores mistakes and negates all separating thoughts and will surround all fellow men with a protecting wall of love which, as far as possible, will endeavour to relieve all need.

Much more could be written about Love but to what avail if these words do not reach the inner being? The gist of the subject has been expressed – try to absorb these thoughts and 'take them to heart'. Do not rush through these pages but carefully weigh the contents and ponder on their deeper meaning and implications. The way some of these thoughts have been expressed in words may be rather crude but try to reach beyond the words and to arrive at their inner significance.

Those fortunate ones who have been able to gain the deeper purport of these thoughts, those who have discovered the first glimmerings of the inner Light of Love, should cherish it and make every endeavour to kindle it, till it finally flares up into a beaming light, not only sufficient to guide the man surely and safely along his own Path but, of much greater importance, also to be able to supply his fellow man with Light and Love and thus eventually to contribute towards helping humanity as a whole to advance on its way towards the manifestation of the Divine Plan.

VIII. 3 (b) **Goodwill**

What an excellent portent that the word 'goodwill' is today being bandied about and used fast and loose in many public speeches and journalistic articles throughout the world. It is realised only too well that on many occasions it is used insincerely and even falsely, merely with the purpose of influencing and pandering to public opinion but this is already sufficient indication that the broader public, the man in the street, is increasingly becoming aware of the role that goodwill is playing in universal human relations and that this is the only way open to attain that peace for which the masses are yearning. The average man has had enough of this perpetual fighting amongst individuals, groups and nations and is longing for goodwill and peace.

Goodwill is the directing of the energies of Light, Love and Understanding to all men. Actually it represents only one facet of Love and is a potent energy at the disposal of every human being intending to use it to good effect. It is the projecting of positive, helpful and constructive thoughts to others, with the sincere purpose of producing good – where possible these thoughts should be vigorously supported by commensurate action.

When attitudes of understanding and goodwill become the keynote of a man's life, it is bound to affect and change the whole of his outlook and personality – 'no man liveth unto himself'. It will inevitably bring forth more harmonious conditions, both within himself and in his circle of influence, than could be encompassed by any form of physical demonstration.

The man who decides to live a life based on the principles of goodwill, will find that because it is such a beautiful ideal, it will demand stern sacrifices and at first will prove difficult to apply in practice. On the other hand it is a life bringing rich rewards. Such a life will demand:

(a) Right thoughts, based on intelligent love.
(b) Right and constructive speech, which will not hurt or harm unnecessarily and must therefore be governed by self-control.
(c) Skill in action, which will prove harmless but at the same time effective towards improving human relations.

It will be found that these endeavours, if seriously undertaken, will call forth every resource of a man's being and will certainly take time and persistence to achieve.

Goodwill can only be the product of true and loving understanding and will be an indication of a personality coming increasingly under the influence of the soul – therefore *it is the criterion of a soul-infused personality*. The practice of goodwill will also attract to the disciple those energies which are beneficent and which may then be applied for the helping of others. These salutary forces will simultaneously react upon and transmute any harmful vibrations which might still lurk in his etheric aura.

In esoteric literature reference is often made to the '*Will-to-Good*' – this is that dynamic energy with which man is irradiated and inspired, either from the Hierarchy or direct from Shamballa. It is this primary force of the Divine Will with which man is animated and which he transmutes and expresses as goodwill. The student should, however, not brood unduly over these distinctions – greater clarity will come with continued study.

Goodwill, which is automatically coupled with right human relations, is rapidly becoming the ideal of the masses. This is demonstrated by the many movements throughout the world for the supply of relief in its variety of forms – for the poor, the sick, the aged, the backward and the uneducated. In all spheres of life where distress of any kind occurs, steps are being taken towards its alleviation. Undoubtedly a great deal remains to be done and new problems and needs arise daily but nevertheless the spirit of goodwill that has been awakened in the human race is unmistakable, is rapidly spreading and is often unexpectedly disclosed where least expected. It has a contagious influence and one act of goodwill is so often reciprocated by another, thus oft initiating a chain effect.

The inclination is to think of goodwill as a form of sentimental kindness but it may be displayed in numberless ways. A scientist may dedicate his work and the fruit of his research to human welfare; a man may offer his physical body for the testing of certain treatments, which might lead to the permanent undermining of his health or even to death; many instances may thus be enumerated where men willingly sacrifice their all – property, reputation, status, health and even life on behalf of their family, nation or humanity as a whole. These may all be regarded as expressions of goodwill and so there are many, many more. In our news media the inclination is to focus the attention on that which is sensational and thrilling, as these news items usually have the best sales value with the masses, whereas acts of goodwill or sacrifice as a rule draw much less attention and may even be ignored. But even in this respect changes are becoming noticeable.

At the suggestion of the Tibetan, a movement was initiated by Alice A. Bailey to unite all men of goodwill throughout the world under one banner, which could then act and speak with one voice on matters concerning the good of humanity. This movement has grown over the years and today functions under the title of **WORLD GOODWILL**; it is reticulated throughout the world and has numerous members in all principal countries. The idea of locating and linking, as far as possible, all men and women of goodwill is excellent but so far this association is apparently not fulfilling its underlying purpose. To hold such a conglomerate group together requires something more than mere talking and writing about the ideals of goodwill and better human relationships. To retain the active interest of members will demand inspired leadership, which will result in imaginative and constructive service activities. The feeling must be inculcated in members that they severally and jointly are working towards a worthwhile objective, for which they must not only exert themselves but which will also demand sacrifices. *The idealist wants to make sacrifices* for what he considers to be a good cause and these opportunities should be provided. Some of the '*Units of Service*' do undertake smaller service activities but seemingly most of this work is of a routine and unimaginative nature, not inspiring members to concentrated exertion and sacrificial effort. This must inevitably lead to waning enthusiasm, which is unfortunate because the movement contains vast potentialities. Basically the organisation appears to be sound and ready to undertake more responsible work but it needs to be aroused and infused with fresh energy, to become that effective channel through which the Masters can work more actively and constructively.

Goodwill is man's attempt to express the Love of God, which will eventually result in peace on Earth. One of the snags in its practical application lies in the actual simplicity of its principles – people consequently fail to appreciate its potency and dynamic possibilities. The only way, however, for mankind to establish good human relations and finally peace, is through the application of the principles of goodwill. It is an attitude which should therefore be deliberately cultivated, thereby establishing its principles in the consciousness of the masses. The inner good is already present in every human being but as a rule it is smothered by evil influences, materialism and selfish desire. A great deal can, however, be achieved by proper education and training and the best place to start is with the younger generation. From the earliest stages our youth should be made aware of the power of love and goodwill and that much more can be attained by the use of these energies for the manifestation of a better life on Earth, than by applying the forces of hate, greed, envy and intolerance.

The **Law of Cause and Effect** should be stressed and its effects demonstrated to the younger people. They should be taught that life ever repays in the same coin which it receives and therefore that when love and goodwill are offered to your fellow man these are the energies which in the end will be returned to you – and what is even more important, it will not only be repaid with interest but will also be passed on along the line to the next man!

Some *apparent* exceptions will occur, such as for instance the initial negative reactions by those who are still unprepared, who have in their lives encountered nothing but hate and frustration and who have rarely if ever experienced real love; however, with perseverance even the most hardened cases will begin to react and will gradually recognise the possibilities and wonders of goodwill. Even the most perverted 'sinner' has that tender inner core which *can* be exposed with correct treatment and which once revealed can be worked upon and influenced to the good. It must constantly be stressed, till man eventually learns and consciously concedes that 'hatred ceases not by hatred but that hatred ceaseth by love' – by love expressed as practical goodwill.

It is not so much that human nature has to be *changed* but rather that the good that is always present must be uncovered; the hard layers of the dark outer appearance must be softened and penetrated and the inner centre, the heart of love, must be exposed. This *must* and *will* finally be achieved, so why not begin with it right now and thus share in the advantages which will inevitably accrue! What a wonderful new world we can and are going to create; a world in which it will be a pleasure to live – for each and every individual; a world of peace, without hate, constant fighting and starvation; a world of goodwill, love and harmonious human relations; a world of plenty, where everything will be shared and where the work that is done will not be for selfish acquisition but a work of joy for serving fellow human beings and contributing one's small share towards expressing the Divine Plan. All this real 'Heaven on Earth' is there for the taking, if man could but open his eyes and begin to identify himself with the forces that are at his disposal, by appropriating and applying the energies of Love and Goodwill.

When men and women can meet in a spirit of goodwill, no matter what their political affiliation, religion or nation, there is no single problem that cannot be solved to mutual benefit and satisfaction. They must only be inspired with the divine energy of the will-to-good and this energy is today far more widespread than is realised. It is only for the infused men and women to take the initiative and to discover and reveal this quality in others and then to train and guide these forces and bring them to effective action. No problems of any nature can in the long run withstand the pervasive effects of goodwill when suitably organised and expressed with loving discrimination and steadfastness.

A Call!

The Hierarchy calls all men to end their lives of vague dreaming and to come to the practical asssistance of humanity by commencing in the place and circumstances to which they have been assigned by the decrees of life, by demonstrating the potentials of love and goodwill in their own immediate surroundings, in their own homes and social circles. This task should then be extended systematically to include the community and the nation, until ultimately it must also affect international relations. In this work the effort of each and every individual is needed and will prove effective, acting cumulatively, until with the course of time all opposing forces must inevitably be overwhelmed by an ever growing and irresistible tidal wave of goodwill. This dynamic power, when trained to arouse the potency of public opinion, demanding the greatest good for the greatest number, must and will carry everything before it, to save humanity and to prepare a better world for posterity.

It is realised that the whole world certainly cannot be suddenly converted to such a new approach in the course of a few years but this ideal has already taken hold of the imagination of certain important sections of world opinion and it will not take many decades from now before these principles will be accorded world-wide recognition. Meanwhile let every man and woman of goodwill lend his *active* support towards investing the existing World Goodwill movement with new life and energy, thus enabling it to become more practical and dynamic and with loving understanding to shape it into a useful instrument in the hands of the Hierarchy, by means of which improved human relations may then be encompassed on all levels. Once greater enthusiasm for this movement has been engendered, it is bound to gather rapid momentum and to show world-wide effects. Here lies a wonderful *field of service* for many of those enthusiastic disciples who so often are on the lookout for some sphere of work in which their energies may be expressed on behalf of humanity.

A considerable amount of work has already been accomplished in contacting the men of goodwill in every country. This should be followed up on a broader basis so as to include an ever larger percentage of the men of goodwill who are available. When this latent force, with its enormous potentialities, begins to assert itself by being swung into concerted, intelligent and well considered activity, it will rapidly lead to a closer synthesis of all nations and races, to unite them finally into the One Humanity.

Every care should, however, be exercised that the World Goodwill movement must at no stage be brought under suspicion of promoting or supporting any specific political faction and even more particularly where such parties tend toward opposing or undermining the government in authority. Goodwill does not function through partisanship and attack but through intelligent reasoning, understanding and collaboration, and by systematically applying these principles, all opposition must and will be demolished.

To summarise it might be stated that the objectives of World Goodwill should be:

(a) To inculcate the principles of goodwill in the minds of the leaders in all areas of human activity.

(b) To educate the youth of the world in these thoughts.

(c) To infuse public opinion or the masses, with these basic principles.

It should be remembered, however, that it is only the Law of Love, translated and expressed as Goodwill which, when applied with discrimination and loving understanding, will lead to these improved human relations.

Let every disciple therefore contribute his share according to his particular circumstances, to get this terrific force of goodwill into motion. Goodwill is contagious and nothing will be able to stop its momentum – this is how the New Era could be inaugurated, an era which will ensure prosperity, world unity, peace and plenty for all!

VIII. 3 (c) **Forgiveness**

To be able to forgive is surely one of man's most winning traits. It is the willingness to surrender of one's self and of one's convictions, for the sake of others and is therefore closely associated with both sacrifice and goodwill. Forgiveness is ever the attribute of the greater who is willing to make some sacrifice or concession on behalf of the lesser, in order that the lesser may be enabled to continue towards its objective. Achievement of the greater is typically characterised by some form of concession to the lesser.

Forgiveness must really be regarded as a divine attribute and that is why its degree of manifestation keeps pace with man's development on the Path of Life; the highly evolved will therefore reveal this characteristic to a far greater extent than the unevolved savage. It symbolises a forgetting of the bad and unpleasant of the past and a passing forward to the better that is visualised for the future.

VIII. 3 (d) **Sacrifice**

By sacrifice should be understood that joyful rendering of what one has, in service of others; it therefore implies spontaneous giving from the heart and is thus a gesture of love and goodwill, leaving no after effects of pain or regret. Should sacrifice, however, be regarded as an obligation or liability, only reluctantly made under some form of duress, resulting in regrets, pain and suffering, then from the spiritual point of view it becomes meaningless and should rather be avoided.

Sacrifice therefore should be a spontaneous inner urge and is not something that can be taught and, moreover, should never be demanded of disciples. If exacted and grudgingly granted, it actually may have a negative effect by causing a feeling of antipathy or even of animosity. Similarly, if too much stress is applied in teaching the principle of sacrifice, the disciple – rightly or wrongly – may develop a feeling of guilt because of non-sacrifice and although this may then lead to so-called sacrifice, it will no longer be the genuine article – it will be of a forced, unwilling and therefore of an undesirable nature.

To the disciple there should therefore be no such thing as 'sacrifice' in the ordinary sense of the word. What the average man might regard as an act of sacrifice, will be nothing of the kind to the dedicated disciple; to him the relevant action may merely represent an opportunity for joyful giving or serving, without even for a moment considering the cost. To the materially minded the effect of such a deed might vary between self-pity and self-admiration, being an indication of the selfish-emotional reaction of the personality. The spiritually focussed individual will, however, regard his so-called sacrifice as an opportunity that has been granted him to serve, for which he is sincerely grateful and which might provide that inner joy of the soul but without reflecting any emotional repercussions.

'*Spiritual sacrifice*' is therefore that divine urge to give and surrender that which in the past was of importance but which subsequently has been superseded by other and higher values. It means the impulse towards giving, which usually has been triggered unconsciously by a change in life values because of the ascendancy of soul influence. That which in the past was deemed of such importance has lost its allure and is gladly relinquished.

The spirit of sacrifice will also be evinced through an inclination towards *sharing*. Such sharing will be an indication that selfishness is being superseded and is being sacrificed on the altar of altruism. World stability will ultimately be achieved only when founded on the sublimation of selfishness in general and when a greater willingness is revealed by the nations of the world to share freely both their natural resources and the products of their technical and intellectual proficiency with those who are less fortunately endowed.

Spirituality can of course never be bought by tendering a sacrificial offering. When man is, however, approaching spiritual life and spiritual consciousness, his sense of values also changes and, step by step, the old material and emotional merits are 'sacrificed' and surrendered, to be superseded by that which is spiritual.

No individual ever exists entirely on his own – he always forms an inseparable part of mankind, even though he may be leading some cloistered existence. The majority of men have their family ties and responsibilities and beyond that they usually fulfil some role in their surrounding community. Their attitude or any change of approach to life, must therefore invariably also affect those who surround them. The extent of this influence will depend on the strength of the forces which they are radiating. Therefore when some sacrifice is contemplated, this should not solely be determined by personal considerations, as its effect on others is just as important and should be carefully weighed. On the other hand, no sacrifice, when purely inspired by spiritual considerations, could ever be really detrimental to others; effects which might *appear* to be harmful, will only be apparently so, because of man's limited perspective and inaccurate discernment and evaluation of circumstances. When there is any doubt whether the impulse to sacrifice springs from astral levels and is therefore prompted by selfish desire or emotion or whether it is of spiritual origin, then the final decision must be left to the guidance of the soul.

Different meanings will therefore be attached to the concept of 'sacrifice', depending on the level and aspect from which it is being considered and the motivating incentives:

(a) The motive may be selfish and for personal advantage, by surrendering some possession, whether material or subjective, with the hope of exchanging this for something which is regarded of greater value. This indicates an orientation towards either material acquisition or the satisfying of emotional desires. It therefore more resembles a form of bartering than what esoterically would be regarded as sacrifice.

(b) It may be the instinct to be of help to others, which in its turn may arise from either (i) a basically selfish motive in trying to avoid personal distress at the sight of suffering, but this is already an indication of the unfoldment of compassion; or (ii) it may purely arise as an urge towards impersonal service, in which case it must be regarded as soul inspired.

(c) The stage is finally reached where there is a total revaluation of the qualities and purposes of life. The disciple becomes spiritually orientated and material values fade away and are 'sacrificed' for that which is higher, resulting in what may be termed 'the exquisite agony of sacrifice'. This eventually leads to the stage where all forms of pain are transcended and where neither sorrow, rebellion or suffering are experienced and ecstasy and exaltation are attained.

IX

DISCIPLESHIP

IX. 1. The Disciple

After man has tasted both the joys and afflictions of life in the world of matter and illusion, he begins to realise their emptiness and that they fail to satisfy some inner hunger which has been urging him along to seek physical expression. Unconsciously he has been seeking for something indefinable during the course of many incarnations; seeking it in every possible physical, sensual, emotional and mental experience, each individual experience contributing towards rounding out of soul needs – the soul of whose hidden presence he has for so long remained unaware. But, at last, he begins to see 'double' and becomes aware of duality, of an inner and outer existence; he is awakening to the consciousness that, apart from the sensory life of the personality, there exists a deeper and stronger urge, an even more vital driving force – that of the inner man, the soul, who no longer craves for material satisfactions but is unfolding in him unexpected new fields of consciousness and perception. These revelations then shed new light on his Path and new vistas are opening up to his vision – vistas of self-improvement and service to humanity: a disciple is being born!

The word 'disciple' is used to denote all grades or workers on behalf of humanity and the Hierarchy of Masters, from the probationary disciple or aspirant who is tentatively beginning to feel his way, up to and including the Christ himself – 'the Master of all Masters and the Teacher alike of Angels and of men' and therefore the *First Disciple*.

The disciple is an individual whose whole outlook on life has been reoriented and who has radically changed his sense of values. He finds, however, that these new values do not remain stationary but are in a constant process of adjustment to keep pace with an ever expanding consciousness. The rate of this expansion will vary and might undergo periods of stagnation but, notwithstanding temporary intermissions, this cyclic development will continue to include ever higher and wider realms of consciousness.

Although the disciple has been concentrating on his individual effort, there will be a growing awareness that he forms an innate and intimate part of a greater whole and that in the past undue stress has been laid on the separateness of his existence. He is becoming aware that he belongs to a group of workers with whom he should co-operate as a team and that the focus of his attention should be changed to group work, whereby the combined individual efforts will be considerably enhanced.

As the man develops, as a deeper knowledge is acquired of the self and a more expanded consciousness is evoked of that which this self sees, hears, knows and contacts, the man will also increasingly make contact with this group to which he subjectively belongs and with which he is to collaborate. He will also become consciously aware of the guidance and support which he is receiving from the Master.

The disciple thus progressively adapts himself to a new rhythm of life and discovers and enters new fields of experience. He becomes aware of the presence of an advanced group of beings functioning on subjective levels, known as the Hierarchy of Masters, who have already cleared and paved a Path from darkness to light, from the unreal to the real and he is making every effort to prepare and qualify himself to follow this Path. He finds himself in a state of transition between the old and the new concepts of being and this frequently causes doubt and uncertainty. With growing spiritual perception and as the soul gradually brings greater illumination to the brain via the mind, more confidence will however, be gained leading to more effective service to the fellow man.

One of the first aspects on which the student of the Ancient Wisdom teachings gains a clearer insight, is the constitution of man. This leads to a deeper understanding of his own nature and some conception of the extent to which he has in the past been imprisoned in the worlds of glamour and illusion. When after further perseverance on the Path he becomes aware of the soul and the spiritual realms, his whole outlook and approach to life becomes revolutionised and a new world of endeavour opens up before him.

It should always be kept in mind, however, that there is no short-cut on this road towards the light and that every forward step will have to be carved and cleared by the disciple's own painstaking efforts, applied with the greatest persistence.

It will be found that all development follows a *rhythmic pattern* and the disciple must therefore learn to adapt himself to this in- and out-breathing of the soul life. Times of vision and unfoldment, when the aspirant will be lifted to the crest of a wave of ecstasy, must inevitably be followed by the subsequent period of the cycle when he will sink down into the trough of the wave and will be surrounded by utter spiritual darkness. For this he must be prepared, as it might prevent his sinking into profound depression. This realisation will simultaneously bring the assurance that such ebbing of the forces is quite normal and should rather be regarded as moments of recovery during which the disciple is granted a short breathing space and during which fresh forces may be gathered, enabling him to make the best use of his opportunities when in the course of the next cycle he is again lifted to the crest of the wave.

This ebb and flow can be observed in every sphere of existence and is even demonstrated in the sequence of man's incarnations – lives will occur which will be relatively static and uneventful, while subsequent lives might be crowded and vibrant with experience, leading to rapid growth. This factor should be duly considered when workers are seeking to help others – too much energy should not be directed to those lives not yet ready to absorb it, as this might not only be wasting of energy but might even prove harmful. Rather concentrate available forces where the best results may be produced, thus leading to fruitful service.

The Hierarchy is responsible for the expression of the Plan. The Masters are, however, dependent on disciples in physical incarnation to serve as channels and instruments for bringing the subjective designs into outer manifestation. Should these physical workers fail to respond or else make mistakes, this will result in temporary delays. Meanwhile the energies which should have been utilised in this process keep on streaming forth because of the never ending pulsations of the One Life and these might then evoke catastrophic results by being misapplied. A great responsibility therefore rests on the shoulders of those disciples whose eyes have been opened and who, because of their knowledge and sensitivity, have automatically become the hierarchical servers on the outer planes.

It is only by a combination of hard work, intellectual unfoldment, steady aspiration and spiritual orientation, that title to discipleship may be acquired; these qualities must in addition be supported by positive goodwill and an inner eye that is opening to the worlds of reality.

The true disciple will not regard his work as a marvellous opportunity for spiritual advancement – this would be the selfish approach and could not lead to efficient service. The genuine worker will apply himself to his indicated task with all the energy at his disposal, forgetful of his own personality, with the one purpose of contributing all that lies within him towards serving and the realisation of the Plan. This must inevitably also lead to his own progress – not towards self-satisfaction but by evoking dormant capacities that will mould him into an ever more efficient instrument of service in the hands of the Masters.

An essential requirement of the disciple is that he should ever retain an open mind and that he should be ready to relinquish many of the pet theories as to life, his work and his concepts about the hidden worlds, when new aspects are revealed to him. He should ever remain receptive to unexpected new impressions and interpretations and when these prove convincing, he must be prepared to reverse or adapt his preconceived ideas. He must consequently assume an expectant attitude, knowing that new visions *will* appear, new revelations *will* be made and new versions of the Truth will emerge to guide him along the Way. Care should therefore be exercised that the temporary interpretation does not crystallise and develop into a barrier separating him from the unfolding Truth and from the recognition of truer vision.

The life of the disciple is one of constant risks and dangers to which he is deliberately and willingly subjecting himself for spiritual unfoldment and for preparing himself for service. Disciples are severely tested and only a pure heart, true love of his fellow beings and the practical and intelligent application of mental activity, will qualify him to overcome his dilemmas. The emotional life in particular should be watched with care to prevent the generation of new glamours. The appearance of such glamours is not necessarily an indication of failure – failure only occurs when the disciple identifies himself with such astral demonstrations and subsequently succumbs and reverses to past rhythms of life. In these instances the Master will not interfere, as there are problems which the disciple has to overcome by his own powers. These obstacles are set in his path as tests of his consecration, will and perseverance. He will either overcome these problems and move forward to the door of light where the Master awaits him or he will *temporarily* stagnate in his evolution, till sufficient fresh forces have been gathered for a renewed assault against the obstructing barriers.

The disciple must be willing to face life as he finds it at any given time, with the equipment at his disposal. He must then proceed to subordinate himself, his affairs, circumstances and time to the needs of the day, with special reference to his group and the nature of their activities and requirements. When this is consciously undertaken, forgetting about himself, he will find that his personal affairs are miraculously taken care of and that his capacities for service are increasing beyond all expectation. It is through work, study, meditation and service that the disciple progressively acquires a deeper insight into reality. It is through altruistic service, rendered unstintingly, that fresh powers and energies will be manifested in him, increasingly qualifying the server to greater efficiency and a wider range of work.

The nature of the disciple's work may sometimes draw public attention but his spiritual reward will certainly not be commensurate to the publicity he acquires. The man who quietly works behind the scenes, unknown, unrecognised and unacclaimed, with sacrifice of all identity, is often the man who renders the greatest service to humanity. Such a man will receive no public homage but will have the greater inner compensation of knowing that he has contributed towards the salvage of struggling souls, that he has helped with the rebuilding of lives and that he has succeeded in generating some brighter light for focussing on humanity's Path of Return.

During the early stages of his experience the disciple as yet has very little self-confidence. The time will arrive, however, when he *must* assume that he has acquired more knowledge in some respects than is available to his less favoured brother and when it therefore becomes his duty to share with the latter what he has already received or to utilise his knowledge in some other way that will prove beneficial to others. His first experience in this direction might lead to awkward situations or a feeling of clumsiness but greater proficiency will be gained with practice. It is surprising how shrouded knowledge will well up when required and there is much that will be more clearly understood when needed to present to others. Actually the best way of learning is by teaching. 'Think humbly, speak wisely and work ceaselessly.'

When the head and the heart of the disciple begin to function as a team, he automatically becomes spiritually magnetic, his radiation will make itself felt in his environment and will evoke response from others who will be attracted to him. This will consciously or unconsciously lead to the forming of his own little group, which may prove the initial stages of what in a later life may be extended into a full-fledged esoteric group under his direction.

There are instances where disciples are sent into incarnation with a particular mandate. As a rule they will be unaware of this mission, although in exceptional instances there may be a 'conviction of mission' from early youth. Usually, however, disciples will be born with certain innate gifts and talents, which will progressively develop into firmly rooted ideas and ideals and combined with a brain responsive to these incentives. Normally these men or women will unknowingly be guided into that field of human activity wherein they are destined to play their role and in which they are meant to effect certain fundamental changes in accordance with hierarchical intent. As these disciples mentally mature and spiritually unfold, the work to be done will be felt or impressed on the mind as an irresistible urge. Whether this work is to be political, financial, educational, scientific or spiritual, they will unconsciously be guided by the Masters, who will also see to it that the necessary doors are opened, contacts are arranged and facilities are provided for implementing the work, without there being any evidence of this inner manipulation.

Although in exceptional instances consciousness of such a mission may be developed, the usual procedure is that the disciple reacts and works in response to impression but without being aware of the origin of such impression, which he regards as the products of his own mind.

All these disciples are, however, characterised by their humanitarianism and goodwill and their determination to promote the well-being of humanity, each according to his specific capacities and in the environment where he has been placed. Their every effort will be motivated by their innate love for their fellow men.

IX. 2. Need for Disciples

While the Masters are still mainly operating from etheric levels, they are dependent on the sensitivity of a limited number of human beings who are susceptible to hierarchical impression and who may thus serve as channels for the transmission of ideas from the Hierarchy to humanity.

The world is at present passing through a phase of preparation and adjustment for the coming New Age and one of the principal activities of the Masters is the gathering and training of those disciples who show the needed aptitude and who are urgently needed as bridges and instruments for constructive work on behalf of mankind. It is the responsibility of the modern disciple to become aware of these needs and to respond to the best of his ability. The extent to which this response is evoked, will be reflected by the increased love he expresses towards his fellow men and the simultaneous decrease in his self-interest.

IX. 3. **Attributes of the Disciple**

In the previous chapter, under the title 'Human Virtues', those outstanding qualities of *Love, Goodwill, Forgiveness* and *Sacrifice* have already been dealt with. These are the primary attributes on which good human relationships are founded and should therefore also be characteristic of every disciple.

The human character is, however, composed of many additional qualities, of which some of the more prominent will be briefly outlined in the following pages. Although it is hoped that this analysis will furnish a clearer picture of the complexity of the human character, it should at the same time be realised that in practice these components are not always clearly distinguishable and that they often overlap and merge. Some of these qualities may become accentuated during particular circumstances but they will remain part of the character as a whole. Actually the germ of each of these attributes is present in every individual but often lies dormant until needed or stimulated by outer circumstances. Those qualities which do become prominent will be evoked by:

(a) The Rays of Energy to which the vehicles of the personality and the soul are subject.

(b) The stage of development attained.
(c) The circumstances under which the disciple is functioning.
(d) The exigencies of the service as inspired by the soul.

It will therefore be realised that the qualities briefly described below, will not necessarily be apparent in all disciples. On the contrary, each disciple will exhibit his own combination and the pattern of his character will be determined by those attributes on which the main accent falls and which become manifested as the result of the demands of life.

IX. 3 (a) **Responsibility**

Man's responsibility in life is determined by the degree of self-consciousness that has been achieved. There can be no responsibility when there is an absence of self-consciousness. Animals therefore cannot be held responsible and though they suffer pain on the physical plane, they are free from karma on the subtler levels. Man, on the other hand, is self-conscious and therefore becomes responsible for his actions – both good and bad. But all men cannot be held equally accountable, because they differ widely in mental development and therefore also in consciousness. Responsibility increases in direct ratio to the expansion of intelligence and consciousness and the undeveloped savage consequently does not carry nearly the same responsibility as the more advanced disciple. The latter is far better aware of the fact when he infringes the laws of nature or the ethical demands of social standards, than is the savage, and his responsibility towards his environment and his fellow human beings is therefore also increased to a corresponding degree. The result is, that for the same trespass, the evolved man will have to pay a much severer penalty than the unevolved or in other words his negative karma will receive a heavier debit.

Man cannot be relieved of his liabilities by his brother – each individual must shoulder his own responsibilities and acquit himself of these obligations to the best of his ability but at the same time he should refrain from interference in the responsibility of others. True love therefore sometimes has to stand aside with detachment, having to look on whilst others are learning life's lessons – this at times may be hard to accomplish but may be mitigated by rendering moral support and the understanding of a loving heart.

Responsibility is one of the most prominent characteristics of the soul and there consequently arrives the time when the disciple becomes aware of his *spiritual responsibilities*, which actually far outweigh the physical aspects, which only relate to personality issues. The effect of man's spiritual influence will prove far more penetrating and of a more lasting nature, than the discharging of physical obligations.

IX. 3 (b) Discrimination

To enable the soul to liberate itself from the trammels of matter, man must learn to discriminate between illusion itself and that which is veiled by the illusion. Discrimination is the talent of the mind to observe, analyse, separate and then to decide between various qualities.

In the earlier stages of his development, man's discrimination or judgement and his consequent choice of roads to be followed, will often be at fault but it is through these mistakes and subsequent pain and suffering that life's lessons are learned.

Discrimination indicates that the disciple has in the first instance become aware of the plurality of forces that are affecting an issue. It now remains for him to distinguish clearly the nature and direction of these forces and then to choose the correct path which must lead him to the determining of true values and thus to the soul's destination. It often means that a choice has to be made between primary and secondary principles, the weighing of greater and lesser rights or deciding between essentials and non-essentials.

Closely associated with discrimination are such qualities as intelligence, esoteric sense, balance, dispassion, detachment, selflessness, love and goodwill – these will all contribute towards correct discrimination and the activation of the 'third eye', thereby providing clear vision of the path to be followed. Add to these acceptance and the emotional nature will be rendered immune to the disturbing appeals of desire and the influences of the senses.

Sound discrimination is but the evidence of growing wisdom and will evoke right choice and this will lead to right action – all these being determined by true alignment with the soul.

IX. 3 (c) **Free Will**

Repeated reference has already been made to this salient human characteristic – the free will, which for centuries has been one of the most contentious subjects for discussion in religious philosophy – to what extent can man determine his own destiny by exerting his free will?

There can be no doubt that, within certain limits, man has control of and determines his own destiny. But here comes the moot question – where do these limits lie and how and by what are they defined? Man can definitely initiate action that will evoke certain recognisable effects, which can again be diverted into specific directions or channels by conscious action or otherwise they can be allowed to develop 'naturally' without further interference from his side. Therefore, though man and his immediate etheric environment may be the meeting place of constant streams of forces from beyond his control, he is in the position to utilise many of these forces and by the implementation of his 'will' through the mind, brain and personality, he can turn many of these forces to his own ends *as far as circumstances and environment will allow*.

And this is where the crux of the matter lies – there are so many circumstances conditioning his environment, over which he has no direct control whatsoever. Even though he might still have been able to influence certain of these factors if he had the opportunity to give them the necessary attention, there are so many and varying energies which come into play on his 'circumstances', that in practice he can, with the directing force of his will, only attend to a relatively limited portion of these influences. In addition the vast majority of energies to which man is constantly subjected lie beyond his comparatively narrow range of sensitivity and consciousness and because he is not consciously aware of these influences they cannot be opposed or influenced by his will.

It should furthermore also be taken into consideration that the individual forms part of his local community, which in turn constitutes a component of the greater humanity. He therefore has to share his 'circumstances and environment' with many others, each of whom will individually and jointly also exercise and contribute their respective share of 'free will'. What so often happens in practice is that these 'wills' are supporting opposing aspects or interests, which then lead to a clashing of will-forces which might produce a wide range of unexpected results. In other instances this clashing of opposing wills might have a mutually neutralising effect and that is why it becomes so important to co-ordinate efforts and thus to obtain group and mass collaboration for invocative appeals to promote the common weal of humanity. Such a synthesis of will-force, expressed as a united appeal to Higher Entities or Deity, must inevitably evoke favourable responses.

The effect of the free will also depends on the strength with which it is sent forth, its singleness of purpose and its effective direction. In this respect it will be found that will-force can range between wide limits. The weak-willed may exert little or no influence even on his immediate environment, whereas the strong-willed might play a role in world affairs and make his influence felt on international levels.

Attention has so far been limited to the effects of the expression of the human will. But what about the Divine Will? It is this Will which determines the Purpose and the Plan for humanity. The final execution of the Divine Plan can certainly not be allowed to be subjected to the inconsistencies of man's deliberations and activities. It appears that in certain respects man's performances may exert some limited effect on the tempo at which the Plan unfolds but it definitely cannot affect its ultimate manifestation. If looked at from the broader aspects, man is comparatively such a puny factor in the Universe, that the direct influence exerted by his free will must be absolutely negligible and may be disregarded; in this respect he may be compared with a minute atom that is being swept along by the mighty forces of nature to some unknown destiny.

As man evolves, his will-power also consistently increases; what is more important, however, is not so much the increased power of the will but the fact of his improved control over this force and that with his progressive advance along the Path, there is also being coupled a closer co-ordination and synthesis with supernal Forces. Therefore, as the disciple develops and the first rudiments of the Plan become discernible to him, his every effort and all his free will, will be directed towards realising the exigencies of the Plan and there will no longer be any question of opposing it in any respect.

Generally speaking it may therefore be said that the evolving human being has no control with regard to his ultimate destiny – that is determined by Higher Authority. What he does control, however, is the rate of his personal development and this may be retarded or considerably expedited, as he chooses. It is for this reason that even the Hierarchy cannot incontrovertibly ascertain what the immediate future holds in store, either for the individual, the group, the nation or for humanity as a whole. This decision lies in the hands of men and it is for them to decide and to determine the course and rate of their development. The Hierarchy will certainly help and guide as far as possible but they may not interfere with man's and humanity's free will – it therefore remains for the latter to determine the immediate course of events. Should the Hierarchy assume authoritative control, it would mean that they would deprive men of all initiative and men would consequently be changed from responsible, self-directing and aspiring beings to a race of automatons. Man must therefore at all costs be allowed to retain his responsibility and learn to stand and act on his own initiative.

The danger of infringing on the human free will is not from subjective sources but will be encountered in the imposition of ideas, dogmas and ideologies on the untrained and susceptible minds of large sections of the population, by corporate bodies, churches or governments, whereby the development of the mind and free will of the individual is restricted. Any form of totalitarianism or of the imposition of the will of the few on to that of the masses, whether exercised in the home, in religion, education or government, must therefore be regarded as wrong and obstructive to growth and these energies should be qualified and diverted to more appropriate purpose.

IX. 3 (d) Humility

A clear distinction should be made between humility and an inferiority complex. The latter is a negative approach to life and is an attitude that should definitely be avoided; it contains the seeds of intellectual or spiritual jealousy in that the sufferer gains the impression that others are his mental or spiritual superiors – this may then subtly drive him to obtruding his personality on those *he* considers his superiors and thus to assert himself and impress any onlookers. Humility on the other hand is that adjusted sense of right proportion, which will equip the disciple with a balanced point of view with regard to his capacities, his responsibilities and his work. This will enable him to view and evaluate himself with detachment and the opportunities with which he is presented with dispassion.

The fear of arrogance, pride, bombast and a general over-estimation of one's capacities, may sometimes however over-balance the scale, with the consequence that the disciple is inclined to assume an attitude which is too humble, with the result that he underestimates himself, becomes untrue to reality and belittles the power of the soul-infused personality. This in turn may lead to wasted opportunities, loss of time and ineffective service. To be able to walk humbly in spiritual life but nevertheless to serve with full effectiveness, involves discrimination and the true recognition of one's capacities, as well as of the opportunities that life has to offer – therefore accept yourself as you are, in the circumstances and environment where you have been placed and love and serve to full capacity.

The humble disciple will give all he has in service but will then in detachment disregard that he has given of himself. He therefore only considers the service to be rendered and not the role the personality is playing in its implementation – he thus serves with utter self-forgetfulness.

True humility is always based on fact and clear vision – a vision which can only be correctly interpreted with humility. There is therefore nothing wrong in recognising oneself as a disciple but this is entirely a personal matter, which should be faced, accepted and then shelved into the background, so as not to interfere with the work that is waiting to be done. No man who has gained any true concept of the relevant position he occupies in the greater Whole, can ever again be anything but humble; the deeper his vision and the greater the expression of his consciousness, the more acute will be the realisation of his own relative insignificance.

IX 3 (e) **Simplicity**

Modern life is inclined to become ever more complex, but the disciple should never allow these complexities to drive him to frenzy. The secret is to cultivate a simplicity of thought-life by systematically acquiring an attitude of acceptance and of complete abandon to the will of the soul, which as far as the individual is concerned, represents the Will of God.

Simplicity stands for a one-pointed outlook, free from the glamours produced by the intricacies of the thought-producing mind; it represents clarity of purpose and steadfastness of effort, without the complications of undue questioning and introspection; it means a life of loving sacrifice, forgetting to ask or expect anything in return; in short simplicity is merely following the dictates of the soul. In practice this will be demonstrated by the disciple as a spirit of co-operative goodwill and loving but intelligent understanding towards all with whom life and destiny bring him into contact.

Our present age has been characterised by materialism of a degree that has never been known before and which, for the sake of humanity, it is hoped will never again be equalled. Human values have largely been reckoned in terms of possessions and with many there has been the tendency to shove spiritual values into the background. These attempts at disparagement of all that is spiritual will fortunately never be successful – man is evolving on the Path of Light and these are merely phases which mankind must experience to recognise for himself the uselessness and emptiness of the material possessions for which he has been striving so passionately. It is therefore expected that there will be a gradual return to a simpler way of life, with less attention being paid to possessions in their many forms and that increasing interest will again be displayed in spiritual progress.

IX. 3 (f) **Detachment, Impersonality and Acceptance**

One of the most valuable tools which the disciple must learn to use with effect on his evolutionary path, is the art of detachment, impersonality and acceptance. The worker must learn to stand apart and hold himself free from that which he is trying to create. He must learn to cultivate the attitude of the Onlooker and the silent Observer. Mental detachment will enable him to obtain a calm and impersonal view of that which he wishes to accomplish.

This detachment must not be seen as a form of self-protection, of self-immunisation or of aloofness but as an attempt to arrive at true perspectives and to see the real values involved as viewed from the level of the soul. It is only from this altitude that circumstances and people will be seen as they really are – with their shortcomings and their virtues, their divinity and humanity; it is only through this attitude that man may escape from violent emotional and mental responses which must inevitably result in unbalanced discernment. Detachment may of course also be carried to excess, when it will constitute a vice and it is therefore for the true server of the Plan to find and walk the middle way.

The gaining of true impersonality and detachment is but another way of saying that the disciple has succeeded in lifting himself above the problems of the personality and is now enabled to work from the level of the soul. He has learnt acceptance and can therefore handle every situation in a spirit of love, refusing to take hasty action that might permit any form of separation to creep into his relationships with his fellow man. This must inevitably lead to true service and the fulfilment of that small section of the Plan for which he is responsible.

Impersonality is achieved by eliminating all personal ambition and love of power. It means relinquishing many cherished ideas, hard won qualities, carefully nurtured ideals or powerfully formulated beliefs and accepting conditions as they are.

The cultivation of an attitude of 'divine indifference' with regard to personal desires, contacts and goals, will contribute considerably towards the attainment of impersonality. Acceptance will mean emotional control, which is one of the most difficult tasks to which the evolving disciple is subjected and which usually takes considerable time to achieve; once attained, however, it will prove to be worth all the effort expended.

This divine indifference will only be fully achieved when the disciple becomes consciously aware of his duality and realises that the soul is the real Self and that the material body is merely an instrument through which he is temporarily functioning; when he becomes aware of the fact that from his position of Observer, he can with serene detachment act as the Director of forces on behalf of humanity – that in fact he is the Soul. The disciple finally comes to the discovery that impersonality is not based on indifference or preoccupation but upon deep understanding, a dynamic focus on world service, upon a sense of proportion and upon a detachment which will enable him to render true help to his fellow man.

IX. 3 (g) Serenity

The two concepts, *serenity* and *peace*, should not be confused. Peace is a condition of temporary nature and refers to the world of feeling, which is susceptible to disturbance. Wherever there is progress, on whatever terrain, it is inevitable that every forward step will be marked by changed conditions and consequently by disturbances. Evolution must unavoidably lead to points of crisis, to a breaking down of previously existing conditions and to a substitution or reconstruction of the new. All this must result in disturbed conditions and will not be characterised by peace but the disciple must learn to experience all such changes with perfect serenity.

To develop a state of serenity, the disciple must first of all obtain control over his astral body, because serenity is that deep calm, devoid of emotional disturbance, by which the disciple whose mind is 'held steady in the light' is distinguished. His physical life may be marked by violent activities and all his plans might be upset by unforeseen circumstances but none of this should disturb the serenity of the disciple who 'stands firm, poised in soul consciousness'.

Serenity is often coupled with joy, which is a clear indication that the soul is in charge of such a life.

IX. 3 (h)   Selflessness

The main objective of spiritual training is to produce disciples with an increased capacity to serve, thereby building bridges which provide the Masters with readier access to humanity, thus furnishing instruments which can be used for selfless service.

Selflessness is to be dedicated to the service of the fellow man; it denotes that loving understanding of the disciple who identifies himself with others rather than with his own interests.

The disciple must therefore learn to serve with total self-abnegation. He must endeavour to reach the stage of utter self-forgetfulness; to forget the past and all it brought of pain and joy; he should forget the personal self with all its material and emotional claims and simply seek to live a life of joyous and balanced service. He must learn to serve with no thought of the self, giving strength and love without self-reference in either heart or mind, merely serving as the soul – 'possessing nothing and asking nothing for the separated self'; becoming simply a selfless channel for Love and Light.

IX. 3 (i)   Courage

One of the essential requirements of the disciple as he advances along the Path, is to cultivate the capacity to walk alone and for this he will need courage. Unavoidably and consistently he will run counter to the opinions of those who surround him – his relations, friends and associates, his religious contacts and public opinion in general. It will often take courage but he will have to learn to do the right thing as he may see it, according to his honest convictions, no matter whether it clashes with the opinions of those who are dear to him or with that of accepted world authorities. He must learn to arrive at his own conclusions based on spiritual communion and the illumination from his own soul as provided by study and meditation.

This is where so many fail – they do not have the courage to follow in detail the dictates of the Inner Voice and they lack the courage to speak out and say those things which the soul urges them to express. The only way for the dedicated disciple is to take himself as he is at any time, under the circumstances that may be ruling and the equipment at his disposal and then to subordinate himself, his affairs and his time to the needs of the hour and to serve according to the behests of his soul.

IX. 3 (j) **Perseverance**

If the disciple is to attain his objective he will require unrelenting and patient perseverance 'that recks not of time nor hindrance'. It is this capacity of sustained effort which often lifts the unobtrusive worker above his more brilliant co-disciple, who might attract more public notice but who does not have the ability to plod systematically along the indicated way.

Always remember that failure never prevents success and that it is by steady and determined persistence that difficulties will be surmounted and the soul will be strengthened. The secret of success lies in impersonal and undaunted perseverance to accomplish the task which has been set.

The disciple's fortitude is above all determined by his courage and perseverance – his power to endure, to hold out unwaveringly, to stand steady and then to go forward undeterred towards the achievement of his objective.

In the life of all disciples there must unfailingly come those cyclic periods of darkness when the light of his beacon is temporarily dimmed and when nothing remains but to endure uncomplainingly and to persevere faithfully with his work, no matter what his inclinations or how acute his inner turmoil. By following this procedure and provided his efforts are supported by loving solicitude towards his fellow men, all his difficulties will eventually be overcome and nothing will be able to stop him.

IX. 3 (k) **Sharing and Giving**

All disciples should learn to give. The aspirant too often still lays the emphasis on what he may expect *to get* by following the path of spiritual development, instead of putting the accent on the opportunities for serving which will open up to him by sharing and giving all that he has.

One of the first signs of the soul's awakening is the reversal of man's selfish attitudes. This is expressed by an increased sense of responsibility towards others and in some respects he assumes the position as his brother's keeper, because he becomes aware that his own progress, contentment, peace of mind and even prosperity, are closely linked with that of his brother. This consciousness of coherence does not remain limited to the individual but is increasingly being demonstrated in groups, organisations and even nations, where various movements are emerging with the sole objective of promoting or uplifting the welfare of man. There is also a growing recognition in the consciousness of the individual, the group and even of nations, of the brotherhood of man and that they should give and share what they have, instead of selfishly grasping and holding everything for their own benefit.

There is no greater gift than to be guided by a pure, unselfish and loving spirit with the capacity and urge to give and share selflessly all that life has lavishly put at man's disposal. 'To those who give all, all is given'. The uninitiated cannot imagine the joys he is foregoing by not sharing his all with others.

The greatest offerings that the disciple can share and give are, however, not in the first instance those of material nature. No, of far more value are the qualities of a loving heart, of loyalty and friendship, of compassion and understanding and finally the capacity of serving mankind with a mind enriched by study, service and spiritual contact – therefore spiritual sharing.

IX. 3 (l) Harmlessness

The first step with which to counter the forces of evil is by confronting it with an attitude of 'harmlessness'. When the daily thoughts, words and activities are positive and based on love and goodwill, no evil can gain entry into the mind and the results can only be constructive and harmless. It will therefore also be readily understood that if harmlessness is the keynote of life, more will be done to obtain harmonious conditions in the personality, than by any other form of discipline.

The life of the man who consciously lives as the soul is expressed by its quality of harmlessness. This is one of the most potent forces in the world today and will demonstrate in daily living as right motive, goodwill, discriminative judging, reticence in speech, ability to refrain from impulsive action and the manifestation of an uncritical spirit. This will allow free play to the forces of genuine love, as well as to those spiritual energies which vitalise the personality and will give rise to right action and consequent favourable human relations.

The harmlessness referred to is not of a negative, sentimental aspect, based on a loving but weak disposition, which refuses to take action because it dislikes trouble that will disturb existing harmony and bring discomfort. No, it is the harmlessness which arises from a soul-infused personality and a consequent true understanding of the fellow man's problems. It is a *state of mind* which, when justified, might even lead to drastic action; it concerns *motive* and ensures that goodwill will motivate all action. Such action or speech might at times even result in disagreeable reaction but provided the mental approach has been initiated by harmlessness and goodwill, then the final results can yield nothing but good. Such attitude will attract to the disciple only beneficent forces, which may then be used on behalf of others who are in need; these beneficent forces may then also be employed for neutralising all emanations of evil.

IX. 3 (m) Balance and Stability

A warning should perhaps be given that even spiritual aspiration might be carried to excess if over intense. The disciple must ever be balanced in all his endeavours, never running to extremes of any kind. That is one reason why esoteric teachings should emanate from mental rather than from emotional levels. If such teaching is of the required quality and correctly interpreted, then it should have a stabilising effect on the aspirant, by being acceptable to his reason and mind.

What it amounts to is that on the one hand the disciple should avoid the tendency to *crystallise*, as this will restrict further unfoldment but on the other hand he should be very careful to avoid all forms of *fanaticism* which can only cause harm. It is therefore essential that a sound sense of proportion and a true sense of values be preserved, which must ever keep the human mind in balance and must enable him to discriminate between essentials and non-essentials.

Stability and steadfastness may also be regarded as the power to stand with clear directed purpose in the midst of an ever changing world of circumstance. It is only the soul that can thus uphold the personality in its needed poise in a world of stress, strain and catastrophe.

IX. 3 (n) Sense of Humour

This attribute might well have been included under the previous heading, because a fine sense of humour must substantially subscribe to the retention of balance and stability.

A qualification must immediately be made, however, and that is that a clear differentiation should be drawn between emotional, unrestrained hilarity or spurious merriment, which is of an astral nature, as compared to a harmonised sense of humour which springs from a well considered sense of proportion.

Students should therefore cultivate a sense of humour and proportion by not taking themselves and their work too seriously – in this way unnecessary tensions may be prevented or released, resulting in clearer discrimination and more effective work.

IX. 3 (o) Solitude

Man forms part of the greater Whole of humanity and with regard to his work and service it is stressed over and over again that he should find the group to which he belongs, as he should work in close collaboration with the other group members. Nevertheless, the inner man ever remains alone, even when associated with those who are spiritually close to him. It is only in solitude that man can really consciously contact his soul and in solitude that the mind can be sufficiently stilled to be impressed by the Master.

Whenever there is an expansion of consciousness and the disciple takes another forward step, there is a corresponding rise in his vibration, which consequently throws him out of tune with his existing environment and this necessarily evokes some form of discord and isolation. Periods of aloneness, as far as his inner state of mind is concerned, therefore become the unavoidable lot of the man who strives to follow the Path with dedication. He will however, find that the lonely way is also the Lighted Way.

The loneliness to which this discussion refers, is that of the soul. Often the disciple also craves for solitude of the personality, which may be denied to him because the nature of his work demands constant relation with others. At other times loneliness may occur because of maladjustments of the personality in relation to those with whom life is associating him. These are, however, merely forms of personality plights which can be rectified by personality adjustments and they do not really affect present considerations.

The server should be on guard that an illusion of loneliness does not impair his true vision. He must come to the recognition that he is **never really alone**, because his soul always remains closely associated with those who have their being on subjective levels.

Every disciple has to experience periods of spiritual aloneness; it is by standing alone and having to grope for his way in the dark, that the seeker learns and will find his own particular line of approach to the centre of Light. It is in this way that the disciple grows, finds his true field of service and eventually also the group with which he is to collaborate.

IX. 3 (p) Devotion

Each individual, from whatever sphere of life, has some particular devotion – some purpose for which he lives, although there are those to whom their life objective does not yet stand out clearly and who live rather aimlessly from day to day. Others vaguely discern some nebulous goal, which for some persons becomes more distinctly outlined as life advances and greater knowledge and sometimes wisdom, is being gained.

To many this devotion is still purely of a physical or emotional nature and largely focussed in the flesh, such as satisfying sensual lusts or a greed for money or possessions. Other lives are again mainly emotionally centred and devotion is displayed as love of family, of popularity, pride of nation, love of animals or a combination of similar variations, to which a large part of the man's energies may be devoted. Or the devotion may be lifted to mental levels and be exhibited as a love of science, philosophy or religion, to which the physical, astral and mental energies may be dedicated.

In the case of the disciple there should also be devotion but care should be exercised to lift this from emotional to mental levels. The inclination is to develop a personal devotion towards a Master but this should be superseded. The Masters do not want or need personal devotion; all they are striving for is to direct the disciple's energies to his specific task or service on behalf of humanity. An intelligent worker who can walk independently in the light of his own soul, is of far more value to the Great Ones than a devoted follower of their personalities.

Care should be exercised that the devotion, to whatever high ideal it may be consecrated, does not become a glamour, obscuring the wider vision and even leading to fanaticism. The necessary balance must always be retained.

To summarise it can therefore be said that devotion as an expression of the personality, is apt to engender fanaticism, which is separative, unbalanced and frequently cruel. On the other hand devotion that is expressed under influence of the soul, will be evinced as inclusiveness and loving understanding and will correspond with the objectives of the Plan as a whole, instead of placing undue emphasis on only some limited aspect.

IX. 3 (q) Joy

It might be of help to differentiate between the shades of meaning attached to the words 'happiness', 'joy' and 'bliss', as used in the present context:

Happiness is interpreted as being the product of the emotions and is therefore a personality reaction.

Joy denotes a deeper, inner reaction and is evoked by the soul.

Bliss is a spiritual effect and is that indescribable experience which is only realised when the soul merges with the Monad, the Father and is therefore a sensation which lies beyond the conceptions of the average man.

Those who seek to live as souls will, however, have experienced what is meant by joy and the difference which exists between joy and happiness. There is the joy of reaching the objective after struggle, strain and pain; the joy of revelling in the Light after seemingly endless struggling in the dark; the joy of achievement and subsequent temporary peace, after striving and wrestling against opposing forces; the joy of achieving soul contact with a kindred spirit; the joy of self-realisation; the joy of hours well spent in helping the fellow man and the solacing of a needy world; the joy of every selfless and non-acquisitive action performed on behalf of others; the joy of being able to distinguish the first faint outlines of the Plan and the subsequent even greater joy of contributing a small share towards its materialisation.

Yes, the spiritual life is full of joy and joy should be the keynote of the disciple; the joy of the soul will make its presence felt even during periods of profound personality distress and unhappiness. Joy lets in the light, dispels glamour and misunderstanding and evokes strength for the task that lies ahead. Joy in the recognition of inner strength leads to the tackling of tasks which previously seemed insuperable and ensures their successful accomplishment. Joyfulness therefore becomes the hallmark of the server.

(See also: PART ONE – X. 6 (d))

IX. 3 (r) Esoteric Sense

This is not a generally known expression but is a useful term to denote the power which is gradually unfolding in every disciple endeavouring to live and function on subjective levels; it denotes that inner contact and at-one-ment with the soul, which is manifested in the outer life as goodwill and loving understanding; it is expressed as wisdom in daily decisions; it becomes apparent in the capacity of synthesis and of identification with all that breathes. It therefore denotes that interior attitude of mind of the soul-infused individual which can orient itself at will and at need in any direction.

By means of the esoteric sense the disciple gains complete control over his own emotional life and simultaneously also exerts a considerable influence on those with whom life brings him into closer contact. It will furnish the disciple with greater discrimination and will accentuate his sensitivity to impression and will thus mould him into a more efficient instrument in the hands of the Masters and in service of the Plan. It will enable him to become a purer channel for the transfer of hierarchical concepts and to better clothe the inspired ideals with thought-matter to make it more readily recognisable to those still moving in the everyday world of men.

The esoteric sense must become part of the normal equipment of every disciple. Actually it is but another way of expressing the degree to which soul contact has already been established. Esoteric sense may be promoted by steady spiritual orientation, by holding the attitude of the Observer and by study, meditation and service. The degree to which it has been developed will also determine the disciple's true capacity for invocative and evocative living.

IX. 3 (s) Reticence and Silence

It is essential that the disciple should display a measure of discreet reticence with regard to his inner spiritual experiences. This is mainly because comparatively there are still so few who are able to understand these spiritual happenings, with the consequent danger of misunderstandings. The position is of course quite different where co-workers meet and where there is unity of thought; here spiritual matters will be understood and may therefore be freely discussed.

As a general rule it is wise to retain silence with regard to mental work that is still in the creative process; untimely words may tend to shatter delicate thought-forms which are still in the formative stage and the work may thus be rendered abortive.

Instinctive reticence becomes part of the necessary equipment of all who are struggling along the Path but at the same time there should be the discrimination to share knowledge and certain experiences with fellow disciples.

The disciple should develop the judgement to recognise for himself the stage that he has attained on the Path. Recognition of status is, however, purely a personal matter; it is something that he should accept and for the rest he should keep silence and calmly proceed with his activities.

Generally speaking it may be regarded as axiomatic that more harm is caused by injudicious speech than by undue reticence.

IX. 4. **Group Life and Work**

Each person exerts a certain amount of magnetic force through his aura and it is this power which mutually attracts and binds individual units into families and communities. In the early stages of man's development such attraction is largely instinctive without the individual being consciously aware of these tendencies. The average man is in fact more inclined to exhibit selfish and separative rather than group traits and instead of making any endeavours to promote the well being of his fellow man, he will struggle purely for self advancement and in the process will often not hesitate to trample his brother ruthlessly underfoot should he happen to obstruct his way. He might even be prepared to destroy others and to use their bodies or possessions as stepping stones in his selfish striving. Should he, however, avail himself of some group or co-operative effort, the incentive will often remain self-advantage, because he merely regards the community as a convenient medium to be utilised for promoting his schemes.

Yes, not a very pleasant picture to contemplate but nevertheless representative of a large section of humanity who is awakening to the vast possibilities offered by the increased use of mental qualities. As yet these men are, however, still in the ruthless, self-seeking stage.

Fortunately this is merely a phase through which each and all human units have to pass in their progressive unfoldment and before they come to the conscious recognition that they form an integral part of that larger whole – Humanity. The transition between these two stages is as a rule bewildering, because the accent must be changed from 'what is best for myself?' to 'what will prove to be to the advantage of the group or to mankind?'. This means a temporary clashing of the lower and the higher principles and for a longer or shorter period the balance will remain poised between these two alternatives – the weighing of self-interest against that of the group; the advantage of the individual as opposed to that of the community. In this connection it might be of help to keep in mind that it is the lower principles which concern the unit and the higher principles which apply to the group. In the beginning it will be difficult to come to the correct decision but progressively and as the disciple's vision expands, the emphasis on the humanistic attitude will become more spontaneous, till eventually the stage is reached where all personality interests are freely and readily sacrificed in favour of the group.

One of the first signs that the soul is beginning to influence its instrument, is the development of an increased sense of responsibility. The man no longer merely lives to promote his own interests but he also becomes aware of the needs of his neighbour and that he can contribute something to make life more liveable for others. To an increasing extent he assumes the responsibility of becoming his brother's keeper in accordance with his capacities and the circumstances in which he has been placed. He comes to the recognition that his own contentment, peace of mind, spiritual progress and even prosperity are closely correlated with that of his fellow man. This awareness grows and expands from concern for his family and immediate associates, to that of his community, his nation and finally the whole of mankind. It is this spirit of mutual concern and responsibility, which during the past century has given rise to the multiplicity and ever increasing number of local, regional and international movements and organisations for the help, protection, upliftment and welfare of fellow human beings. The principle of giving rather than getting is increasingly finding favour in both the individual and racial consciousness and even the ideal of universal brotherhood is here and there making its first hesitant appearance.

In the previous paragraph it was briefly indicated that there is a slow but sure change in man's general attitude towards his fellow man. A parallel development is taking place in the unfoldment of the individual disciple but with this difference, that an urge is arising within him to find the group with which he can collaborate. Increasing soul control is being expressed in various forms of idealism, as an impulse to sacrifice and to serve, with a particular inclination towards group service.

Discipleship today is primarily an experiment in group work. The idea is therefore not so much the perfecting of the individual disciple but rather that individuals should supplement and complement each other, so that the aggregate of their qualities and efforts should provide a group complex through which spiritual energy can be expressed to the advantage of mankind. For this purpose the mental plane should be the region of contact and the first endeavour should be to weld the group together in such a way that the members can all work in close mental rapport and spiritual co-operation with each other. In this process the disciples will also have to learn to subordinate their individual efforts at personal growth to the group requirements of the moment – this will entail that certain members will have to hasten their progress in some respects, whereas others will temporarily have to slow down to the pace of the majority. The individual members must therefore show their willingness to withdraw claims for personality attention and only to consider group efforts and the enrichment of the group consciousness as being of first moment.

In this connection it should always be remembered that the Masters are not interested in the personality reactions of their disciples – it is only their soul unfoldment which is of vital moment and it is only the souls which the Masters cherish and seek to lift, expand and enlighten.

The combined invocative power of the group is considerably more effective than the total of the separate efforts of the members would have been and so will also be the response evoked through the group channel – a massive two-way bridge will be constructed, suitable for extensive energy traffic, instead of a number of narrow and ineffective one-man bridges.

Groups could be graded into what may be called either preparatory or advanced groups, according to the stage of development that has been attained by most of its members. As in the case of individuals, this stage of development will also determine the effectiveness of the group to act as an invocative or evocative channel for the flow of energies from hierarchical levels.

Large numbers of preparatory groups are today being formed in all countries throughout the world, under the overarching influence of the Hierarchy. The time will come when these smaller groups will be drawn together, to become blended and united into a world-wide movement of goodwill, expressing the power of Love. But the time for this is not yet, although endeavours should now be made to commence with the consolidation of some of the preparatory work that has already been carried forward for several decades.

In this respect, it is regrettable that signs of *spiritual arrogance*, with its separative effects, is making its appearance. This is a pity but must probably be regarded as a normal phase in the unfoldment of the picture and as part of the growth pains which will have to be accepted, eventually to be overcome by patience and goodwill. It is, however, an aspect that should be guarded against very carefully, as it may give rise to spiritual *crystallisation* – of which it may sometimes also be the result! Particular efforts should, however, be made always to keep esoteric work vibrantly alive, expansive and sensitive to the never ending flow and stimulation of impressions from Higher Levels and always to keep the mind ready to register new visions and new revelations. Such receptivity should be accompanied by a corresponding flexibility of mind to provide for correct interpretation of that which has been revealed and to display an adaptability to adjust the new vision into a fresh approach to life and its problems. Any form of spiritual stagnation must unavoidably lead to spiritual deterioration.

When the true disciple compares his insignificant knowledge with that limitless arcana of mysteries which as yet remains securely hidden to him but of which he is faintly becoming aware, he can never be anything but humble, even though he might for the time being be somewhat in advance of some of his less favoured brothers. Furthermore each individual disciple has his shortcomings but also his special aptitudes, depending on the capacity of his physical computer, on his circumstances, the Rays under which he works and his stage of development. Let the members therefore guard themselves against fatuous, negative and even envious comparisons of each other and let there rather be an attitude of gratitude if an individual displays aptitudes which temporarily may be lacking in others; such attributes can only contribute towards more effective functioning of the group as a whole and must therefore be regarded as to the benefit of mankind.

In these groups the members must learn to supplement and fortify each other. The work should largely remain on mental levels and each member must learn to remain in close mental and spiritual contact with the others. Each has to learn to subordinate his own personality, ideas and growth to the group requirements and this will certainly require reciprocal bonds of goodwill. It is only through inner subjective coherence that these groups can be held together; only subjective links and work will determine the success to be attained. Thus a small group of say only three people, who prove to be spiritually sympathetic and who closely collaborate in their service efforts, may prove a far more effective channel for the purposes of the Masters, than a much larger group, which may be imbued with sincerity but where for some reason or other co-ordination and mutual trust are lacking.

The aggregate of the forces of aspiration, consecration and dedication expressed by a group, will carry the individual members to greater spiritual heights than could ever be attained by the individual efforts. Such invocative appeals from a group must unavoidably evoke corresponding force impulses from the Hierarchy, which will be manifested as light, inspiration and spiritual revelation and will effect definite changes in human consciousness and will therefore contribute to ameliorate conditions in this needy world of ours.

Group Will:

Just as the previous age – the Piscean – was characterised by personality unfoldment, with the emphasis on individual effort, so the Aquarian Age will predominantly be the age of group interplay, group idealism, group consciousness and group activity. Selfishness as known at present, will gradually fade, for the 'individual will' which underlies selfish concern, will progressively be superseded and voluntarily blended into the 'group will'.

It stands to reason that because of its increased potency, this group consciousness and 'group will', contains even greater dangers than was the case with the far weaker individual will. It is therefore of the utmost importance that this 'group will' should be guided by steadfast consecration of the spiritually minded to goodwill and the fostering of the interests of the masses instead of those of localised groups or sectional interests. Group selfishness, owing to its potency, might even have worse effects on communal life than has been the case with individual selfishness.

Inner Groups:

Although for the most part unaware of it, all disciples are associated with inner esoteric groups. These groups are constituted on inner planes and all the members do not simultaneously come into incarnation, with the result that each group is represented on both the physical and etheric levels. These groups are under the direct guidance of a Master and are held together by a common objective, similarity of vibration, ancient karmic links and the ability to work harmoniously on higher levels.

The disciple in physical incarnation would be able to work much more effectively if he could recognise his fellow group members and join them for concerted service activities. Mistakes in this respect, however, do occur when disciples indiscriminately join groups to which they do not inherently belong and this may lead to unhappy results and wasted effort.

On the other hand it should be remembered that the souls of group members have assumed outer personalities which often fail to harmonise. In such instances the only solution is that the souls should obtain a stronger grip over their personalities, to enable the esoteric group relation to be manifested more effectively on the physical plane.

The individual disciple is incarnated with the divine urge to accomplish some particular task; his life has – mostly unconsciously – been guided by his own soul, which in turn has been working in close and conscious co-operation with his subjective group and the Hierarchy. Usually, however, the individual remains unaware of his association with this inner group and of the divine mission to which he has to contribute his modest part. In all these instances the workers are building for posterity and their particular field of service will unknowingly dove-tail with that of other workers.

According to D.K. the establishment of these outer groups as a reflection and externalisation of the inner groups, was only sanctioned by the Hierarchy in the year 1931 and is therefore still in the experimental stage and therefore subject to growing pains and adaptation.

Group Relationships:

For groups to function efficiently it is essential that harmonious interrelations are maintained. On inner planes there are no problems in this respect, as those groups are in the fortunate position that they do not have to cope with the problems of separative minds and the emotional tribulations of desire bodies which constantly tend to disturb cordial relations on the planes of personality expression.

To make a success of group work it is, however, essential that sound inner relationships be maintained even though outer clashes or divergences of opinion might periodically disturb the even tenor. For this purpose an inner link of love *must* be held and disciples should relinquish all sense of authority over each other. Although there must be close collaboration, each individual should retain full responsibility for his own activities.

In this connection there are three general rules of conduct which, if closely attended to, might help appreciably in overcoming points of disagreement:

(a) Notwithstanding outer differences, allow no breaches of the inner bonds of love which spiritually integrates the group.

(b) Carry on with your own work and leave your brother to attend to his responsibilities. Give each other mutual support where possible but do not interfere and criticise.

(c) You have your own standards and approach to life, which are adapted to your personality and Rays of Energy and which are right for you but will probably differ radically from those of your brother. Let each follow his own Path in accordance with the dictates of his soul – but let there be loving understanding and co-operation.

Group members should therefore watch their mutual relationships with care; this particularly refers to the thought-life, and every inclination towards suspicion or criticism should immediately be smothered by vibrations of intelligent love and goodwill. The only form of criticism that is allowed is when it is unquestionably based on a recognition of fact. Furthermore the judgement must be based to such an extent on love, that it will produce no personality effects in either his own life or that of his fellow disciples. It therefore merely becomes a loving recognition of a limitation or in other words an **understanding** of attitudes and conditions. Understanding is of course the secret power that will achieve firstly identification and subsequently cohesion.

From the hierarchical point of view the effectiveness of these groups has so far apparently been rather disappointing; individual members have on the whole shown little inclination towards making the necessary sacrifices, and personality differences have been allowed to obtrude themselves far too much. Eventually these group efforts **must**, however, succeed and it therefore remains for both new and older members to persist with their efforts and to learn from past experience and mistakes. Every attempt should be made to provide more efficient channels of communication between the Hierarchy and Humanity, not only to obtain closer direct contact but primarily to promote an unobstructed flow and distribution of energy.

For this purpose it is essential, however, that group members should show greater willingness to sacrifice personality concerns to secure enhanced group effects. What should be stressed are the oft repeated essentials of Aspiration, Invocation, Sensitivity, Impersonality, Sacrifice, Selflessness – all these to be intelligently applied with Love, Understanding and Goodwill. Should these impulses be applied with dedication, they must eventually evoke an urge to Serve and to ensure better group relations.

Group Unity:

The best way to ensure group unity is to begin with *group meditation* in an effort to absorb the individual souls into the One Soul and thus to attain greater synthesis in the group, resulting in better co-ordinated action. The second essential is that this synthesis of purpose should be demonstrated in concerted activity as *group service*, which is the real objective of the Masters.

The advantage and strength of the group will lie in the diversity of its component parts and their collective endeavour. This range in characteristics will at the same time also constitute one of its potential weaknesses when members are reacting on the personality level; this is where each member should do his utmost to stand together and to avoid all clashes when personalities evince the inclination towards self assertion. Group coherence and integrity must be ensured by exhibiting the spirit of mutual goodwill, and love must overrule all personality differences.

Groups founded only on personality ties, are very vulnerable and unstable and are bound to be constantly disrupted by emotional clashes. The only sound basis for synthesis is through spiritual bonds, which are forged on soul levels and therefore lie beyond personality differences. Furthermore soul attraction would also indicate a similarity of soul-ray between members and a loyalty towards a Master working under the corresponding Ray. One of the strongest bonds, however, is that of a common objective as expressed in collective activities in serving fellow human beings.

Therefore when serving ever try to act as a group, forgetting about the role the self is playing in such service. The self ever strives for recognition of every little act of service, whilst subjective service should avoid all forms of personal recognition. Service, although effected by an individual member, should still be regarded as part of the group contribution which has merely been channelled through the individual.

As a rule groups are composed of disciples who are at different levels of development but such diversity should not prove an insuperable obstacle to unity of objective and activity. To give efficient service under a variety of circumstances, it is just as well if the group disposes of a miscellaneous range of qualities and potencies from which to draw strength and adaptability.

Group Contact with the Master:

The days of personal messages and personality attention by the Masters on behalf of individual disciples undergoing *preliminary or probationary training*, is something of the past and has been so for several decades. There are of course those disciples who work on astral instead of mental levels and who may therefore be under the illusion that they are still favoured by such contact but in due course they will be disillusioned.

This does not mean, however, that there no longer exists any direct communication between the Hierarchy and Humanity or that the Masters have broken off all contact with their disciples. Such a condition would be inconceivable and in direct conflict with the expressed policy of the Hierarchy which, on the contrary, has provided for *increased communication*, because Humanity has to be prepared for the gradual externalisation of the Hierarchy into the physical world. It is only that there has been a change in policy with regard to the procedure which is being followed. Whereas, up till about the end of the previous century, the Hierarchy could afford to give individual and personal attention to disciples, because of their fairly limited numbers, the position is now being radically changed. Larger numbers of disciples are being trained to expedite humanity's spiritual progress and to effect this training on a broader basis, the Hierarchy has decided to work only through the newly devised group system.

The Master thus communicates his messages to these groups by telepathically impressing a selected member who possesses the necessary sensitivity. This is the same technique which yielded such excellent results with A.A.B. So far sensitives with the needed close affinity and with vibrations which correspond with those of the Master have, however, proved to be of only rare occurrence. A few are, however, available and more will be brought into incarnation as and when required, to serve as links for transmitting the Masters' thoughts. These messages are then communicated for the benefit of the group as a whole but will often refer to the needs of individual members in particular.

IX. 5. Master and Disciple Relationships

Just as professors are not used to teach school children, so the Hierarchy cannot afford to allow its senior members to spend their valuable time and energy on training junior disciples. If the relatively high mental level of the present day esoteric student is taken into consideration, together with the abundance of literature that is available from which suitable material can be selected to fit every stage of development, then it will be seen that the earlier training can to a large extent be self-implemented. When the student is ready for the subsequent stage, where guidance and teachings are needed beyond his personal capacity, then the help and guidance of an advanced disciple will be made available to him, on either the exoteric or esoteric level, depending on circumstances. It is only after disciples have attained certain minimum spiritual qualifications that they will come under consideration for personal instruction by the Master.

The grading of disciples is a relatively simple process. The Masters do not need special records or have to study progress reports for this purpose – they can immediately recognise the stage of development reached by a disciple, simply by studying the quality of the light radiated by the worker. When the man's aura attains a certain hue and his vibrations reach the required intensity, he will automatically draw the attention of some particular Master, who will then submit him to tests to determine whether he has reached the stage that will justify personal attention. The choice of a pupil by a Master will depend on the Master's needs, the quality of the available disciples, the control of a mutual Ray and past karmic associations.

The average student cannot possibly conceive how preoccupied the members of the Hierarchy are in guiding the fortunes of man towards its destiny, in accordance with the divine Plan. The Masters do not have the time, the interest or any intention of intruding or interfering with the details of the disciple's personality life on Earth. All that concerns them is the growth of man's inner light and the extent to which this is reflected in the quality of his service. They therefore only deal with the man on mental or soul levels and do not concern themselves with any hasty or thoughtless deed or word which the man himself can rectify again. The ultimate responsibility for the guiding of the individual lies with the soul and even the soul can only exert a minimum of influence until the lower man is ready and willing to accept such help.

The disciple who is in touch with the Masters will soon find that he will not be subjected to flattery and promises, because nothing is said to feed the disciple's pride or which might foster self-satisfaction and which might consequently lead to future slackness. When the disciple's life and deeds produce a growing radiatory light, such progress will be amply rewarded by increased opportunities for service being put in his way, together with the needed capacities to fulfil the task satisfactorily.

In the life of a disciple periods will possibly come when he seems to have lost all contact with his Master and when it is as if all relations have been severed. Should this happen, the disciple must realise that such severance can only be of a temporary nature and must be due to some lack or excessive disturbance in the disciple's environment or etheric surround and that the condition certainly does not originate from the Master's side. Before a disciple is admitted into a Master's group, he will already have been kept under observation for a considerable time and the Master will be well aware of all his qualities – both his virtues and shortcomings. So when he is finally accepted, the Master's decision will be irrevocable as far as his own standpoint is concerned and this arrangement could then only be broken by deliberate and conscious action on the part of the disciple.

The Masters do not want adoration or veneration from any man; they desire the disciple to be impersonal in all his dealings, as it is an attitude of *impersonality* that will lead to spiritual love and understanding. What the Masters are looking for is intelligent dedication to the needs of mankind.

This same attitude of impersonality is also maintained by the Master himself in his dealings with his disciples and it certainly does not form part of his objective to make his pupils self-satisfied with their status or activities by undue complimentary words. If he wants to guide them it is his responsibility to focus their attention upon their failures and limitations; it is for him to help them to detach themselves from the form aspect of life and equip them to recognise and correctly utilise any expansions of consciousness. He therefore has to keep a close watch on the waxing and waning of the disciple's inner light and on the vibrations that are radiated; it is then for him to make suggestions for improvement of his pupil's attitudes and life expressions and to point out where personality adjustments could be effected to lead to greater freedom from personality dominance and therefore to an intensification of the spiritual life as displayed by acts of service. If in this process of impersonal admonishment the student should take offence and show resentment, it is but an indication that such a student is as yet too deeply immersed in personality reactions and is therefore not yet ready for more advanced work. Disciples should thus learn to work from soul or spiritual focus and not from personality focus.

Disciples must learn to stand on their own feet, to use their own discretion, not to lean too heavily on the Master's support and not to distract his attention unduly from his own pressing activities. The Masters are fully occupied with the many aspects of the constantly changing world picture and with the guiding of the minds of world leaders who must unconsciously be steered to conform to the Plan and Purpose of the Lord of the World. The more advanced the disciple and the closer he approaches to the Master, the deeper his understanding of the position and the greater his endeavour to fulfil his own duties to the best of his ability and to relieve the Master of as much of his minor duties as the disciple's aptitudes and circumstances will allow.

In the olden days when in the East the disciple worked under direct instructions of a Master, implicit *obedience* was exacted and the Master literally assumed full responsibility for the destiny of his pupil. Since then the position has, however, been radically changed; the disciple now works from the mental level and with his free will he retains full responsibility for all his personal decisions and actions. The Master is merely responsible for offering opportunity and the more profound versions of the Truth but nothing more. Under such circumstances no teacher could exact blind obedience. What the Master does expect, however, if the disciple wishes to work under his guidance, is that his instructions must then – of the disciple's own free will – be accurately followed or otherwise such collaboration becomes futile.

More and more groups will inconspicuously make their appearance all over the world, whose members will be better prepared for collaborating with the Masters. There are in fact already more of these actively functioning disciples than is generally known.

These groups will only be able to effect regular contact with a Master if amongst their members they happen to include an advanced disciple who is favoured with a highly developed sensitivity to impression and who can then serve as a channel through which the Master can pass his telepathic communications.

Should such a channel not be available, then each individual disciple will have to depend on:

(a) Soul communication with the Master during the hours of sleep or
(b) Communication during the disciple's periods of meditation, provided the student has developed the ability to lift himself to egoic levels. If the disciple does not succeed in providing these conditions through self-effort, the Master will remain inaccessible.

This self-preparation can only be achieved in the course of time and through persistent efforts at purifying the lower vehicles by regular and painstaking meditation and dedicated service. But once the disciple has purified and equipped himself and has thus reached an adequate inner vibration, then nothing can restrain him and the portals to the higher life will automatically open up before him.

It is man's own soul which will guide and introduce him to the Master and it is only on soul levels that communication between these two worlds of being can take place. The disciple should therefore endeavour to ensure that the connection between soul and brain, via the mind, is well established and remains unobstructed. The Master's work is often frustrated because the channels of contact are sometimes closed for prolonged periods through lack of rapport between soul and personality.

During their early stages of approach to the Masters, disciples will find that the Masters are extremely busy and that they are not readily accessible to attend to trifling matters relating to the personality – for problems which the disciple should be able to solve by his own efforts and with the light supplied by his own soul. Older and tried disciples have far more ready access to the Master but they pride themselves on not wasting the Master's time with trivial affairs and will only go to him for major decisions concerning their service activities on behalf of others.

It should be thoroughly understood by the student that the Masters are not concerned with the personality aspects of individuals. Their only interest is to acquire useful channels through which they can work and direct their energies for the benefit of mankind as a whole. A disciple will therefore enter a Master's group in the first instance because he already has acquired the capacity to render some service and not because he is to receive some cultural training for self advancement. But it stands to reason that in the course of his service he will gain experience and thus gradually he will be shaped into an ever more effective instrument in the hands of the Master.

There are instances where disciples receive specific training but again this will only be done to better qualify them for the expression of some aspect of the Plan.

A disciple is weighed by the *motives* which impel him. The Master is not impressed by the worker's status amongst men or the influence he wields in worldly circles by means of qualities of the personality but merely in his subjective attributes and the motives which prompt his activities. It is only when selfless love, understanding and goodwill arouse him to altruistic service, that he is recognised and brought to the attention of the Master.

X

SERVICE

The important role played by service in the disciple's spiritual development, has been repeatedly emphasised. Actually the degree of progress on the Path of Light will to a considerable extent be reflected by the nature and quality of the disciple's service to his fellow men and in how far he is able to contribute towards the realisation of the hierarchical Plan. This is, however, a criterion that should be used with discretion because true service is often rendered without ostentation or even without any outer demonstration.

The beauty of service is that it is rewarding in all directions. There is for instance the direct benefit to those who are being served; the effect of this will depend on the stage of development of the server, how well he is qualified for the particular task, the energy and dedication with which the work is undertaken and the love and understanding underlying the effort. In due course the server will find that his own rewards are also commensurate with the service rendered to others; he will gain valuable experience that will deepen his insight and which must inevitably lead to further expansions of consciousness and to fresh opportunities for ever more effective service; his Inner Light will burn brighter, not only serving to light his own Way but also irradiating the path for his younger brother whom he serves as a guide. Greater rewards are therefore gained by serving others than by being served.

As far as the Hierarchy and their objective for the realisation of the Plan is concerned, their difficulty is that for much of their work they are dependent on men as their instruments and on the whole these instruments are most erratic and unreliable. As a rule disciples are aware of world need and the desire to meet this is genuine and sincere; there also exists a real longing to lift and serve but, from the hierarchical point of view, the characters and temperaments of these men often present well-nigh insuperable difficulties.

These disturbing characteristics are often latent and only make their appearance after some task has already been undertaken, which may then lead to failure, tragedy and unnecessary suffering. In this connection it can but be reiterated that the disciple should endeavour to retain his balance under all circumstances and must guard against undue stimulation when contact is made with inner spiritual forces. He will also have to deal with men from all walks of life, with their selfish greed, their adulation and praise and their criticism – these will tend to obscure his mind and action if not approached with sufficient detachment. Under pressure of the work his latent personality weaknesses will tend to emerge and will encourage partially submerged inclinations such as pride, ambition and love of power. Continued mental strain may cause a state of bewilderment and clouding of the vision and of truth; in other cases the personality asserts itself to such an extent that it leads to attitudes of self-importance, separativeness and the spoiling of good work by self-glorification.

Service is not something that the disciple should pursue. It is in fact a soul instinct, an unrestrainable urge of the soul that must somehow be brought to expression. It is not something that can be taught or imposed upon a person but is an impulse that is manifested spontaneously and only needs guiding towards a suitable objective.

On the Path of the world server there will always be obstacles which will have to be surmounted but, notwithstanding all the cares and struggles, there will ever remain the joy of attainment, the satisfaction of work accomplished to best ability and above all the knowledge and at times the conscious awareness that the Great Master, the Christ, is looking on sympathetically and understandingly, because he too travelled this same arduous Path.

Yet it is surprising how the labours of the man who is serving selflessly and one-pointedly will be relieved of impediments and how unexpected assistance will often lighten his task and make his work more effective but such help will only come to those who have transcended personal aspiration and, in their desire to serve, have lost sight of considerations of personal progress.

For service to be really effective, *it must be rendered with absolute selflessness*, that is by forgetting the past with its pains and joy; by forgetting the personal self with all that it has to give or to withhold; by forgetting both the kind words, the words of encouragement and the words of criticism of the bystanders. Therefore in service be willing to sacrifice the self, time, money and personal interests, in utter self-forgetfulness. Merely serve – with joy, with all your heart and with all you have to give!

X. 1. Motives for Service

What are the disciple's motives from which arises that inner impulse to help and serve others? All true spiritual service, whatever its nature of expression, is selflessly motivated and issues from the soul and the heart. Therefore as soon as selfish objectives occur it is obviously only the semblance of genuine esoteric service and can thus be regarded as exoteric or commercialised service, which is something totally different and a product of the personality.

The service considered in these studies only concerns the altruistic or esoteric aspects and may be motivated by:

(a) An awakening to the first faint vision of the outlines of the divine Plan and a growing urge to contribute that which one has, even though still imperfect, towards the
realisation of that which is being contemplated.
(b) The accomplishment of some personal ideal, which will demand the soul's highest
endeavour.
(c) An inner welling up of love, manifesting itself as an impulse to serve all that which is
Divine, whether designated as man, the Christ or as God – therefore an aspiration to
serve the Good.
(d) The disciple comes to the recognition that he has acquired something, some capacity
or knowledge which might help to enrich or throw light on the paths of others and
he feels the urge to transmit and share this with them.

It should ever be kept in mind that with service the *effort* and the *motive* are at least equal
in importance to the *accomplishment* of the objective.

X. 2. Field of Service

Each man must find his own field of service, that terrain where under his particular circumstances, his combination of aptitudes and his background and training can be blended and used to maximum advantage. Fortunately there is an unending range of possibilities towards which man's efforts may be profitably directed and every individual will be
able to find his proper niche provided he is really infused to serve and his motives are
impelled by that inner love which, come what may, must find expression.

So often those who show the first signs of awakening and begin to display a half-heart-
ed interest in esoteric work, will remark that: "I would also like to serve and to do something for humanity but what is there that I could do?" With these persons there is an
apparent inner incitement by their souls but their hearts are not yet fully awakened and
there is as yet no real inner love that is looking for expression; wherever there is genuine
soul-love seeking utterance, a suitable outlet will be found.

Care should be taken not to make comparisons regarding the quality of service rendered by different persons. The real inner value of service cannot be gauged by its outer
appearance or effect and will only be finally judged by those who are sympathetically
looking on from subjective levels. Its true value therefore does not lie in the visible outer
activity but in the inner motivating force; an apparently simple gesture of love, which
may pass unnoticed by the outside world, may indeed have a more far-reaching inner
effect than some spectacular act of public service.

When serving concentrate all your energies on your task. If others need assistance
from you in the execution of their responsibilities, then give help freely wherever possible but always remember that in the first instance you are responsible for the work that
your own soul has assigned to you and that you should *never interfere* in the work of oth-

ers. Therefore, allow others the same privilege of doing their work in their own way, as you are demanding for yourself.

All disciples have their limitations and this should be kept in mind when choosing a task of service. The work should be determined in accordance with the disciple's capacities and it would be foolish to attempt that which altogether lies beyond his limits, as this would but lead to frustrations, unsatisfactory results and wasted time and energy. It is far better to accomplish a smaller task effectively than to tackle an apparently more important task and leave it unfinished or badly rounded off.

On the other hand the server is often inclined to underrate the talents with which the soul has endowed him; he tends to weigh only the aptitudes of the personality, not yet being fully aware of the powers lying latent in the soul and which have there accrued in the course of many lives. So when choosing a new field of service, leave the final decision to your intuition – to the dictates of your soul!

X. 3. Methods of Service

Each potential server must find his own particular level and method of service. The form of his service is of secondary importance – that which counts is the motive by which he is inspired. If arising from the heart and soul, it will be based on love for his fellow human beings and, whatever the nature or details of the service, it will be the right thing for him under his specific circumstances.

It should also be realised that, as with all else, *man must learn to serve* and that he must therefore preferably start with the small and relatively simple activities. As experience is gained, fresh opportunities will be presented and, provided these are recognised, there will prove to be no end to the possibilities of service. Once the joy of true service has been tasted, it will prove so infectious that nothing will be able to withhold him from a future all-out career of service.

The efficient server must at all times display *discrimination* in his approach to his work. He must be able to evaluate his own capacities and aptitudes and should realise his limitations; in his zeal he should therefore not rush into fields of work for which his past training and experience has not qualified him and of which he cannot make a success. Such unconsidered action will only lead to waste of time, opportunity and effort and may have harmful and frustrating effects.

X. 4. Money in Service

Every intelligent and balanced approach will recognise the esoteric value of money for purposes of service. There is nothing wrong as such with money, which is merely a convenient and symbolic state of temporarily converted energy or power. As with all energy, the crux of the matter is – how will it be applied? In its essence energy or money is an impersonal or blind force and may be used for either good or evil, depending on how it is directed. Today there is some stigma attached to money but this is only because money is involuntarily associated with so much that is evil or representative of selfish desire, greed and sharp business practice. But the time is rapidly approaching when money will, to an ever increasing extent, be applied to better purposes, to serving the genuine needs of man and to provide those conditions which will be to his spiritual and lasting benefit.

Where in the past money might be regarded as the symbol of man's selfishness, so in the New Age it must become the symbol of man's goodwill, demanding a total reversal of his attitude towards it. Money must therefore be transmuted to a real spiritual asset and responsibility, thus becoming a potent means for achieving world service.

(See also: III. 6 (a))

X. 5. Service and Old Age

When the disciple reaches the years when he may normally expect to be nearing the end of another span of physical life, then there are several attitudes which may be adopted:

(a) A tired and physically worn out personality will tend to settle down, with the attitude that having experienced a complete and comprehensive life, the time has now arrived for a period of well deserved relaxation. This will render the remaining years simply an expression of established habit, of marking time and probably showing signs of losing some of the already acquired spiritual contact.

(b) There may be a recognition that the personality has reached its high-water mark for the present life but there should also be the realisation that in the life of the soul this is merely an intermediate phase and that the evolution of the immortal Self never comes to a standstill.

(c) There should be no undue preoccupation with the processes of growing old, which would indicate too much emphasis on the physical being. Give the body the consideration it requires to maintain it in reasonable functioning order but otherwise concentrate the attention on the mind, persistently feeding and programming the computer and thus stimulating it to full and effective capacity, until the time arrives for closing down and the soul switches off the current, liberating itself and temporarily moving on to better equipped and brighter lit apartments.

(d) Actually old age is the stage when the soul, after having garnered the experiences from a full and rich life, becomes partly relieved of many of the routine commitments of a busy life and now stands free to serve with fewer impediments. No new problems need be undertaken or new disciplines applied and for the rest of his years the disciple can now quietly and steadily devote that which he has gained to the service of humanity, to the Great Ones and to the Plan. It is quite possible that under such circumstances he may cross the 'dividing line' with 'continuity of consciousness', carrying on with existing tasks and only approaching them from a different level.

X. 6. **Recognition of Service Rendered**

One of the earliest lessons that the server has to learn, is that he must never look for gratitude, recognition or reward for what he is doing – he must learn to serve with impersonality. Instead of recognition for services rendered, he must even be prepared to receive ingratitude, rebuffs, direct opposition from friends and relations and even humiliation and contumely. None of this will, however, deter the true server once he has firmly set his feet on the Path, has become aware of the light ahead and has consciously come to the realisation of his objective.

The disciple will therefore do his utmost to fulfil that small part of the Plan for which he has assumed responsibility. Having accomplished his self-set task to the best of his ability and with utter selflessness, he does not look for recognition of his action or waste time on retrospective contemplation of his mistakes or observe with pride what he has achieved but instead he will once again gather his forces and press forward to the next duty, the next opportunity that lies in wait for him. He will taste that inner joy of having given of the best that was within him for what he considered a worthwhile objective; he will realise that Wiser Eyes will weigh the fruit of his efforts with deeper love and appreciation than is known to man. What matters it then whether *apparent* results are not up to expectation or whether there is criticism or lack of understanding from his fellow human beings, providing his own soul is without reproach.

X. 7. **The New Group of World Servers**

X. 7 (a) **The Birth of the Group:**

Since the earliest times of man's spiritual awakening, there have always been disciples at varying stages of development. Although such unfoldment as a rule took place under the guidance of a teacher or some senior disciple, it remained mainly an individual effort.

In 1925, at one of the great quarter-century meetings which the Hierarchy convenes every twenty-five years, it was decided, however, that in view of the rapidly increasing number of disciples and also in consideration of the prospective reappearance of the Christ and the simultaneous externalisation of the Hierarchy, that it would prove much more effective if all disciples, aspirants and men and women of goodwill, were linked more closely on subjective levels.

To implement this decision the Masters arranged that all individuals and groups under their control, should be brought into intuitive and telepathic contact on etheric levels. This originated that comprehensive body which subsequently became known as the New Group of World Servers. On subjective levels this New Group has become closely interrelated and is functioning as a unit but this association is not yet manifested as such on the physical plane, where the individual members have not yet been tied into a single world-wide organisation. Apart from localised groups, they mostly remain unaware of each other. In some instances, however, individuals or groups are loosely associated by mutual goodwill and understanding and also by common service objectives, aiming at better living conditions for all and striving for improved human relationships, tolerance and world peace.

On the same occasion the Masters also organised an intermediate group of senior disciples who could act in a liaison capacity, to mediate between members of the Hierarchy and the thinkers of the world and who could serve as linking agents between various groups, movements and countries.

This New Group has therefore been vested with the responsibility of being the builders of the New Age. Theirs is the task of preserving the spirit of truth and of re-organising the thoughts of men to a meditative and reflective state, which will make them receptive to the recognition of the progressive manifestation of greater Light.

The New Group of World Servers acts as the link between the Hierarchy and humanity and all invocative pleas from humanity and the energies that are evoked, have to be channelled through this Group. It is for this reason that each individual should do his utmost to raise his mental and meditative life to the highest possible levels, to ensure that communication will flow through him as smoothly as possible and with a minimum of distortion.

X. 7 (b) Membership of the New Group:

As constituted at present, this Group consists of a subjective association of conscious, living souls, whose one objective is the upliftment and serving of mankind. On physical levels they are represented by a number of individuals and smaller groups who are responsible for transmitting or bringing into practice the ideas and plans conceived by the Masters on subjective levels.

Those men and women who form the ranks of the New Group are not selected by existing group members or by a watching Hierarchy. No, they select themselves by their power of response to spiritual opportunity and their way and approach to life and circumstance. These men are progressively emerging from all races and nations; from churches, religions and political parties; from young and old, male and female, from rich and poor – literally from all walks of life. The motivating force which impels them on to and along this Path is certainly not ambition or any form of personal advantage but merely a growing awareness of the Light, the Christ within, which then develops into loving understanding and is expressed as goodwill and an urge towards selfless service.

The New Group includes scientists who may violently repudiate any 'unproven' subjective beliefs but who yet cherish an all pervading love for their fellow men and in the course of their work are sacrificing all they have in time, knowledge and scientific ability to humanity. It includes financial giants who may have no conscious knowledge whatsoever of the esoteric world and who merely see themselves as the trustees of the money under their control and who regard it as their responsibility to wisely dispense these funds on behalf of humanity. Similarly there will be those educators, politicians and representatives from all branches of human association who will exhibit these traits of goodwill, loving understanding and service of their fellow men, that will mark them as members of this New Group. Although these men may remain totally unaware of their subjective relations and the source from which they obtain the inspiration for their activities, they will continue to be inspired, provided their motives remain pure and they persist with intelligent meditation.

The main requirement for such inspiration is **meditation** but not necessarily the form of meditation as practised by the esoteric student. All that is needed is that the man acquires the habit of concentrated reflection along a line of thought related to the relief of some human need. By such focussed attention the contemplator unconsciously opens the mind to impression from the subjective guides. This is then real intuition or inspiration which the uninitiated is manifesting through an unconscious technique, whereas the trained disciple arrives at the same results through consciously applied practices.

All aspirants, disciples and initiates therefore belong to this Group, as well as many other men of goodwill who are expressing their gift in some specific field of service; in fact all those who are dedicated in some or other capacity to the well-being of humanity are thus consciously or unconsciously collaborating with the Group and are helping to prepare for the return of the Christ.

Because the membership of the New Group of World Servers is spread throughout all levels of the community and also covers all races in every country of the world, it stands to reason that many different points of view will be expressed and that fields of service and techniques will vary within wide limits. Each server will, however, emit his own light to fulfil some particular purpose, even if apparently minute, in the realisation of the overall Plan.

Broadly speaking the New Group members may be classified into four main divisions:
1. There are those who, owing to their mental approach and spiritual qualities, must definitely be regarded as world servers but who are as yet unaware of this relationship. Some of these men and women may already be well advanced disciples, who for some particular reason have remained unaware of their spiritual status and function.

2. There is a rapidly growing group of aspirants whose members have been imbued with the Christ-consciousness, whose souls are becoming closer aligned with their personalities and who are increasingly becoming aware of an inner spirit of goodwill and an urge to be of service to mankind. Their effectiveness is, however, being restricted by periodic domination of personality influences, causing a certain measure of separativeness.

3. There are the more advanced and consecrated servers who have become aware of some of the main outlines of the Plan. They are in varying degree sensitive and subject to hierarchical impression and are dedicated world servers, free from all separativeness and controlled by loving understanding of all men.

4. Finally there is a small number who may be regarded as the seniors of the New Group, who are in direct communication with the Teachers on the inner side by means of telepathic contact and sensitivity to higher impression. They are the illumined minds of humanity who fulfil a most responsible position as they serve as direct links with the Hierarchy.

Every man and woman, in every nation or country throughout the world, who is contributing his or her share to heal the breaches between man and man and is thus evoking the sense of brotherhood and mutual interrelation and who discards all feelings of separativeness caused by personal, national and racial barriers, belongs to the New Group of World Servers, even though he may never have heard of such an organisation. These individuals will avoid saying or writing words that could lead to separation between man and man or nation and nation. These men therefore represent an *attitude of mind* and they will be encountered in all walks of life.

They are the men of goodwill all over the world, who are slowly but surely uniting their energies into a growing body of influence and who will apply these combined energies and efforts on behalf of humanity as a whole, rather than to the immediate benefit of some local group. It is therefore this Group which will finally be responsible for establishing the One World Religion, which will serve to unite the many nations and races, with all their divergences, into the One Humanity.

X. 7 (c) The Activities of the New Group:

The basic function of the New Group of World Servers will be to prepare humanity for the reappearance of the Christ. This was the prime incentive which led to the formation of the Group during the early part of this century. This preparation is certainly not limited to the field of religion but comprises every sphere of human activity, such as education, economics, science and politics – every terrain which may contribute to the improvement of human relations and all activities which will lead to unity of purpose to ensure true human progress and welfare throughout the world.

In his position as Leader of the Hierarchy, the Christ also automatically becomes the Leader of the New Group and therefore is also the guiding spirit of their activities and service rendered on behalf of humanity. It is through this Group that the energies of the Christ-consciousness are being released to the masses of mankind and it is through these servers that the energy of the will-to-good will reach the masses, where it will manifest itself in the average man and woman as goodwill.

The task of the New Group is therefore to usher in the New Age. Briefly stated, the objective of this new era is that the five kingdoms of nature, the mineral, vegetable, animal, human and spiritual kingdoms, shall ultimately function as one harmonious whole – the Kingdom of God. The Group is thus striving to attain:

1. Improved human relationships, leading to co-operation and sharing on all levels and the recognition of the **One Humanity**.
2. Congenial interrelation of all aspects of activity and sympathetic association with the sub-human kingdoms, will lead to the recognition of the **One World**.
3. With the reappearance of the Christ and the externalisation of the Hierarchy, the reality of the **Kingdom of God** will become established.

Towards the centre of this New Group are found those who are relatively in close touch with the Masters and who have principally a meditative function. They are responsible for the reception of thoughts and ideas concerning the realisation of the Plan and the transferring of these ideas to the minds of those working on the outer areas of the Group; it is the role of the latter again to attend to the proliferation and materialisation of these ideas in the world at large. Each individual member of the Group has to determine for himself what position he occupies in this structure, where his meditative responsibilities lie and in which direction his capacities may be most effectively applied. In this respect disciples are particularly warned never to allow their judgement to be guided by *spiritual ambition*, as this must lead to failure and wasted opportunity which can only harm the greater cause.

The New Group provides the training ground and a field of experience for all those showing inclinations for spiritual unfoldment and who can finally fit themselves as disciples under direction of the Christ.

The activity of this Group is not primarily concerned with the petty interests and problems of the individual; their responsibility is the upliftment and well-being of mankind as a whole. Their attitude towards their immediate environment should therefore be somewhat impersonal and this sometimes subjects the server to criticism of the casual bystander who cannot understand his deeper insight and broader objectives.

The Hierarchy and therefore the Group, fundamentally work to effect *changes in consciousness;* it is man's consciousness which must be expanded to enable him to obtain a deeper recognition of the subjective worlds by which he is surrounded and by which he is constantly being influenced but of which his lack of vision leaves him largely unaware.

XI

White And Black Magic

XI. 1. White Magic

The art of the esotericist is to become a 'white magician', that is, to avail himself of the unseen energies and forces of the spiritual universe and by means of the creative powers of the soul, to bring these energies down to Earth in some desired material form. It is therefore the bringing together of Spirit and Matter under controlled and harmonious conditions and in accordance with the laws of nature. As far as man is concerned, this means increasing the inner vibration, which is displayed as expanding consciousness, rising progressively from physical and self-consciousness, to emotional, mental, egoic and finally spiritual consciousness. When spiritual consciousness is attained the physical sheaths are rejected or in other words there will be no further need for the soul to reincarnate.

The white magician further concerns himself with the intelligent interpretation of all that relates to nature and, with the co-operation of these forces, he achieves the objectives of the divine Plan to the extent that its outlines can be discerned by him.

The ideal of the esoteric student should therefore be to produce organised creative work by utilising subjective energies according to the laws of nature. If this is to be achieved, one of the first essentials is to cultivate *emotional stability*. This cannot be attained by an effort of will but solely by submitting the personality to the dictates of the soul, thereby overcoming astral domination.

The work of the white magician will include all that is conducive to the expansion of consciousness and to increased sensitivity to impression; it will comprise all that tends to dissolve and remove that separating veil which hides the etheric world from those who are temporarily held within the physical body; all that will promote the production of better vehicles through which the Christ-principle or the soul can express itself.

The Hierarchy of Masters is the guiding force or source of inspiration for the manifestation of white magic on the physical plane. As the opposite pole to the Dark Forces, the Hierarchy is also referred to as the Great White Lodge. The members of both the White and Black Lodges use man as their instruments for manipulating their powers. Both these groups avail themselves of the same energies and forces but these powers are applied from a totally different point of approach and with diametrically opposed motives.

The average man as a rule is unaware that the broad area covered by modern education and the progressive and sometimes fantastic new scientific discoveries made over a very wide area of research, may be associated with the breaking down of the existing barriers between humanity and the subjective world. There are for instance the rapid strides which have been made in the various systems of communication, such as the development of radio and television; telepathy is in process of receiving scientific acknowledgement and is now being seriously investigated; the prophecies of the Tibetan with regard to the discovery by science of the etheric world, have at last come true and there is an increasing awareness not only of the existence of the vital surround of every form but also of the predominating role this vital body fulfils in all of creation.

Great changes in man's attitude towards the hidden worlds must be expected during the coming years and this should in the first instance become apparent in psychological expression – this whole science will become revolutionised to play a far more important role in human enterprise. All these developments must be seen as manifestations of white magic, which is destined to be emphasised by the incoming Seventh Ray – the Ray of the Magician – which Ray will dominate life on Earth for the next several centuries.

XI. 2. Forces of Light

The Supreme Being is man's ultimate Source of Light. In its pristine form this Light would, however, be of such potency and brilliance, that all on Earth would be consumed by it. Its power is consequently reduced by stepping it down through various celestial Entities, until it reaches our Solar Deity, who supplies the Lord of the World with that much of the Light as is required for the Earth's evolutionary development. This Light is then adapted by the Hierarchy, serving as man's immediate Source of Light, for final transmission by him to the rest of nature.

The men of goodwill, by reacting to the needs of humanity, demonstrate their responsiveness to the Forces of Light and they may thus also be regarded as reflections of this Light and its energy – the will-to-good. This energy is consistently being radiated to man, influencing the minds of the New Group of World Servers and of all selfless workers for humanity. The minds of the selfish, self-centred and separative individuals, however, remain sealed to many of the beneficial qualities of this Light. This will also prove to be the case with those whose reasoning has been crystallised by dogma and doctrine – whether of political, social, scientific or religious nature. Little can therefore be done for those whose vision and minds are limited to their own personal requirements, to their immediate environment or who are vested in sectional interests instead of working on behalf of mankind as a whole.

XI. 3. **The Dark Forces and Black Magic**

The problem of the Dark Forces and the evil they perpetrate, is deep seated and obscure and partly originates from world or even cosmic karma and therefore goes far beyond the relatively simple considerations of the present treatise. There are, however, a few aspects to which attention should be drawn, because they fall within the control of the human being.

One of the most prominent characteristics of the black magician is that he works alone, because all his acts are motivated by intense selfishness. Should he at times co-operate with others, there will definitely be some ulterior motive, hoping to draw some additional advantage and ultimately to outwit his collaborator. He will furthermore always be found in opposition to the White Brothers, because he abhors the Truth. These dark forces do not endeavour to co-operate with the laws of nature but try to turn these laws to personal profit or to satisfy their physical desires.

Where the White Brother deals with the soul, the Dark Brother only concerns himself with the form, the outer manifestation. His power is derived by preying on the form – by breaking it down and destroying it and utilising the energy or essence that is released. Black magic thus is destructive of nature and will blight and destroy all it contacts.

The Forces of Darkness deliberately work to retain ancient and crystallised material forms. They will consequently endeavour to prevent the inflow of new and life-giving energies which will promote unfoldment and progress; they will do all they can to keep humanity enshrouded in astral vapours, with its distorting glamours, and to feed the fires of selfish desire, hate, separateness, suspicion, cruelty and criticism. The disciple should learn to recognise the existence of these evil forces and should as far as possible evade their harmful influences by the purity of his activities and thought-life, or in other words, by concentrating on the life of the soul and not on that which is material. The problem of directly opposing these evil forces is, however, not the concern of man and should be left entirely in the able hands of the Hierarchy, the White Lodge.

XI. 4. **Evil**

Every form of creation is a materialisation of Spirit and therefore an aspect of God. Man's perceptions are, however, limited and owing to imperfections of the senses and inadequate interpretations by the physical brain, he obtains a distorted image of the created form. Without this distortion there would have been the recognition of perfection, the Divine or the actual reflection of God in each creation, with the result that all of creation would have been recognised for what it is in fact – nothing but God. With such clear perception man would see all with which he is surrounded, including himself, in its true perfection – its true reflection of God. There would then remain nothing further for him to experience, to learn or to strive for – he would have become merged in God, in Perfection. Somehow this seems to be the ultimate objective for man but meanwhile the average individual still has a long way to go and a great deal to experience because of his limited and astrally distorted perception.

It is this limited perception, with its consequent distortion of Reality or the Truth, which has led to the concept of 'Evil'. Or, to express it differently, for man to recognise Good or God, there must be the contrasting aspect of Evil. It is the task of the disciple to come to the realisation that good may be wrested from apparent evil, because evil is merely an astral illusion. Evil primarily originates through a warped perception of the true facts and this is then aggravated by the selfish and separative motives of the personality, thus abusing the opportunities presented by life. By using a different approach and applying right motives under the same circumstances, good may be engendered.

With regard to mankind in general it might be said that the inclination of the masses is towards the good but 'the door where evil dwells' is still kept wide open because of man's selfish desire, greed, hatred, personal ambition and love of power and by the creation of artificial racial and national barriers. These evil forces, however, can and finally will be submerged and transmuted by the energies of the will-to-good which today are streaming forth into the hearts of men. It is this immanent good in man that should be encouraged and developed in an attempt to swell it into a rising tide of right human relationships with which to swamp all evil. Hate and fear can only be offset by intelligent goodwill and loving understanding.

In an attempt to obstruct the successful progress of the Forces of Light, the Evil Forces will sometimes resort to direct attack on the physical bodies of the disciples who are employed by the Hierarchy as their instruments for transmitting their ideas and energies to mankind. By causing distress in the physical body of a worker, they seek to limit the disciple's output. In such cases the Masters will often decide to intervene by protecting their disciples against attacks which might result in effects of an obstructive nature – it is one of the main tasks of the Hierarchy to stand between the forces of evil and humanity and to expose such evil to the Light.

In the past the forces of evil have played havoc in the ranks of human existence, because the majority of human beings were materially and astrally oriented, thus offering an ideal opportunity for attack by these forces. The forces of good and of light are now, however, rapidly being organised and must inevitably triumph over the forces of darkness; the 'Lights which carry out the Will of God' are now only waiting for the concerted and decisive invocative cry from humanity!

XII

SPIRITUALITY

XII. 1. Material Living

The world has ever belonged to the strong. In primitive times it was physical strength which counted but with the passing aeons the developing intellect began to play an increasing role and for many centuries it has now been the mentally strong who have managed to dominate the world. But even mental dominance must be seen as merely a passing phase in the evolutionary plan. The next stage which must inevitably follow, is that mental supremacy will be superseded by spiritual strength and that man's activities will be guided by the energies of Love and Light. These will form the criteria of the New Age which man is now entering but, meanwhile during the transitional stage, a last desperate battle is being fought between the vested interests of materialism and the invading forces of spirituality.

The majority of men still regard their future hope of happiness to be closely linked with material welfare and possessions. This unavoidably leads to selfish striving to possess as great a share of the worldly goods as their grasping hands can lay hold of, with relatively little concern for the loser or for the under-dog who in the process is being trampled underfoot.

It is this selfish, greedy and often ruthless striving for money and power which unavoidably leads to hate and envy, to war and fighting with all its atrocities and misery, instead of the happiness that was envisaged. And so the wheel keeps on turning, generation after generation, life after life, until it gradually seeps through to the mind that there *must* be something even beyond the intellect. Gradually man's consciousness expands and for brief spells he becomes aware of the light of the soul and of its energy – the will-to-good; gradually there is a growing awareness that there could be much more to life than just selfish striving for the material, and that far greater possibilities of gaining happiness are being offered by sharing and surrendering rather than by holding. And thus, step by step, another soul gains dominion over the material world and joins the ranks of those who have discovered the Path towards the Mountain Top.

Those who have become aware of these new values and of the existence of duality –

the material life and the life of the soul – are still in the minority but their ranks are rapidly being swollen by new recruits. The influence of goodwill, loving understanding, sharing and serving, is permeating the world of human relationships and although on occasion still regarded with some mistrust, the possibilities of this new approach are increasingly being recognised and are gaining ground.

XII. 2. **Spirituality**

As used in the present context 'spirituality' refers to that inclusive striving for human betterment, uplift and understanding; of tolerance on all levels, including political and religious relations and also embracing all that may contribute towards the expansion of human consciousness. The motivating impulse is that vague inner urge which, for lack of better words, is often described as the 'Love of God' and which displays itself in daily life as love of the fellow man. The man who has been gripped by this spirit becomes aware of the true meaning of brotherhood and goodwill, of selflessness and service.

Spirituality is an inward retreating and the achievement of a deepening conception of the values of life, which in turn will lead to wisdom, truth and reality. While man's destiny binds him to Earth, he must pursue and fulfil his physical responsibilities but simultaneously he must learn to combine these with a life of intense aspiration and a questing for the light of the soul – for spirituality!

Throughout the world there is today a search and demand for truer values, a rejection of the norms which conditioned the past and an urge for demonstrating those virtues, spiritual impulses and incentives, which it is realised must supersede material values if happiness is to be found. It is everywhere becoming apparent that humanity as a whole is experiencing an expansion of consciousness and that man is rapidly being equipped to absorb more light and is expectant of a coming revelation and a new dispensation. Man is already so far advanced that these demands and expectations, which are largely being unconsciously invoked, do not merely concern material benefits but primarily encompass spiritual vision, true values and improved human relationships. This invocative call, when it becomes more clearly defined and accentuated, cannot be ignored by the Hierarchy and will be the deciding factor which will lead to the reappearance of the Christ.

All the qualities which relate man to man and man to Deity and which will lead to a better world, should be included in the concept of spirituality. It refers to attitudes and relationships and to all aspects of the evolutionary process driving man forward from one range of sensitivity and awareness to the next.

The myopic view is often expressed that humanity has reached a very low level of spirituality. This mistaken impression is mainly due to the noticeable loss of interest exhibited by many in the orthodox presentation of truth in most of the world's churches. What is happening is that organised religion has failed to keep pace with man's growing demands for spiritual leadership. Man's evolution is not restricted to mental levels and should also be reflected in his approach to that which is spiritual. Therefore if the churches wish to retain their position as the spiritual leaders of the people, it is essential that they should guard against crystallisation of their tenets and obstinate clinging to dogmatic interpretations which sufficed in the past but which are now being outgrown. The present defection in church attendance can therefore as a rule be ascribed to lack of vitality in religious presentation of the Truth and an inability to meet the spiritual needs of the masses, rather than to a falling off in spirituality of the masses. Actually an ardent search for spiritual verities is today encountered throughout the world and the truly religious spirit is now more essentially alive than at any previous time in human history.

If religion is to serve a really useful purpose, it must ever remain vital and should it wish to retain spiritual leadership, then it must always keep a few steps ahead of the public's spiritual development and demand, instead of lagging behind and waiting to be pulled along unwillingly by progressive public thought.

XII. 3. Spiritual Man

When a man living the life of the material world has become aware of the spiritual realms and is consequently endeavouring to adjust his physical life to conform to his interpretation of the subjective demands, then such a man may be called 'spiritual'. It is the man who has come to a recognition of the One Source and is now concentrating every effort to a better understanding of this Source and by adapting his life is hoping to effect a closer relationship with this Unknown.

With a growing consciousness of the existence of more exalted realms, the spiritual man lifts his eyes from his circumscribed personality experiences, to study the nature of the Greater Whole which is unfolding before him. His breadth of vision is developing, thus expanding his horizons and providing deeper understanding. He is recognising the basic unity of creation, all of which is focussed in the One Life.

The life of the spiritual man should be an expression of positive goodwill towards all and towards every expression of life; he should be free of all personal ambition and selfishness; he should endeavour to live consciously as the soul whose nature is love and inclusiveness and who is aware of the Light of the Creator in all forms. Such realisation will result in true understanding of the needs of his fellow men, without obscuring this discernment by undue sentiment. It will prevent needless talk, criticism and comparison with the self or with others and will evoke immediate response to genuine need. This spirituality is the ability to evaluate the inner motives and causes responsible for outer conditions and then from this point of discrimination and wisdom to provide true help and guidance.

To allow for the free passage of the energy of Love, as well as those other spiritual energies which vitalise the personality and lead to right action, there should be:

(a) *A thought-life guided by goodwill* – this will lead to caution in judgement and criticism and reticence in speech.

(b) *Emotional goodwill*, which will provide a channel for the expression of the love of the soul.

(c) *Goodwill in action*, which will prevent impulsive or hasty deeds, will release the creative will and will produce balance and skill in action.

The ideal is that the man should develop such conscious control of himself, that he will be able to focus his consciousness at will either in the soul or in his form aspect, according to some particular objective of service. The spiritual man will ever seek to further the Plan as far as this can be identified and as far as possible to relate himself with the divine in creation; he will seek to reach the hearts of men and provide those in need with the Light at his disposal.

There are three significant faculties which the spiritual man should develop – these are:

(a) The capacity consciously to receive and transmit telepathic communications from both higher levels and from fellow disciples.

(b) The capacity of intuitive recognition of truth, its formulation into thought-forms and subsequently, by means of the creative mind, to materialise these thoughts into tangible form.

(c) The capacity to heal, which means the understanding of forces and energies and knowing how to manipulate them to provide relief of specific physical or mental limitations of fellow human beings.

A further notable characteristic of the spiritual man is that he is controlled by what may be termed a *'divine discontent'*. The life of the Spirit entails an irresistible urge to betterment, which never becomes completely satisfied; he is constantly impelled from an existent state to some more enticing vision, till he finally enters the Path, after which there is no longer any question of turning back – even if he would. He automatically develops the *habit* of right action, supported by goodwill, instinctual understanding and correct reaction, which become established as part of his nature and therefore grow into 'spiritual habits'.

XII. 4. Spiritual Development

The evolutionary urge of the human being, that irresistible impulse to push forward along the Lighted Way 'from darkness into light, from the unreal to the real and from death to immortality', is a divine attribute inherent in all created forms and for which the human mind can give no satisfactory explanation.

The life of the evolving personality may be divided into five progressive steps, which are determined by the condition of the indwelling spiritual flame and the quality of the light that is being radiated.

It should be realised, however, that although these stages are here only sketchily indicated in a few paragraphs, their sequence actually covers innumerable incarnations, spread over vast periods of time which may be reckoned in terms of millions of years. Especially during the early stages of existence, man's development is extremely slow and it is only when nearing its culmination and when the soul is beginning to take hold, that a marked increase in the rate of unfoldment will occur.

Furthermore, students should realise that the classification as set out below, is artificial and is merely given to provide an overall picture of the general process of development. The procedure will vary considerably from soul to soul, both in rate and characteristics and in some instances the periods described might partly overlap or even show a somewhat simultaneous development.

The *First Period* – the recognition of man as a human being dates from that prehistoric time when animal-man was provided with an individual soul and thus gained 'self'-consciousness – he was 'individualised'. In this early stage man was still polarised purely in his physical body and was learning to control it by means of the desire or emotional body. This corresponds with the ancient historical periods of Lemuria and Atlantis. During this period man as yet had no knowledge or awareness of any higher existence and his aspirations did not go beyond pandering to the lusts and pleasures of the flesh.

This period may be compared with that of a child between the ages of one and seven years. At this stage the inner flame of the soul is as yet hardly noticeable to the Teachers of the race and only appears as a small pin-point of light and the driving force of evolution is still largely instinctive.

The *Second Period* is characterised by a polarisation in the emotional body and is associated with the first signs of an awakening lower mind of desire. This occurred during the later Atlantean days. With the mind beginning to permeate the personality, the desires no longer remain solely focussed on the physical life but become directed towards the astral level and a capacity arises for a deep love and unreasoning devotion for those exhibiting greater intelligence and wisdom or in wild and unreasonable hatred towards some associates. The balance which the reasoning mind will later achieve is, however, still lacking and the life during this period will therefore be characterised by emotional extremes. The mental aspect is unfolding but the man is still dominated by the emotions.

If this period is symbolically compared with that of a single life, it will correspond with the life of a child of seven to fourteen years old – the period covering adolescence and the maturing of the child. The inner light of the soul remains dim during this stage and still hardly noticeable.

The *Third Period* is that vital phase when the mind is being developed and the life is polarised in the mental body.

The man by now has full control of the physical body and each incarnation provides better equipment, with the accent primarily on the quality of the brain as the instrument of the mind. Simultaneously the emotional body becomes more refined in its life of desire and instead of as in the past turning downwards to the material for its satisfaction, it now tends upwards and desire becomes transmuted into aspiration – at first mental aspiration, till later there comes an awareness of the existence of the subjective worlds. The man also becomes conscious of the joys of the intellect and therefore ever strives for greater adequacy of the mind.

Meanwhile the divine spark of the soul, which for so long has remained dormant, has commenced to glow and to develop into a small flame. This spiritual fire is permeating the body of the soul, supplying it with warmth, radiating its energies and allowing the soul to gain in consciousness on its own plane. The physical brain, however, does not yet become consciously aware of impressions issuing from this indwelling force.

This period will correspond with the individual age of between fourteen and twenty – the reaching of adulthood.

The *Fourth Period* is that wherein the Personality, as a co-ordinated whole, is for the first time being recognised – the three lower bodies, the physical, emotional and mental, have become synthesised into a single working unit under mental control. The consummation of the personality life has been attained and its attention is now being consciously focussed towards the soul.

This is the stage where the *disciple is born* and where he takes his first hesitant steps on the Path. He has become aware of his duality; he comes to the realisation that his whole being will finally have to become centred in the soul and that the soul must come into complete control of the lower planes. He therefore commences to work on this transmutation and the expansion of his consciousness; he finds this a laborious and painful task, marked by constant reverses and which can only be achieved by dedication and persistence. He finds that his most effective tools in this demanding task are study, meditation and service to his fellow man.

In the course of these struggles and without the disciple being aware of it, his inner fire has systematically been receiving more fuel and is now burning so much brighter, that the inner light is beginning to attract the attention of the Masters.

This marks the maturing adult stage of twenty-eight to thirty-five years.

The *Fifth Period* marks the consummation of the human being on the physical plane. It is the stage where he enters the Path of Initiation – initiation into the conscious recognition of the spiritual worlds.

Through sustained meditation, supported by its two helpmeets, study and service, the disciple is increasingly making direct contact with the soul's vibration and more and more the soul-consciousness is being incorporated to include the lower planes. The soul light is burning ever brighter and its radiation is lighting up the disciple's Path.

During this period the polarisation shifts entirely form the Personality to the Soul, until towards the end of the fifth stage, liberation is complete and the man is set free. The next step is that the polarisation shifts even higher, to become centred in the Spiritual Triad but this only occurs after the Third Initiation.

The fifth period may be compared with the symbolic age of forty-two.

It is often found that disciples become impatient or discouraged with their slow spiritual progress but it should always be remembered that all truly esoteric effects are slowly achieved and that only after consistent and painstaking work. Should a man make apparently rapid progress in any one incarnation, this will be due to the fact that he is only recapitulating that which has already been acquired in earlier incarnations and that he is preparing for his next arduous task.

The whole path of spiritual evolution is therefore a successive range of expansions of consciousness, of recognitions and succeeding revelations, until the world of matter and form stand revealed in the light of the soul and illumination is achieved. The disciple then gradually establishes his conscious life in the subjective world, the world of reality; his sense of values becomes radically changed and his time and capacities are devoted to higher objectives.

XIII

INITIATION

XIII. 1. **The Nature of Initiation**

The student should be on his guard not to place undue emphasis on the subject of initiation, as this might readily lead to too much self-interest. 'Man should work *towards* initiation and not *for* initiation'. Initiation as such should therefore never be the objective of the disciple – he should work, discipline himself and study to equip himself mentally as best he can to become an efficient instrument in the hands of the Masters for serving humanity. With such striving and serving, the disciple will automatically gain experience, knowledge, expansion of consciousness and finally wisdom, resulting in proportionate spiritual stature. For descriptive purposes, various sequential stages of spiritual development are referred to as 'initiations'.

Each successive initiation will be an indication that the disciple's inner flame is burning ever brighter; this will result in achieving closer union, not only with his fellow man but with all that lives, with all of God's creation. It will result in constantly expanding horizons, widening fields of service and consequently increasing responsibility. It will lead to ever clearer vision and consciousness and a resulting sharper projection of the Divine Plan on the screen of life and a better conception of that small fraction of the Plan for which the initiate is assuming responsibility.

Once the 'stream of initiation' has been entered, there may occur temporary delays and deviations and the process will certainly take many lives to be accomplished but there will be no turning back and the man will be swept onwards until eventually he may touch the feet of the Father.

In this saga of development the distinction between good and evil will be revealed; the disciple will be offered the opportunity of *utter sacrifice*, which must first be experienced before perfect liberation will be granted and before the initiate will stand free of all Earth's fetters. Then will the initiate be granted complete Wisdom and will he be handed the key to All Knowledge, which will be put at his disposal in graduated sequence. As succeeding states of consciousness are entered and as these expansions lead to the vision of one new horizon after another, all the hidden mysteries of the solar system will step by step be revealed to him.

The evolution of the human spirit is a process of progressive *at-one-ment*. At first it is the gradual unification of the personality with the soul, followed subsequently by at-one-ment with the Monad, the Father. Every instance of merging must, however, be preceded by a burning or destruction of the partition that had been separating the bodies; this burning of all barriers is effected by the inner spiritual fire.

Before entering the Path of Initiation the cost will have to be carefully counted, because this entry will demand a total readjustment of values and each step forward, every move from one plane of activity to the succeeding higher plane, will demand the voluntary sacrifice of all that the heart held dear on that plane.

Expansions of consciousness will come with the course of time to every individual according to the laws of nature but in this process distinction should be made between expansions of knowledge and expansions of wisdom. Accrued knowledge can only be transmuted into wisdom and thus lead to initiation, if such knowledge is consciously sought for, if applied to life with selfless sacrifice and if willingly used on behalf of others and intelligently applied towards realisation of the Plan.

With each fresh expansion of consciousness, new revelations will be disclosed to the initiate's vision, new inner powers will be evoked and new fields of service will be recognised – and all this will of course be accompanied by corresponding increased responsibility. The effect of initiation is to enable man to live as the soul and progressively to become the distributor of divine energy towards its planned destination.

The Master never directly informs the disciple as to which stage of spiritual advancement he has reached. That is something which each disciple must determine for himself and it is for him to ascertain which is the next initiation that lies ahead and for which he must prepare himself. This he will be able to establish by a careful study of his circumstances and a recognition of the tests and experiences to which he is being subjected.

Since the end of the previous century there has been a marked shift in approach to initiation. Whereas previously initiation was approached mainly from the emotional angle, the accent is now being placed on mental and service aspects, as well as on a clear understanding of what initiation implies. The disciple must come to the realisation that he is being taught to become a white magician or in other words how to work with energy, and how creative and dynamic energy may be applied in accordance with the hierarchical Plan in order to manifest the Divine Purpose in the material world. As he advances along the Lighted Way, new forces and energies, of which previously he had been unaware, will be placed into the hands of the initiate and these he must progressively learn to apply for fulfilling the Plan.

For aeons the soul has been gaining experience in the three worlds but mainly in a passive sense and without playing an active role in the development of the personality. Initiation is, however, an indication of the degree to which the soul has managed to reverse this role and is now succeeding to prevail over the personality and in manifesting its true nature and character.

It is the disciple's capacity to recognise the different lights encountered along the Path of Light which indicates his readiness for initiation. The extent to which the Light will permeate his being will depend on his development and will determine the clarity of revelation of that which up till now remained hidden and which will now form the basis for his next step towards his objective. Each initiation will immerse the initiate into ever brighter light, thus subduing the light previously acquired.

XIII. 2. **Preparing for Initiation**

The life of the probationer and disciple prepares the individual for the Path of Initiation. It marks that phase in the man's unfoldment when he deliberately and consciously begins to co-operate with the evolutionary forces and works at the reconstruction and strengthening of his character. He becomes aware of certain of his shortcomings and systematically tries to rectify what is lacking, to cultivate better qualities and bring the co-ordinated personality under control of the soul.

In past times the training of disciples usually took place under direct instruction of a senior disciple or 'Guru'. This training was largely of a mystical nature. With changing world conditions and particularly with the rapidly increasing intelligence of the masses, especially in the Western races, the disciple is today obtaining a much better mental grasp of the underlying principles of life and, with available literature, is in the position to make considerable esoteric progress by self-study.

Improved mental equipment has, however, also resulted in raising the standards of discipleship and the Masters are now demanding correspondingly higher qualities from their pupils than was previously the case.

Students who have become interested in the field of esotericism, will find that somehow – and often apparently unaccountably or 'by chance' – just the right book will be put into their hands. This manipulation of conditions is usually the work of *invisible helpers* from the 'other side' – senior disciples on etheric levels who are appointed by the Master to help younger disciples who are struggling under physical handicaps. In this respect it should, however, be remembered that the soul is and always will remain, man's mainstay and principal guide with regard to all decisions and attitudes concerning the spiritual aspects of being or the quality of life. But there are also many other aspects affecting the disciple's environmental conditions and circumstances, over which the soul has no direct control and where this 'invisible helper' can prove of inestimable assistance. This guide so often unknowingly contributes to smooth over all kinds of external difficulties and in many instances he is the unseen factor behind the screen who is responsible for those happenings which are often lightly passed over as our 'lucky fate'. People who believe in their good fortune are as a rule those who co-operate with their helpers in a positive way, whilst the 'unlucky' ones usually have a negative approach and consequently make matters difficult for both their guides and themselves.

But to revert to the subject of esoteric studies. The dedicated student will find that by some means or other he can always acquire the literature needed for his particular stage of development. He may, furthermore, rest assured that if his genuine spiritual needs should happen to exceed the scope of the literature at his disposal, then the Master will supervene and somehow his requirements will be met. No disciple, under whatever circumstances his 'destiny' may have placed him, remains unobserved and when through self-effort his inner light begins to attract attention, his Master will provide the facilities by which he will be guided along the Path of Initiation.

Although the occasional student will be found who for some reason is working alone, there is something which mutually attracts esoteric students and there will be the inclination for students to join some esoteric school or to link up with a local group who may prove to be compatible and where the individual feels that he 'belongs'.

It should always be remembered that the Master is not in the first instance interested in the personal development of the disciple but that he sees his pupil as a potential channel through which the hierarchical energies may be transmitted to humanity. As the disciple progresses, this should also increasingly become his personal attitude towards spiritual evolution and initiation – not so much how to promote his personal advantage but rather how to improve himself to become a more efficient server.

XIII. 3. Group Initiation

Entry into the Aquarian Age is accentuating the general tendency towards synthesis, grouping of interests, collaboration in all spheres and moving away from the separative attitudes which so often characterised human relationships in the past. This inclination is also finding expression with regard to initiation.

Some salient aspects of group work have already been dealt with and it will therefore suffice to point out that these principles are also applicable to the training of initiates. Whereas in previous ages the emphasis has been on individual training and the single admission of initiates, the Hierarchy has now adopted a policy of group admission. The Masters have been forced to this revised attitude because of the rapidly increasing number of candidates for initiation and because many more are expected in the years that lie ahead.

In future initiation will therefore become a joint effort. This will be based on the principle that through close collaboration, loyalty, interdependence and loving understanding, united groups will be created which will be consecrated to the serving of humanity. The idea is that these disciples will then unitedly be able to stand before the Initiator and that they will unitedly be able to enter their new sphere of consciousness and activities and that they will assume their new fields of service as united groups.

As might have been expected, these initial attempts are not yet working smoothly and according to plan. Man is as yet not quite equal to future expectations, as the average disciple still has to overcome several of his inherent selfish traits before he will be able to adapt himself to this new approach to initiation. The general principle of group effort on various terrains is, however, rapidly permeating the human mind and with further changes now being effected for improving human relationships, it should not be very long before initiation will be able to function more satisfactorily.

Actually the soul, forming part of that larger group synthesised in the One Soul, is in its own nature already group-conscious and has no individual ambitions, not being interested in any personality concerns. *It is the soul which is being initiated.* The First Initiation is that process when the spiritual man within the personality becomes aware of himself as the soul, of the duality of personality existence, and that this inner subjective entity has its own powers, relationships and destiny. The moment the individual becomes even faintly or only periodically aware of this, his group-consciousness also awakens. Every further step along the Path of Initiation accentuates this group recognition and will facilitate group activity and initiation.

Meanwhile each and every disciple should do his utmost to conform by suppressing individualistic inclinations and ensuring that he is contributing his full share to make this new group system a success.

Although on the whole disciples are not yet consciously aware of it, they already belong to a group of souls constituted on etheric levels. One of the reasons why so many groups on physical levels fail is because their members have been gathered haphazardly and often prove to be uncongenial, which unavoidably leads to personality clashes. Such groups are therefore artificial and will not meet esoteric requirements. For real initiate training the disciple must find the group to which he belongs subjectively and when he is ready for this work, he will be guided to his spiritual group but it will be left to his own sense of affinity to recognise his soul-mates and fellow group members.

As is the case with any Master's group (ashram), these training groups will consist of members at various levels of development and all of them will certainly not be simultaneously trained for the same initiation.

It may be expected that so-called training groups will arise here and there under self-seeking or be-glamoured leaders, who might even proclaim themselves as Masters. These spurious teachers may temporarily attract the notice of the general public and perhaps even of early beginners but few genuine disciples will feel attracted to them or will be duped or impressed by their glib arguments. It will be found that in the majority of instances these groups are commercially motivated, which factor alone should be sufficient to ward off the authentic aspirant.

XIII. 4. **The Initiate**

The ever increasing number of initiates on Earth must be regarded as one of the first indications of the gradual externalisation of the Hierarchy and therefore as a preparation for that period when the Perfected Ones will again walk the Earth in physical presence and in direct conscious contact with man. Meanwhile these initiates are serving as a connecting link, transmitting the wishes and energies from the Hierarchy to humanity. Each initiate, according to his development and capabilities, serves as a smaller or larger centre of light and power for the group or community for which he consciously or unconsciously has assumed responsibility.

The initiate should ever be ready to evince the sensitivity needed for registering and recognising impressions intended for his reception. He should be ready to translate these communications and to bring them down to Earth with a minimum distortion. Each additional revelation should be regarded as but a further step intended for the unfoldment of the human consciousness. This constant flow of new and ever superseding concepts is provided to ensure the steady and systematic evolution of mankind and, if correctly intercepted, transmitted and interpreted, will satisfy every need. The initiate should be prepared to relinquish instantly all that appears to be futile, superfluous or inadequate to man's need and to utilise the power with which he is endowed to break and disperse that which has served its purpose, has become crystallised and is obstructing man's progress along the Path and is not in accordance with the prescriptions of the Plan. In contrast to the vague and uncertain attitude of the mystical idealist, the initiate must be prepared to fulfil the practical and decisive duties of the esotericist, both on subjective levels and on that of daily human requirements.

The true initiate will never make any public claim as to his status. Such claims by the unqualified have already caused much harm and only lead to loss of public confidence, sowing distrust in man's belief in many aspects of esoteric work and of the subjective worlds in general. Even within the relative privacy of esoteric groups, any claims as to spiritual status will only lead to competition, jealousy and criticism by those still standing on the lower rungs of the ladder. And of what importance is worldly status and title? All that matters is the quality of the service and work produced by the initiate and this is what will really determine his spiritual status. It is his life activity, the truth and intuitive appeal of his words and teachings which will reflect his actual inner status.

Humility is therefore an attribute of the true initiate but at the same time this humility should be firmly based on fact, on vision and the need of circumstances. The initiate must therefore have a sense of right proportion, a balanced point of view, a dispassionate and impersonal attitude and lastly discrimination or the ability to recognise and truthfully to consider the pros and cons of each situation.

By constantly focussing his consciousness in the subjective world of thought and no longer predominantly occupying himself with the world of outer perceptions, the initiate, the spiritual seeker, arrives at the realisation that the world of spirit is in truth the world of meaning and the sole world of reality for humanity. It becomes his task to assist in establishing the recognition of this concept in the consciousness of the race.

The term 'initiate' actually refers to the Soul. The initiate therefore ever was and still is, present in every human being. Viewed from this standpoint the initiate is therefore not the product of the evolutionary process but its underlying cause.

XIII. 5. **First Initiation** (The Birth of the Initiate)

For aeons of time and during the course of innumerable incarnations, the soul has over and over returned to human existence, to gain every possible experience which life in the physical world could offer, till at long last the stage arrives when it decides to enter the Path of Return, leading back to the House of the Father.

This decision by the soul is marked by the man turning his back on exclusively human activities and taking the first hesitant steps towards the super-human or spiritual kingdom, which is esoterically known as the First Initiation. It is the entering of the fifth phase of evolution, the first four being the mineral, vegetable, animal and human phases and now the spiritual is being entered.

The First Initiation is the stage when the soul is gaining a considerable degree of control over the physical vehicle and when various forms of excess, such as gluttony, drink and licentiousness are no longer allowed full sway and are brought under conscious and willing control and are being disciplined by the dictates of the soul. This means that the bridge between the lower and higher minds is being firmly established and that obedience by the flesh is increasingly becoming automatic.

Many phases of progress will be encountered during this early stage on the Path of Initiation and it stands to reason that in the beginning the young initiate is bound to succumb periodically to earlier appetites and temptations. That is why the Path of the First Initiation is so long and tedious – it is always a difficult struggle and remains characterised by many relapses and disappointments, is full of suffering and usually stretches over several lives. What matters is that the man has arrived at the stage where his shortcomings are self-recognised and when willingness is shown to fight and overcome these failings and imperfections.

On the other hand, because the disciple has become aware of the requirements of the straight Path, any lapses or deviations from this Path will be more severely judged and penalised than was the case when he still erred in ignorance – *knowledge bringing responsibility*.

No hard and fast rules can be laid down for the development of individuals who have found the Path, because each man will follow his own pattern according to the Rays which influence his life and determine his character in the circumstances prepared by destiny. The main interest of aspirants, however, becomes centred on self-discipline and on limiting lapses in the control of the physical nature, thus step by step gaining ascendancy over the sensual body. This mastery over the astral body is essential, because the Second Initiation cannot follow until the emotions are well under control. During the First Initiation the main objective is therefore the subjection of all forms of desire but as man has been feeding and indulging these selfish desires during his many lives over the past millennia, it is understandable that these inclinations are not going to be lightly suppressed and overcome and that this process will only be laboriously accomplished, probably covering several incarnations.

Taking these first tentative steps on the Path of Return is sometimes symbolically described as the 'Birth of the Indwelling Christ' and entails achieving certain minimum standards of right living, thinking and conduct. The germ of this Inner Christ, the Soul, has ever been present but was lying dormant and is only now beginning to manifest its presence.

Large numbers of aspirants throughout the world have already taken the First Initiation, either in the present or in some previous life. The Christ-consciousness becomes apparent by aliveness to spiritual issues, intensity of aspiration, inclination to self-sacrifice and a loving nature. These men and women are therefore sincerely moving forward upon the Way, although several lives may still be needed before noticeable progress will be registered.

It stands to reason that no Master will accept a candidate as disciple till he clearly shows that the Christ-spirit has been born in him. That such a man will still have many failings, is only normal and expected, otherwise he would already be occupying a higher position on the ladder of initiation. The Master therefore is not concerned about occasional failings – what he is looking for is whether the right motives and intentions exist and whether these are supported by conscientious effort.

Most of those who are demonstrating the presence of the Christ-spirit, are not even aware of the existence of esoteric teachings and some may even be ignorant about the Christ teachings. These are therefore not the criteria which determine entrance to the Path of Spirit. It is the content of the heart that counts, the consequent life discipline and the conscious motivation with which man is striving towards his spiritual objective, no matter by what name this goal may be identified.

During the First Initiation the aspirant must gain control over his emotional life and the only means to effect this is by developing a more pronounced mental approach, thus enabling the mind to supersede the emotions.

The fact that hundreds of thousands of men and women from all over the world and from all nations and races and all walks of life, have already taken or are preparing for the First Initiation, is evidenced by world-wide spiritual reorientation, by the interest exhibited everywhere in human welfare, the perseverance shown in search of Light and by the longing and desire amongst average people for true peace, based on goodwill and right human relations. Even the unsettled condition of the world's youth must be seen as mainly caused by spiritual awakening and a search for more Light. The same holds good for the revolt which is everywhere displayed against crystallised, dogmatised and even materialistic forms of religion. People are searching for a religion that is vital, adaptive to the evolving consciousness and deeply spiritual, instead of stale phrases, hackneyed words, ritual and ceremony that has largely become empty and meaningless.

Very few aspirants who have attained their First Initiation, are consciously aware of this or realise that esoterically they may be regarded as disciples of the Masters. That they have reached this stage is evidenced by their life activities, their ideals, motives and objectives and their attitude of goodwill and loving understanding towards their fellow men. Most of these individuals would, however, be surprised if they were told that they have already attained the First Initiation.

The individual who has completed this first step – even though unknowingly – will experience great changes in his general outlook on life, and his attitude towards both himself and his fellow men will be radically altered. There will be a growing awareness of the duality of existence – his life hitherto has been centred in the personality and characterised by a selfish striving for material objectives but this will now increasingly be opposed by the spiritual urges of the soul.

The Tibetan points out that the Seventh Ray is now in process of superseding the Sixth Ray as one of the principal Rays of Energy that will command world conditions during the Aquarian Age. One of the outstanding qualities of this Seventh Ray is that it operates as a synthesising agent between spirit and matter. As far as humanity is concerned, this characteristic will be reflected by the strong influence it exerts in relating soul and personality, thus leading to the emergence of the 'new man' in ever growing numbers. D.K. states that whereas today First Initiates exist in their thousands, they will be present in their millions towards the early part of the coming century; nothing will be able to arrest this activity, which will form part of the transformation of humanity and the establishing of a new world order, with its radical change in approach to human relationships, leading eventually to a better world and peace on Earth.

XIII. 6. **Second Initiation** (The Baptism of the Initiate)

Most of the numerous aspirants and disciples today walking the face of the Earth and represented by men and women from every race, nation and country, functioning in every religion and in every phase of social and political life, have already attained their First Initiation. Those on the other hand who have in addition attained reasonable control over their emotional bodies and may therefore be regarded as initiates of the second degree, occur in far smaller numbers, whilst only a very small percentage of disciples have reached the stage of the Third Initiation.

After aspirants have entered the Path of Return and demonstrate the inner Christ-consciousness, they start working, usually unconsciously, to rid their personalities of that reprehensible quality, common to all at that stage – *selfish desire.* This reprehensible characteristic which is still present to some extent in every individual disciple, may find expression in many different forms and intensities and embraces many defects of which the dark forces avail themselves to lead man to evil. The product of this life of desire is in turn expressed in the astral body and it is now the task of each individual soul to gain mastery over these many aspects of the desire life and thus eventually to still the turbulent waters of the emotions.

Another prelude to the Second Initiation and a direct result of the submerging of the emotions, is that the initiate is largely set free from glamour – those glamours which up till this stage have proved such a handicap to progress and have caused so much unnecessary suffering. The most efficient agent for this purpose is the energy of the mind, which must consistently be directed towards the turbulent waters and mists of the astral body. Through the light of the soul the mind may be illuminated, thus serving to dissipate astral glamours.

During the last stages of the First Initiation period, the disciple often undergoes the most acute emotional distresses of his whole existence. This may perhaps be seen as the last desperate efforts of the astral body to retain its hold and is demonstrated by inner turmoil and uncertainty, self-discrimination, deep subjective discontent and an intense longing to be freed from those emotional limitations.

As a reward for perseverance through all these tests and trials, these stormy astral experiences will finally be weathered and will land the disciple in the relatively calm world of realities, free from disturbing emotions and only now learning the meaning of real spiritual love for all of creation.

The Second Initiation must therefore be regarded as an important milestone on the Path and once this hurdle has been cleared, progress, although remaining difficult and painstaking and demanding all the initiate has to offer should, relatively speaking, take much less time.

With the control of the astral elemental, the emotional body should become pure and limpid, with the lower nature losing its influence. A fresh impulse of aspiration and an urge to serve, love and demonstrate goodwill to all will be felt and this expression must unavoidably result in rapid unfoldment. This is why this initiation and the Third may quite often occur in the same life.

Mastery over the emotional forces indicates the release of the soul from its astral prison. From now on the soul will be able to use the astral body by moulding desire and emotion to conform to spiritual purpose. With the breaking of the hold of the astral body, the intuition, that higher counterpart of aspiration, can begin to play an active role in the disciple's future decisions and conduct of life.

Because of the many facets through which desire may be manifested and which must be brought under control, several lives will as a rule intervene between the First and Second Initiations – a long period of struggle and strain to overcome the desires and emotions of the astral body. Once the Second Initiation is attained, however, the progress towards the Third should be relatively rapid, with the Fourth following possibly in the same life or otherwise in the succeeding.

XIII. 7. **Third Initiation** (The Transfiguration of the Initiate)

With the subduing of the desire and emotional life which led to the Second Initiation, with the welling up of the spirit of altruism and the urge to sacrifice, to give and to share, the opportunity to serve will be revealed to the candidate. He will be accorded a vision of that part of the world's need and of the Plan to which he can contribute his small share, with the capacities at his disposal and in the circumstances under which he is functioning. If this opportunity is recognised and faithfully reacted to, this work may provide that mental control which has still been lacking in the disciple's make-up to prepare him for the Third Initiation.

Mental control means that the capacity has been acquired to manipulate thought-matter, which includes the laws of creative thought building. For the Third Initiation the disciple must also have a profound theoretic and practical knowledge of the nature of the material worlds and of the laws governing his own lower nature.

The intervening period between the Second and Third Initiations is usually characterised by intense suffering, brought about by factors of glamour and illusion which have not yet been completely eliminated and which involve the disciple in situations which for the time being leave him bewildered. Meanwhile the frustrated candidate, under the right guidance and with spiritual determination, strains forward persistently but still largely feeling his way in the dark; he has the advantage to dispose over a logical and understanding mind but as yet only intermittently obtaining spiritual inspiration. Unrelenting efforts and growing powers of the mind, however, lead him to success, bringing the emotions ever more effectively under control.

At first the soul only makes its presence felt periodically but this influence will progressively be increased by focussing the light of the soul on the disciple's path. This may frequently add to the complications of the man's life but will eventually provide the control needed to effect the liberation of the soul. It is this liberation which opens the portals to the Third Initiation.

To the Hierarchy, the first two initiations recognised by esotericists in describing the spiritual development of man, are merely preliminary or preparatory stages. What man knows as the Third Initiation, they regard as the *First Major Initiation*, because it is at this stage that the disciple really becomes 'transfigured' and consciously enters the spiritual kingdom. It marks the stage when the soul gains control over the mental vehicle which, together with the physical and emotional bodies, constitute the 'personality'. It means that for the first time the soul is then in full control of the personality and that personality and soul become united and fused into a single unit – *the soul-infused being*. For man this is the consummation of his life and for the soul it means liberation.

To the soul this liberation means that henceforth it will no longer respond to the lower vibrations of the three worlds, which in the past were transmitted to it by the personality. The soul comes to the recognition that in future it will merely serve as a link, a vibrating invocative and evocative centre between the Hierarchy and Humanity – until with the Fourth Initiation it ultimately becomes absorbed into the Spiritual Triad.

With transfiguration the entire soul-infused personality is flooded with light, which now for the first time reaches him directly from the Monad, who can now pour its divine energies into this newly prepared channel. The transfiguration of the personality liberates it from the alluring attractions of the three lower worlds and it becomes exclusively an agent of the soul. The initiate now irrevocably enters the Kingdom of God and thus serves the Hierarchy as another point of anchorage on Earth, providing another channel for transmitting the divine energies into the three worlds of human endeavour.

The physical vehicle is changed to a totally different consistency and quality and all its aspects now exclusively serve the purposes of the soul; it is no longer even subject to the laws of health which apply to the lower bodies of the average human being. What used to be the 'personality' now becomes merely a practical instrument to serve the purposes of the soul, with no personal desires, ambition and powers of thought. It is only a physical sheath vitalised by the soul but still perfectly adapted to the circumstances and the role it has to play for rendering the service activities amongst men as planned by the soul.

When reaching this stage, the disciple's consciousness is also completely liberated and can function freely either in or out of form, according to the requirements of the Plan. The initiate can now at will pass in full consciousness to higher worlds, leaving the lower worlds far behind. The spiritual and material have been merged and are at-one, opening the way to a still higher union with the Monad, which will lead to complete emancipation from the three worlds. The 'way of escape' now becomes the 'way of daily living' and all pain is steadily transcended, with the result that neither pleasure nor pain retain any hold over the disciple.

Esoterically speaking the 'Transfiguration' also indicates the final 'parting of the ways' between the black and white magicians. For his selfish and ambitious purposes the 'brother of darkness' can largely simulate the requirements of physical and emotional control needed for the first two initiations but his evil intent cannot tolerate and survive the truly spiritual atmosphere which will be engendered at the time of the transfiguration by the loving Will of God, emanating from the Monad. The 'black brother' therefore will never be able to penetrate the precincts of the Third Initiation.

XIII. 8. **Fourth Initiation**   (The Renunciation)

After the soul has assumed full responsibility for the 'transfigured personality', a period of intensive training is entered and an unbelievable amount of knowledge is rapidly absorbed and accumulated. The initiate must now learn to thoroughly grasp the laws of the three lower planes and how to wield them intelligently for furthering the hierarchical scheme of evolution. He must become versed in esoteric technicalities and has to develop fourth dimensional vision. He is not only working constantly at expanding his spiritual nature but he is simultaneously learning to direct the activities of the building devas.

With the Fourth Initiation the initiate is at last brought face to face with his own Monad, his 'Father in Heaven', who so far has only been known as the spiritual Entity inspiring the soul. As a result of this direct contact between the Monad and the soul-infused personality, the functions of that vague concept, the Soul, which for aeons has served as the intermediary between the Monad and its instrument of manifestation in the three lower worlds, now becomes redundant. The soul is consequently absorbed within the Monad and disappears as a separate entity and in its place naught is left but the energy of Love-Wisdom and the dynamic Divine Will as directed by the Monad.

The Fourth Initiate therefore is directly controlled by his Monad, by means of the 'Bridge of Light' (the Antahkarana). For as long as the initiate has to function or appear in the three worlds of men, he avails himself of a 'personality' which to the average man will have a perfectly normal appearance. The form side of existence is, however, no longer needed as a medium for gaining experience; from now on it will only serve as an outer mask through which the initiate or the Master may unobtrusively work among men to fulfil his spiritual purpose. This personality or body of expression will therefore not be the product of physical procreation but will be *self-created* by the focussed Will and Purpose of the Monad and it will thus not be subject to the normal laws of nature.

This *body of manifestation* will not in any way limit the initiate or hold him prisoner; by means of the applied Will it can at any time and according to the requirements of circumstances be 'dissolved' or made to fade away from human vision; it can be radically changed in outer appearance or can be transferred at a moment's notice from one part of the world to another.

With the Great Renunciation everything that used to shackle the disciple to the material world is relinquished in order that the energies and powers which the initiate controls may be applied to the benefit of mankind as a whole. He is now dominated by the energy of the will-to-good. He is still aware of the experiences gleaned from his numerous physical incarnations but he has discarded all that proved insignificant, retaining only the essence which has been transmuted into wisdom. As the purified distillation of the past, his destiny now faces new realms of experience and spiritual adventures, which will lead him from human evolution to Spiritual Evolution and ultimately to the choice of one of the Seven Cosmic Paths.

XIII. 9. **Fifth Initiation** (The Initiation of Revelation)

According to human standards, man has attained perfection when he is ready for the Fifth Initiation. This also marks the time when the initiate has gained sufficient wisdom, love and spirituality to be admitted to the acknowledged ranks of the Masters of Wisdom.

The Initiation of Revelation will place in the initiate's hands the power to wield Light as the carrier of Life to all in the three worlds; to his vision will also be revealed the next step to be taken upon the Way of Higher Evolution. The Way is then revealed to him in a totally new light and it therefore signifies the true emergence of the initiate from the tomb of darkness of material being and the entrance into the world of Reality and of Spiritual Being which lies beyond all that man has hitherto sensed or known.

These are of course realms of thought and being which are as yet far beyond human conception and comprehension and these representations are only briefly expressed to round off the picture which has so far been sketched. It is realised that to the man in the street these thoughts of the Tibetan's will be just ludicrous nonsense or the more sympathetic might regard them as the whimsical fantasies of a fanciful dreamer!

XIII. 10. **Higher Evolution** (The Seven Cosmic Paths)

As pointed out before, the Path of Evolution is never ending. When from the human standpoint liberation has been achieved after the Fifth Initiation, new realms of expansion will be revealed to the initiate. The realms to be trodden will ultimately include the whole cosmic sphere and are divided into Seven Cosmic Paths of Evolution, each Path being determined by one of the Seven Cosmic Rays of Energy.

Each initiate has the free decision to follow whichever Path he chooses but the probability is that as a result of the Law of Attraction, the initiate's choice will be strongly influenced by his vibration as induced by his Monadic Ray. Some of these Paths may keep the initiate linked to the Hierarchy and to Earth service for many aeons to come, whilst others may lead to wider planetary activities within our solar system or even to outer-planetary or cosmic activities. The final decision as to the Path to be followed, must be made at the consummation of the Sixth Initiation – the Initiation of Decision. From this decision there will be no turning back.

XIV

THE KINGDOM OF GOD

The Kingdom of God on Earth already exists within the hearts of numerous men and women but will not be publicly recognised till there exists a preponderance of spiritual men in the world. Eventually their influence and the force they transmit, will be felt in all the kingdoms of nature. In this New Era man will then obtain dominion over all forms and with the power to transmit the spiritual energies of love and the will-to-good, the whole physical plane will become transformed, inaugurating that symbolic period known as the 'Millennium'.

So far the spiritual kingdom has mainly had its seat in the inner subjective worlds – on the hierarchical plane of the Masters and of the Perfected Men and Angels. However, every soul-infused human being on Earth is also a junior member of the Kingdom of Souls and is therefore serving to anchor this Kingdom more firmly in the worlds of human endeavour. There have always been outposts of God's Kingdom among men, those who served to link the Hierarchy with the physical worlds and who have served as channels for the flow of loving understanding, goodwill and service and who have been responsible for the spiritual evolution of man. These have been the men, present in every country, who were infused with the Christ-consciousness, no matter by what name this consciousness was known.

These soul-infused men are at present constituting a vital 'bridge of souls' between the heavenly realm and the world of human beings. This bridge is already firmly established and is daily being extended and strengthened by new recruits. The result is that although the human kingdom still dominates all fields of human thought and activity, the Kingdom of God has already established a firm foothold on Earth and is growing progressively as a result of the spiritual forces which are steadily flowing across the Bridge of Souls. Each new soul incorporated into this exalted Kingdom, will increase its power and effect, because each soul represents an additional channel for transmitting spiritual energy from the higher to the lower planes.

The Kingdom of God on Earth must therefore be regarded as an established fact and it is only its public recognition that is still lacking. This recognition will be withheld till it can be protected against the narrow claims of individual churches, religions or organisations, who will profess that admittance may only be gained through their specifically prescribed rules and regulations and separative approach. Humanity will, however, come to the realisation that the Kingdom of God is neither of Christian or Buddhist origin, nor is it related to any other specific church, religion or organisation but is constituted of that integrated group of soul-infused individuals who are consistently radiating love and are solely motivated by the will-to-good.

The New Group of World Servers, that loosely constituted group of spiritual men on Earth, may be regarded as the symbolic outpost of the Fifth Kingdom. They are the fore-runners of the Hierarchy which is now slowly being externalised and are serving to pre-pare the way for the reappearance amongst men of the Master of all Masters. The van-guard of these liberated souls is already with mankind; unobtrusively and largely unknown, they are persistently exerting their influence by slowly guiding the human race towards its joyful destiny.

It should be realised that in this higher kingdom there only exist spiritual relationships and man is only assessed by the content of his heart. All material criteria fall away and it matters not whether a man, according to human standards is rich or poor, high or low on the ladder of status or whether his skin is yellow, black or white. No, all men and women are considered children of the One Father and therefore all are brothers; all of them are on their way towards the Kingdom of God but many of them have not yet become aware of their Destination; they are still temporarily blinded by the dense astral miasma by which they are surrounded, and as yet are only conscious of physical and emo-tional desire, with all their energies focussed on selfishly satisfying these demands. There are thus many stages of development and the only meaningful difference between indi-viduals is the extent to which they are still wrapped in darkness or otherwise the degree of Light that has penetrated their minds, leading to various degrees of consciousness.

On the other hand, part of the responsibility of those fortunate ones who have found the Light and who have entered the Realm of Souls, is to focus the Light they have received back into the regions of darkness in which they themselves have been cloistered for aeons and thus to illumine the way for those who must still follow in their tracks.

It is through the concerted and sustained efforts of all those who are spiritually inclined, of all men and women whose hearts are guided by love and goodwill, that mankind as a whole will be uplifted. In this respect each disciple will make his own contribution, each according to the Light he has received, according to the qualities and aptitudes with which he has been endowed and each according to his particular circumstances as determined by time and place. People must be brought to the realisation that the Kingdom of God will only be found by recognising its presence; that this Kingdom must not be sought for in outer appearance but that it will primarily be found by recognising the Christ within the heart. Therefore do not hesitate to express the energies of Love and Goodwill with which you are inspired – they will provide the opportunities for which to live, to work and to serve and for fulfilling your dreams and aspirations, thus contributing your share to make this a better world for all and for the final manifestation of the Kingdom of God on Earth.

AFTERWORD

If ‚BRIDGES‘ has satisfied the reader‘s demands for esoteric knowledge, then it has failed in its purpose. The objective has been to open up new visions, and to stir the student to deeper exploration of the fascinating search for the verities of life, and the wonders of a more profound knowledge of the Self and of the Truth. In this book only a small corner has been lifted of the veil hiding so much of the enthralling inner realities, the awareness of which make life really worth living. Let the present studies therefore only prove to be a stimulant to provide the impetus to delve ever deeper into the original works of the Tibetan.

This treatise has been based nearly exclusively on the writings of the Tibetan Sage, as his work is considered to be not only the most comprehensive with which humanity has so far been entrusted, but also as containing the most modern and advanced version of the Ancient Wisdom. When making this statement the intention is certainly not to belittle or detract in any way whatsoever from the value of the numerous other esoteric publications.

To the contrary – it should be recognised that the actual source of knowledge is not of primary importance, and that all that matters is the quality of the Truth that is conveyed. Many disciples in the past have attained perfection without any knowledge of the Tibetan and his teachings, and neither will these in future be the only venue to attainment. In this respect let each man follow those teachings to which he intuitively feels attracted – there are many paths leading to the mountain top!

For the production of ‚BRIDGES‘ some 8,000 references from the Tibetan‘s writings were compiled and classified. As these references might prove equally useful to students who would like to deepen their knowledge of certain aspects, they are included and have been arranged sequentially to correspond with the classified contents of the present study.

APPENDIX

REFERENCE INDEX

BOOKS BY THE TIBETAN
(DJWHAL KHUL)
through ALICE A. BAILEY

Book. Ref. No	Title	First Edition	Reference Edition	Pages
1.	*Initiation, Human and Solar*	1922	8th 1967	225
2.	*Letters on Occult Meditation*	1922	8th 1966	360
3.	*A Treatise on Cosmic Fire*	1925	6th 1964	1,283
4.	*A Treatise on White Magic*	1934	8th 1967	640
5.	*Discipleship in the New Age – Vol. I*	1944	6th 1966	790
6.	*Discipleship in the New Age – Vol. II*	1955	2nd 1955	768
7.	*The Problems of Humanity*	1947	3rd 1964	181
8.	*The Reappearance of The Christ*	1948	3rd 1960	189
9.	*The Destiny of Nations*	1949	2nd 1960	152
10.	*Glamour: A World Problem*	1950	3rd 1967	272
11.	*Telepathy and the Etheric Vehicle*	1950	3rd 1963	197
12.	*Education in the New Age*	1954	1st 1954	153
13.	*The Externalisation of the Hierarchy*	1957	2nd 1958	701
	A Treatise on the Seven Rays:			
14.	Vol. I – *Esoteric Psychology I*	1936	5th 1967	430
15.	Vol. II – *Esoteric Psychology II*	1942	2nd 1960	751
16.	Vol. III – *Esoteric Astrology*	1951	5th 1965	695
17.	Vol. IV – *Esoteric Healing*	1953	4th 1967	715
18.	Vol. V – *The Rays and the Initiations*	1960	2nd 1965	769

NOTE

Reference Example: A reference number, such as for instance (12-135/6) at the end of a quotation, would refer to a quotation taken from *"Education in the New Age"* (12) starting on page 135, and continued on page 136.

Bridges

PART ONE
MAN IN THE UNIVERSE

I.   SUMMARY

II. THE ANCIENT WISDOM: 4-7/10, *377/82*; 5-700; 6-85, 87; 9-132.
     The Mysteries: *3-847*; 4-30/2; 6-511, 528, 767/8; 8-71, 94, 121/3; 13-574; 15-280; 18-260, 330/2, 18-334, 337, 345.
     Truth: 3-xiv; 4-32/3, 114/9, 408, 490; 5-240, 347; 6-86/7, 238; 7-75, 123, 126/8, 138/9, 141/52; 8-138/40, 144; 10-145, 146, 170, 176/7; 11-4, 106; *15-20*, 86; 16-9, 215; 17-*567*, 611/4; 18-77/8, 18-303, *378*, 389.
     Points of View: 4-33; 5-48/9; 6-*681/2*; 10-146; 14-268; 15-106/7, 108/9, *740*; 17-*353*.
     Reality: 2-300; 9-47; 10-190, 191, 198, 200, 246/7; 13-115, 136, 285; 14-15; 15-234, 239, 246/7; 16-7, 422; 18-41, 78, *304*.
     Limitation of Words: 3-150, 568, 802; 4-22, 32, *523*; 9-118; 11-182; 14-24, 59; 15-216, *425*; 17-320; 18-50, 167, 172, 287.
     Limited Comprehension: 3-597/8; 4-24/5, 363/4; 6-263; 16-629; 18-147, 173, 203, 304, 646.
     Paradoxes and Contradictions: 11-66; 16-64/5, 453; 18-*412/3*.

III. ALL IS ENERGY: 3-601 (footnote); 4-220, 291, 320; 6-181, 396/7; 7-161; 8-78, *88/95*; 9-93/4, 9-128; 10-165, 247/8; 11-2, 114, 118, 122, 129, 130, 142/3, 144, *149*, 162, 173, 177; 12-24, 60/2; 13-85, 644/7, 655/9, 673/5; 14-7, 152, 194, 282, 315; 15-68, 79, 184, 283/90, 411/2, 424/5; 16-9, 10, 16-11, 14/5, 22/3, 27, 30, 266/7, 458/9; 17-*141/2*, 210, 241, 327/9, *584, 586, 615*; 18-4, 14, 75, *230/2*, 18-234/5, 482, 549, *556/7*, 588, 689, 691, *708/14, 715/6*.
     Energy and Forces: 3-862, 1236/7; 4-291, 581; 5-700, 760; 6-62, 132/3, 163; *9-16*, 129; 10-243; *12-143*; 13-278/80; 15-452; *17-136/7, 583/4*, 586/8, 595; 18-57, 353, 469.
     Sources of Energy: 6-374/5; 9-128; 16-26, 28, 422; 18-690.
     Future Power Resources: 3-426/9, 434, *909/10*; 14-364.
     Atomic Energy: 3-492, 496; 4-332/4; 6-163; 7-67, 75, 81/3; 13-*491/500*, 548; 14-224; 228; 17-503, 17-713; 18-412, 646/8.
     1. The Etheric World: (See also: X. 1. - The Etheric Body) 3-57, 79, 81/7, 87/90, 474; 11-114, 11-124, 151, 153, 155, 178/80; 17-424.
     2. The Seven Rays of Energy: 3-152, 437/8; 4-32, 111/2, 194/6; 6-582/3, 698, 710; 9-3/5, 9-57, 135, 145; 10-120/3, 221/3; 11-81; 12-70; 14-3/4, 22/6, 59, 60, 118/29, 157/215, 266, 316, 14-347, 401/7; 15-21, *39/44*, 80/1, 140/5, 288, 290/3, 295/6, 298/9, 341, 351/78, 358; 16-26, 16-422; 17-583, 590/1, 597; 18-343, 557/66, 558, 642, 709.
     First Ray: 9-12/8; 10-6; 13-*334/5*, 644/7; 14-*201/2*, 227; 15-214; 16-596; 18-*645/53*.
     Second Ray: 9-18/21, 644/7; 14-*202/4*; 15-110/1, 214; 18-560, 611.
     Third Ray: 9-21, 644/7; 14-*204/5*, 337/42; 15-214; 17-590/1, 597; *18-560*.
     Fourth Ray: 14-*205/7*; 18-602/5, 611/4, 639/40.
     Fifth Ray: 14-*75/9, 207/8*; 18-590/602, *592*, 596/7.
     Sixth Ray: 9-29, 39; 14-79/83, *208/10*, 358/63; 18-569, 575/89, 583.
     Seventh Ray: 9-29/30, 41, 644/7; 14-83/8, *210/1*, 225/8, 279/80, 282, 363/75, 390/1; 18-551, 18-*569/75*, 672.

17-*578/9*; 18-345, *477*, 479, 664.

Atlantis: 4-360/1, 374, 380, 382, 399, 478/9; 6-160, 409, 467; 8-121; 9-13, 43/4, 46, 48; 10-32, 109; 11-17; 12-*39/40*, 42, 54; 13-40/1, 72, *120/4*; 14-354, 356/7, 378, 381, 401; 15-22, 25/6, 205, 209, 15-211, 350, 557/8, 575/6, 578, 580; 17-58/9, 199/200, *226/31*, 232/42, 252, 487, 576/7, *579/80*, 594 18-345, *477*, 480, 560/1, 603, 664, 732.

Aryan: 6-160; 15-22, 26, 350, *575/6*, 580; 17-59, 576, *580*; 18-478, *559*, 560/1, 658, 664.

Root Races: 3-121/2(Footnote), 714(Footnote), 187, 386, 456, 458/9, 463; 4-88/9; 12-118/9; 14-*263*, 316, 345, 354, 357, 400/1; 18-272.

Nations and Races: 6-232; 7-42/3, 85/121, 114/21; 8-93; 9-47, 60/1, 64; 13-241/2; 14-316, 14-400/1; 15-52; 17-*222/4*; 18-*620/36*.

Race Problems: 3-825/6; 7-85/121; 9-64/5; 13-194/6.

IX. MAN KNOW THYSELF: 4-*29/31*, 412, 451/2; 14-348.

What is Man?: 3-228/31, 397/8, 814/6; 4-13/4, 382; 11-61; 14-20/1, 267, *311*, 339, 405.

The Nature of Man: 3-809/11; 4-*30/1*; 10-242, 247; 11-61; 13-221; 14-5, 90/4, 230; 15-340, 15-*405/7*.

Equality of Man: 7-101, 148; 10-*132*; 13-190, 272.

Individual Differences: 4-*111*; 12-45; 13-190.

X. THE CONSTITUTION OF MAN: *1-xv*; 3-261, *283*; 4-18, 451/2; 14-*20/1*, 56; 15-7, 284/5, 434/5; 17-2/3, 33, 43, 163.

 1. The Etheric Body (Vital Body): (See also: III. 1 - The Etheric World)
    2-337; 3-97, 104, 122, 794, 910; 4-44/6, *76/7*, 289/90, 293, 372, 500, 566, 569; 5-209, 699; 6-20; 9-119, 133/4; 10-246; 11-2, 16, 32, *139/97*, 140, 141, 142/4, 148/58, 162, 177; 14-124, 132, 14-183/4; 374; 15-63/4, 184/5, 293/4, 302, 309, 434, 512, 519, 520/1, 533, 592; 16-*9/11*; 17-2/3, 71/2, 74, *76/88*, 141, 190, 273, 274/5, 288, 326/7, 332/3, 461, 466, 474/5, 477, 484, 17-539/40, 613, 617, 626/8.

    (a) Centres of Energy: 3-99, 162/78, 166, 283, 437, 474/5, *537*, 790/1, 857/9, 964, 1155/65; 4-190/208, 205, 285, 362/3, 587/8, 590, *595/6*; 5-264; 6-604; 10-261; 11-143, 146, 162, 11-167/76, 172/3; 13-18; 15-66, 294, 304/13, 338/40, 413, 514/5, 519, 520/2, 523/7, 15-575, 592; 16-11, 25, 76/7, 425, 453; 17-37, 47, 72/3, 75/88, 140, 144, *202*, 203/4, 207, 210, 17-241, 461, 465/6, 593, 595, 602, 618, 620, 622/3, 628, 644/5; 18-162/3, *336*, 669.

    (b) Carriers of Energy (Nadis): 11-145, 146, 152, 162; 15-64, 591, 594; 17-*195/8*, 333, 473/5, 17-628.

    (c) The Third Eye: 3-894, *965/6*, 974/5, 1007/9, *1008/13*, 1129/30, 1160/1; 4-*212/4*; 6-289/90, *292/3*, 374, 399/401; 10-250; 14-184; 17-525, 571.

    (d) Kundalini Fire: 3-134, *139, 183*, 894, 1129; 4-391; 13-*18/9*; 14-370; 15-66, 302, 340, 15-*528/30*, 539; 17-*181/9*.

    (e) The Etheric Web: 3-184, 864, 944; 6-61; 11-163; 14-102, 125, 370; 15-594/5.
    Etheric Vision: 3-475, 1096/7, 1164; 14-*124/5*.

    (f) Radiation: 3-*478*, 809, 863, *1060/83*; 5-185, 382, 740, 752/7; 6-78, 537/8, 540, 560, 752; 9-123, 124, 133; 11-173/5, 176, 180; 14-130, 197, 199/200, 225/6, 235, 369; 17-7, 17/8, 17-369/70, 526/7, 578, 580, 604, 643/4, 646, *653/8*; 18-98, 261, 375.
    Radio Activity: 3-1068; 14-225/6;
    Magnetism: 14-234, 244; 17-7, 17, 368/70, 526/7, 578/9, 642, 644, 646; 18-262, 375.

    (g) The Aura: 3-84; 5-98, 230, 386, 752; 6-538; 10-28, 35; 11-*95/8*, 99/100, 108, 115/8, 145, 11-*173/5*; 17-466, 527, 644, 655/7.
    Extra Sensory Perception (E.S.P.): 9-134/5; 11-9.

 2. The Physical Body: 2-334/6; 3-283; 4-20/1, 41/3, 226, 281/3, 293, 304/5; 5-56; 6-697; 9-125, 9-

131; 10-261; 14-20; 15-22, 24, 330; 17-2, 39, 111, *163*, 190, 578/9, *612/4*, 616/7, 634; 18-705.

Diet: 3-645/6, 1012; 4-84, 420; 14-220, 241, 374; 17-311, 334; 18-*125/6*.

Recreation and Amusement: 4-348; 17-62.

  (a) The Nervous System: 4-18/9; 11-145, 152/3; 15-63; 17-46, 86, 107, 129, 141, 196, *333*, 17-628.

  (b) The Brain: 3-287; 10-1; 14-132, 371/2; 17-332; 18-*431/4*, 442, 451.

  (c) The Endocrine Glands: 11-147, 152, 163; 15-64, *412*, 434; 17-45/6, *84/7*, 140, 141, *197*, 17-*202*, 204, 208, 213, 219, 614, 617/8, 623/6; 18-*431*.

    The Spleen: 3-84, 86; 15-64/5; 17-203.

  (d) The Blood Stream: 11-147; 15-62; 17-*85*, 141, 142, 189, 197, 211, 240, *331/2*, 337/8, 17-345, 474, 561, 617/8, 626/8; 18-451.

  (e) The Senses: 1-113/4; 3-164, *186/200*, 351, 1009/10; 11-54, 58/60; 14-132/3; 15-561/3.

  (f) Pain: 2-37; 4-304/5, 357/8, 531/3; 5-100/1, 127, 677; 6-29, 650, 767; 12-120; 13-154/5; 14-80, *250*; 15-*102/3*; 17-12, 346/7, 399, 502, 569/70; 18-67, 243, *499*, 701, 702, 723.

  (g) Sex: 4-241; 14-244, 262, *268/307*; 15-154, 235, 496, 530/2, 538; 16-212, *234/6*; 17-60/1, 17-89, 176, 180, 229, 231, 562; 18-*552*, 571/2, *668/70*.

    Celibacy: 14-304/6; 15-536; 16-212; 18-670.

    Homosexuality: 17-*62/4*.

3. The Astral Body: 2-337/9, 346; 3-955; 4-220/2, *225/51*, 232/7, 293/310, *315/7*, 344/5, 612/4; 5-56/7, 118; 6-544; 10-*66*, 106, 140/1; 15-22; 17-3, 33/4, 38, 42/3, 65, 88, 488/9, *579/80*; 18-673.

  Emotions: 6-623/5; 10-114/5, 149; 15-588; 17-38, 60, 92, 95/6, 594, 672/3; 18-5, 576/7, 582, 18-679, 681/2.

  (a) Fear: 4-238/42, 293, 297/306, 344/9, 625/7, 629; 5-504; 6-748/9; 7-127; 10-46; 13-75/6, 13-81, 245, 255; 15-645; 17-388, 393.

    Fear of Death: 4-300/2, 494, 626; 9-45; 17-384, 393/4, 397, 425, 432, 475; 18-731/2.

    Fear of Failure: 2-311, 343; 4-305/6, 630, *634*; 5-240, 267, 604; 6-732; 18-678.

  (b) Depression: 4-306/10, 341/3, 348/50; 15-512/3.

  (c) Hatred and Antagonism: 4-488; 6-22; 13-63, 75/6, 246, 381, 436; 15-123, 547, 680, 683; 17-38, 92, 432, 561.

  (d) Love: See PART TWO: .(a)

  (e) Psychic Powers: 1-59; 3-886; 4-12; 5-*49/50*, 66, 111, 634/6, 733, *741/2*; 6-9; 9-44/5; 13-*8/9*, 10/5, 516, 587; 14-97, 381; 15-555/6, *558/98*; 16-123/4, 216; 17-236, 395/6, 17-398; 18-477.

    Psychic Mediums: 3-757/8, 904/5; 4-166, 168, 179/80, 249/50, 301/2, 501; 10-184; 11-88, 11-104; 13-8/15; 15-568/9, 583/6; 17-377.

    Spiritualism: See PART TWO – III. 4.

4. The Mental Body: 2-340/1, 346; 3-1102/3; 4-141, 216, *227*, 357, 361, 363/5; 5-56; 14-55; 15-22, 290/3; 17-3, 88/95, 489, 580.

  (a) The Mind: 3-268, 287, 308, 310, 334/5, 337/8, 354/5, 401, 418/24, 1100/1; 4-*80/1*, 125, 4-361, 363/8, 378; 5-50, 340, 593, 698, 720; 6-623/6; 10-83, 144/5, 173/5, 205; 11-26/8, 48, 11-71, *152*; 12-4/5, 7/8, 11/2, 16/7, 35/7, 69/98; 13-29; 14-55, 76, 179, 231, 331; 15-68, 15-71, 286; 17-577, 580, 588, 589; 18-38, 63, 107, 216, 272, *432/3*, 443, 460/1, *464/7*, 478, 18-*537*, 574, 599, 691/2, 705, *713*, 748/9.

  (b) The Three Aspects of Mind: 4-361, 365; 12-4/5; 17-511; 18-*457/70*, 465.

5. The Personality: 2-347; 4-40/1, 262, *391/4*, 396, 493; 10-268/70; 11-152, 167/76; 12-140/2; 14-39, 76, 112/3; 15-68, 104, *263*, 264/7, 324, 415/37; 16-111; 17-506/7, *515/9*, 642, 681; 18-44, *57*, 61, 96/7, 98, 109, 161, 434, 457, 466, 468, 497, *562/3*, 571, 599, 669, 688, 710.

6. The Lord of the World: 1-28/9; 18-16, 83, 417, 462, 714.

Sanat Kumara: 1-28, 40/9, 104, 106; 3-221, 366, 412, 509, 728, *751/3*; 4-432; 6-159, *286/8*, 6-385, 419; 8-39; 9-25; 10-266; 11-66, 68, 119, 159, *183*; 13-464/5, *676*; 17-*298*, 610, 620, 17-636/7, *679/80*; 18-130, *205*, 242, 246/7, 267/8, 273, 277, *366/8*, 394, *412*, 421, 652, 657/60, 18-714, 717.

(a) Shamballa: 1-33; 3-753; 4-378/9; 6-135/6, 159, 197, 206, 209, 217, 222/3, 233, 260/1, 6-292/3, 519/20; 8-38/9; 9-12/3, 24, 119/20; 11-42/3, 68, 81, 134, 149, 155, 159, 183/4; 13-*407/8*, 455, 522, 532/3, 535/8, 545, 560/1, 567; 16-22, 593; 17-615, 619, 637; 18-68/9, 18*84*, 89, 112, 118, 120, 139/41, 150, 162, 204, 231, 240, 380, 412, 659/60, 735.

(b) Shamballa Energy: (Energy of Will) 9-*13, 17*, 18/21; 13-71/2, 106/8, 126, 151, 165, *343/6*, 13-438/41, 525, 536, 561; 16-371/3, 583/4, 586/8; 17-667; 18-35, 85, 86, 94, 110, 120, 130, 18*144/6, 159/60*, 230/1, 235, 240, *376/7*, 471/2, 550, 580, 646, 648/9, 651, 715/6.

(c) The Divine Purpose: 6-172, 398, 401, 667; 9-25, 98/9; 10-181; 11-7, 68, 69, 71, 95, 119/23; 11-183; 13-260, 533, 541; 14-59; 18-69, 246, 270, *307*, 315, 370/1, 496/7, 652, *714/7*.

(d) The Hierarchical Plan: 2-309/10; 4-130/3, *403*, 605; 5-25, 54, 289; 6-138, 154, 159, 167, 6-210/1, 223, 233/4, 261, 361/2, 371, 373/4, 390/2, 498, 596, 667; 8-25; 9-12, 120; 11-68, 11-70, 71, 73, *95, 118/23*, 196; 12-106, 111; 13-332, 533, 589, *670*, 672; 14-*141/3, 170/9*, 14-356; 15-*28/9*, 72/3, 185, *218/9*, 221/2, 241/6, 251, 287, 333, 649/50, 652/3, 656, 665/6, 15-684; 16-*115*, 325, 327, 371/2, 388; 18-*130*, 246, *307*, 315, 368, 370/1, 469, 712.

7. (a) The Hierarchy of Masters: 1-20/25, 49/62; 2-256/95; 3-1078/9; 4-79, 276/7, 527, *608*, 4-638; 5-23/4, 43, 685, 778, 787/9; 6-64, 65, *102*, 135, 137, 166, 172, 211, 217, 223, 233, 260, 6-314/7, 358, 351, 429, 761; 7-144/7; 8-19, 37, 57/8, 148, 153, 157; 9-18/21, 36, 139; 10-185/6, 266; 11-43/6, 66, *69*, 70, 149, 159, 184, 187, 197; 12-126; 13-108, 124, 125, 150/2, 13-169, 218, 225, 232, 393/8, 407, 416/7, 420, 453/6, *472/4*, 515, *519/22*, 524/6, 541/5, 549, 13-550, 560/1, 565, 567, *588*; 15-185, 224, 241/2, 244/5, 251/2, 259/61, 270, 576, 638, 716, 15-744/51; 17-615, 619; 18-15, 68/9, 88, 89, 119, 128, 133/4, 136, 150, 230/1, 236, 238/9, 18-333/4, 367/70, 374, *380/1*, 700, 702, 706, 712, 717, 753.

Master and Disciple Relationships: See PART TWO – IX. 5.

The Master's Ashram: 5-694/7, 728/9, 731/2, 738/9, 747/8, 789; 6-34, 103/7, 133, 138, 203, 6-205, 330, 357/8, 503, 549/50, 554, 564, 609/10, 631, 652, 664, 676, 679, 720, 742; 11-194; 13-679/81; 18-58, *97/8*, 119, 150, 168/9, 346, 366/72, 374, 378/80, 373/95, *383/4, 386/8*, 18-542/7, 562, 712.

(b) The Masters: 15-578, 582, 596; 18-*103/4, 230*, 398/400, *438/40*, 700, 705, 712/3, *720*.

(c) The Master's Body of Manifestation: (Mayavirupa) 1-117; 2-275, 339; 3-761(footnote); 4-388; 13-697; 15-32/3, 35, 252/3; 17-518; 18-51, *101*, 317, 439/40, 455, 699, *705*.

(d) Individual Masters:

Koot Hoomi: 1-*54/6*; 5-43, 757; 6-246, 465, 503, 564, 596, 609, 668; 11-160; 13-505/6, 13-643/4, 660/2; 14-108; 18-169, 342, 398, 586, 705.

Morya: 1-53/5, 61; 5-226, 622, 624, 730; 6-246, 595, 596; 11-160; 13-307, 505, 577, 578, 13-644, *662/4*; 14-108; 15-80; 18-170, 373, 549, 586.

Rakoczi: 1-46, 49, 58/9, 61; 3-455; 6-593, 596; 11-160; 13-160, 304, 507, 541, 644, 665, 13-*667/8*; 18-169/70, 232, 586.

Jesus: 1-46/7, 49, 55/7, 61; 3-678, 759, 1259, 5-72, 624; 9-37, *59*; 11-5; 13-307, 506, 573; 14-397/8; 18-83, 315, 353/5, *524*, 599, 706.

Hilarion: 1-*59*; 3-455, 759; 5-624; 11-163; 13-*506*; 18-586.

Djwhal Khul: 1-57/8; 3-759; 4-128/9; 5-33, 54, 238, 757; 6-473, 597; 11-160; 13-506/7, 13-522, 644, 669; 17-306; 18-169, 372, 586, 643, 705, 707.

PART TWO
MAN ON THE PATH OF LIFE

248/50, 251, 397, 399, *488/91*, 641, 659; 15-145, 692, 694; 18-95, 611, 616/7, 755/61.

Invocative Festivals: 3-756; 5-743; 7-162/4; 8-45/6, 96, 154/7; 9-147/8, 151; 13-162/3, 13-227/8, 286/8, 347/54, 420/1, 556/7, 641; 15-684/700; 18-760.

3. Meditation: 2-2, 9, 12/7, 18, 22, 48/9, 58, 61, 77, 90, 93, 96/7, 100/3, 112, 4, 115, 145, 147/54, 155, 2-161, 193, 223, 240, 256/95, 276/7, 284/5, 295, 297/331, 299, 303/4, 312/3, 326/7; 3-197, 746 3-961, 998/9; 4-64, 74, 89, 204, 366, 515/7; 5-46, 50, 57, 89, 349, 546/7; 6-154, 180, *197/207*, 6-215/6, 233/6, 313, 488/9; 7-160/1; 10-22, 67; 12-9, *96*; 13-17, 18, 19, 23; 14-12, *375*; 15-118, 15-195, 463/80, *464/6*; 16-615; 17-620; 18-122, 252, 447.

Full Moon Meditation: 5-29/30, 338, 434, 567, 588, 629, 664; 6-*15/6*, 25/6, 54/7; 11-44; 17-*340/1*.

Visualisation: 3-971; 5-89/91, 506, 546; 17-582; 18-123, 442, *488/90*.

Imagination: 3-971; 6-373; 15-222, 243, 246/50.

Creative Imagination: 15-*247/9*, 428; 17-355, 582; 18-442/3, 482, *488/9*, 553, 712.

Living "As If": 5-72; 6-46, 554/5, 556; 18-443/4, 703.

Vision and Contemplation:L 4-211/3, 367/8, 630, 633; 5-620, 648, 687/9; 6-14, 338, 666; 7-49; 11-73; 12-15, 87; 13-103; 15-*219*, 221, 237/41, 244, 248, 256, 605; 18-60, 113, 197/8, 18-200, 241, 297/8, 301.

Prophecies: 3-453, 909/10, 1070, 1080; 9-34, 41, 55, 61, 62, 73, 81; 85; 11-33; 13-508/9; 14-74, 14-83, 97, 123, 184, 367/8; 16-238; 17-48, 370, 374, *376/9*; 18-640.

Prevision: 4-302/4; 9-27/8; 14-96/7, 104.

4. Revelation: 1-119; 5-92/3; 6-14, *252/62*, 268, 291, 294, 306/8, 310/3, 316, 318/9, 346, 367/8, 6-379, 388/9, 417, 434/7, 439, 443, 657; 7-135, 140/1, 154, 158; 8-9/10, 58, 61/2, 133, 138, 148; 10-135/8, 139, 167, 173/7, *182/9*, 205/6; 11-4, 56, 64/74, 91; 13-286, 289, 290, 413, 420; 15-246, 248; 16-589; 18-74/5, 114, 203, 241, 257/8, 298/301, 331, *424*, 538, *644*, 703/4, 707, 18-*708/14*, *716/7*, 727/8, 741/2, 750.

Recognition: 1-114; 5-108/9, 562, 692, 740; 6-164, 247, 257, 293, 319, 421; 7-140/1; 8-41, 44, 8-50.

VIII. HUMAN RELATIONSHIPS

1. Human Relationships: 3-811/3; 4-86/7, 573/4; 5-194, 363, 731/2; 6-297/8; 7-28, 30, 42/3, 7-46, 57, 59, 81/2, 115/6, 118/21, 169, 176/81; 8-12/3, 22, 30/1, 41, 46, 56/7, 83, 95, 108/15, 132 8-149; 9-152; 11-48, 69; 12-84, 88/9; 13-161, 183, *192/3*, 195, *205/11*, 241, 647, 669; 15-86, 15-450, 674/5; 18-88, 394, 499/500, 573, 584, 611/2, 615, 617/8, 641, 748, 750/2, 755.

Brotherhood of Man: 7-*147/8*, *179*; 8-41, 52, 124; 9-138; 12-115; 13-272, 404/5; 14-96, 14-173, 192, 302; 15-662/3.

Values of Life: 3-237; 12-112, 117, 121; 14-284, 340/2; 15-338.

2. Human Shortcomings: 16-206.

(a) Selfishness: 4-238, 260, 627; 5-46, 569, 661; 7-73; 8-171; 10-76; 11-47; 15-159; 16-62, *237*; 17-346; 18-109, 210, 272, 342, 716, 753.

   (i)   Self-centeredness: 4-627; 5-569; 7-12; 13-19/20.

   (ii)   Self Pity: 5-492/4, *511*, 658, 661; 10-111; 15-276; 16-397; 17-346, 563.

   (iii)   Material Desire: 7-79; 9-113, 129; 10-*74/6*, 77/8, 149, 185, 200, 202/3, 211; 12-121; 13-342, 344; 15-154, 156, 158, 159, 224, 329, 346, 496; 16-21, 62, 324, 388/9, 579, 16-583/4; 17-39, 53, 66, 172, 348; 18-246, 468, 469, 477, 670.

   (iv)   Personal Ambition: 4-94/5, 418, 426; 12-74, 105; 15-129, 134, *135/7*, 330, 332/3, 15-496, 607, 713; 16-*173/4*; 18-651/2.

   (v)   Pride: 5-78, 744; 6-696; 10-82.

   (vi)   Crime: 16-*237*.

Motives: 2-344; 4-119, 188, 203, 257/67, 396, 558; 5-241; 6-631, 448; 9-128, 131; 10-149; 13-180; 15-119, 121/2, 157, 160.

Leadership: 4-140; 5-45, 396, 706; 6-704, 707; 7-136; 15-710.

Occult Obedience: 2-309; 4-153; 5-5, 7, 45/6, 208, 686/7; 6-*264*, 549, 586; 10-49; 15-73, 15-157/8, 484; 18-59/60, 67.

Freedom: 5-245, 288/9, 310, 367, 393; 6-740, 758; 7-128, 139, 152; 8-149, 164; 9-25; 10-*46/8*; 11-177; 13-255, 266, 271, 319, 414, 671; 15-108; 17-516, 666; 18-*416/7*, 428, 679/80, *684/7*, 18-749.

Synthesis: 6-650; 8-76/8, 82, 93/4; 13-101/2, 168, 242, 304/5, 413, 516, 535, 648, 663; 14-33/5, 14-178, 222, 234, 280, 282, 294, 360, 368; 15-*231/7*, 239, 243/4, 251, 556/7, 567, 573, 655; 16-6/7, 592; 18-*58*, 110, 112/3, 115, 118, *120/3*, 134, 146, 168, 172/3, *265/6*, 269, 276, 298/301; 18-470, 588, 657, 716, 752.

Outer Obligations: 4-420/1, 425/6; 5-535, 538, 541; 6-410; 15-105.

Bridges: 4-458/9; 5-32, 70; 7-63; 8-76; 12-4/6, 30/1, 32/3, 36, *89/91*, 94, 130, 145/6; 15-67; 18-470, *474, 477*.

Disciplines: 2-310; 4-420; 5-295, 364, 568; 7-49; 10-87/9; 13-432/3; 14-11, 365; 15-161, 15-310/1; 17-578/80, 18-11, 84, *125/6*, 127/8, 575.

Age of Disciple: 5-596; 6-508, 533, 636, 644; 12-50, 91; 15-52/3, 614; 17-463.

Old Age: 4-497; 5-387/8, 465, 517; 6-502/4, 510, 638, 696; 15-76.

Older Age: 5-287, 387/8, 599.

The Sannyasin: 5-295, 314, 391, 454, 464; 6-755, 758.

Tension: 5-734/5, 744/5; 6-243; 8-73; 18-486/8, 496/7, 540.

Crises: 5-229, 338, 534, 539, 665; 6-13/4, 293, 428, 430, 533/4, 628, 637, 644; 8-8, 57/8, 68; 11-44; 13-391, 394; 15-51/62, 215, 449/50; 16-*477*; 18-*393*.

2. Need for Disciples: 4-*428*; 5-680; 10-*271;* 13-314, 467; 14-186/7.

3. Attributes of the Disciple:

   (a) Responsibility: 3-562/3; 4-3, 201; 5-116, 167, 289, 395, 405, 446, 518, 524, 704; 6-89, 316, 6-390, 643; 7-47, 58; 11-82; 12-76/7, 93, 105; 13-207, 214, 220, 244/6; 15-106/8, 711.

   (b) Discrimination: 3-*173*; 4-222, *229, 230*, 357/9; 5-144, 206, 297; 6-736/7; 10-178; 12-104; 13-*412*; 14-281; 15-34, 159, 161, 166, 175, *223*, 244, 251.

   (c) Free Will: 3-804/5, 1053/4; 6-233; 8-113, 164; 11-80, 90; 13-61/2, 113, 125, 126, 252, 13-254/5, 259, 281, 307, 643, 671, 701; 15-29, 483; 16-377; 17-248, 522; 18-231, 251, 393, 18-411, 640, 743.

   (d) Humility: 5-95/6, 417, 562, 769; 6-88, 256/7, 618, 704; 10-145; 15-136, 572.

   (e) Simplicity: 5-391; 6-518; 7-65; 12-91, 121.

   (f) Detachment: 4-*559*, 604, 606; 5-55, 116, 130, 146, 158, *312, 314*, 383, 386, 393, 417, 570; 6-617; 10-4; 11-11, 101; 13-412; 15-34, *103/9*, 604; 18-73, 702/3.

       Impersonality: 4-625, 636; 5-48, 51, 59, 82, 216, 251, 737/8; 6-23, 603; 16-422; 18-72/3, 18-209/10.

       Divine Indifference: 5-57, 59, 66, 88, 97, 429/30, 494, 659, 661, 737; 6-243, 512; 10-172, 10-242/3, 262; 18-210.

   (g) Serenity: 5-750; 7-47; 15-200; 17-92.

       Peace: 13-208, 234/5, 259, *277*, 366, 443/4; 15-200; 16-572.

   (h) Selflessness: 5-*485*, 562, 564, 570, 654/5, 657/8, 685, 690; 6-24, 550, 621/2; 15-*177*; 18-293, 549.

   (i) Courage: 4-586; 5-339; 6-*42/3*; 8-177; 11-195.

   (j) Perseverance: 2-340/1; 4-559, 579/80, 609; 5-419, 516; 6-142/3, 500, 547; 13-577; 16-615; 18-377.

411

BY THE SAME AUTHOR

Life – Now and Hereafter
On the Nature of Life and Death

151 pages, paperback
ISBN 978-3-929345-25-4

Please visit our English
language section on

www.bridges-publishing.de

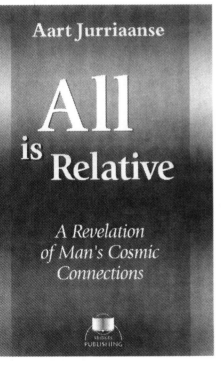

All is Relative
A Revelation of Man's Cosmic Connections

163 pages, paperback
ISBN 978-3-929345-21-6

Printed in the United Kingdom
by Lightning Source UK Ltd.
134388UK00001B/47/A

9 783929 345322